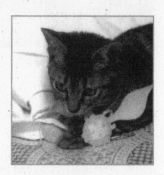

A handmade Timcanpy made by a fan. ...Huh? It's already been caught...

—Katsura Hoshino

Shiga Prefecture native Katsura Hoshino's hit manga series *D.Gray-man* has been serialized in *Weekly Shonen Jump* since 2004. Katsura's first series "Continue" first appeared in *Weekly Shonen Jump* in 2003.

Katsura adores cats.

GRAPH
HOSHINO
NO
V.2

D.GRAY-MAN
VOL. 2
SHONEN JUMP ADVANCED
Manga Edition

STORY AND ART BY
KATSURA HOSHINO

Translation & English Adaptation/Mayumi Kobayashi
Touch-up Art & Lettering/Elizabeth Watasin
Design/Yukiko Whitley
Editor/Michelle Pangilinan

VP, Production/Alvin Lu
VP, Sales & Product Marketing/Gonzalo Ferreyra
VP, Creative/Linda Espinosa
Publisher/Hyoe Narita

Printed in the U.S.A.

Published by VIZ Media, LLC
P.O. Box 77010
San Francisco, CA 94107

10 9 8 7
First printing, August 2006
Seventh printing, April 2010

THE WORLD'S MOST
CUTTING-EDGE MANGA

SHONEN
JUMP
ADVANCED
www.shonenjump.com

VIZ
media
www.viz.com

SHONEN JUMP ADVANCED MANGA EDITION

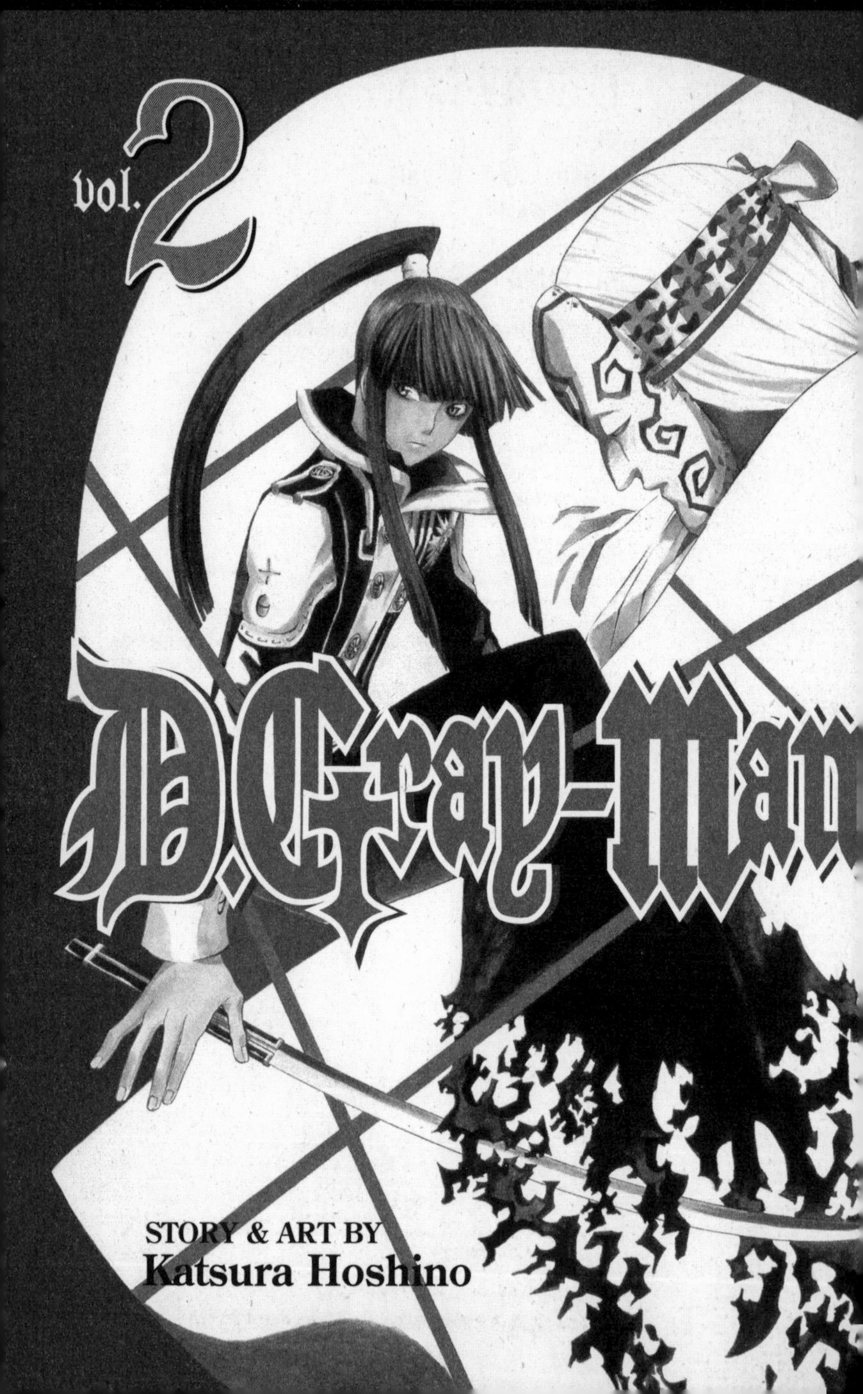
vol. 2
D.Gray-man
STORY & ART BY
Katsura Hoshino

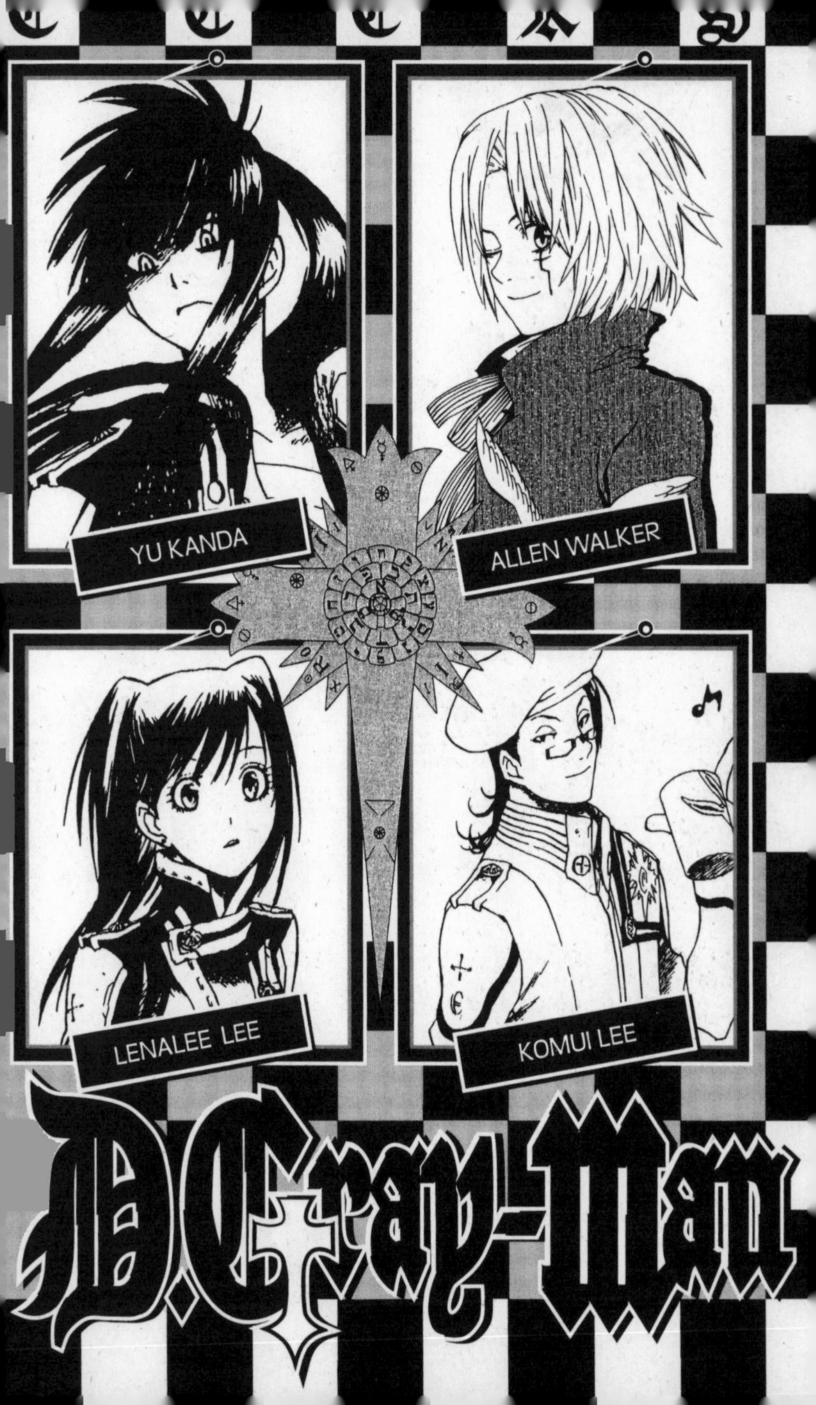
YU KANDA
ALLEN WALKER
LENALEE LEE
KOMUI LEE
D.Gray-man

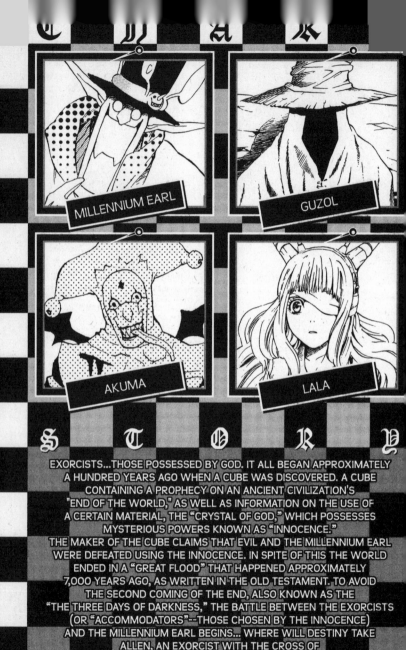

CHAR

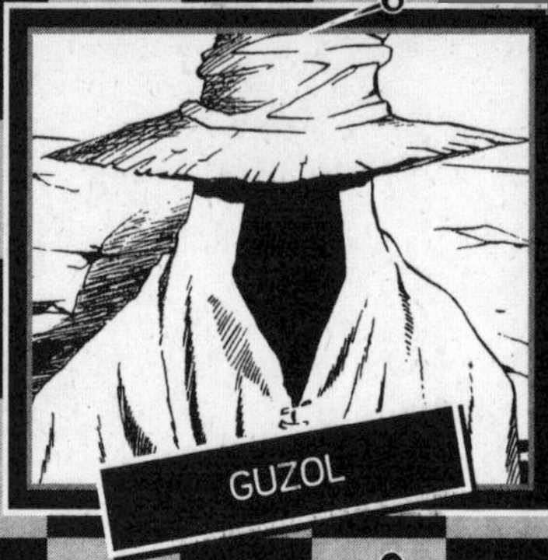
GUZOL

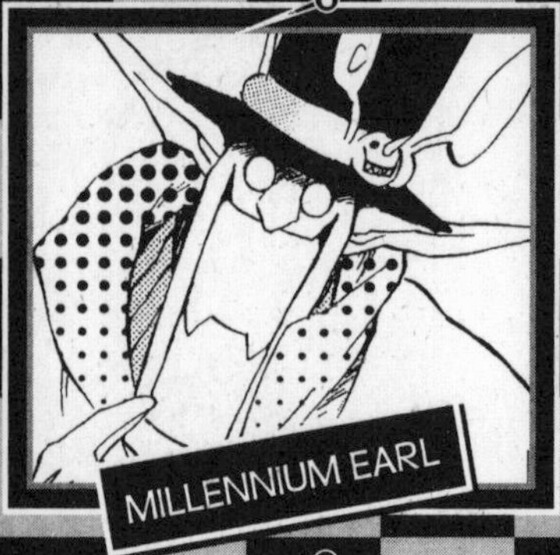
MILLENNIUM EARL

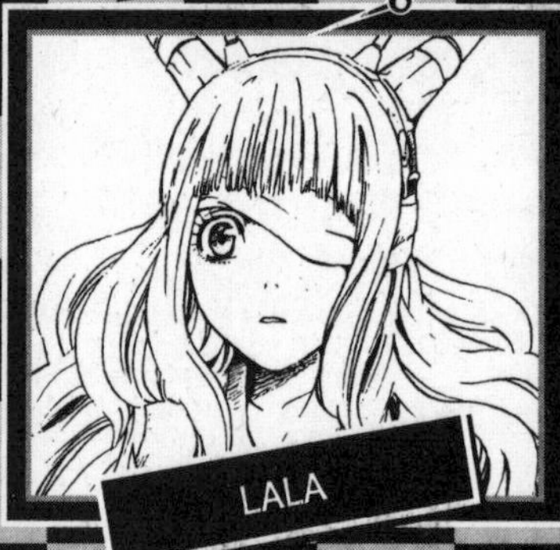
LALA

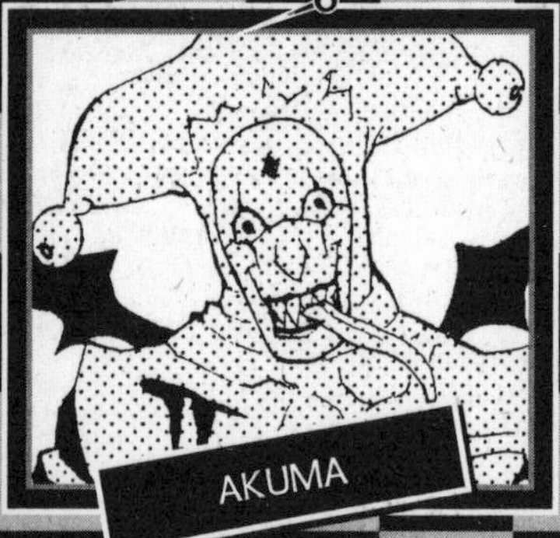
AKUMA

STORY

EXORCISTS...THOSE POSSESSED BY GOD. IT ALL BEGAN APPROXIMATELY A HUNDRED YEARS AGO WHEN A CUBE WAS DISCOVERED. A CUBE CONTAINING A PROPHECY ON AN ANCIENT CIVILIZATION'S "END OF THE WORLD," AS WELL AS INFORMATION ON THE USE OF A CERTAIN MATERIAL, THE "CRYSTAL OF GOD," WHICH POSSESSES MYSTERIOUS POWERS KNOWN AS "INNOCENCE."

THE MAKER OF THE CUBE CLAIMS THAT EVIL AND THE MILLENNIUM EARL WERE DEFEATED USING THE INNOCENCE. IN SPITE OF THIS THE WORLD ENDED IN A "GREAT FLOOD" THAT HAPPENED APPROXIMATELY 7,000 YEARS AGO, AS WRITTEN IN THE OLD TESTAMENT. TO AVOID THE SECOND COMING OF THE END, ALSO KNOWN AS THE "THE THREE DAYS OF DARKNESS," THE BATTLE BETWEEN THE EXORCISTS (OR "ACCOMMODATORS"--THOSE CHOSEN BY THE INNOCENCE) AND THE MILLENNIUM EARL BEGINS... WHERE WILL DESTINY TAKE ALLEN, AN EXORCIST WITH THE CROSS OF GOD ON HIS LEFT HAND?

D.GRAY-MAN
Vol. 2

CONTENTS

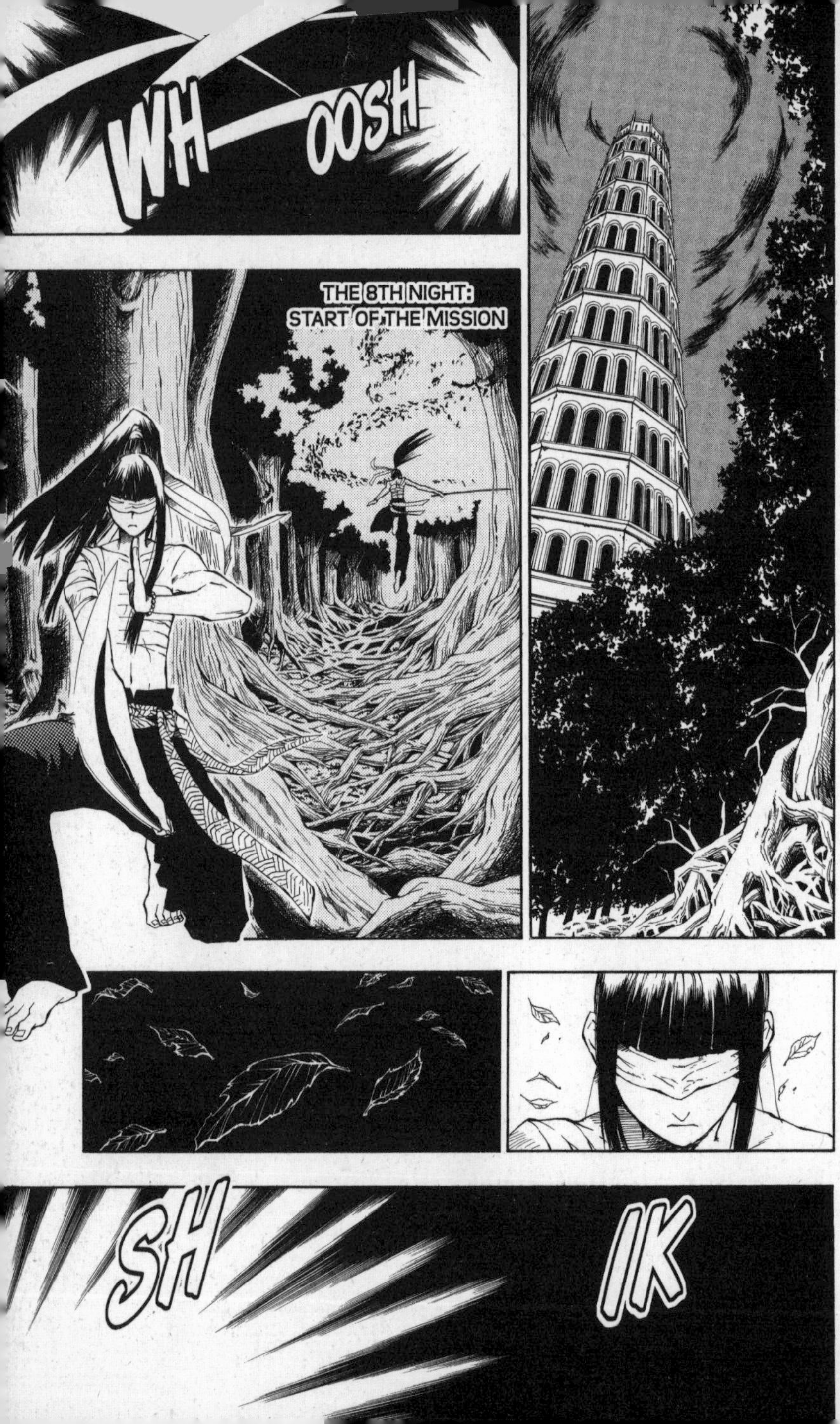
WHOOSH
THE 8TH NIGHT:
START OF THE MISSION
SHIK

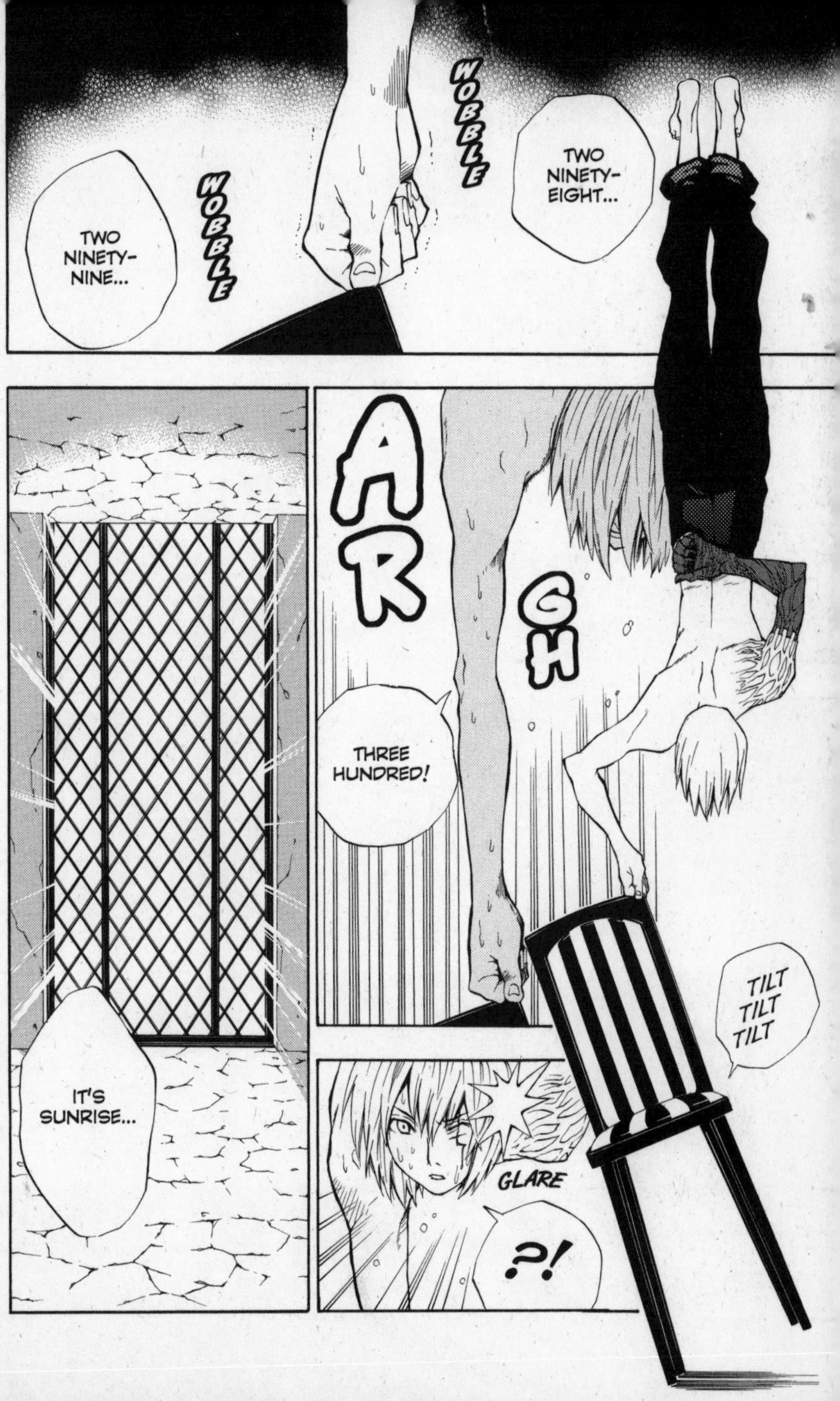
TWO NINETY-EIGHT...
WOBBLE
WOBBLE
TWO NINETY-NINE...
ARGH
THREE HUNDRED!
TILT TILT TILT
GLARE
?!
IT'S SUNRISE...

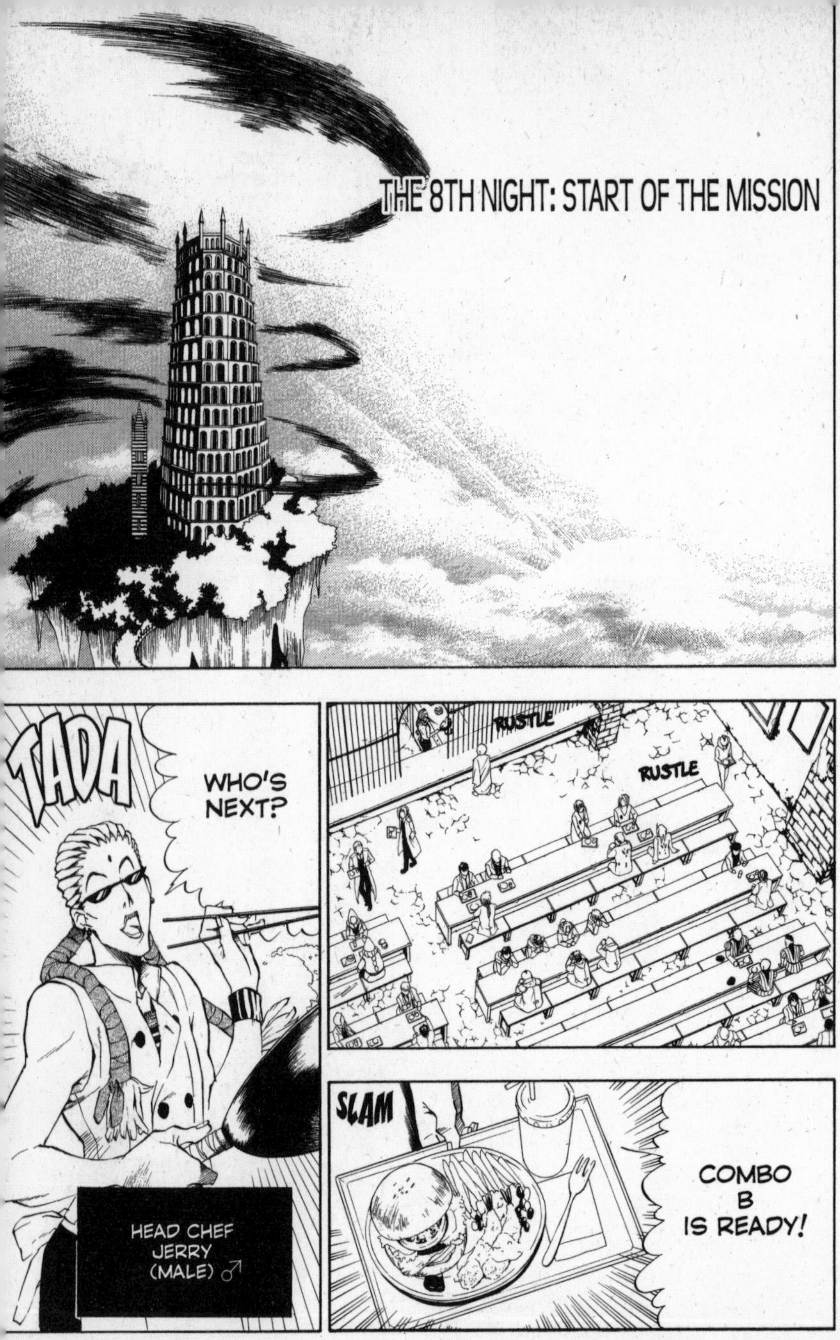
THE 8TH NIGHT: START OF THE MISSION
RUSTLE
RUSTLE
SLAM
COMBO B IS READY!
TADA
WHO'S NEXT?
HEAD CHEF JERRY (MALE) ♂

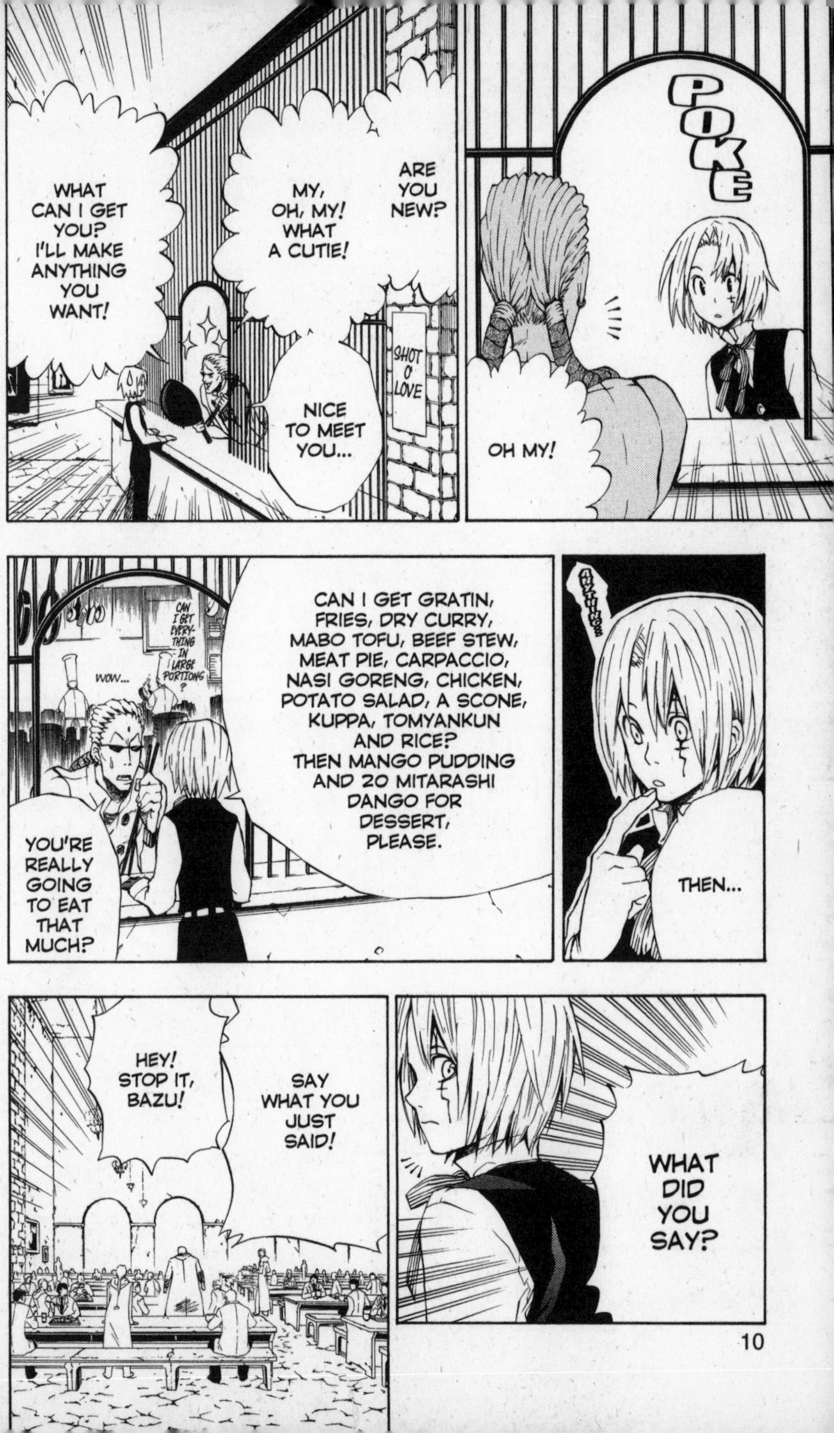
POKE
OH MY!
MY, OH, MY! WHAT A CUTIE!
ARE YOU NEW?
NICE TO MEET YOU...
WHAT CAN I GET YOU? I'LL MAKE ANYTHING YOU WANT!
SHOT O' LOVE
ANYTHING?
THEN...
CAN I GET GRATIN, FRIES, DRY CURRY, MABO TOFU, BEEF STEW, MEAT PIE, CARPACCIO, NASI GORENG, CHICKEN, POTATO SALAD, A SCONE, KUPPA, TOMYANKUN AND RICE? THEN MANGO PUDDING AND 20 MITARASHI DANGO FOR DESSERT, PLEASE.
CAN I GET EVERYTHING IN LARGE PORTIONS?
WOW...
YOU'RE REALLY GOING TO EAT THAT MUCH?
WHAT DID YOU SAY?
HEY! STOP IT, BAZU!
SAY WHAT YOU JUST SAID!

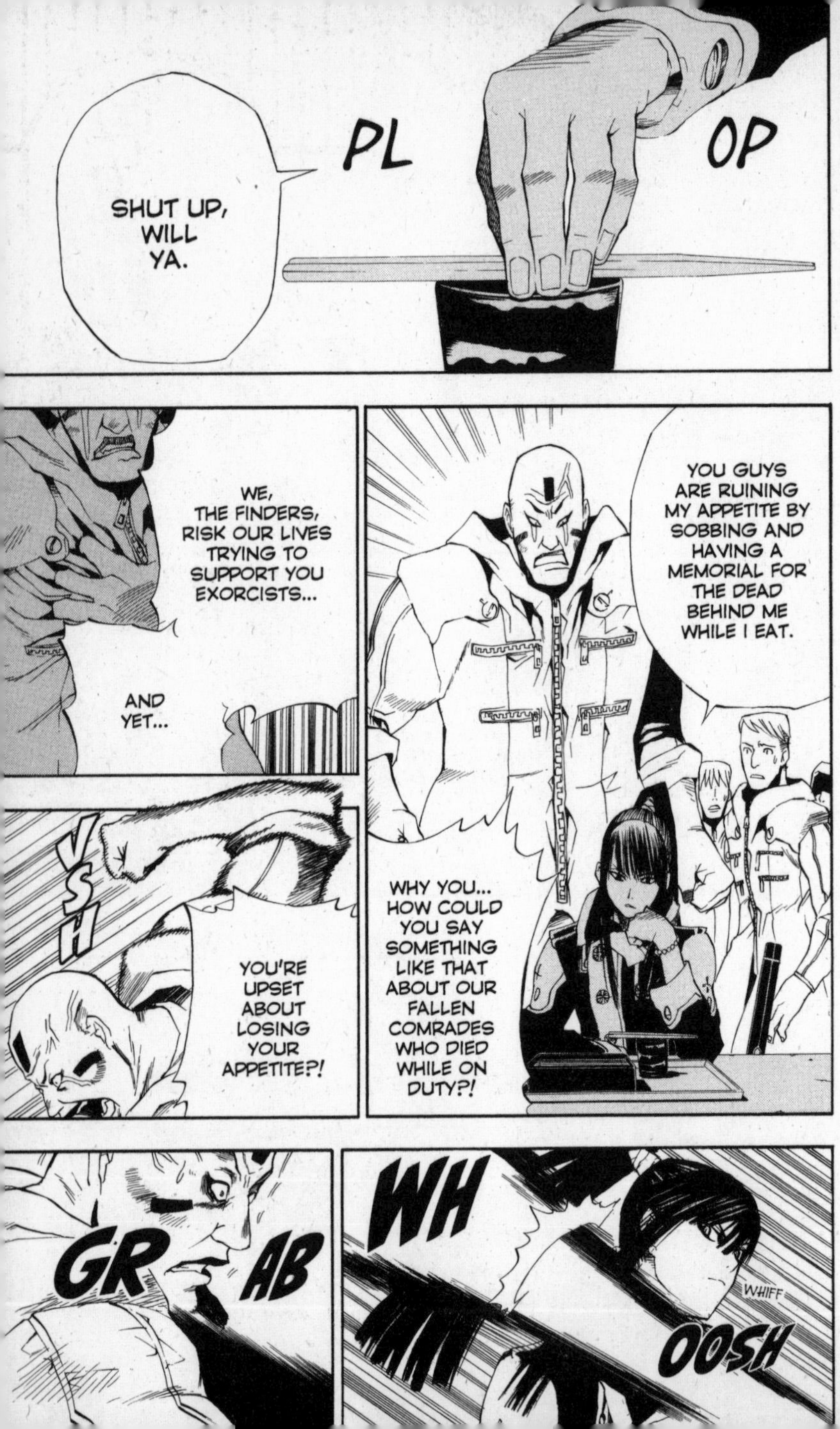
PL
OP
SHUT UP, WILL YA.
YOU GUYS ARE RUINING MY APPETITE BY SOBBING AND HAVING A MEMORIAL FOR THE DEAD BEHIND ME WHILE I EAT.
WHY YOU... HOW COULD YOU SAY SOMETHING LIKE THAT ABOUT OUR FALLEN COMRADES WHO DIED WHILE ON DUTY?!
WE, THE FINDERS, RISK OUR LIVES TRYING TO SUPPORT YOU EXORCISTS...
AND YET...
VSH
YOU'RE UPSET ABOUT LOSING YOUR APPETITE?!
WH
WHIFF
OOSH
GR
AB

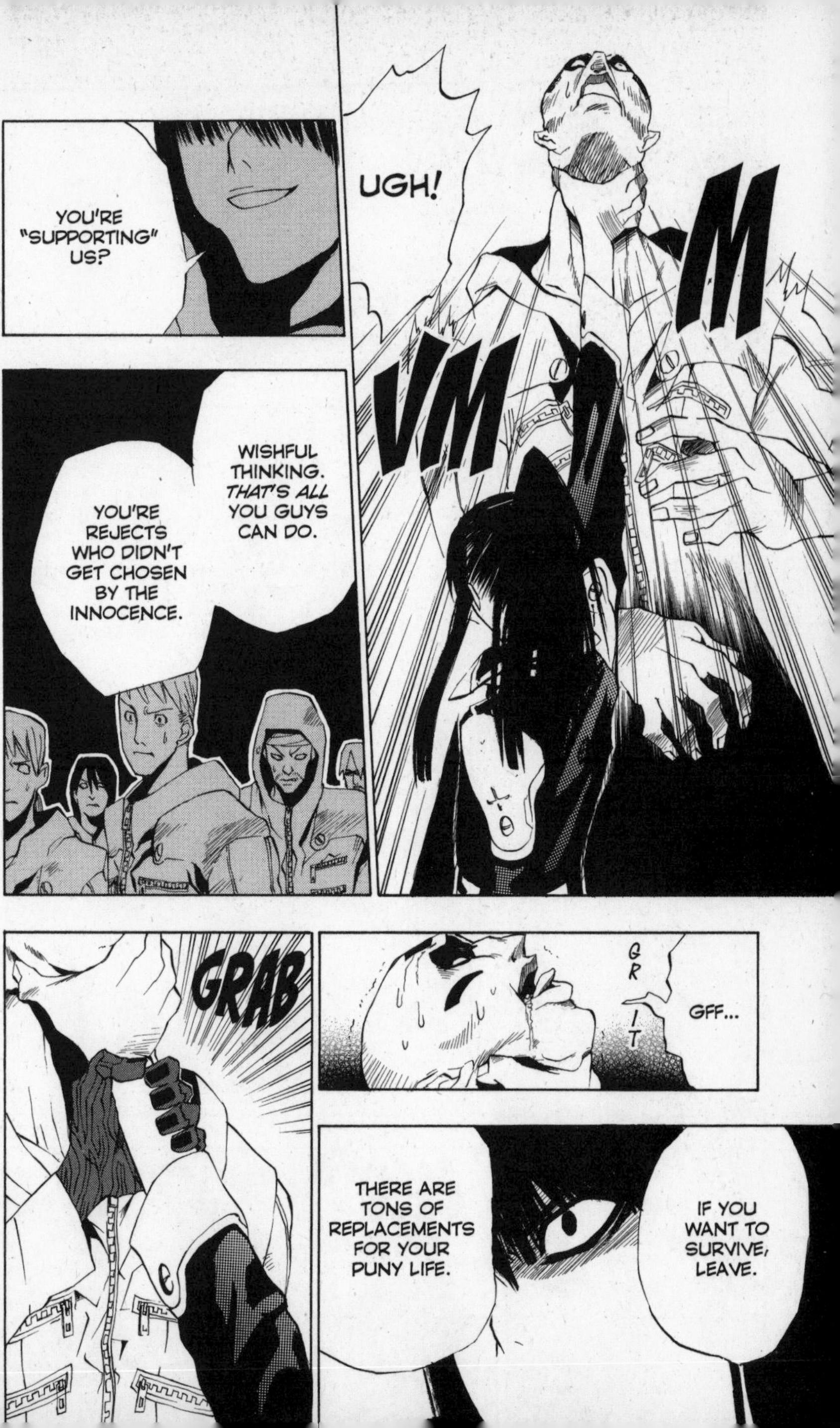
UGH!
VMM
YOU'RE "SUPPORTING" US?
WISHFUL THINKING. *THAT'S ALL* YOU GUYS CAN DO.
YOU'RE REJECTS WHO DIDN'T GET CHOSEN BY THE INNOCENCE.
GFF...
GRIT
IF YOU WANT TO SURVIVE, LEAVE.
THERE ARE TONS OF REPLACEMENTS FOR YOUR PUNY LIFE.
GRAB

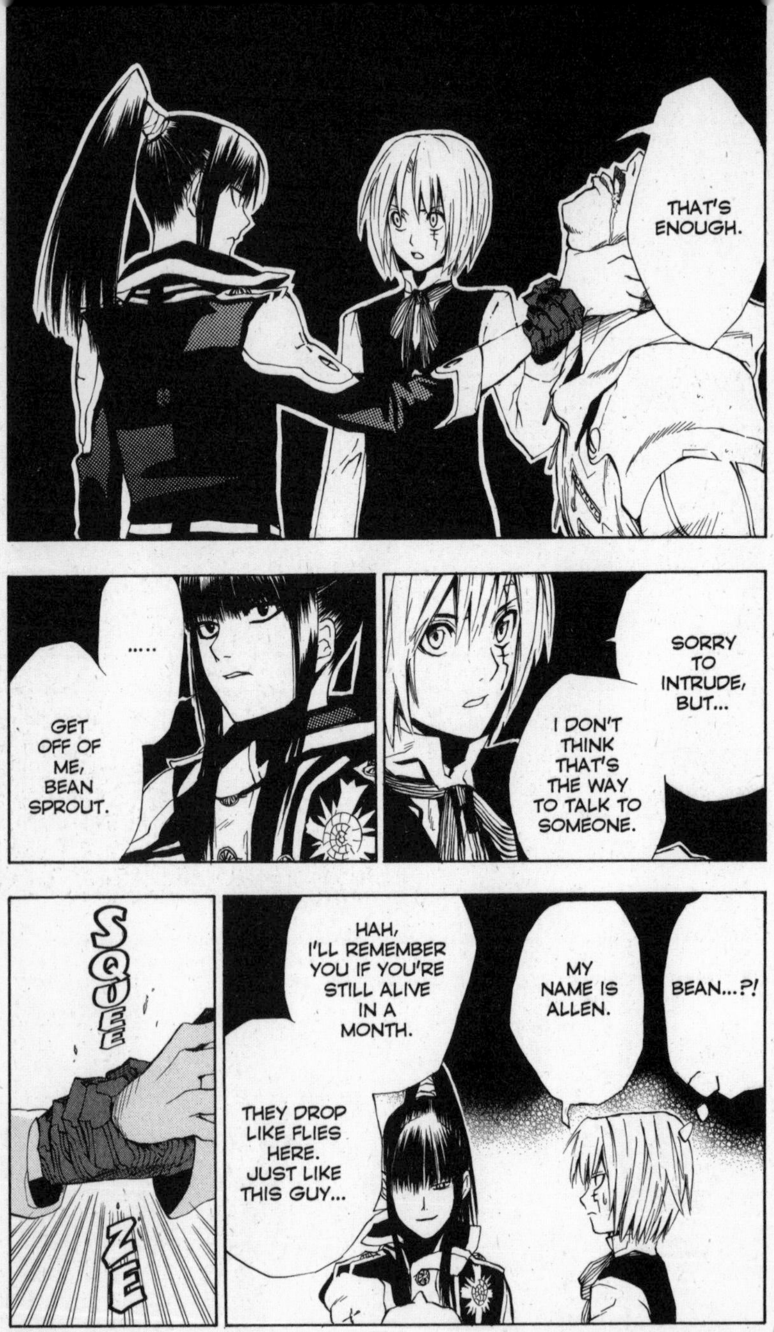
THAT'S ENOUGH.
SORRY TO INTRUDE, BUT...
I DON'T THINK THAT'S THE WAY TO TALK TO SOMEONE.
.....
GET OFF OF ME, BEAN SPROUT.
BEAN...?!
MY NAME IS ALLEN.
HAH, I'LL REMEMBER YOU IF YOU'RE STILL ALIVE IN A MONTH.
THEY DROP LIKE FLIES HERE. JUST LIKE THIS GUY...
SQUEEZE

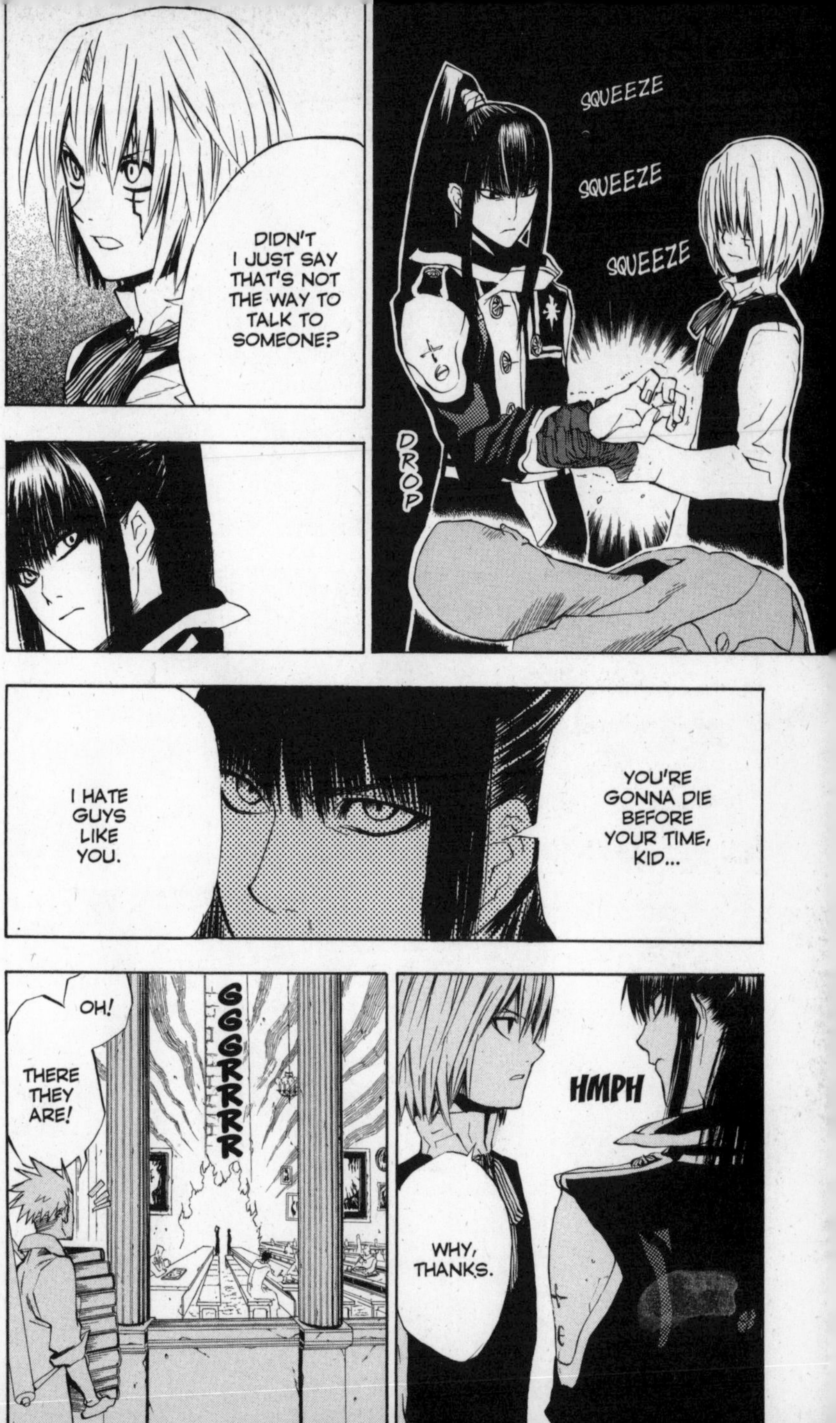
SQUEEZE
SQUEEZE
SQUEEZE
DROP
DIDN'T I JUST SAY THAT'S NOT THE WAY TO TALK TO SOMEONE?
YOU'RE GONNA DIE BEFORE YOUR TIME, KID...
I HATE GUYS LIKE YOU.
HMPH
WHY, THANKS.
GGGRRRR
OH!
THERE THEY ARE!

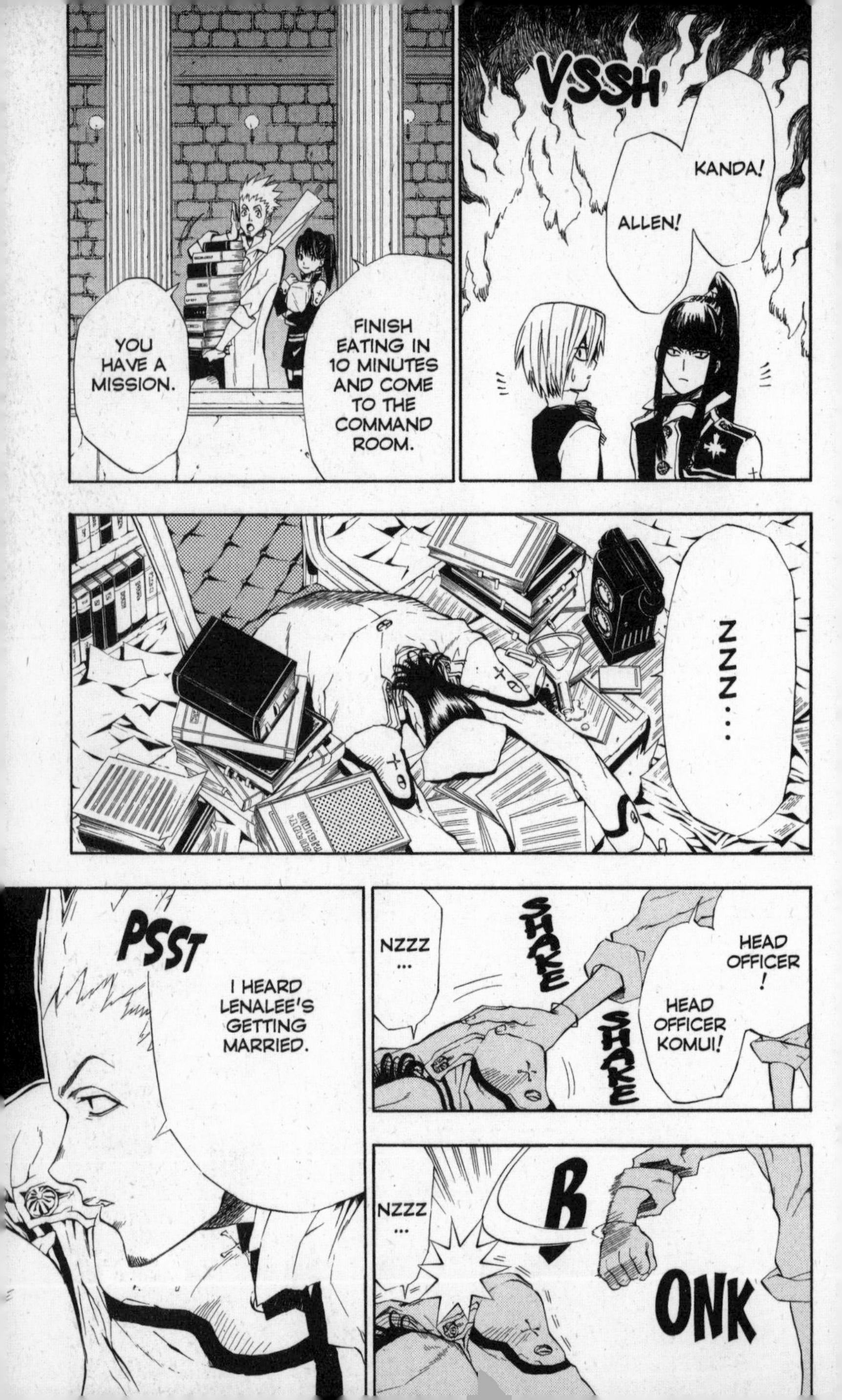
VSSH
KANDA!
ALLEN!
FINISH EATING IN 10 MINUTES AND COME TO THE COMMAND ROOM.
YOU HAVE A MISSION.
ZZZ...
HEAD OFFICER!
SHAKE
HEAD OFFICER KOMUI!
SHAKE
NZZZ...
B
ONK
NZZZ...
PSST
I HEARD LENALEE'S GETTING MARRIED.

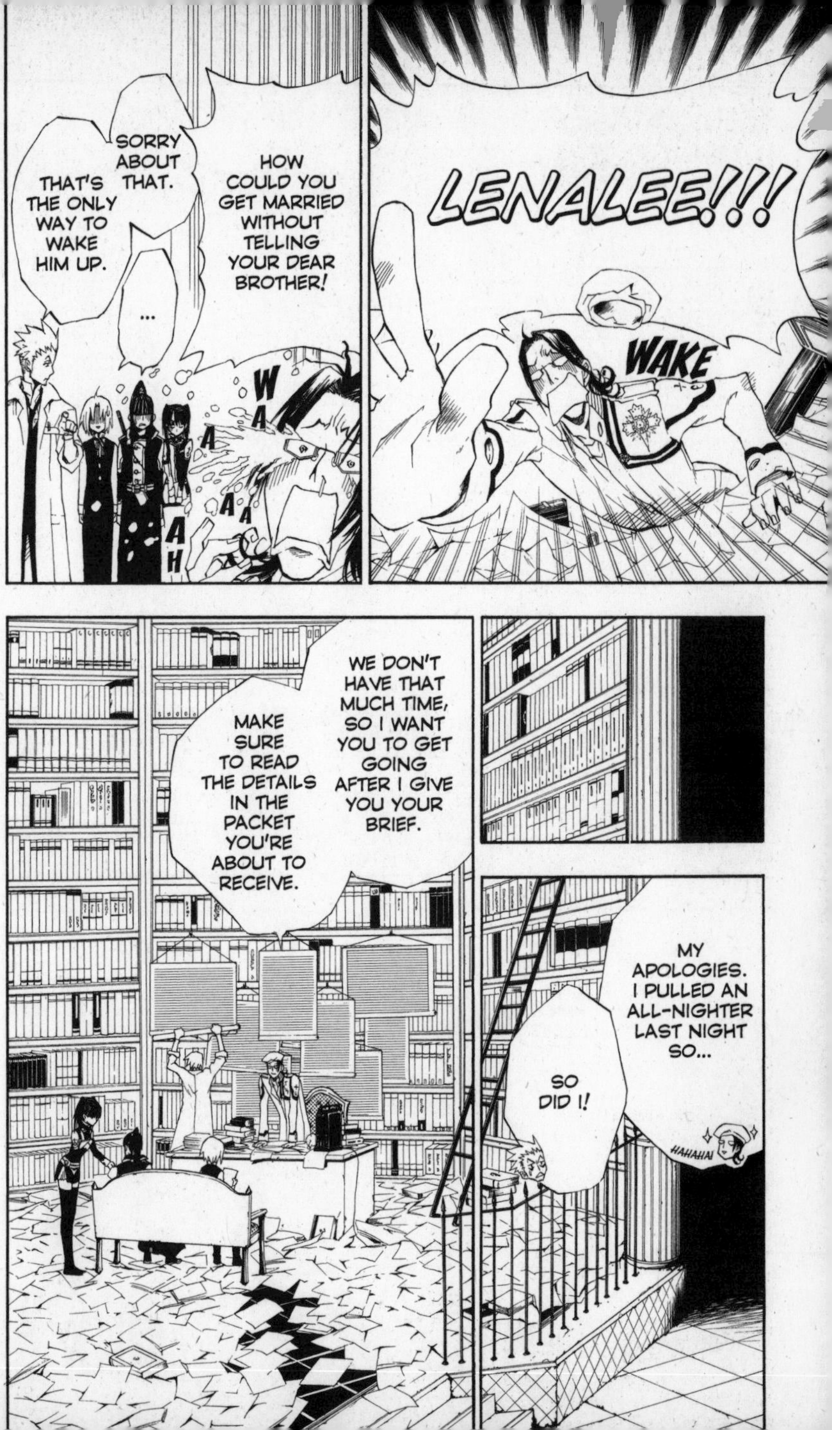
LENALEE!!!
WAKE
HOW COULD YOU GET MARRIED WITHOUT TELLING YOUR DEAR BROTHER!
SORRY ABOUT THAT.
THAT'S THE ONLY WAY TO WAKE HIM UP.
...
WAAAAAH
MY APOLOGIES. I PULLED AN ALL-NIGHTER LAST NIGHT SO...
SO DID I!
HAHAHA!
WE DON'T HAVE THAT MUCH TIME, SO I WANT YOU TO GET GOING AFTER I GIVE YOU YOUR BRIEF.
MAKE SURE TO READ THE DETAILS IN THE PACKET YOU'RE ABOUT TO RECEIVE.

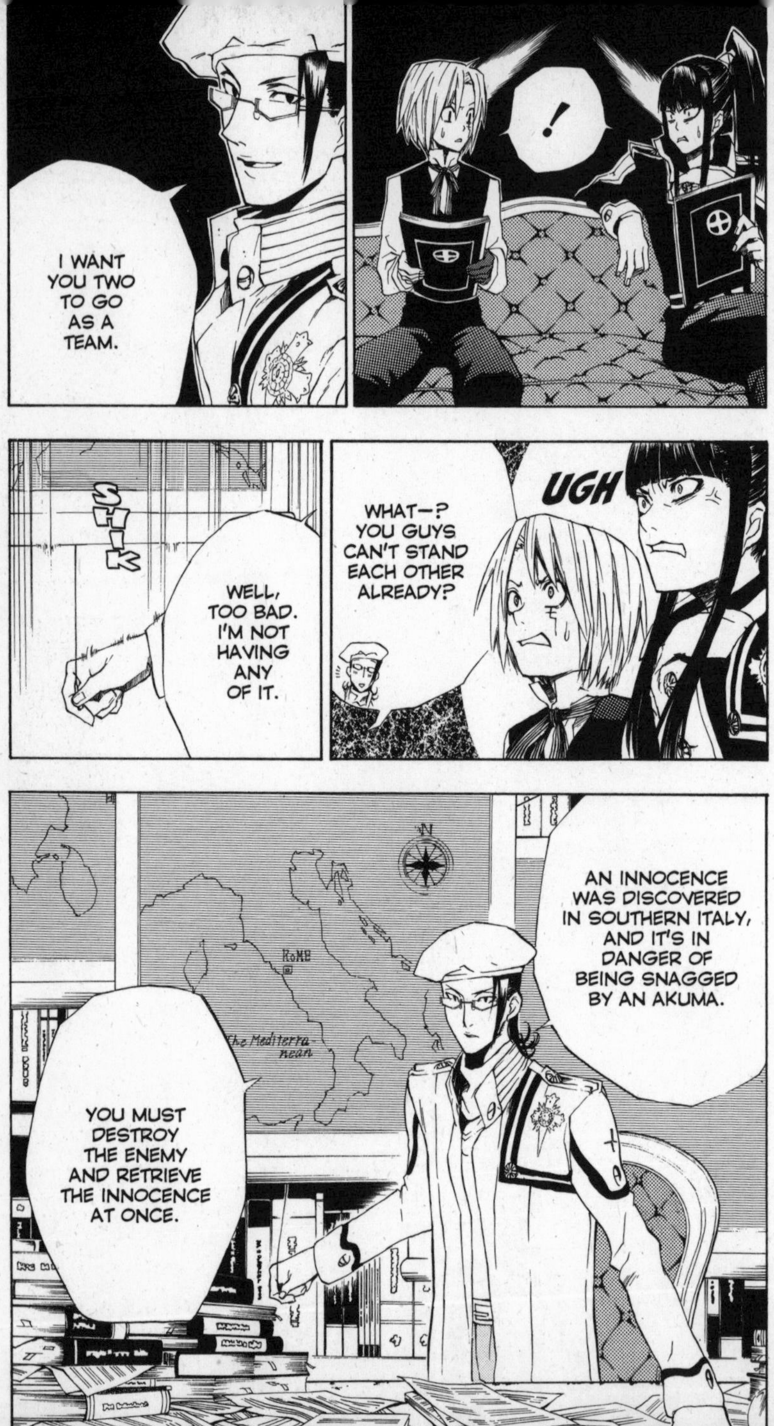
!
I WANT YOU TWO TO GO AS A TEAM.
UGH
WHAT—? YOU GUYS CAN'T STAND EACH OTHER ALREADY?
SHIK
WELL, TOO BAD. I'M NOT HAVING ANY OF IT.
AN INNOCENCE WAS DISCOVERED IN SOUTHERN ITALY, AND IT'S IN DANGER OF BEING SNAGGED BY AN AKUMA.
ROME
The Mediterranean
YOU MUST DESTROY THE ENEMY AND RETRIEVE THE INNOCENCE AT ONCE.

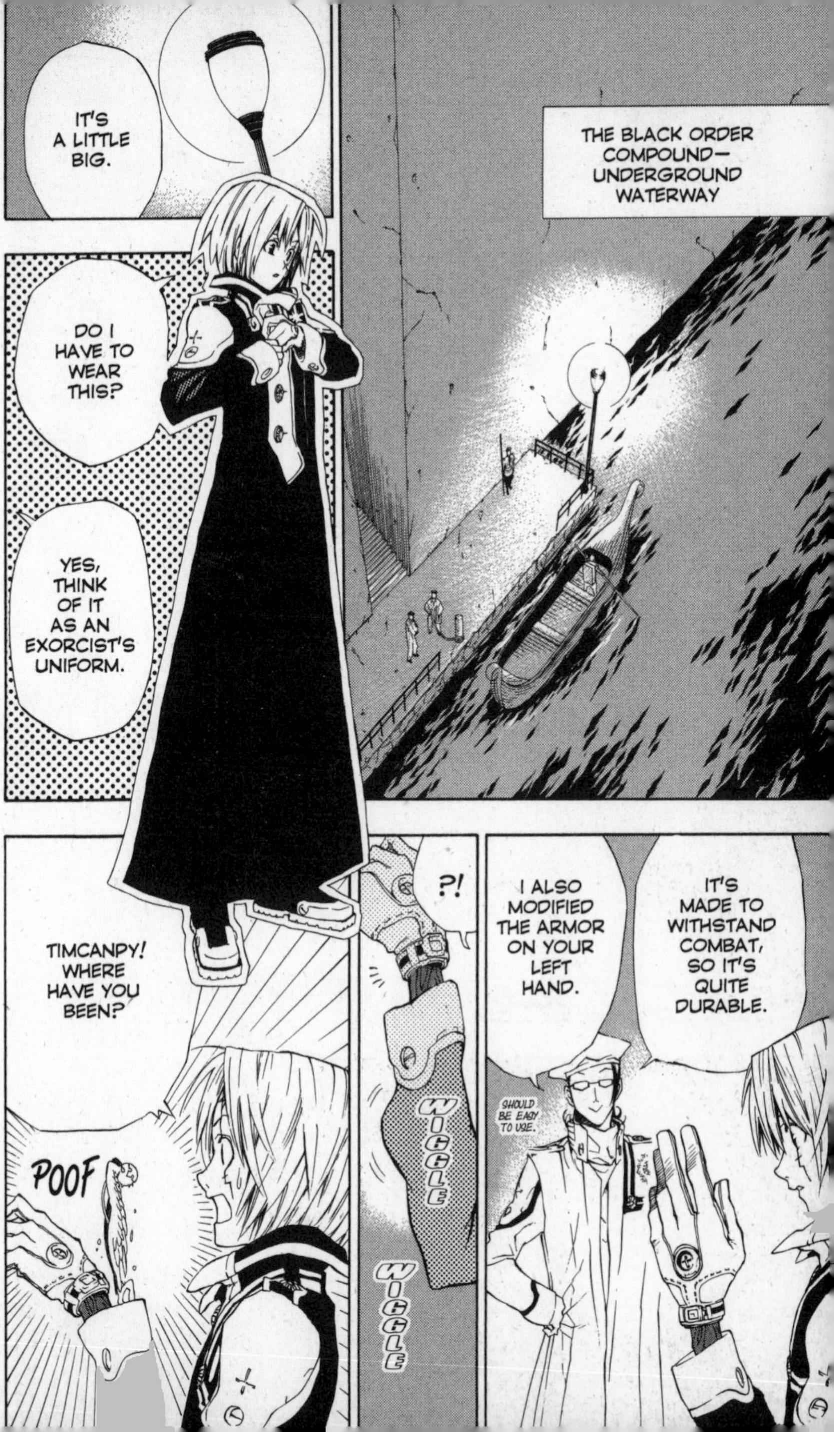
THE BLACK ORDER COMPOUND— UNDERGROUND WATERWAY
IT'S A LITTLE BIG.
DO I HAVE TO WEAR THIS?
YES, THINK OF IT AS AN EXORCIST'S UNIFORM.
IT'S MADE TO WITHSTAND COMBAT, SO IT'S QUITE DURABLE.
I ALSO MODIFIED THE ARMOR ON YOUR LEFT HAND.
SHOULD BE EASY TO USE.
?!
WIGGLE
WIGGLE
TIMCANPY! WHERE HAVE YOU BEEN?
POOF

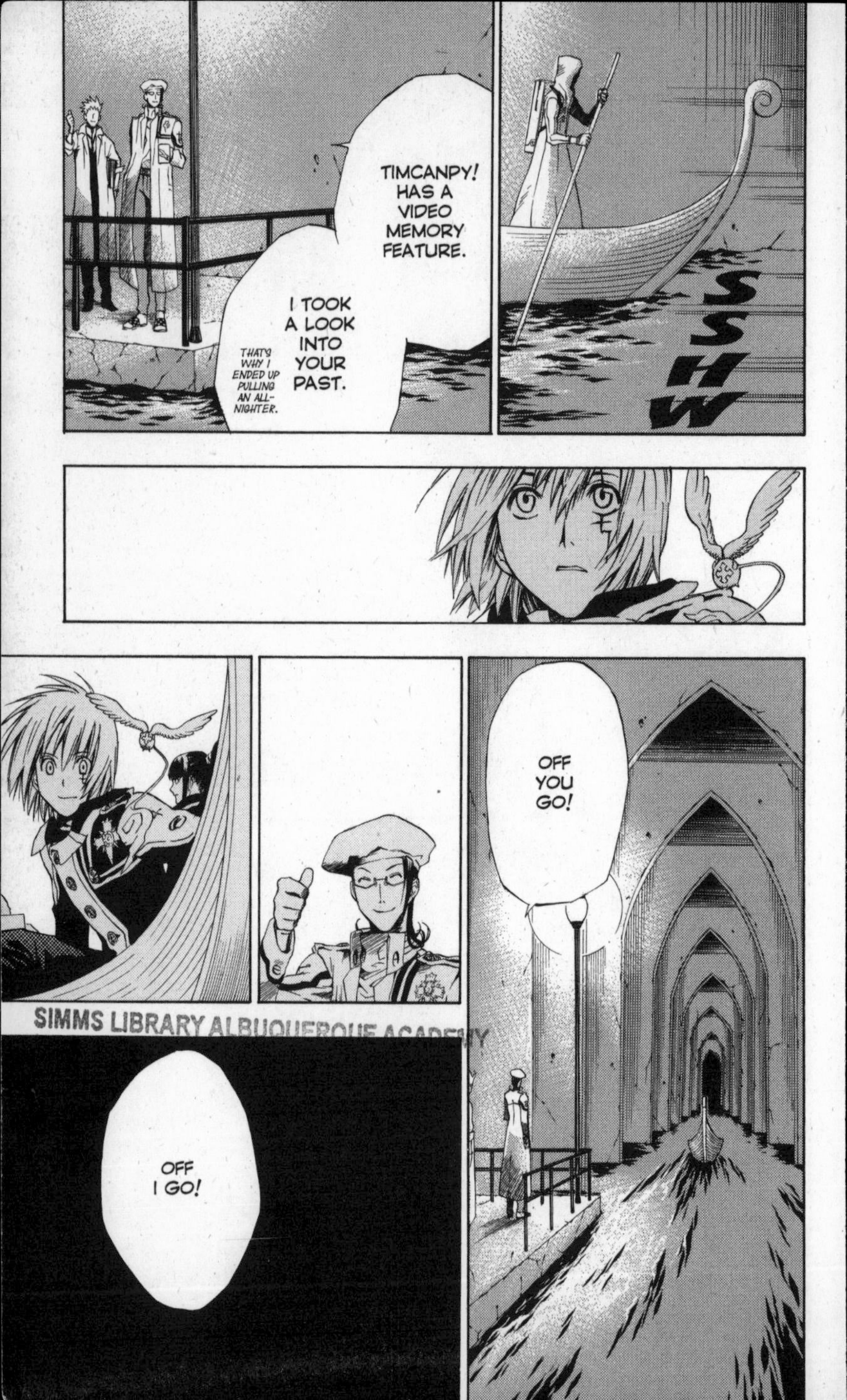
SSHW
TIMCANPY! HAS A VIDEO MEMORY FEATURE.
I TOOK A LOOK INTO YOUR PAST.
THAT'S WHY I ENDED UP PULLING AN ALL-NIGHTER.
OFF YOU GO!
OFF I GO!

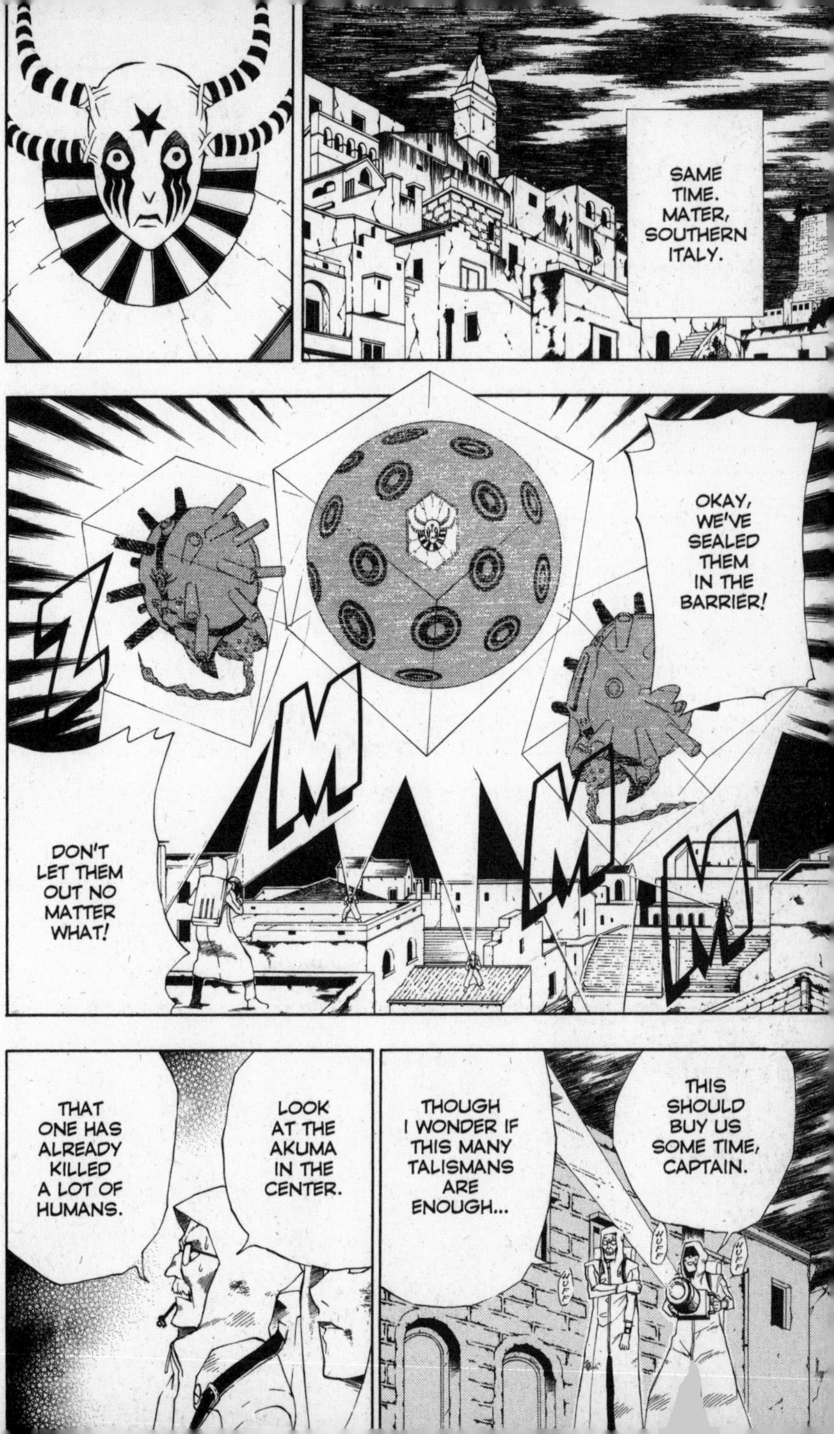
SAME TIME. MATER, SOUTHERN ITALY.
OKAY, WE'VE SEALED THEM IN THE BARRIER!
DON'T LET THEM OUT NO MATTER WHAT!
THIS SHOULD BUY US SOME TIME, CAPTAIN.
HUFF
HUFF
HUFF
THOUGH I WONDER IF THIS MANY TALISMANS ARE ENOUGH...
LOOK AT THE AKUMA IN THE CENTER.
THAT ONE HAS ALREADY KILLED A LOT OF HUMANS.

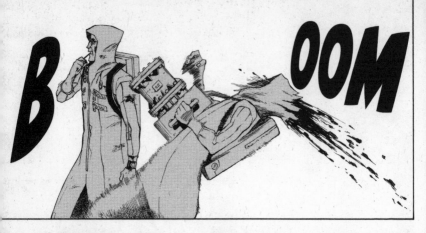

B OOM

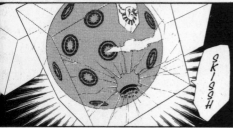

SKIGSH

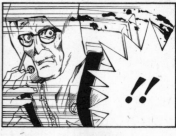

!!

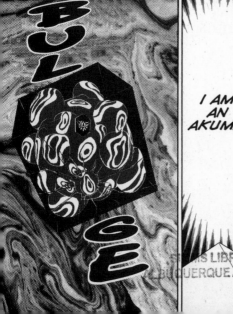

BUL GE

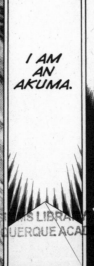

I AM AN AKUMA.

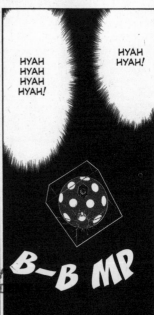

HYAH
HYAH
HYAH
HYAH!

HYAH
HYAH!

B-B MP

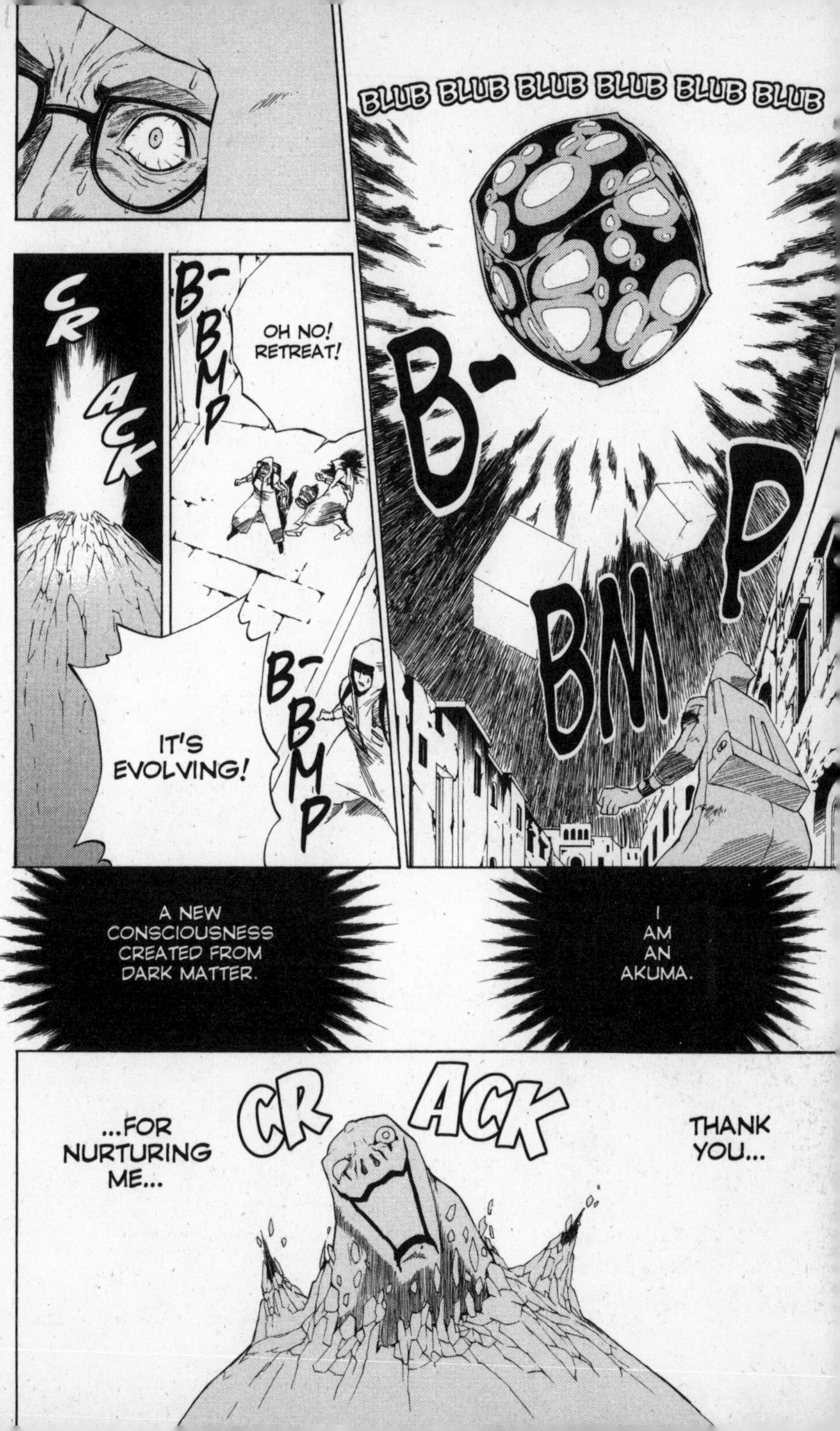
BLUB BLUB BLUB BLUB BLUB BLUB
B-BMP
B-BMP
OH NO! RETREAT!
B-BMP
IT'S EVOLVING!
CRACK
I AM AN AKUMA.
A NEW CONSCIOUSNESS CREATED FROM DARK MATTER.
THANK YOU...
CRACK
...FOR NURTURING ME...

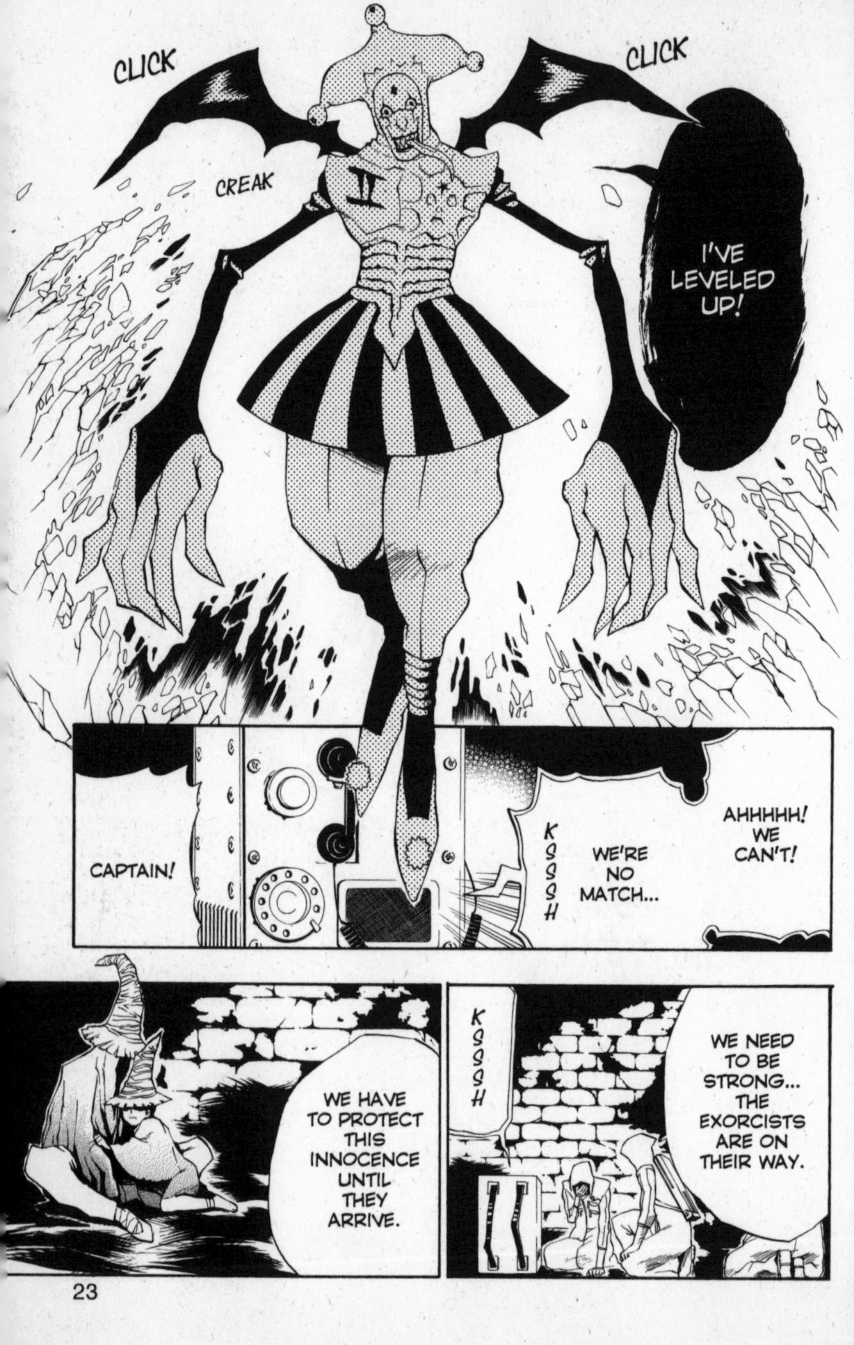
CLICK
CLICK
I'VE LEVELED UP!
CREAK
AHHHHH! WE CAN'T!
KSSSH
WE'RE NO MATCH...
CAPTAIN!
WE NEED TO BE STRONG... THE EXORCISTS ARE ON THEIR WAY.
KSSSH
WE HAVE TO PROTECT THIS INNOCENCE UNTIL THEY ARRIVE.

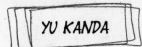

YU KANDA

JAPANESE: 18 YEARS OLD
HEIGHT: 175 CM
WEIGHT: 61 KG
BIRTHDAY: JUNE 6TH
GEMINI: BLOOD TYPE: AB

FAVORITE FOODS: SOBA, TEMPURA
DOESN'T LIKE: TOO MANY TO MENTION
IT'S NOT EASY DRAWING BEAUTIFUL PEOPLE.

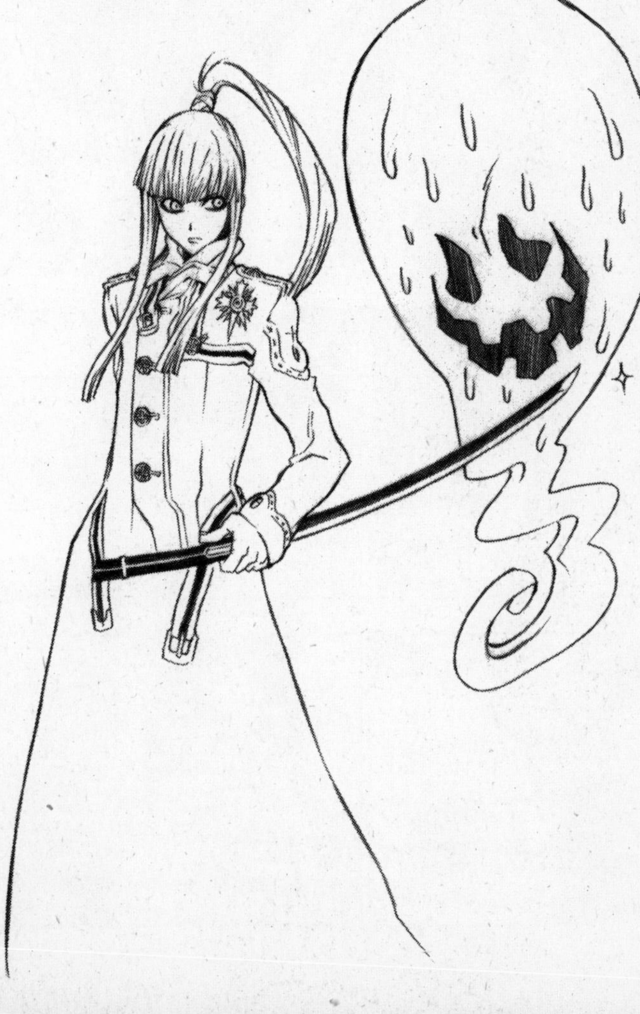

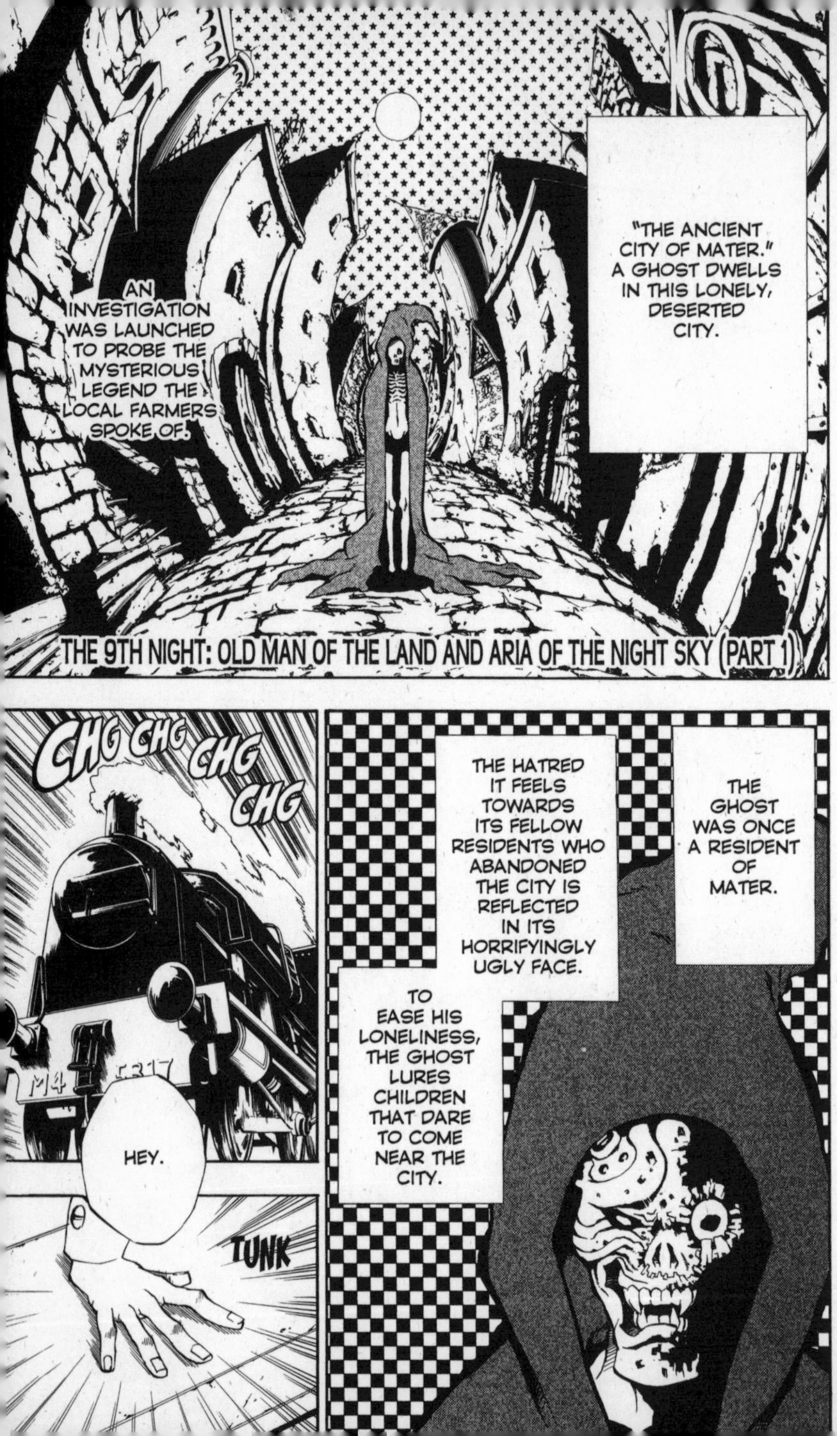
"THE ANCIENT CITY OF MATER." A GHOST DWELLS IN THIS LONELY, DESERTED CITY.
AN INVESTIGATION WAS LAUNCHED TO PROBE THE MYSTERIOUS LEGEND THE LOCAL FARMERS SPOKE OF.
THE 9TH NIGHT: OLD MAN OF THE LAND AND ARIA OF THE NIGHT SKY (PART 1)
THE GHOST WAS ONCE A RESIDENT OF MATER.
THE HATRED IT FEELS TOWARDS ITS FELLOW RESIDENTS WHO ABANDONED THE CITY IS REFLECTED IN ITS HORRIFYINGLY UGLY FACE.
TO EASE HIS LONELINESS, THE GHOST LURES CHILDREN THAT DARE TO COME NEAR THE CITY.
CHG CHG CHG CHG
HEY.
TUNK

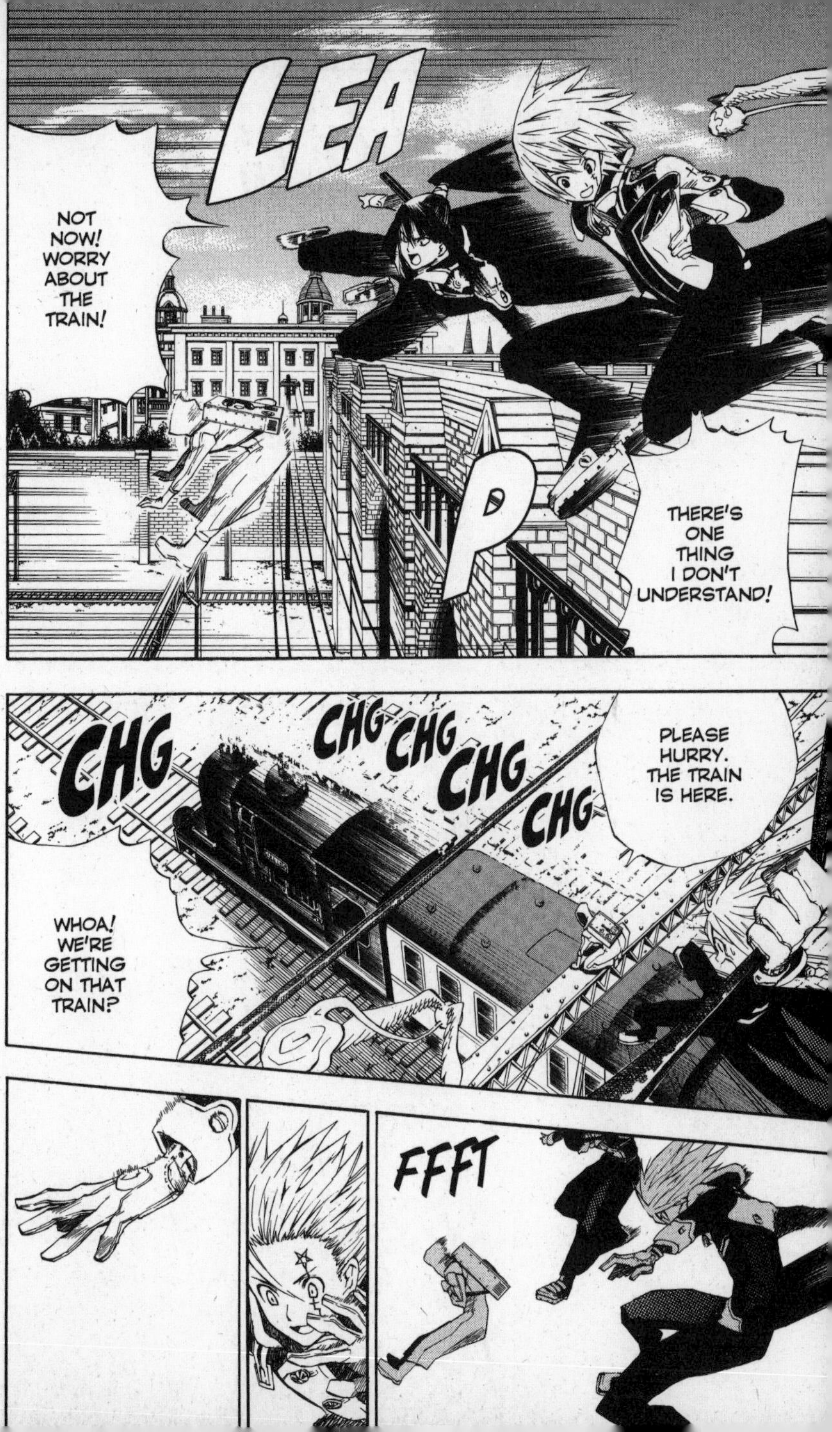
LEA
NOT NOW! WORRY ABOUT THE TRAIN!
P
THERE'S ONE THING I DON'T UNDERSTAND!
CHG
CHG CHG CHG CHG
PLEASE HURRY. THE TRAIN IS HERE.
WHOA! WE'RE GETTING ON THAT TRAIN?
FFFT

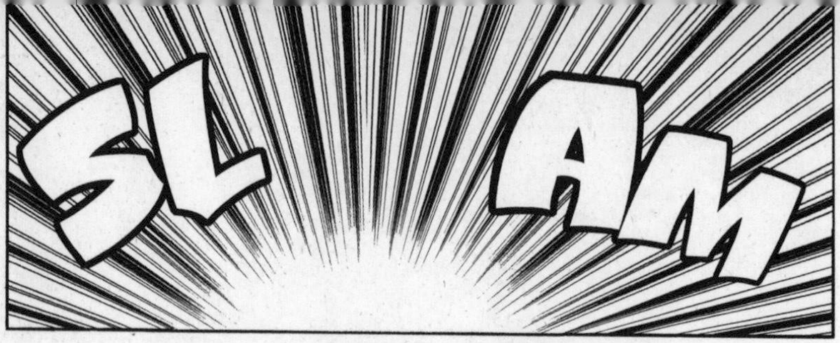
SLAM

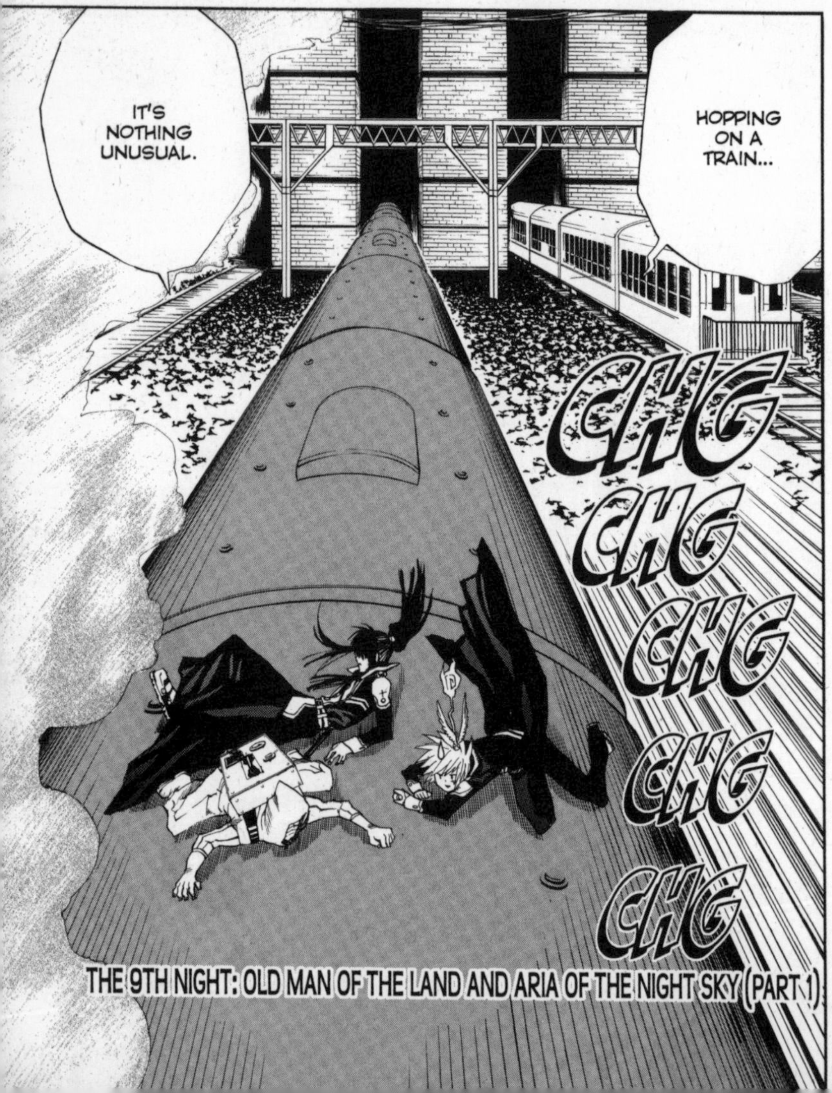
HOPPING ON A TRAIN...
IT'S NOTHING UNUSUAL.
CHG CHG CHG CHG CHG
THE 9TH NIGHT: OLD MAN OF THE LAND AND ARIA OF THE NIGHT SKY (PART 1)

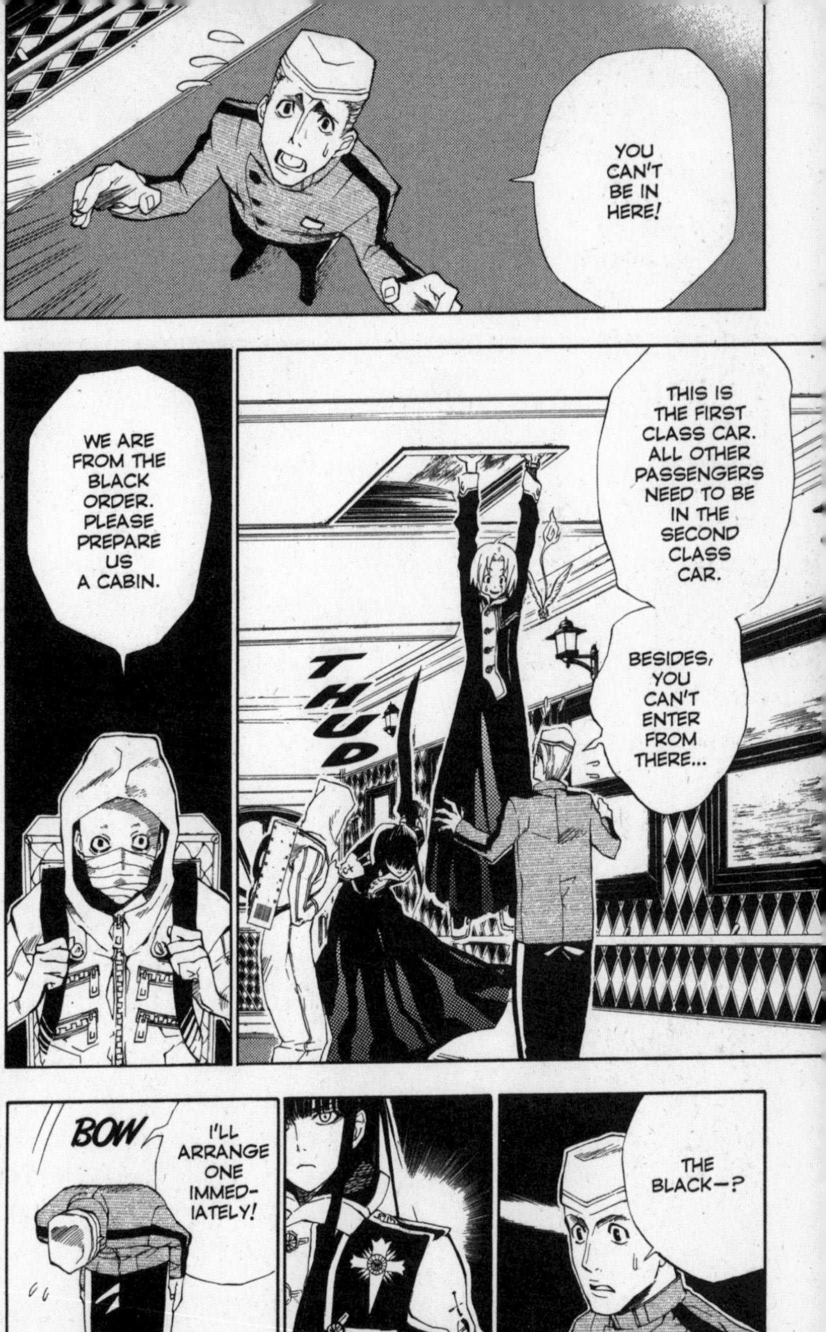
YOU CAN'T BE IN HERE!
THIS IS THE FIRST CLASS CAR. ALL OTHER PASSENGERS NEED TO BE IN THE SECOND CLASS CAR.
BESIDES, YOU CAN'T ENTER FROM THERE...
THUD
WE ARE FROM THE BLACK ORDER. PLEASE PREPARE US A CABIN.
THE BLACK—?
I'LL ARRANGE ONE IMMED-IATELY!
BOW

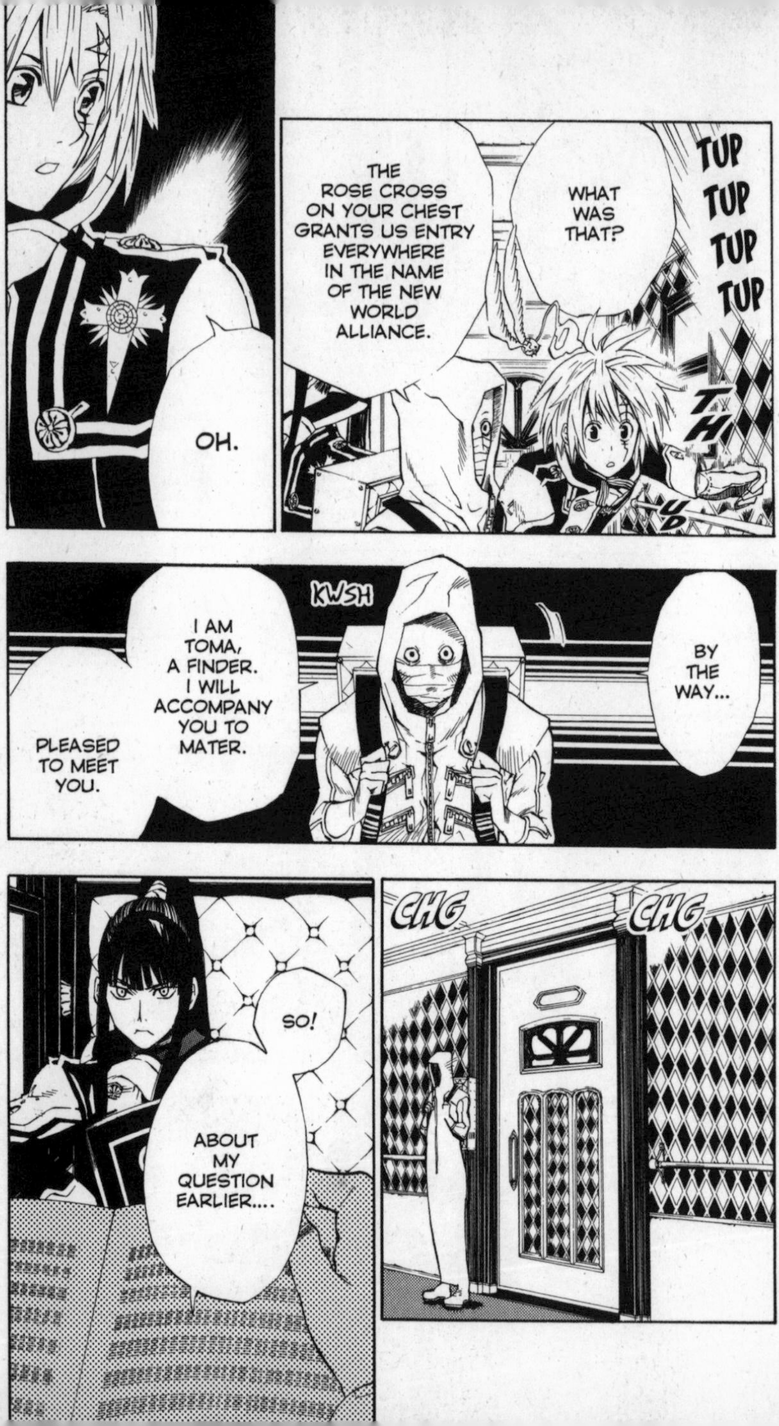
TUP TUP TUP TUP
WHAT WAS THAT?
THE ROSE CROSS ON YOUR CHEST GRANTS US ENTRY EVERYWHERE IN THE NAME OF THE NEW WORLD ALLIANCE.
THUD
OH.
BY THE WAY...
KWSH
I AM TOMA, A FINDER. I WILL ACCOMPANY YOU TO MATER.
PLEASED TO MEET YOU.
CHG
CHG
SO!
ABOUT MY QUESTION EARLIER....

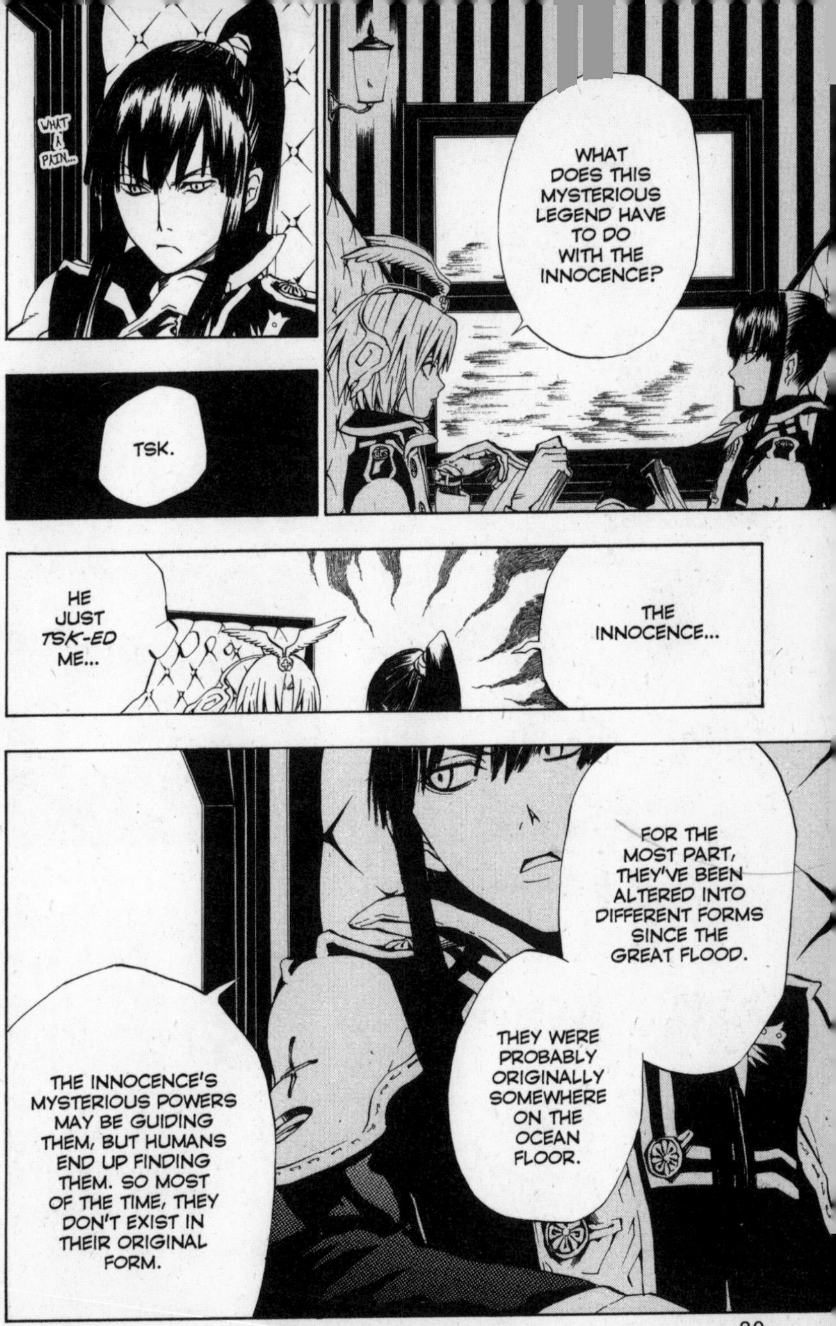
WHAT DOES THIS MYSTERIOUS LEGEND HAVE TO DO WITH THE INNOCENCE?
WHAT A PAIN...
TSK.
THE INNOCENCE...
HE JUST *TSK*-ED ME...
FOR THE MOST PART, THEY'VE BEEN ALTERED INTO DIFFERENT FORMS SINCE THE GREAT FLOOD.
THEY WERE PROBABLY ORIGINALLY SOMEWHERE ON THE OCEAN FLOOR.
THE INNOCENCE'S MYSTERIOUS POWERS MAY BE GUIDING THEM, BUT HUMANS END UP FINDING THEM. SO MOST OF THE TIME, THEY DON'T EXIST IN THEIR ORIGINAL FORM.

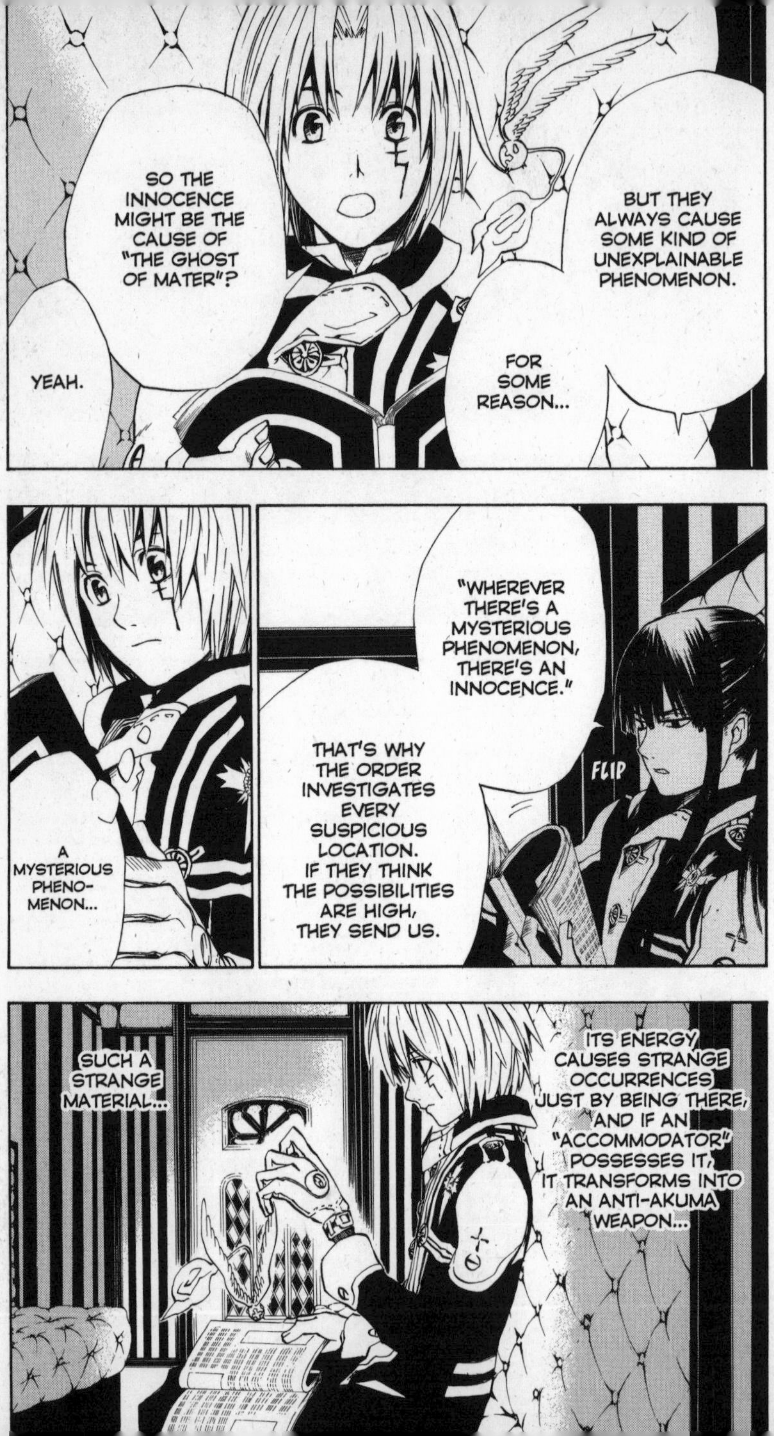
SO THE INNOCENCE MIGHT BE THE CAUSE OF "THE GHOST OF MATER"?
YEAH.
FOR SOME REASON...
BUT THEY ALWAYS CAUSE SOME KIND OF UNEXPLAINABLE PHENOMENON.
A MYSTERIOUS PHENO-MENON...
"WHEREVER THERE'S A MYSTERIOUS PHENOMENON, THERE'S AN INNOCENCE."
THAT'S WHY THE ORDER INVESTIGATES EVERY SUSPICIOUS LOCATION. IF THEY THINK THE POSSIBILITIES ARE HIGH, THEY SEND US.
FLIP
SUCH A STRANGE MATERIAL...
ITS ENERGY CAUSES STRANGE OCCURRENCES JUST BY BEING THERE, AND IF AN "ACCOMMODATOR" POSSESSES IT, IT TRANSFORMS INTO AN ANTI-AKUMA WEAPON...

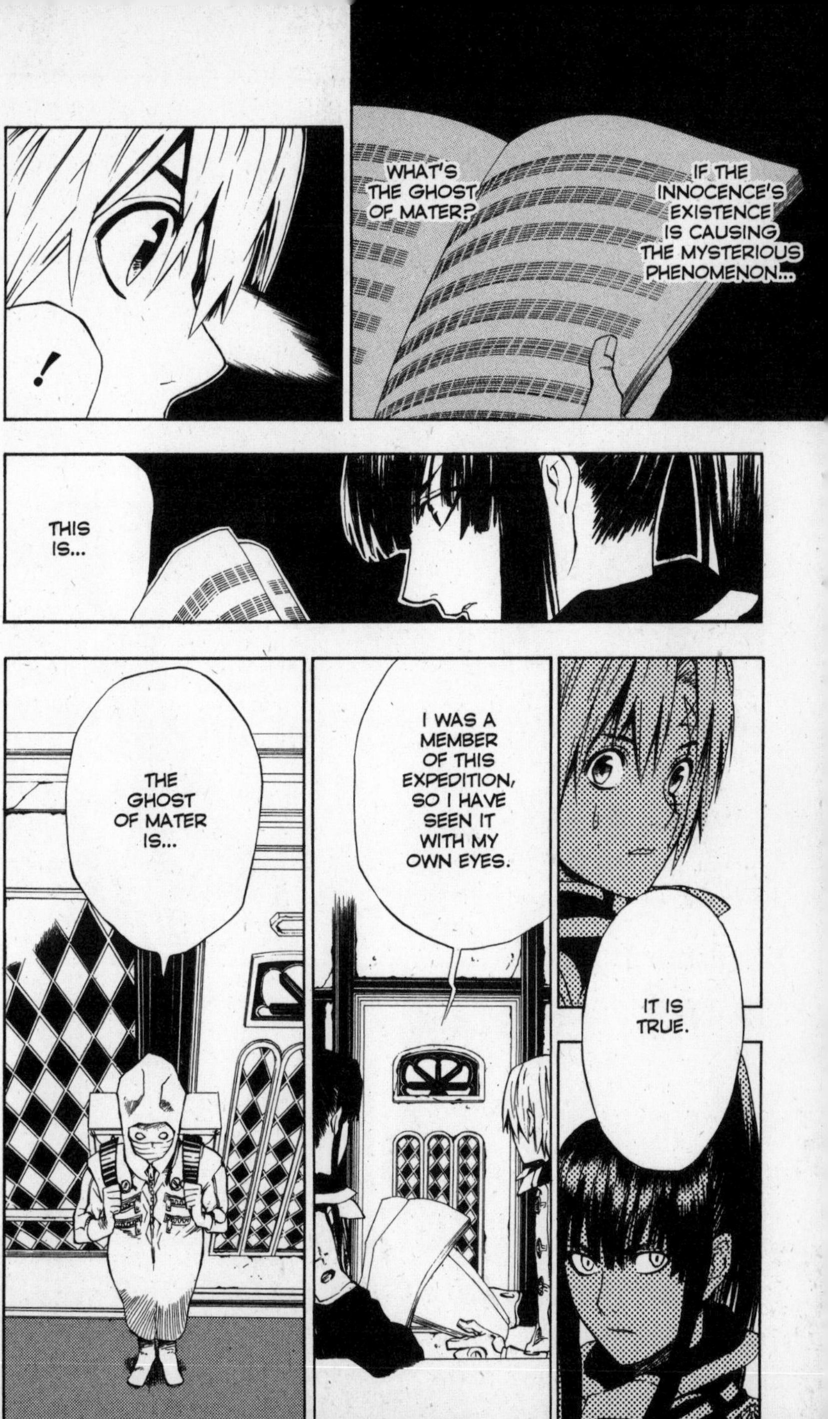
IF THE INNOCENCE'S EXISTENCE IS CAUSING THE MYSTERIOUS PHENOMENON...
WHAT'S THE GHOST OF MATER?
!
THIS IS...
IT IS TRUE.
I WAS A MEMBER OF THIS EXPEDITION, SO I HAVE SEEN IT WITH MY OWN EYES.
THE GHOST OF MATER IS...

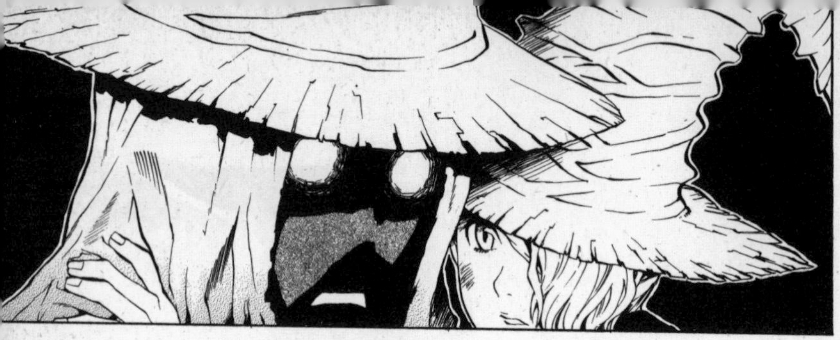

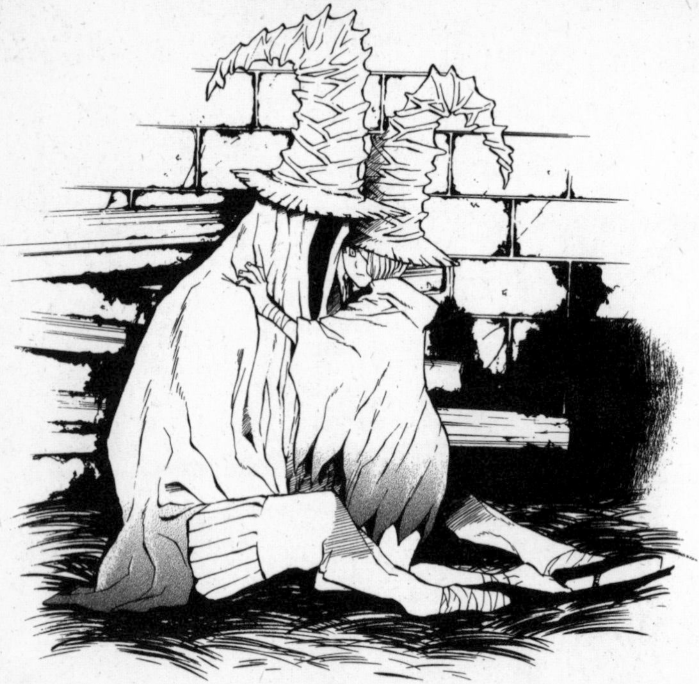

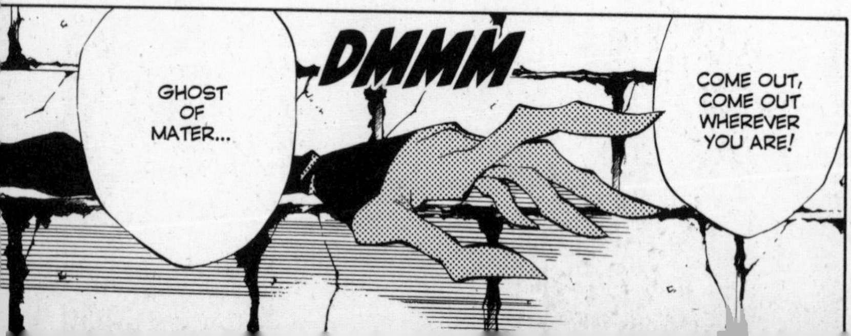
COME OUT, COME OUT WHEREVER YOU ARE!
DMMM
GHOST OF MATER...

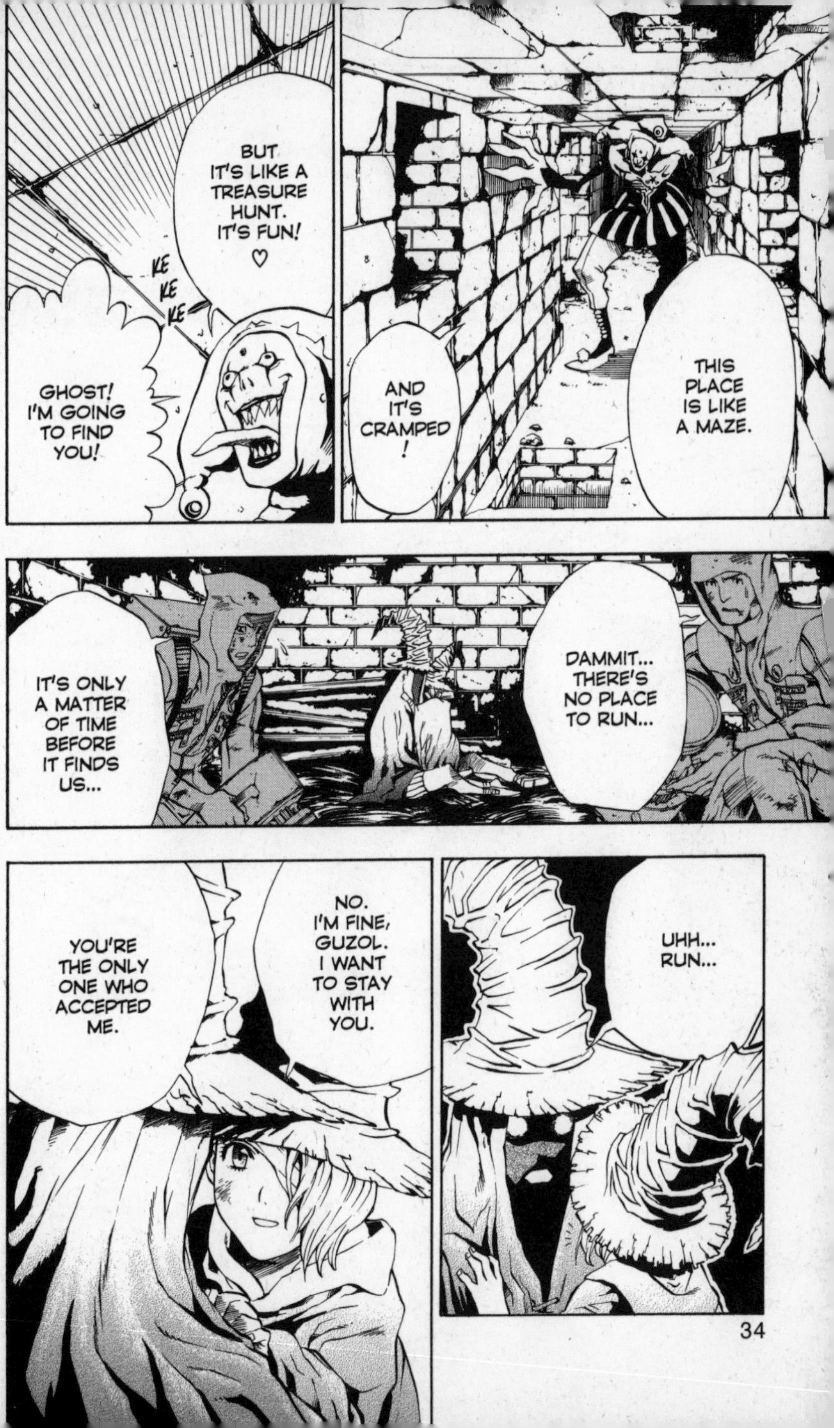
THIS PLACE IS LIKE A MAZE.
AND IT'S CRAMPED!
BUT IT'S LIKE A TREASURE HUNT. IT'S FUN! ♡
KE KE KE
GHOST! I'M GOING TO FIND YOU!
DAMMIT... THERE'S NO PLACE TO RUN...
IT'S ONLY A MATTER OF TIME BEFORE IT FINDS US...
UHH... RUN...
NO. I'M FINE, GUZOL. I WANT TO STAY WITH YOU.
YOU'RE THE ONLY ONE WHO ACCEPTED ME.

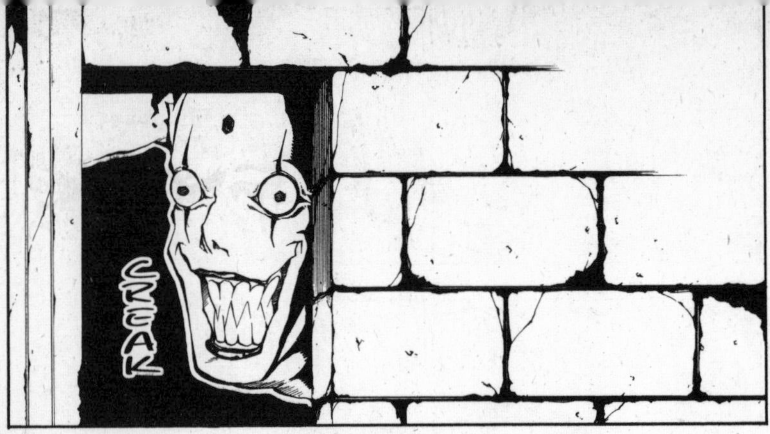
CREAK

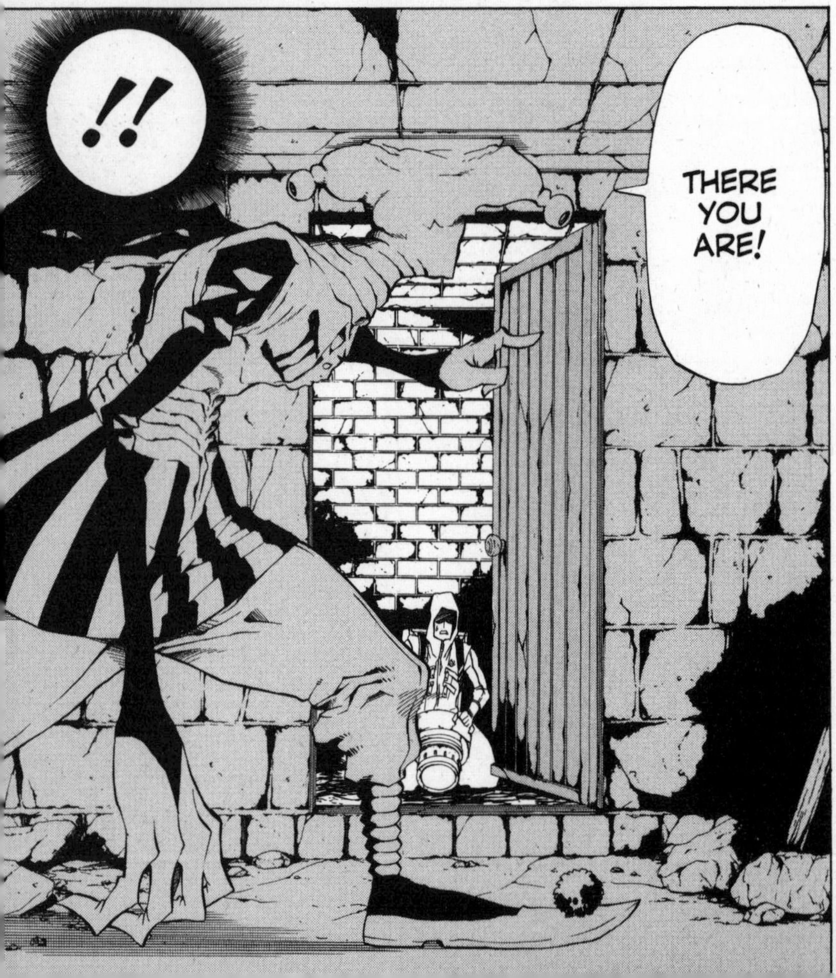
THERE YOU ARE!
!!

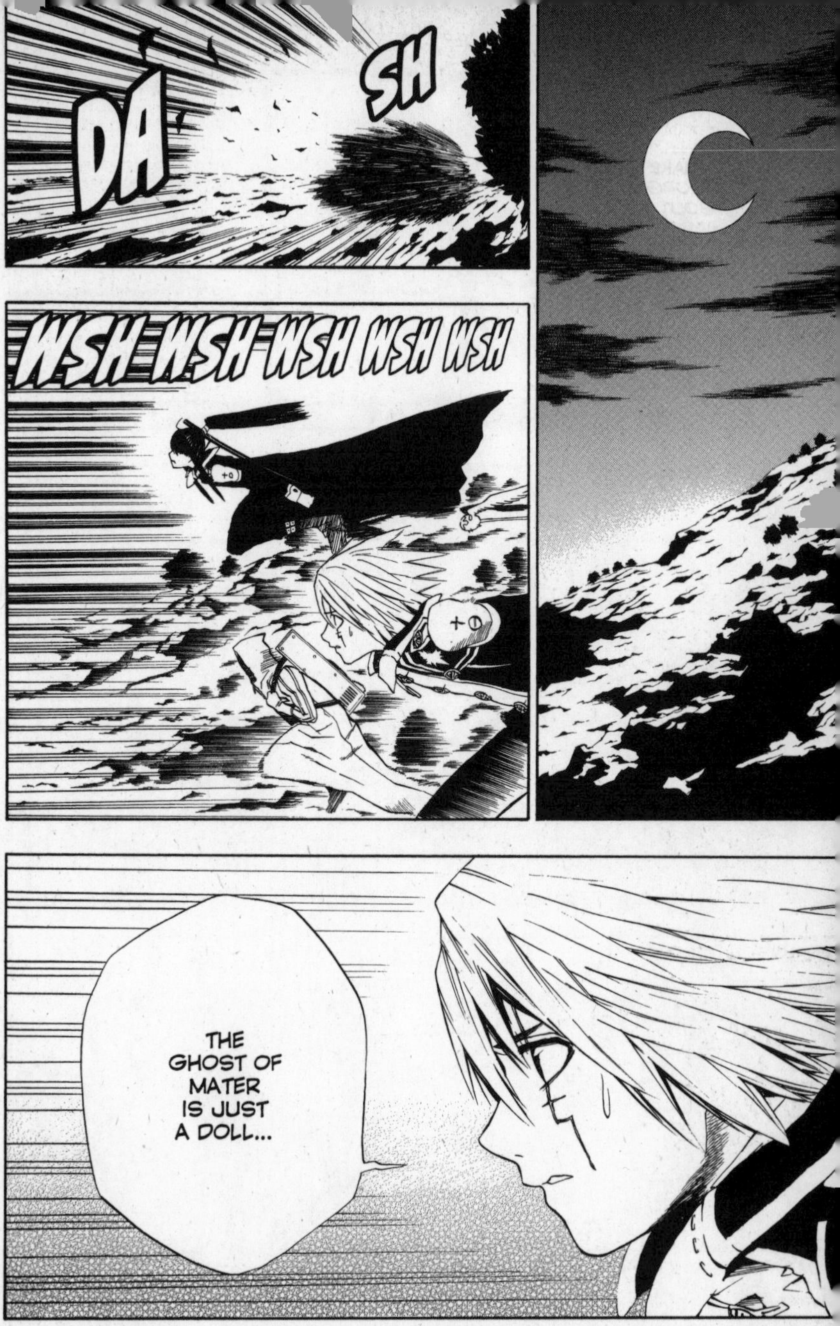
DA
SH
WSH WSH WSH WSH WSH
THE GHOST OF MATER IS JUST A DOLL...

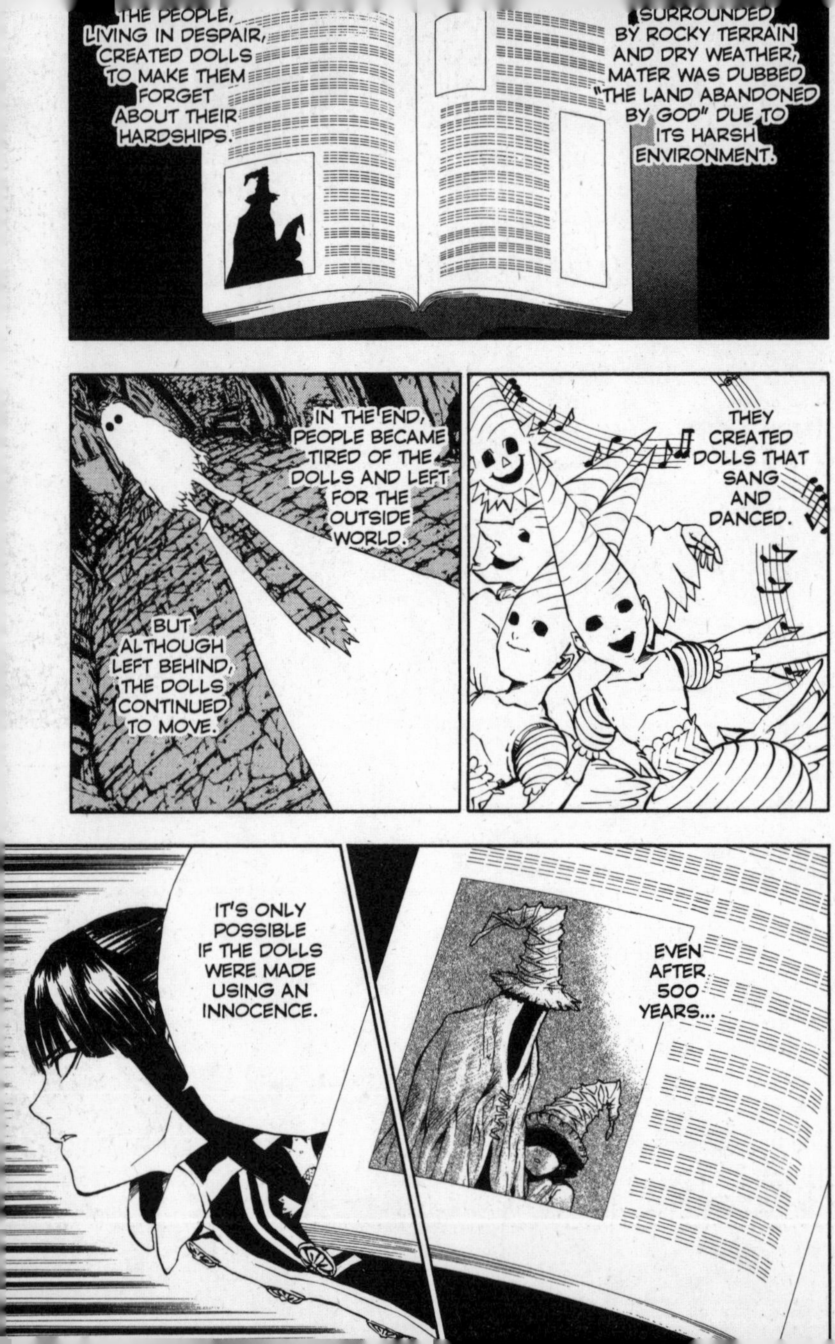
SURROUNDED BY ROCKY TERRAIN AND DRY WEATHER, MATER WAS DUBBED "THE LAND ABANDONED BY GOD" DUE TO ITS HARSH ENVIRONMENT.
THE PEOPLE, LIVING IN DESPAIR, CREATED DOLLS TO MAKE THEM FORGET ABOUT THEIR HARDSHIPS.
THEY CREATED DOLLS THAT SANG AND DANCED.
IN THE END, PEOPLE BECAME TIRED OF THE DOLLS AND LEFT FOR THE OUTSIDE WORLD.
BUT ALTHOUGH LEFT BEHIND, THE DOLLS CONTINUED TO MOVE.
EVEN AFTER 500 YEARS...
IT'S ONLY POSSIBLE IF THE DOLLS WERE MADE USING AN INNOCENCE.

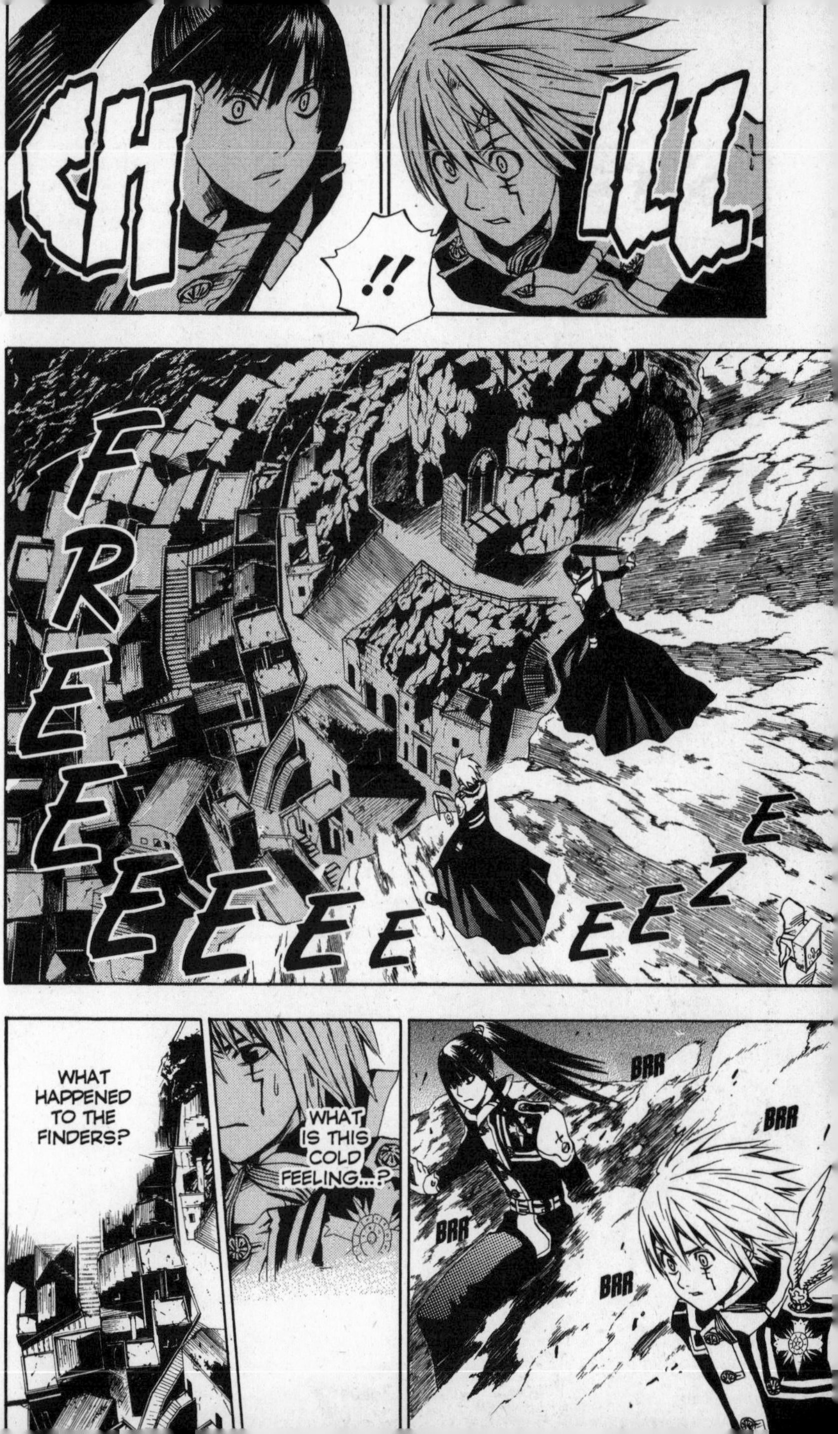

!!
CHILL
FREEEEEEEEEEZE
BRR
BRR
BRR
BRR
WHAT IS THIS COLD FEELING...?
WHAT HAPPENED TO THE FINDERS?

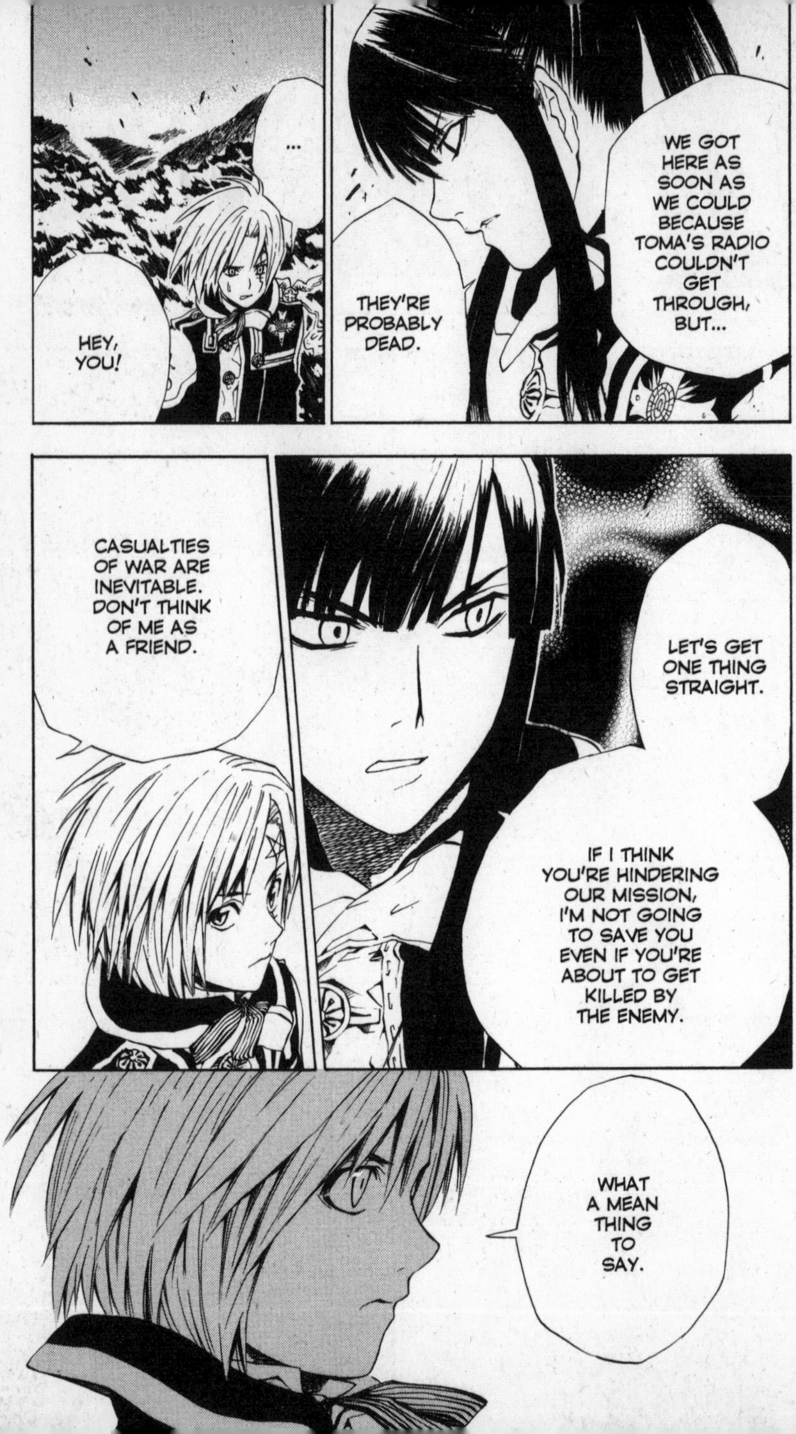
WE GOT HERE AS SOON AS WE COULD BECAUSE TOMA'S RADIO COULDN'T GET THROUGH, BUT...
THEY'RE PROBABLY DEAD.
...
HEY, YOU!
LET'S GET ONE THING STRAIGHT.
IF I THINK YOU'RE HINDERING OUR MISSION, I'M NOT GOING TO SAVE YOU EVEN IF YOU'RE ABOUT TO GET KILLED BY THE ENEMY.
CASUALTIES OF WAR ARE INEVITABLE. DON'T THINK OF ME AS A FRIEND.
WHAT A MEAN THING TO SAY.

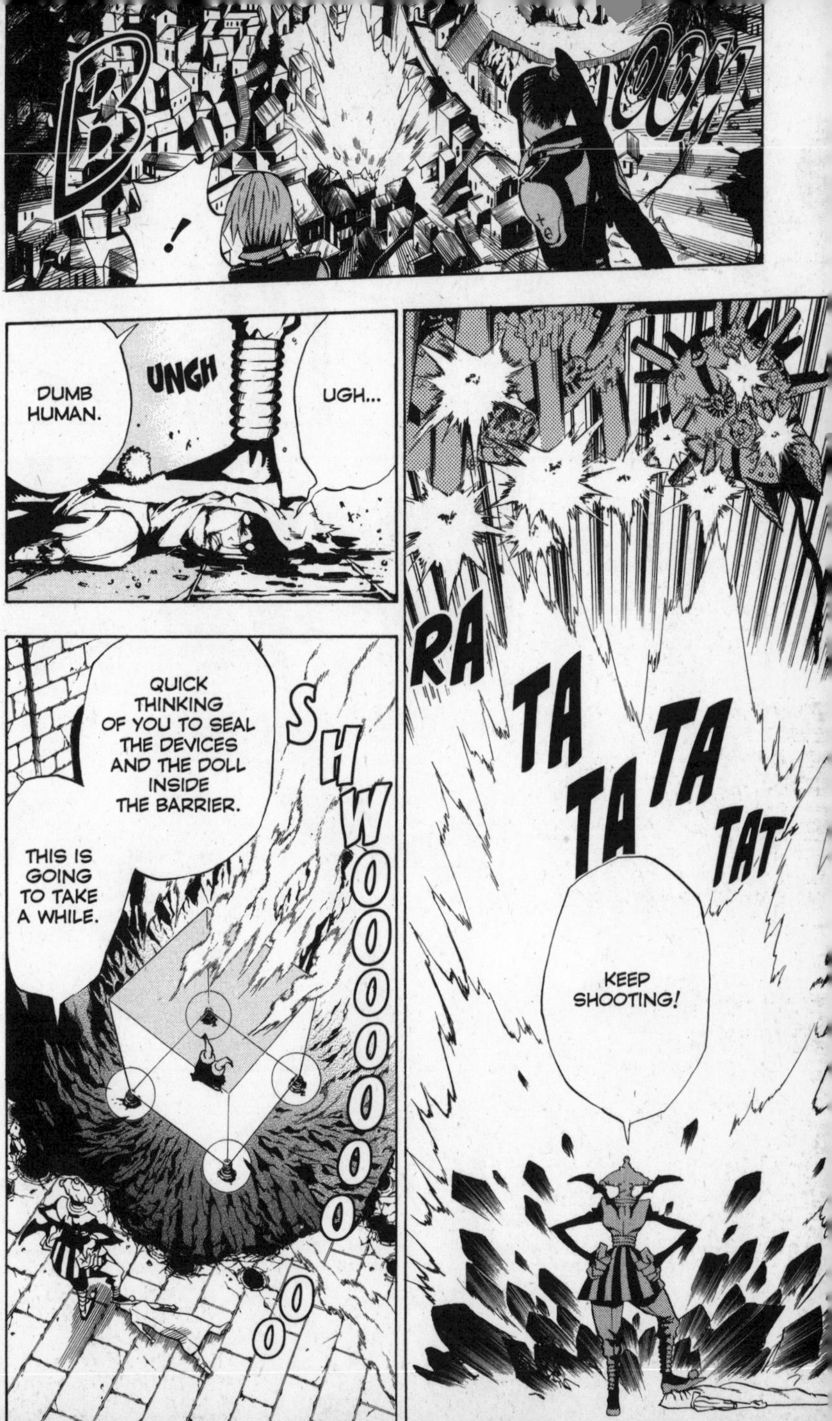
BOOM!
!
RA TA TA TA TA TAT
KEEP SHOOTING!
UGH...
UNGH
DUMB HUMAN.
SHWOOOOOOOOOOO
QUICK THINKING OF YOU TO SEAL THE DEVICES AND THE DOLL INSIDE THE BARRIER.
THIS IS GOING TO TAKE A WHILE.

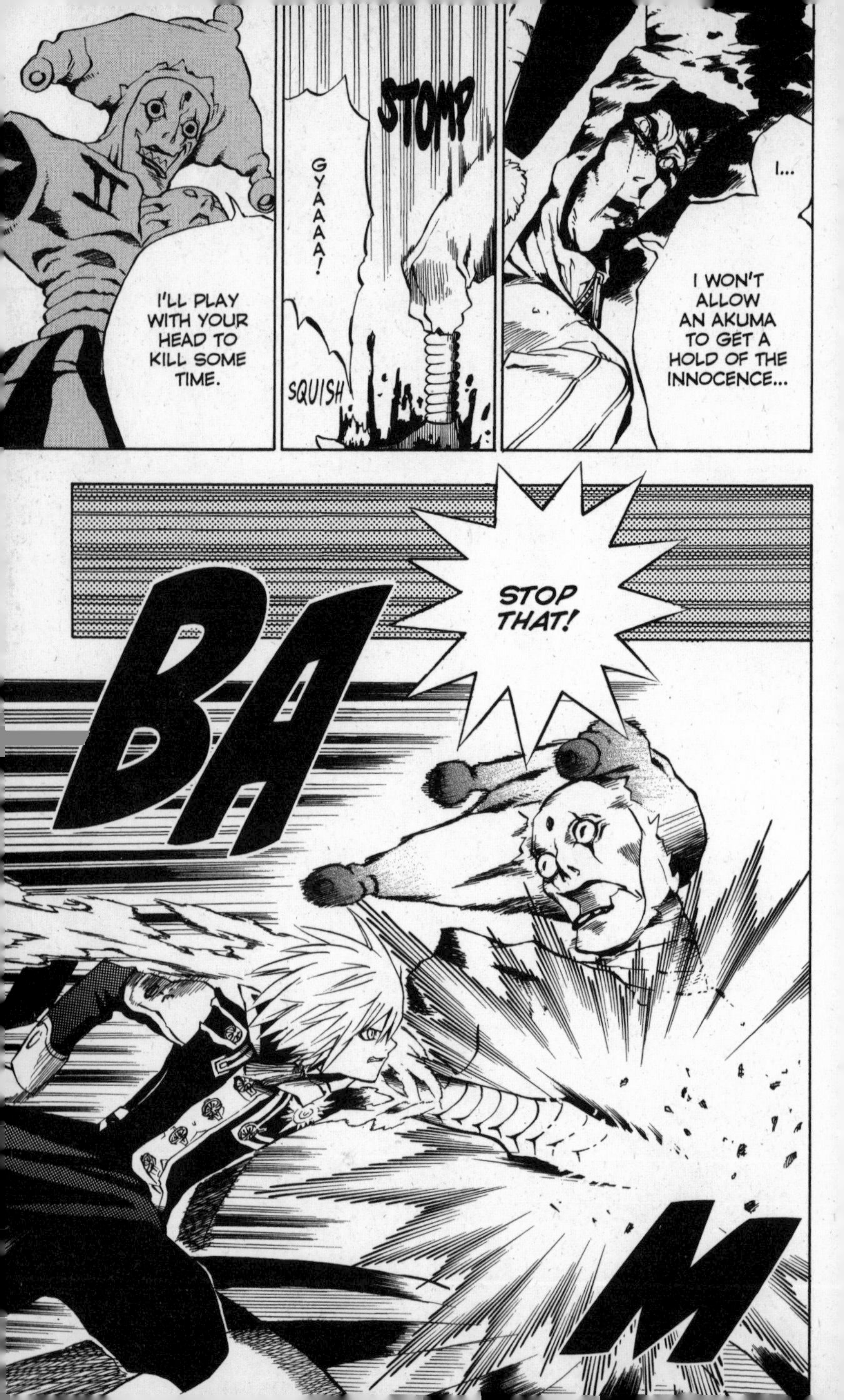
I...
I WON'T ALLOW AN AKUMA TO GET A HOLD OF THE INNOCENCE...
STOMP
GYAAAAA!
SQUISH
I'LL PLAY WITH YOUR HEAD TO KILL SOME TIME.
STOP THAT!
BAM

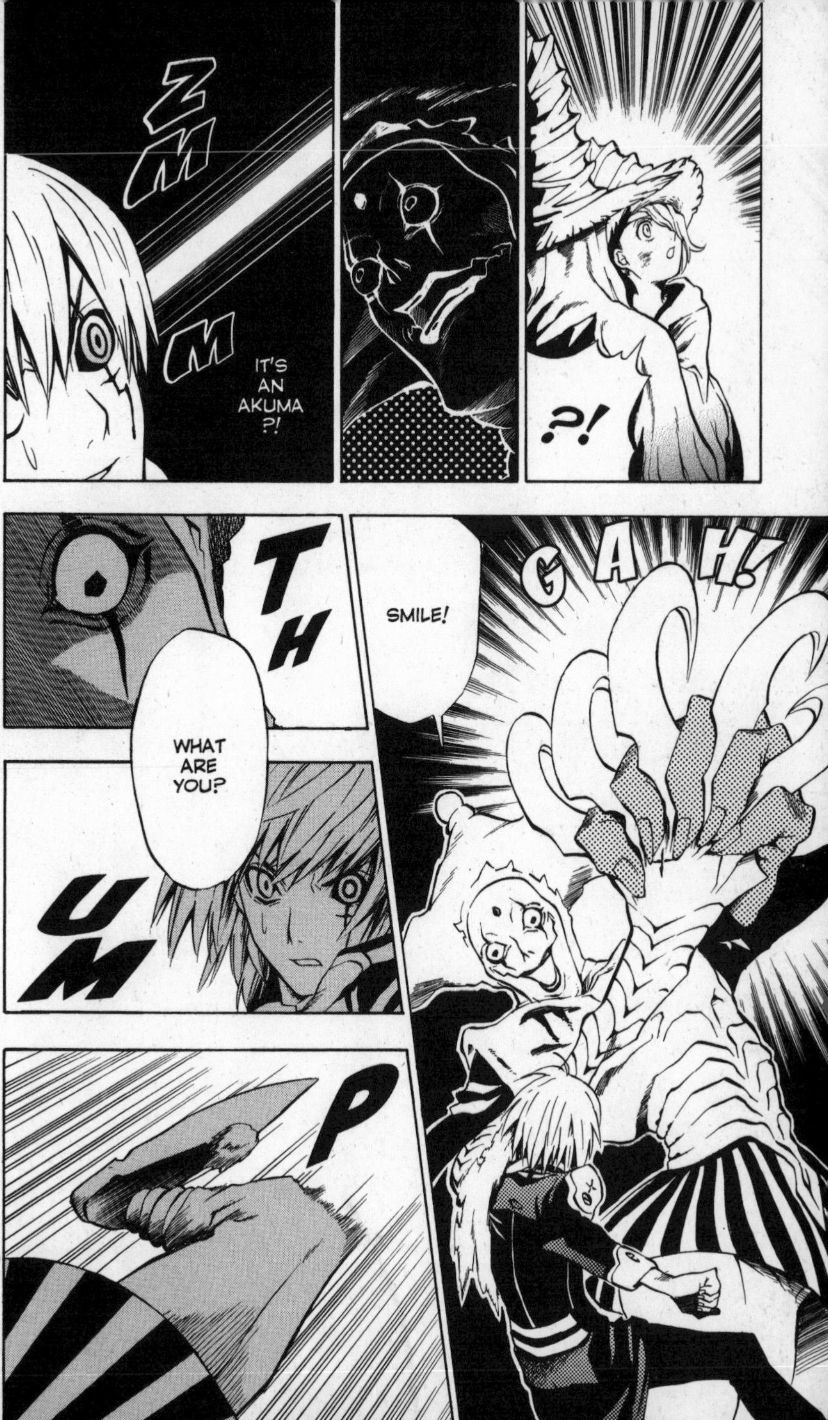
?!
ZMM
IT'S AN AKUMA ?!
GAH!
SMILE!
WHAT ARE YOU?
THUMP

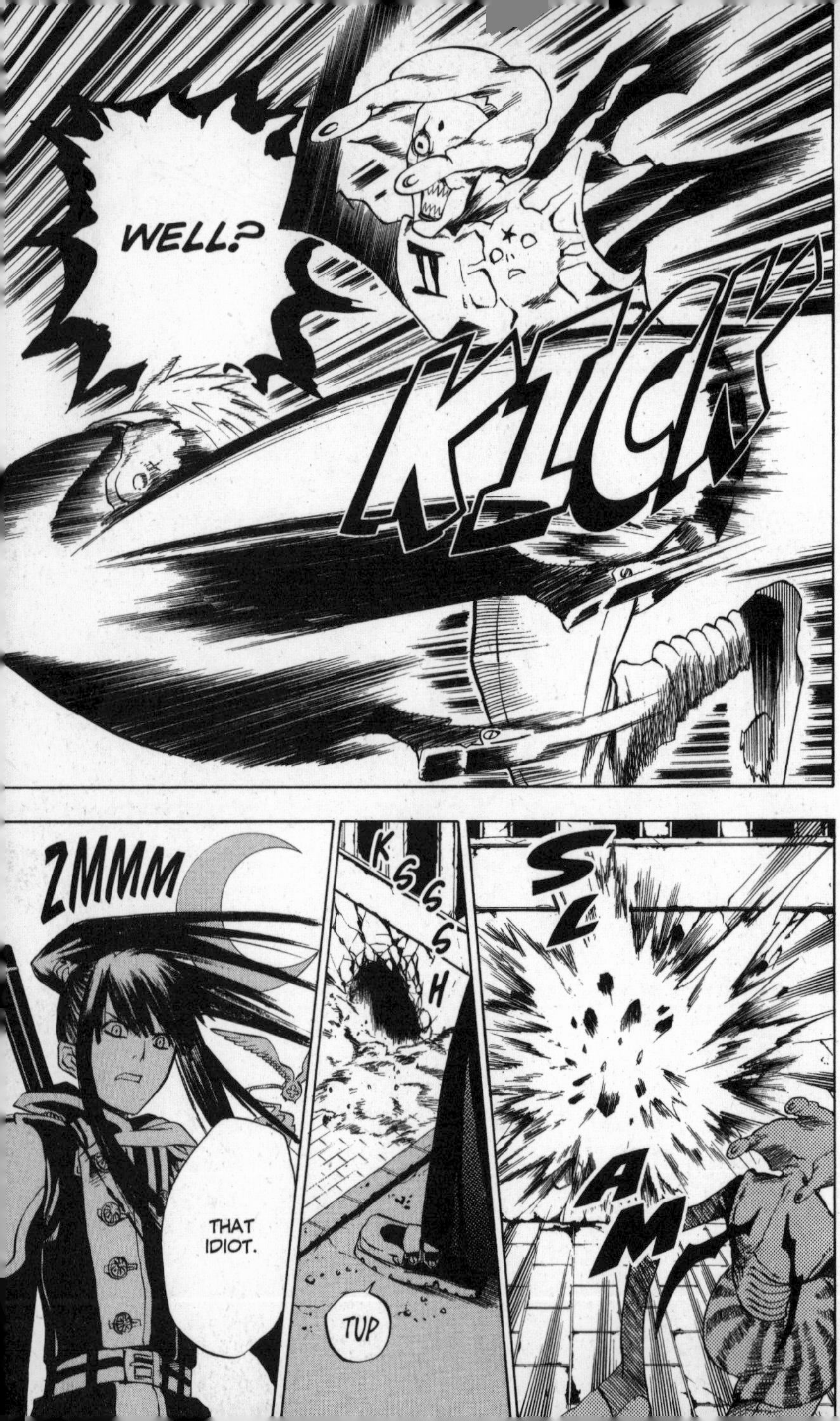
WELL?
KICK
SLAM
KSSSH
TUP
ZMMM
THAT IDIOT.

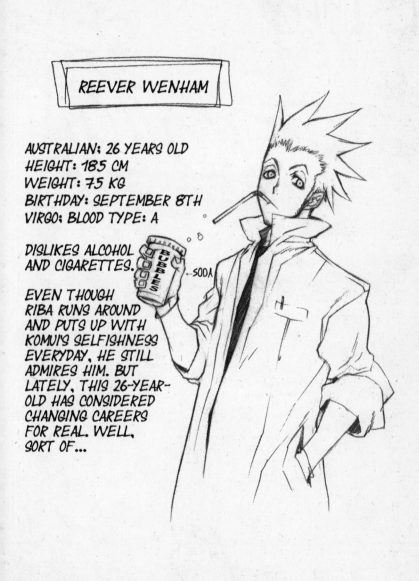

REEVER WENHAM

AUSTRALIAN; 26 YEARS OLD
HEIGHT: 185 CM
WEIGHT: 75 KG
BIRTHDAY: SEPTEMBER 8TH
VIRGO; BLOOD TYPE: A

DISLIKES ALCOHOL
AND CIGARETTES.

←SODA

BUBBLES

EVEN THOUGH
RIBA RUNS AROUND
AND PUTS UP WITH
KOMUI'S SELFISHNESS
EVERYDAY, HE STILL
ADMIRES HIM. BUT
LATELY, THIS 26-YEAR-
OLD HAS CONSIDERED
CHANGING CAREERS
FOR REAL. WELL,
SORT OF...

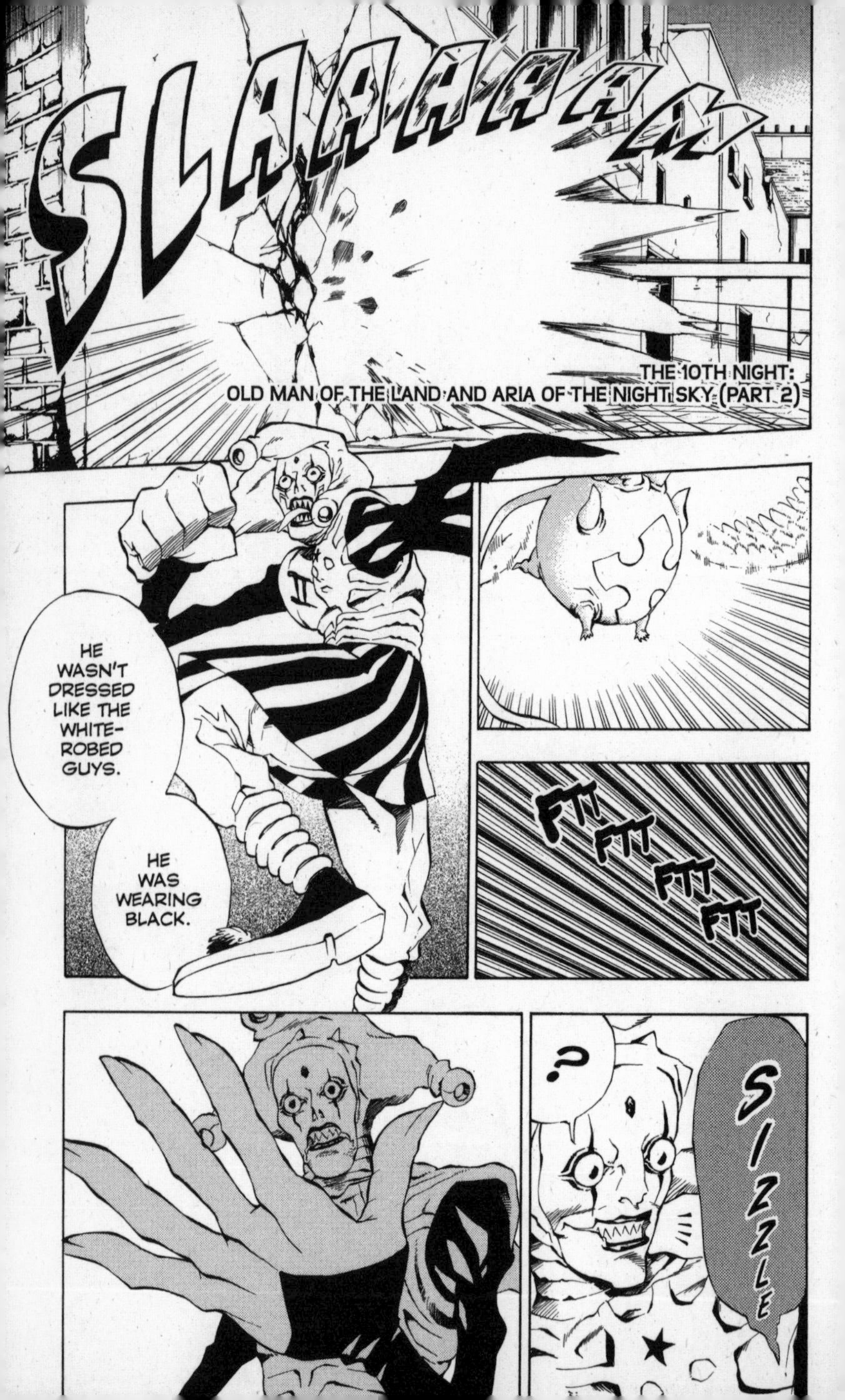
SLAAAAAAM
THE 10TH NIGHT:
OLD MAN OF THE LAND AND ARIA OF THE NIGHT SKY (PART 2)
FTT FTT FTT FTT
HE WASN'T DRESSED LIKE THE WHITE-ROBED GUYS.
HE WAS WEARING BLACK.
?
SIZZLE

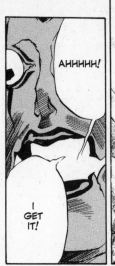

AHHHHH!

I GET IT!

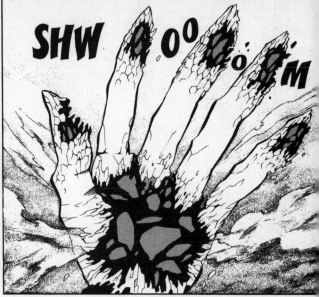

SHW OO OM

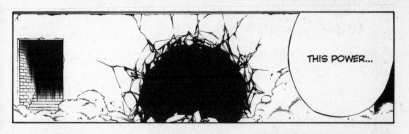

THIS POWER...

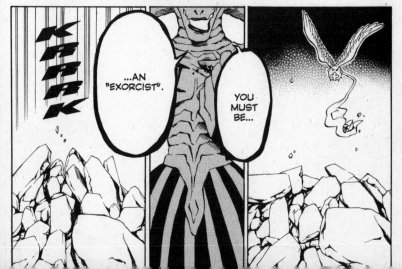

...AN "EXORCIST".

YOU MUST BE...

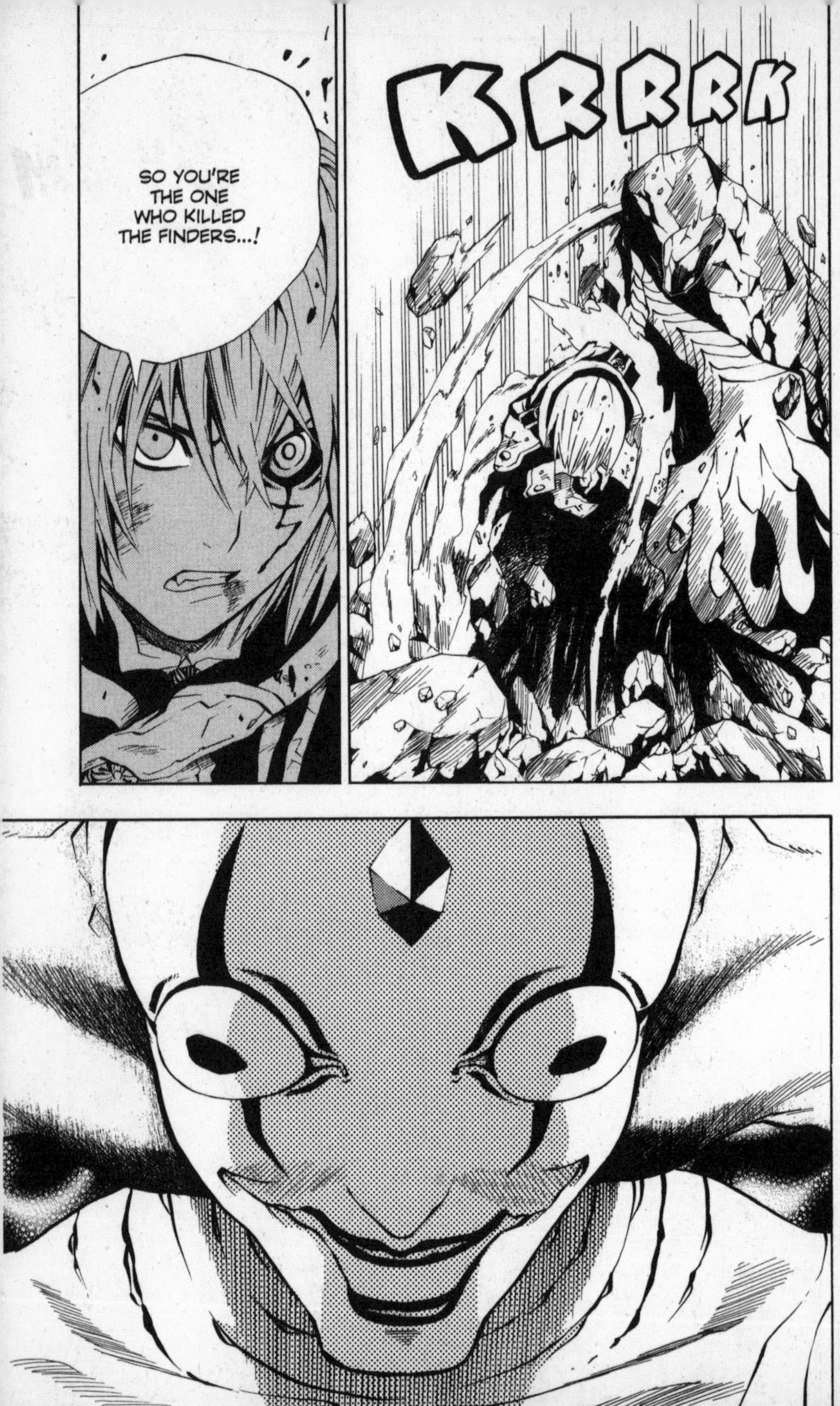
KRRRK
SO YOU'RE THE ONE WHO KILLED THE FINDERS...!

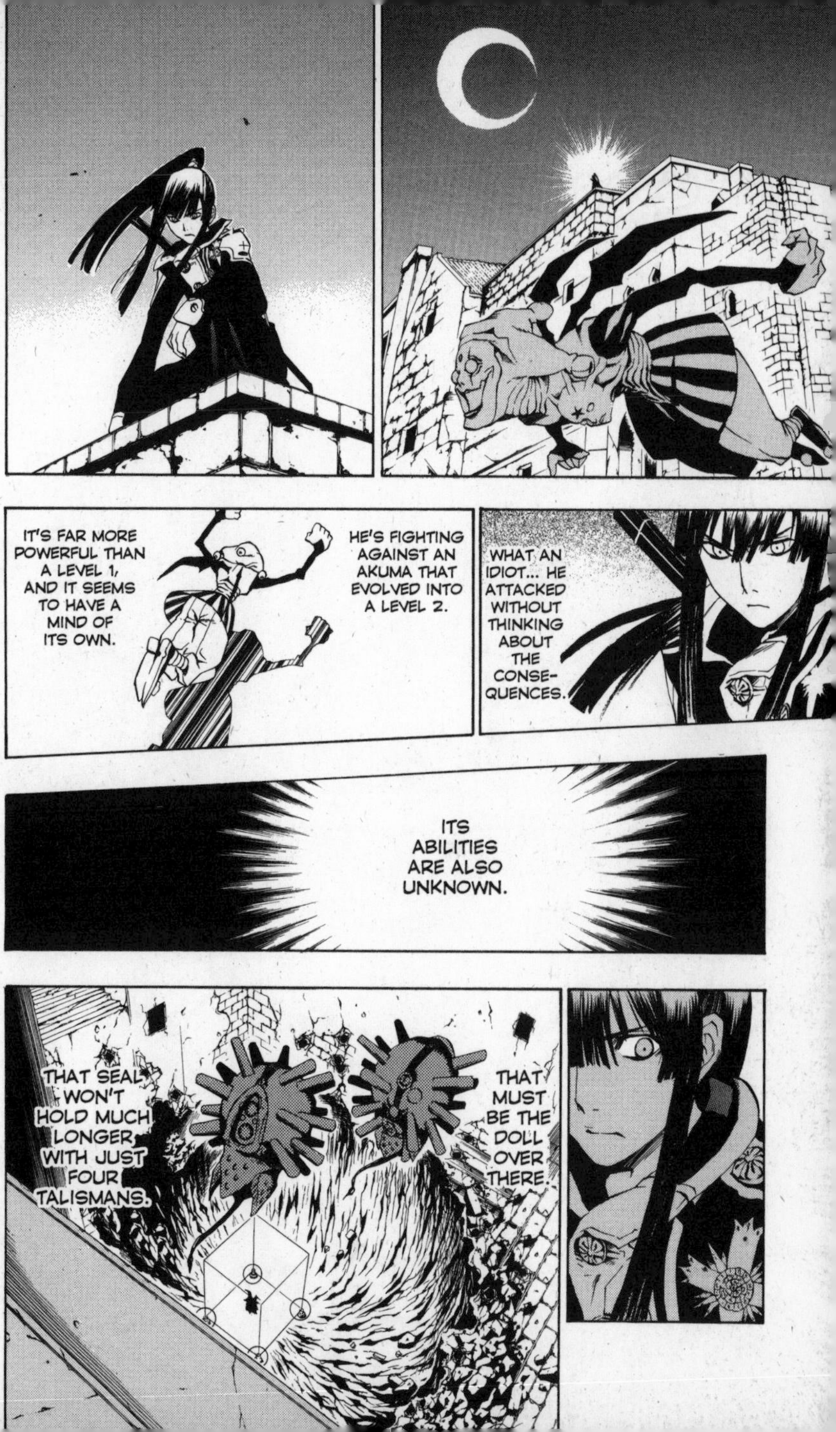
WHAT AN IDIOT... HE ATTACKED WITHOUT THINKING ABOUT THE CONSE-QUENCES.
HE'S FIGHTING AGAINST AN AKUMA THAT EVOLVED INTO A LEVEL 2.
IT'S FAR MORE POWERFUL THAN A LEVEL 1, AND IT SEEMS TO HAVE A MIND OF ITS OWN.
ITS ABILITIES ARE ALSO UNKNOWN.
THAT MUST BE THE DOLL OVER THERE.
THAT SEAL WON'T HOLD MUCH LONGER WITH JUST FOUR TALISMANS.

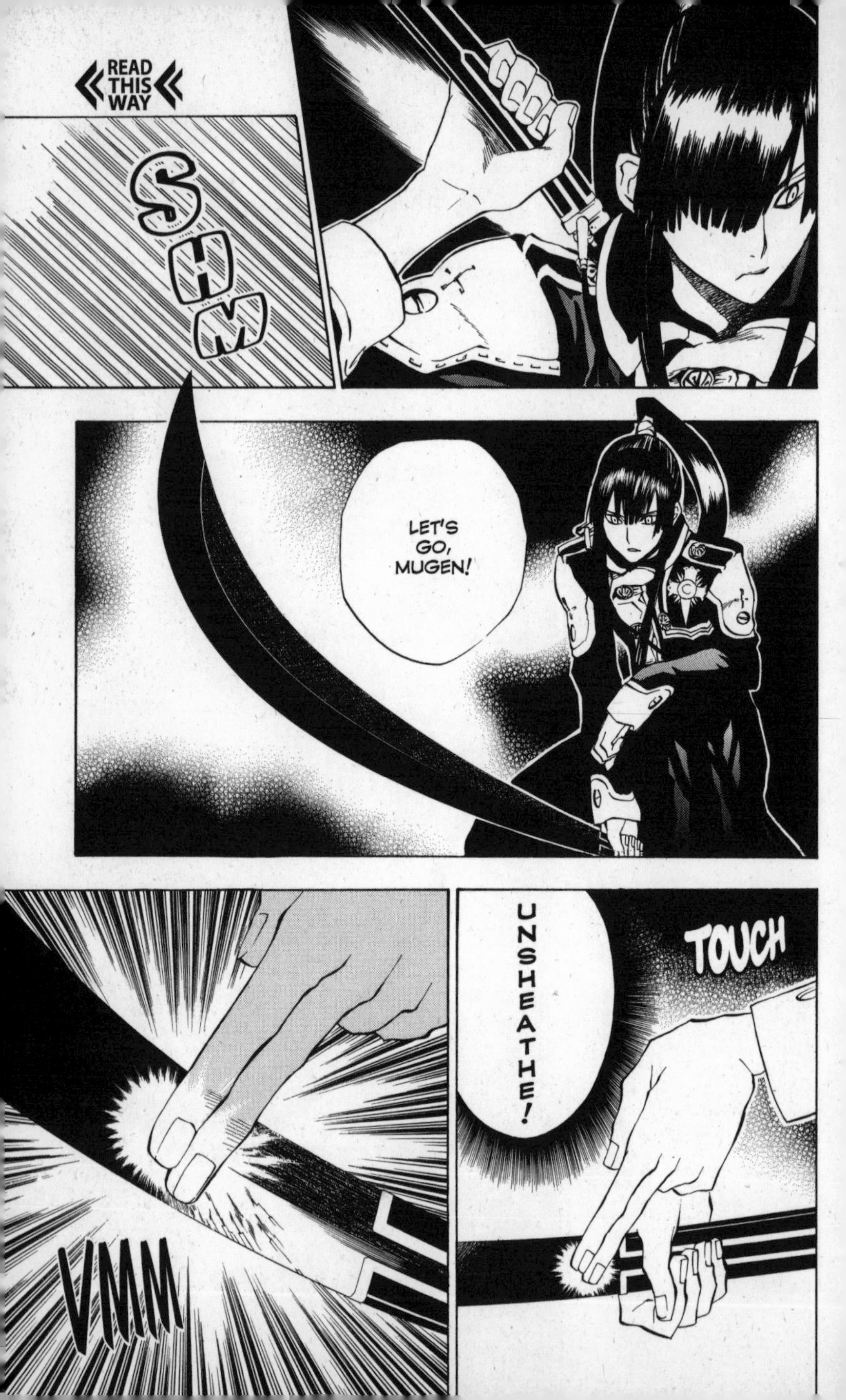
READ THIS WAY
SHM
LET'S GO, MUGEN!
UNSHEATHE!
TOUCH
VMM

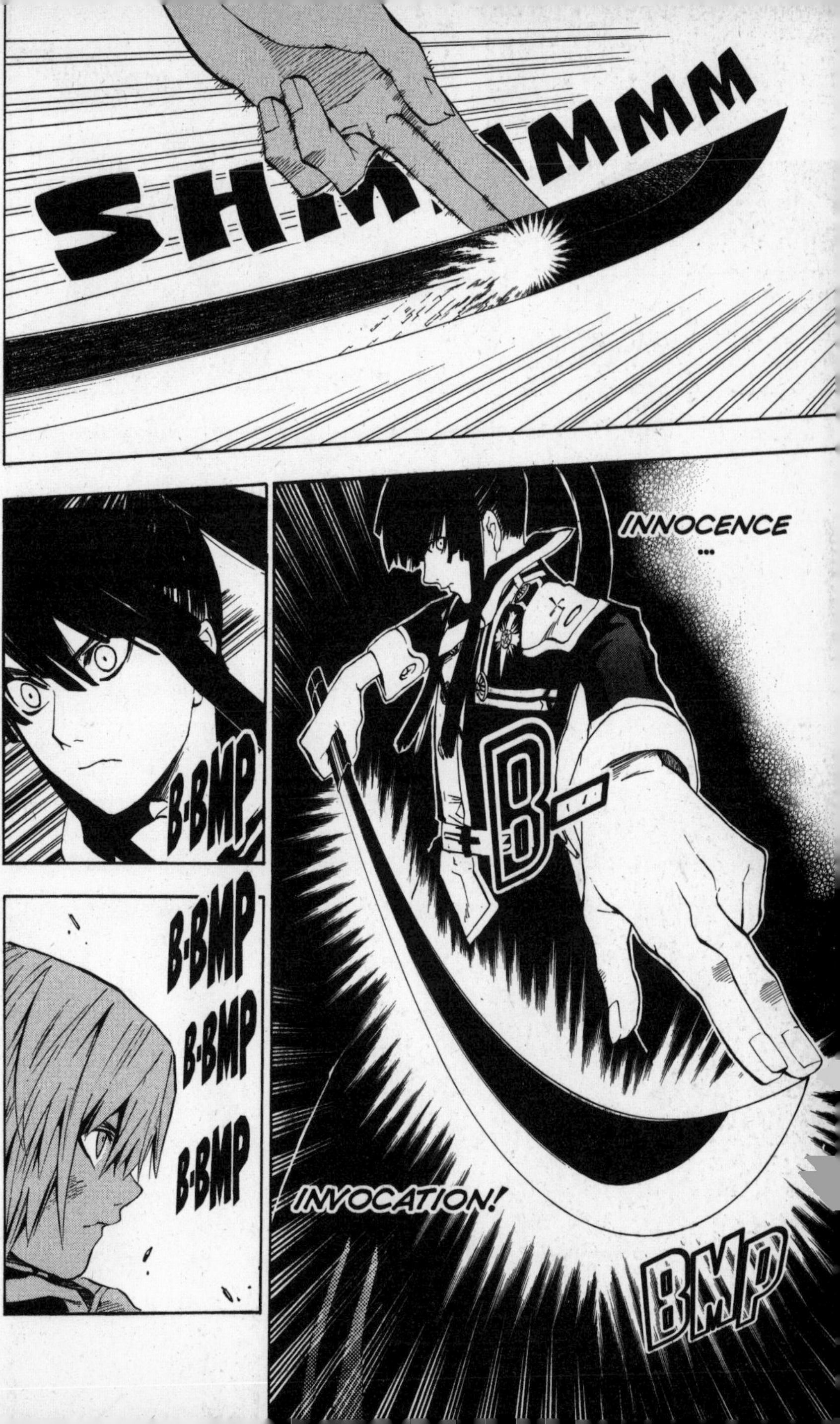

SH MMMM
INNOCENCE ...
INVOCATION!
BMP
B-BMP
B-BMP
B-BMP
B-BMP

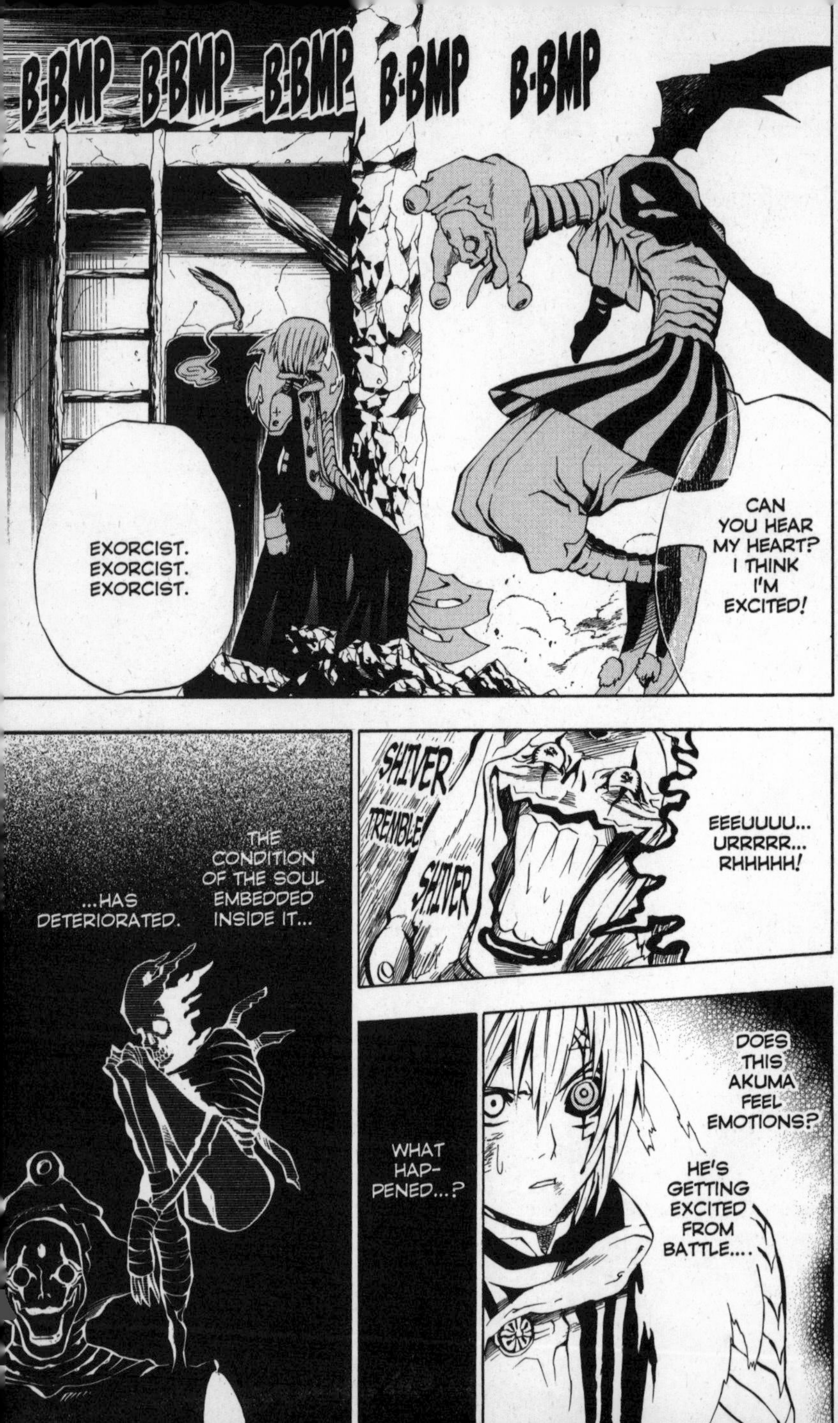
B-BMP B-BMP B-BMP B-BMP B-BMP
CAN YOU HEAR MY HEART? I THINK I'M EXCITED!
EXORCIST. EXORCIST. EXORCIST.
SHIVER
TREMBLE
SHIVER
EEEUUUU... URRRRR... RHHHHH!
DOES THIS AKUMA FEEL EMOTIONS?
HE'S GETTING EXCITED FROM BATTLE....
WHAT HAP-PENED...?
THE CONDITION OF THE SOUL EMBEDDED INSIDE IT...
...HAS DETERIORATED.

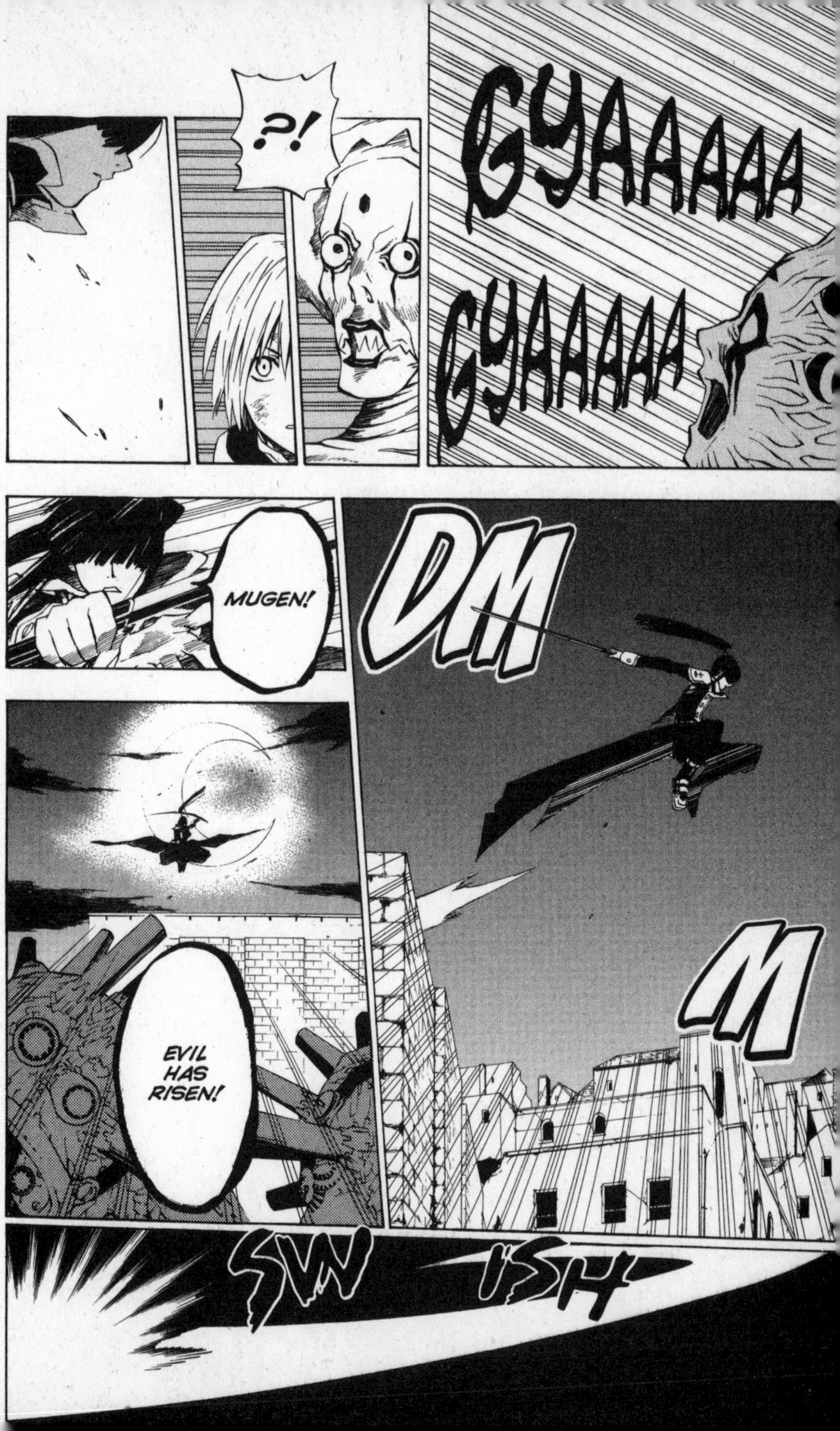
GYAAAAAA
GYAAAAA
?!
DMM
MUGEN!
EVIL HAS RISEN!
SWISH

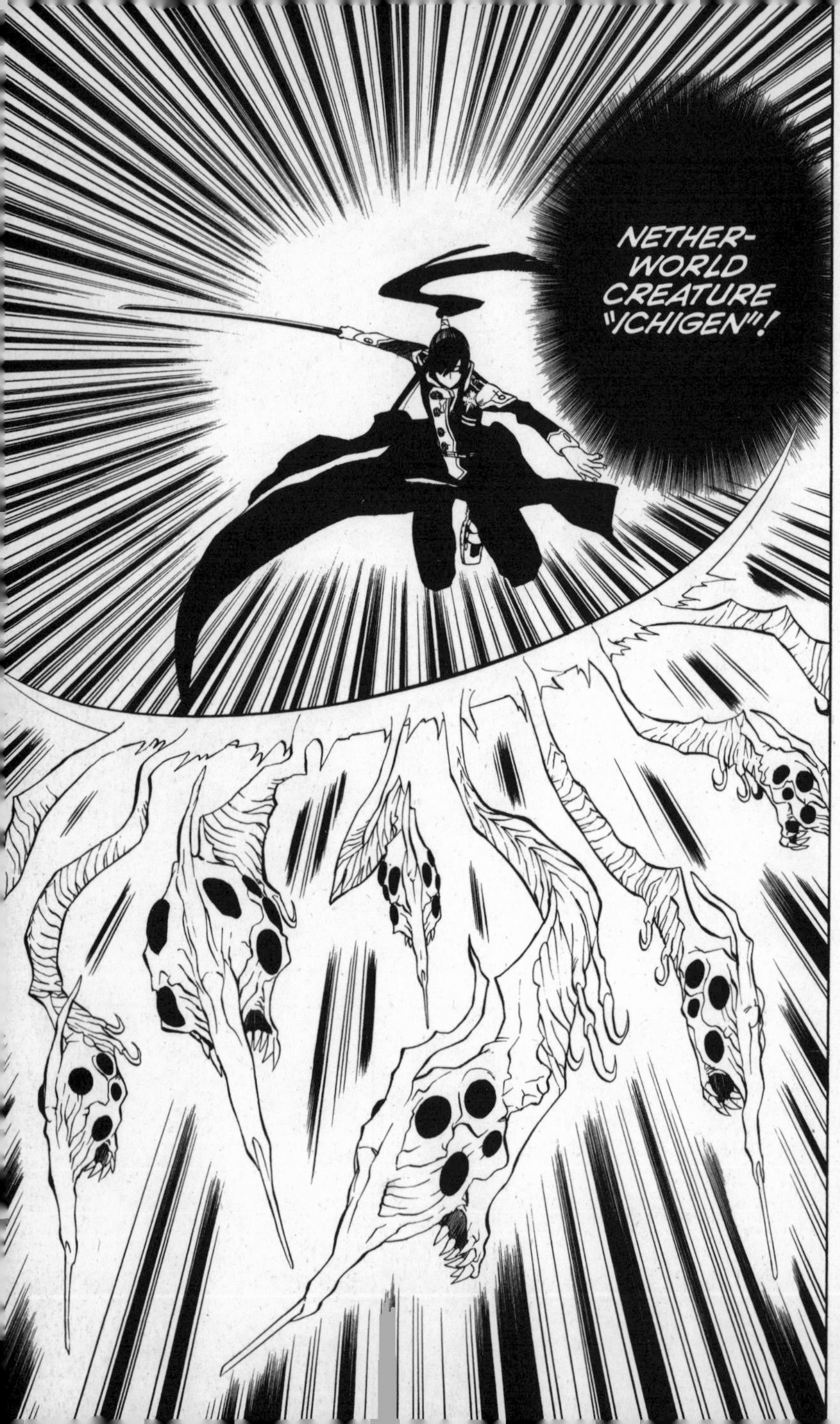
NETHER-WORLD CREATURE "ICHIGEN"!

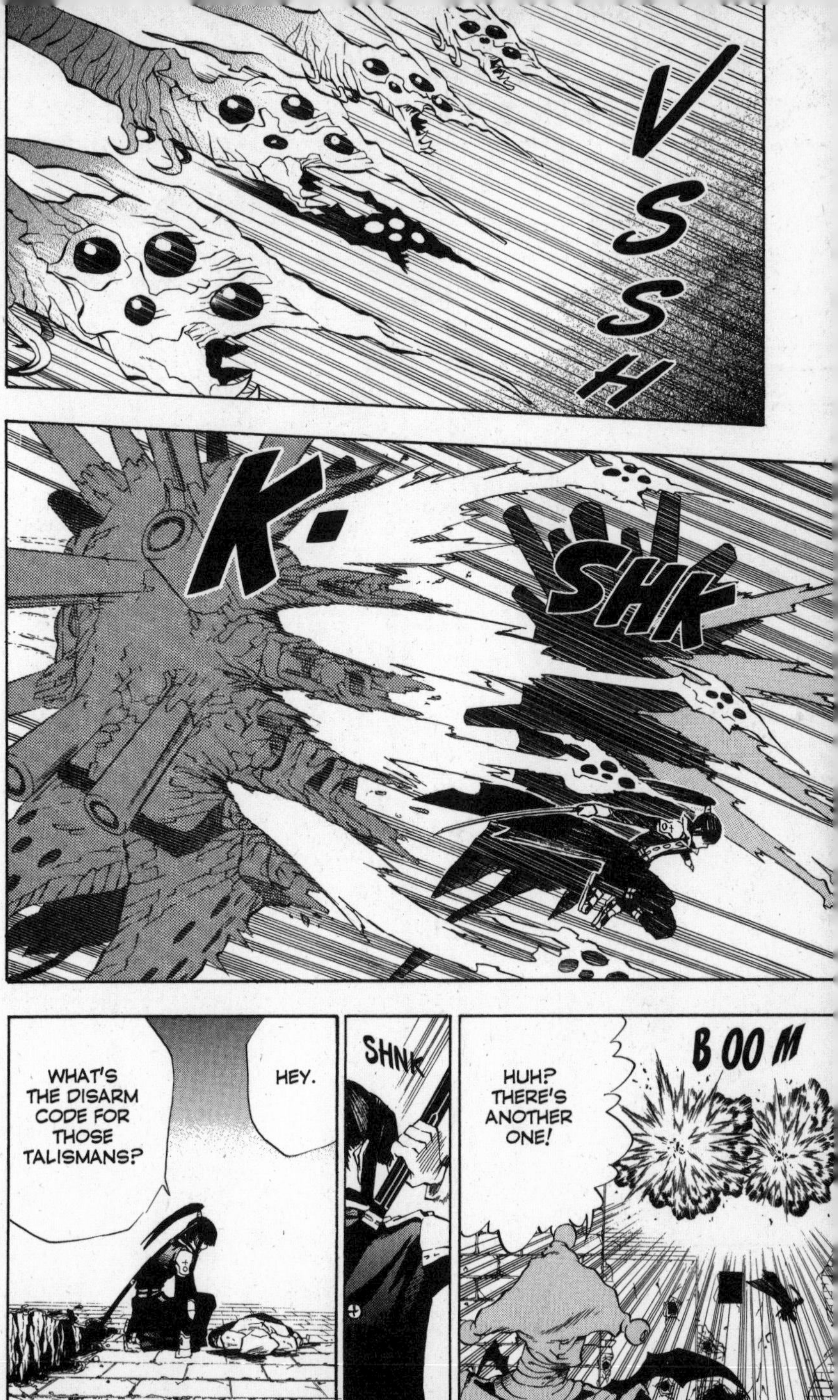
VSSH
K-
SHK
BOOM
HUH? THERE'S ANOTHER ONE!
SHNK
HEY.
WHAT'S THE DISARM CODE FOR THOSE TALISMANS?

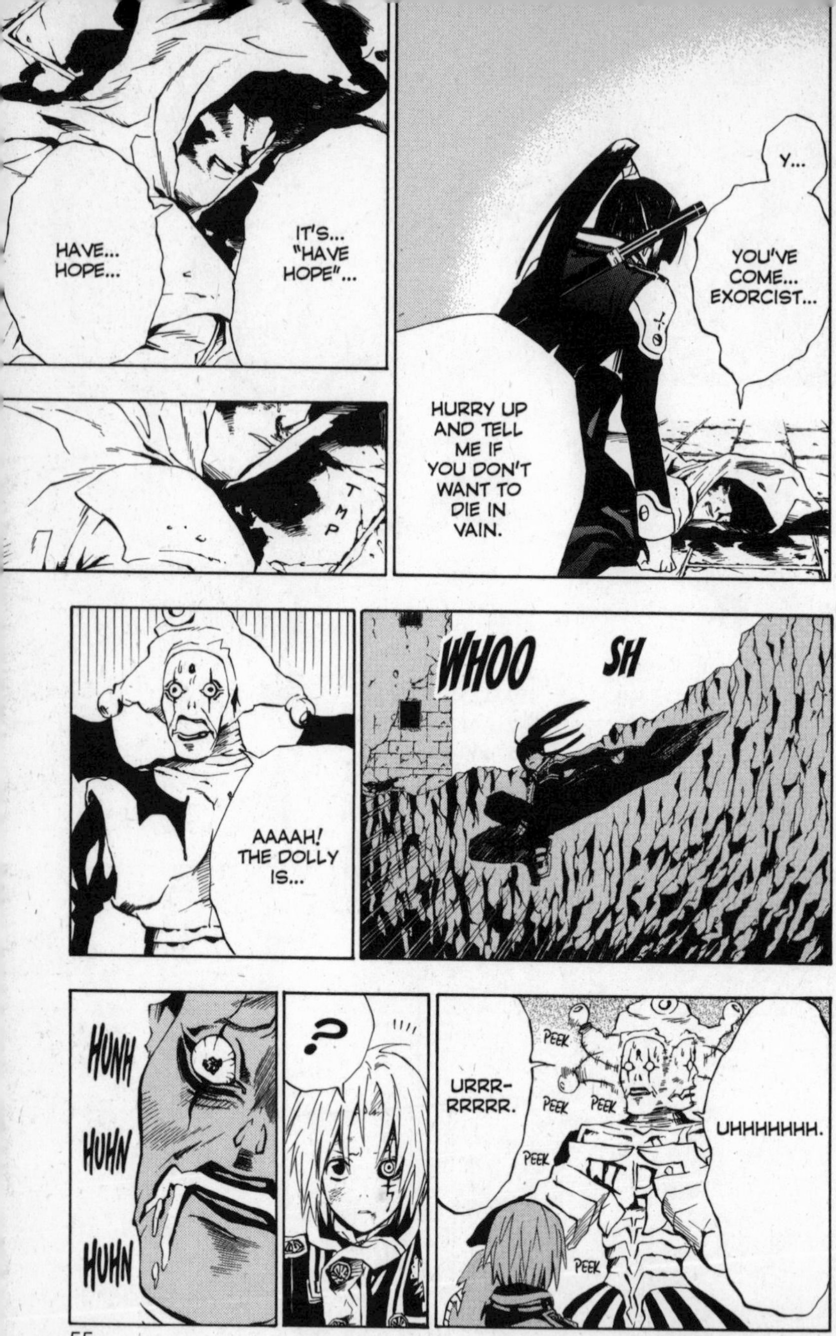
Y...
YOU'VE COME... EXORCIST...
HURRY UP AND TELL ME IF YOU DON'T WANT TO DIE IN VAIN.
IT'S... "HAVE HOPE"...
HAVE... HOPE...
TMP
WHOO SH
AAAAH! THE DOLLY IS...
UHHHHHHH.
PEEK
PEEK
URRR-RRRRR.
PEEK
PEEK
PEEK
?
HUNH
HUHN
HUHN

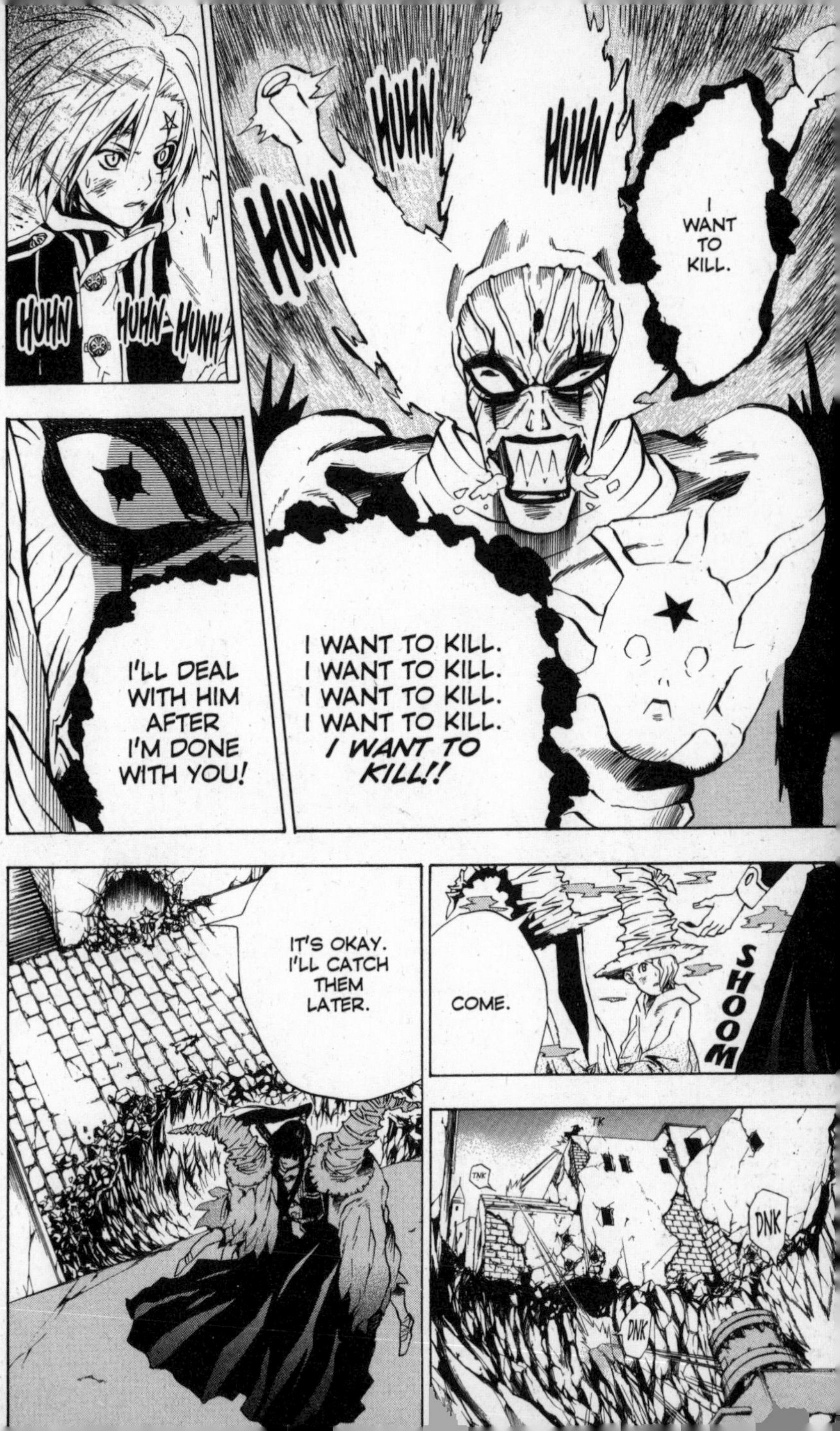
HUHN
HUHN
HUNH
I WANT TO KILL.
I WANT TO KILL.
I WANT TO KILL.
I WANT TO KILL.
I WANT TO KILL.
I WANT TO KILL!!
HUHN
HUHN-HUNH
I'LL DEAL WITH HIM AFTER I'M DONE WITH YOU!
SHOOM
COME.
TK
TNK
DNK
DNK
IT'S OKAY. I'LL CATCH THEM LATER.

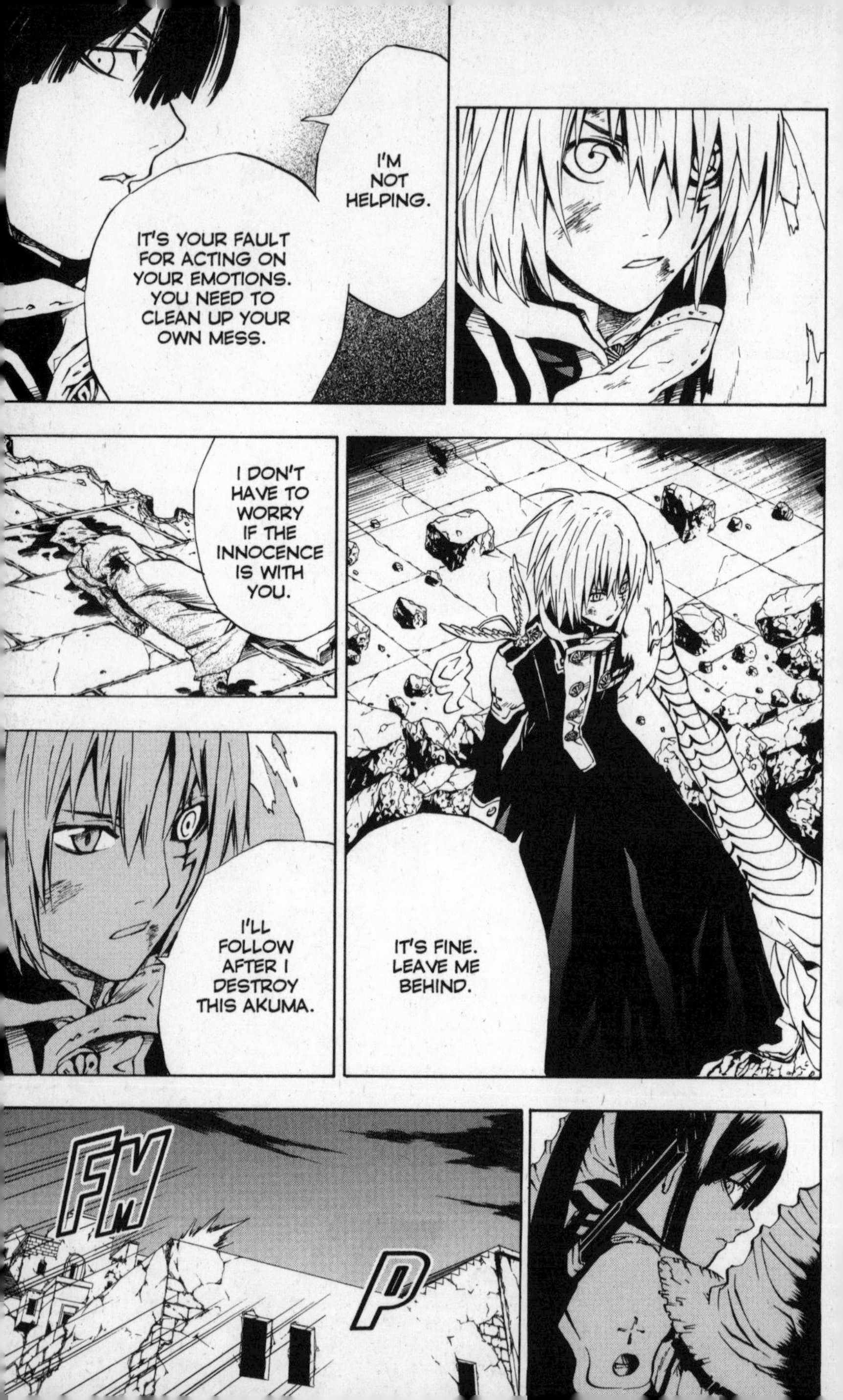
I'M NOT HELPING.
IT'S YOUR FAULT FOR ACTING ON YOUR EMOTIONS. YOU NEED TO CLEAN UP YOUR OWN MESS.
IT'S FINE. LEAVE ME BEHIND.
I DON'T HAVE TO WORRY IF THE INNOCENCE IS WITH YOU.
I'LL FOLLOW AFTER I DESTROY THIS AKUMA.
FM
P

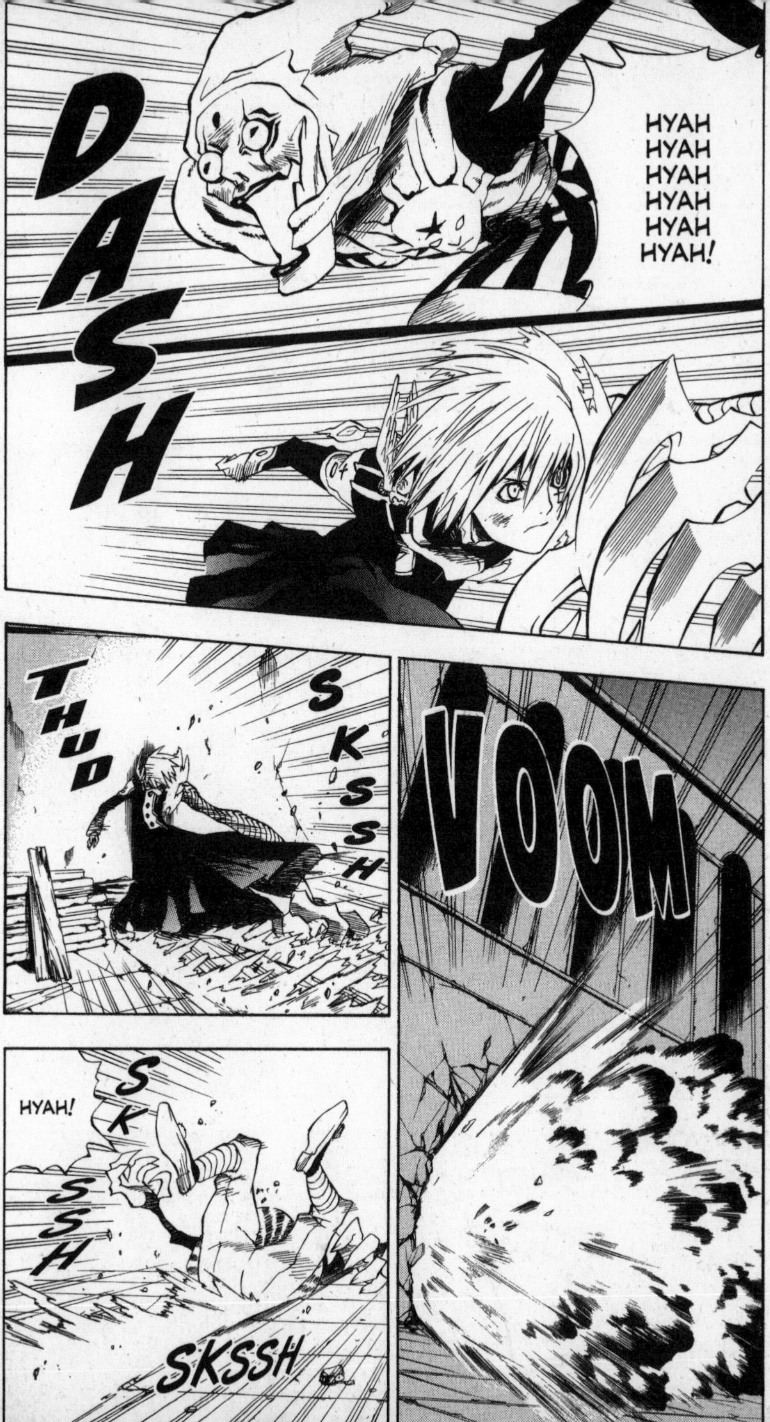
HYAH
HYAH
HYAH
HYAH
HYAH
HYAH!
DASH
VOOM
SKSSH
THUD
HYAH!
SKSSH
SKSSH

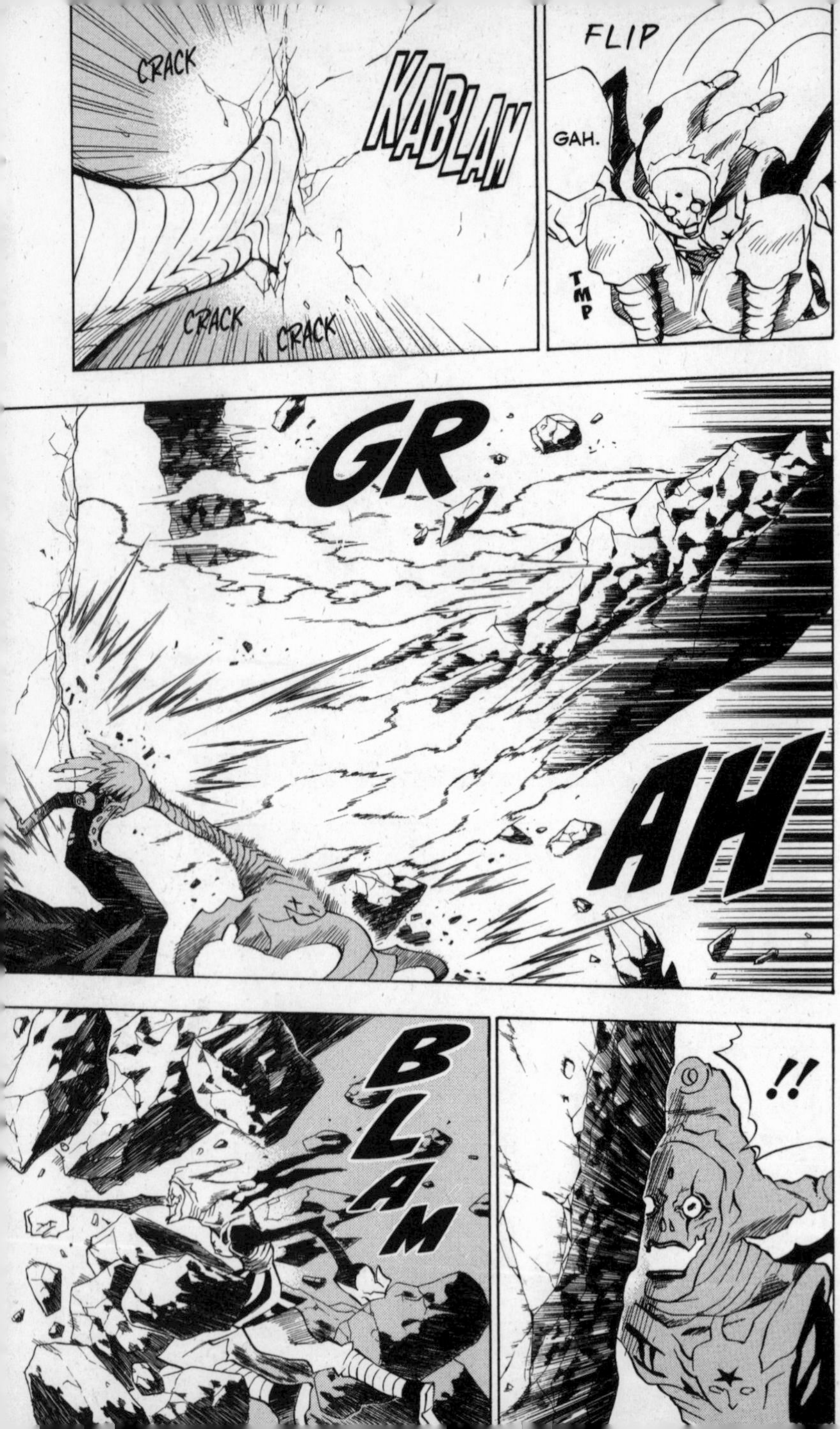
FLIP
GAH.
TMP
KABLAM
CRACK
CRACK
CRACK
GR
AH
!!
BLAM

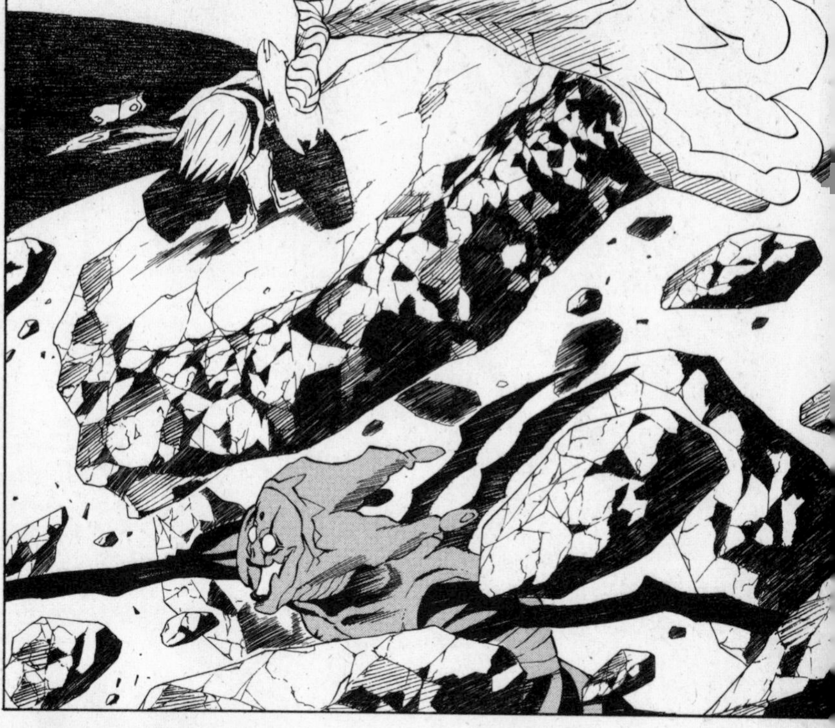

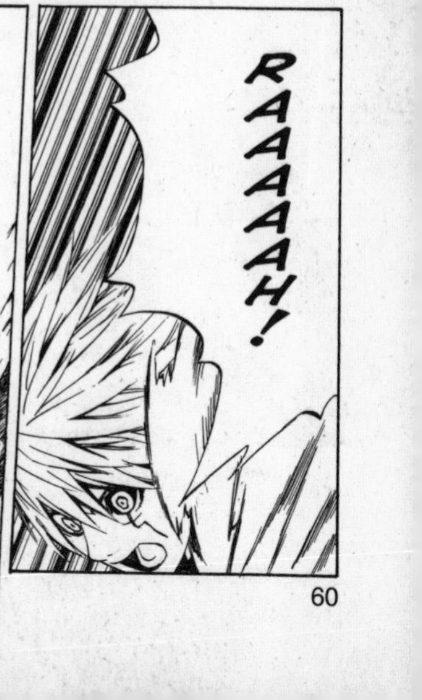
RAAAAAH!

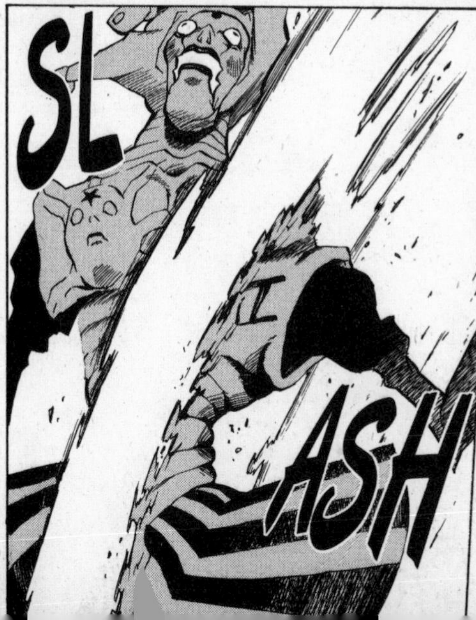
SLASH

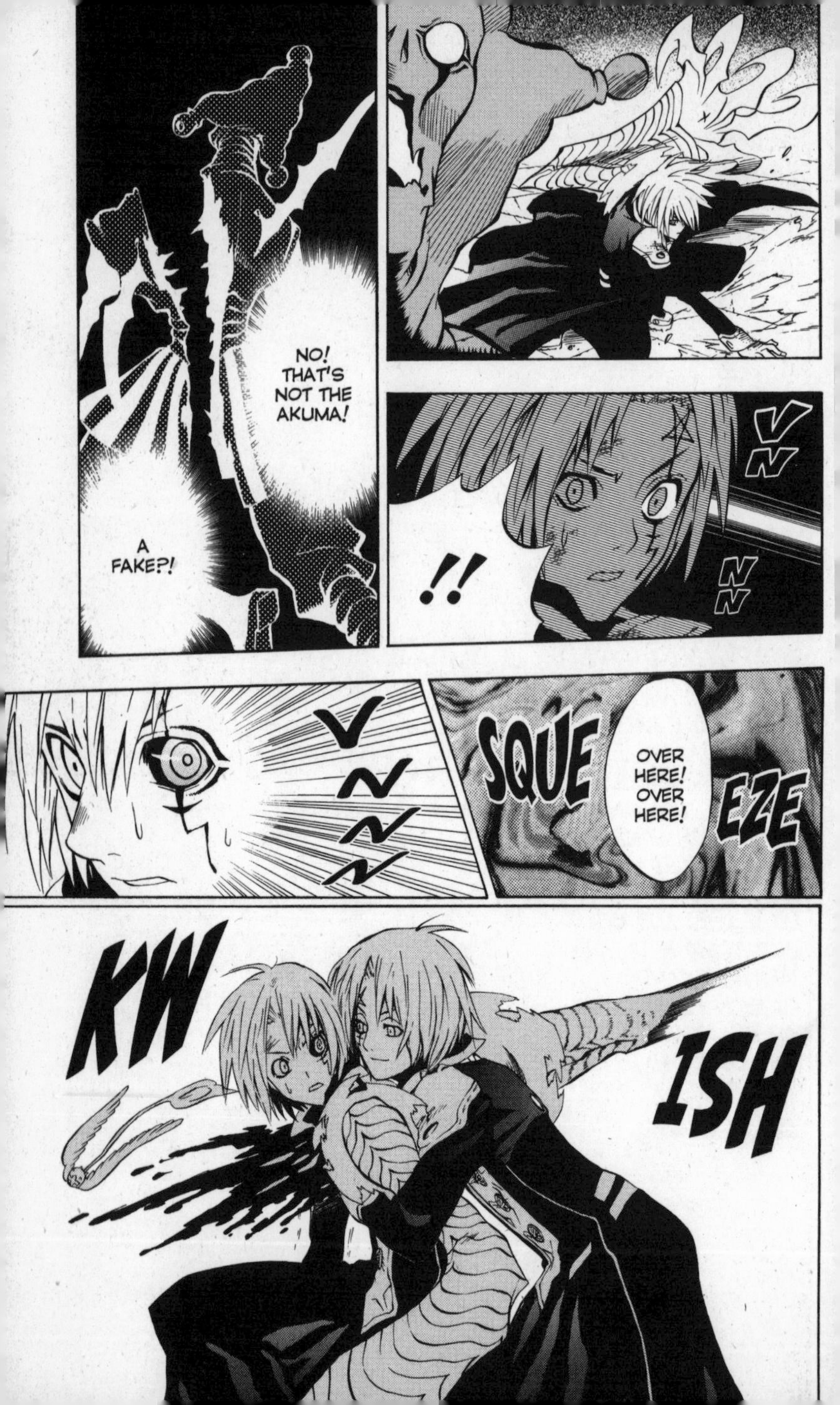
VN
NN
!!
NO! THAT'S NOT THE AKUMA!
A FAKE?!
SQUE
OVER HERE! OVER HERE!
EZE
VNNN
KW
ISH

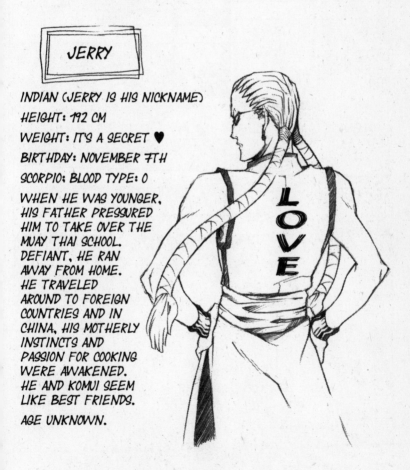

JERRY

INDIAN (JERRY IS HIS NICKNAME)

HEIGHT: 192 CM

WEIGHT: IT'S A SECRET ♥

BIRTHDAY: NOVEMBER 7TH

SCORPIO; BLOOD TYPE: O

WHEN HE WAS YOUNGER, HIS FATHER PRESSURED HIM TO TAKE OVER THE MUAY THAI SCHOOL. DEFIANT, HE RAN AWAY FROM HOME. HE TRAVELED AROUND TO FOREIGN COUNTRIES AND IN CHINA, HIS MOTHERLY INSTINCTS AND PASSION FOR COOKING WERE AWAKENED. HE AND KOMUI SEEM LIKE BEST FRIENDS.

AGE UNKNOWN.

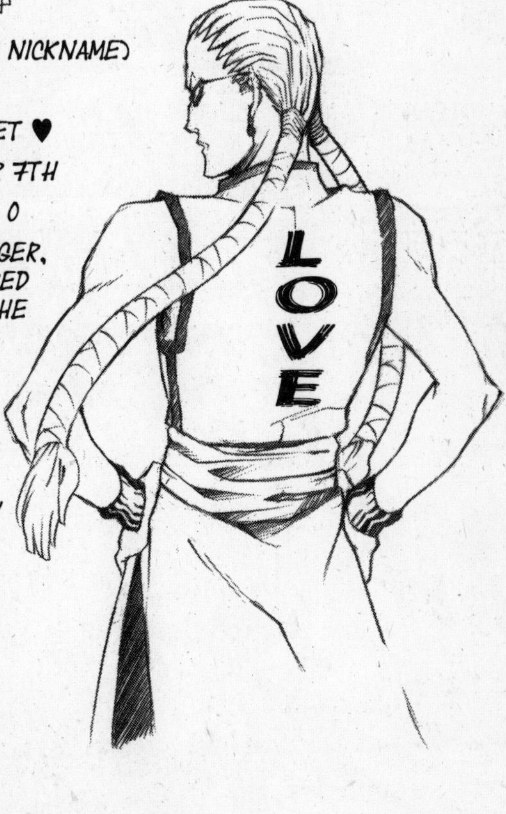
LOVE

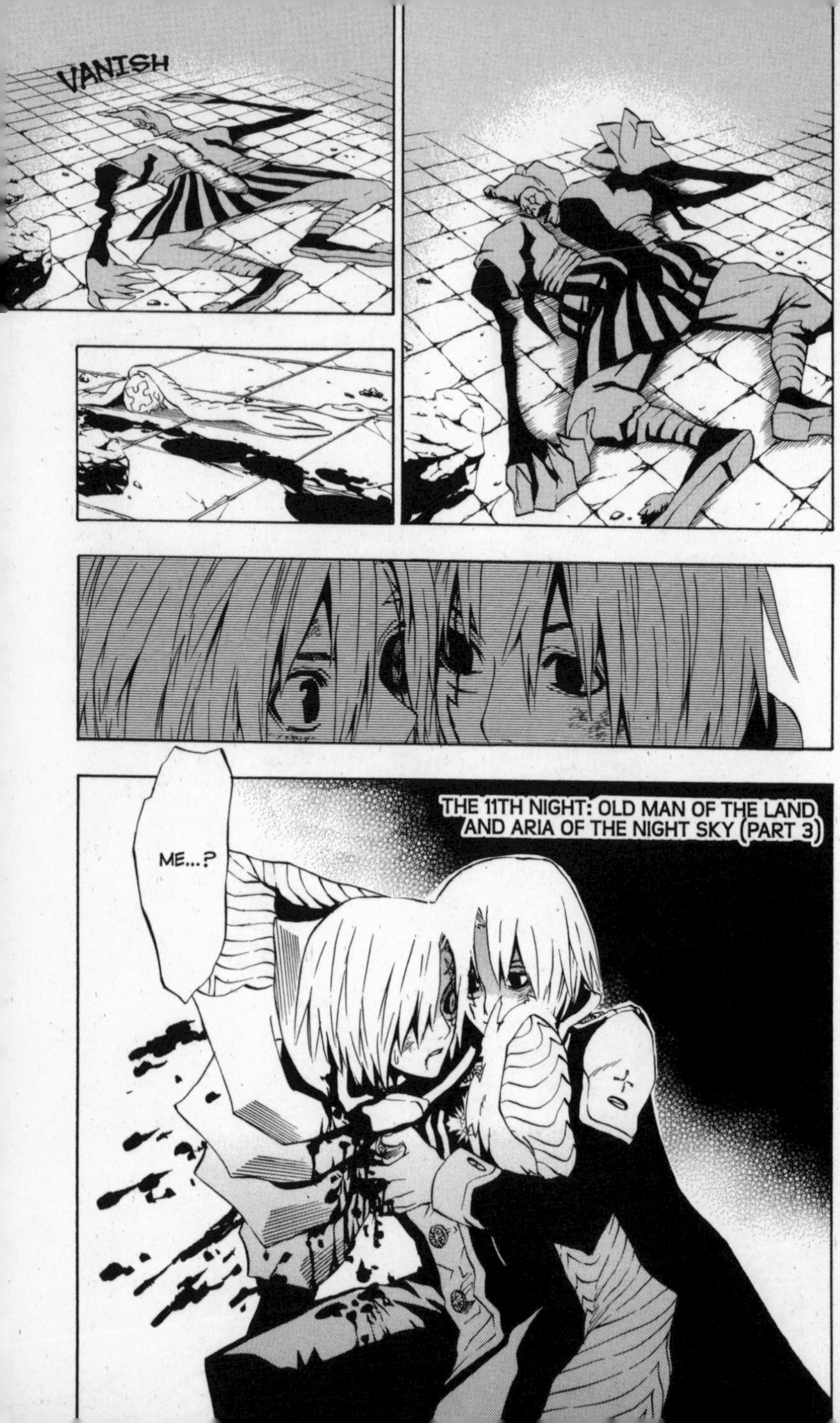
VANISH
THE 11TH NIGHT: OLD MAN OF THE LAND AND ARIA OF THE NIGHT SKY (PART 3)
ME...?

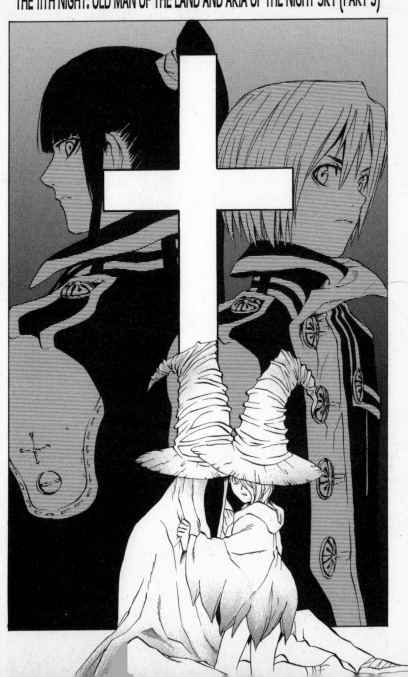

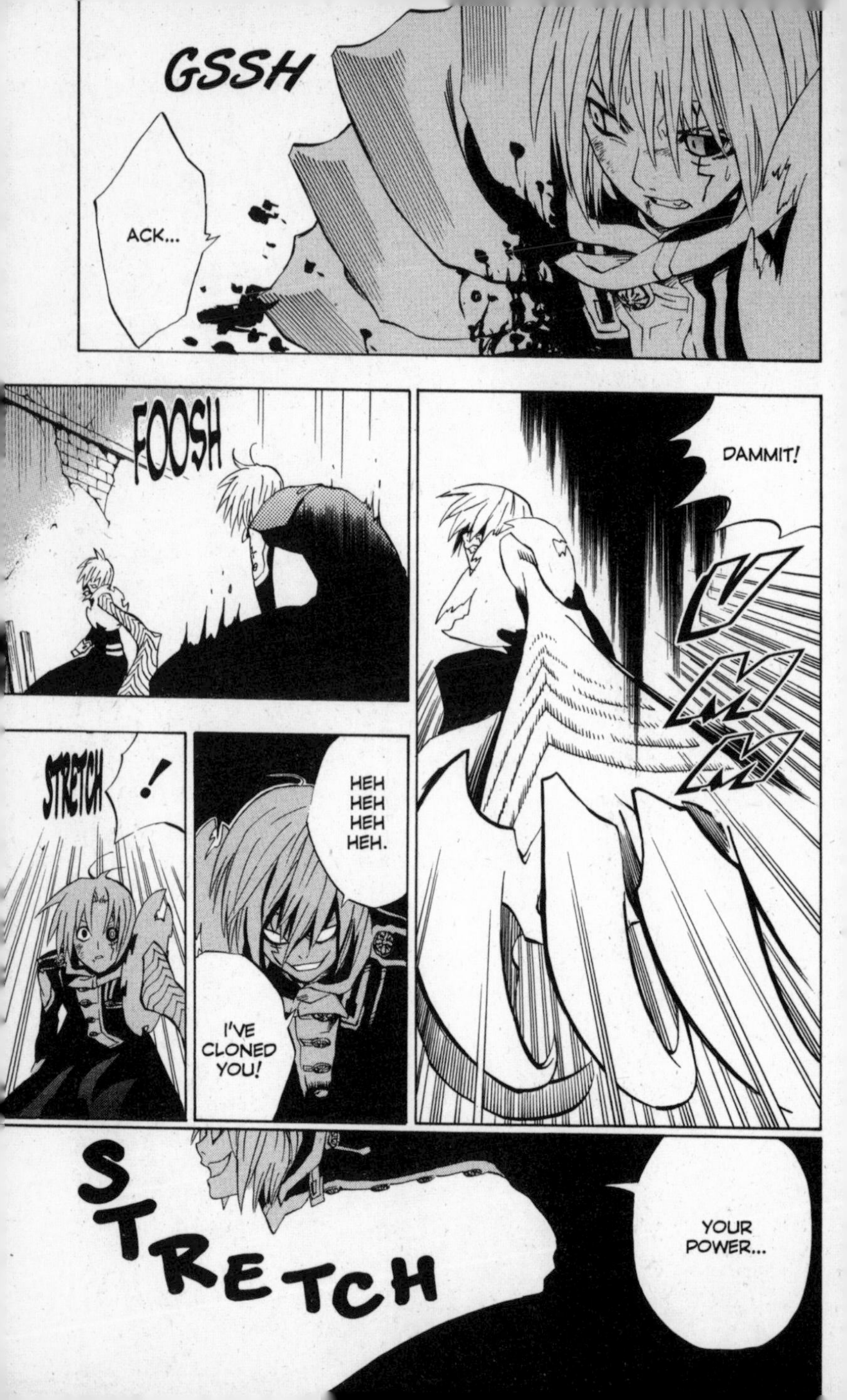
GSSH
ACK...
DAMMIT!
VMMM
FOOSH
HEH HEH HEH HEH.
I'VE CLONED YOU!
STRETCH
!
YOUR POWER...
STRETCH

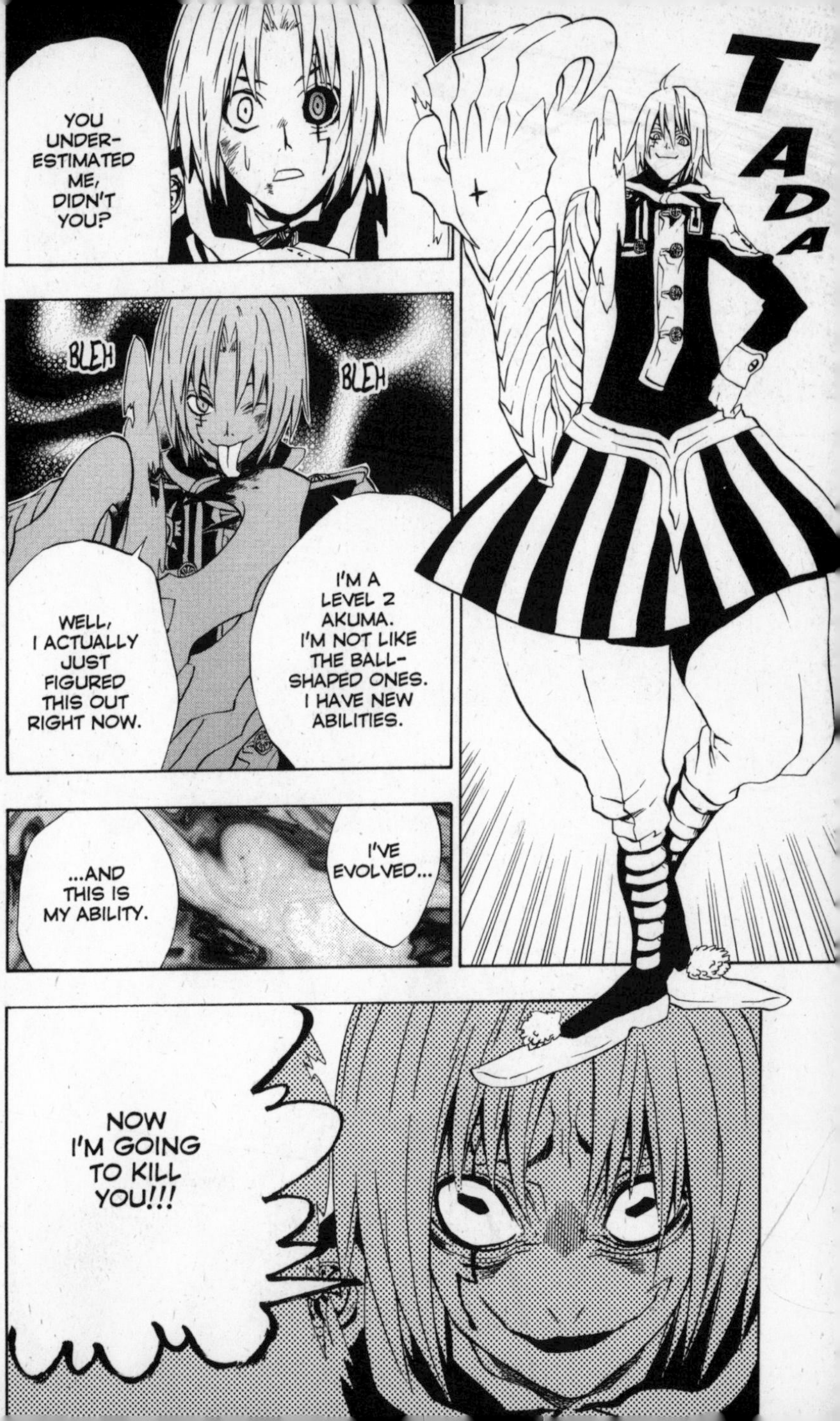
TADA
YOU UNDER-ESTIMATED ME, DIDN'T YOU?
BLEH
BLEH
I'M A LEVEL 2 AKUMA. I'M NOT LIKE THE BALL-SHAPED ONES. I HAVE NEW ABILITIES.
WELL, I ACTUALLY JUST FIGURED THIS OUT RIGHT NOW.
I'VE EVOLVED...
...AND THIS IS MY ABILITY.
NOW I'M GOING TO KILL YOU!!!

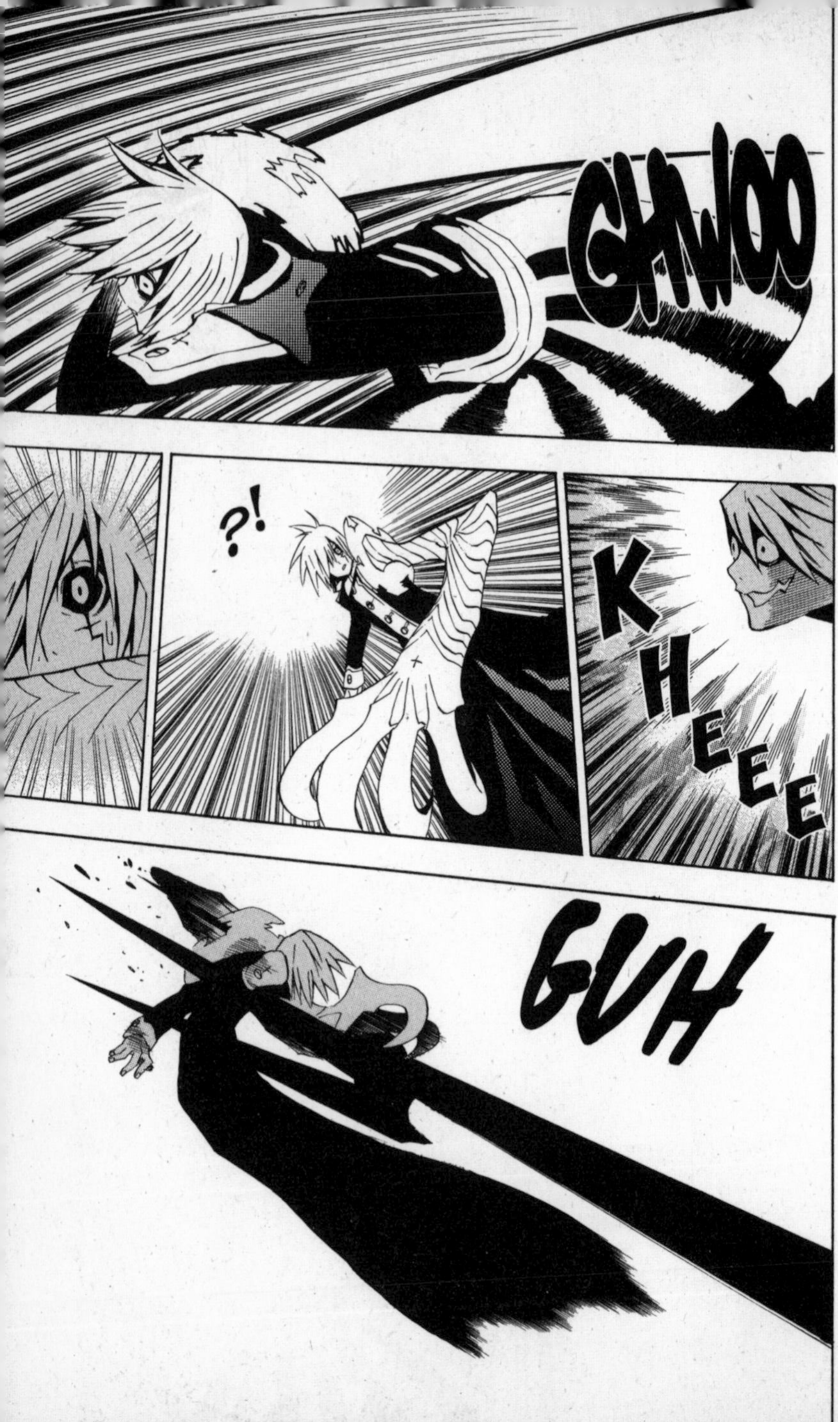
GHWOO
KHEEEE
?!
GUH

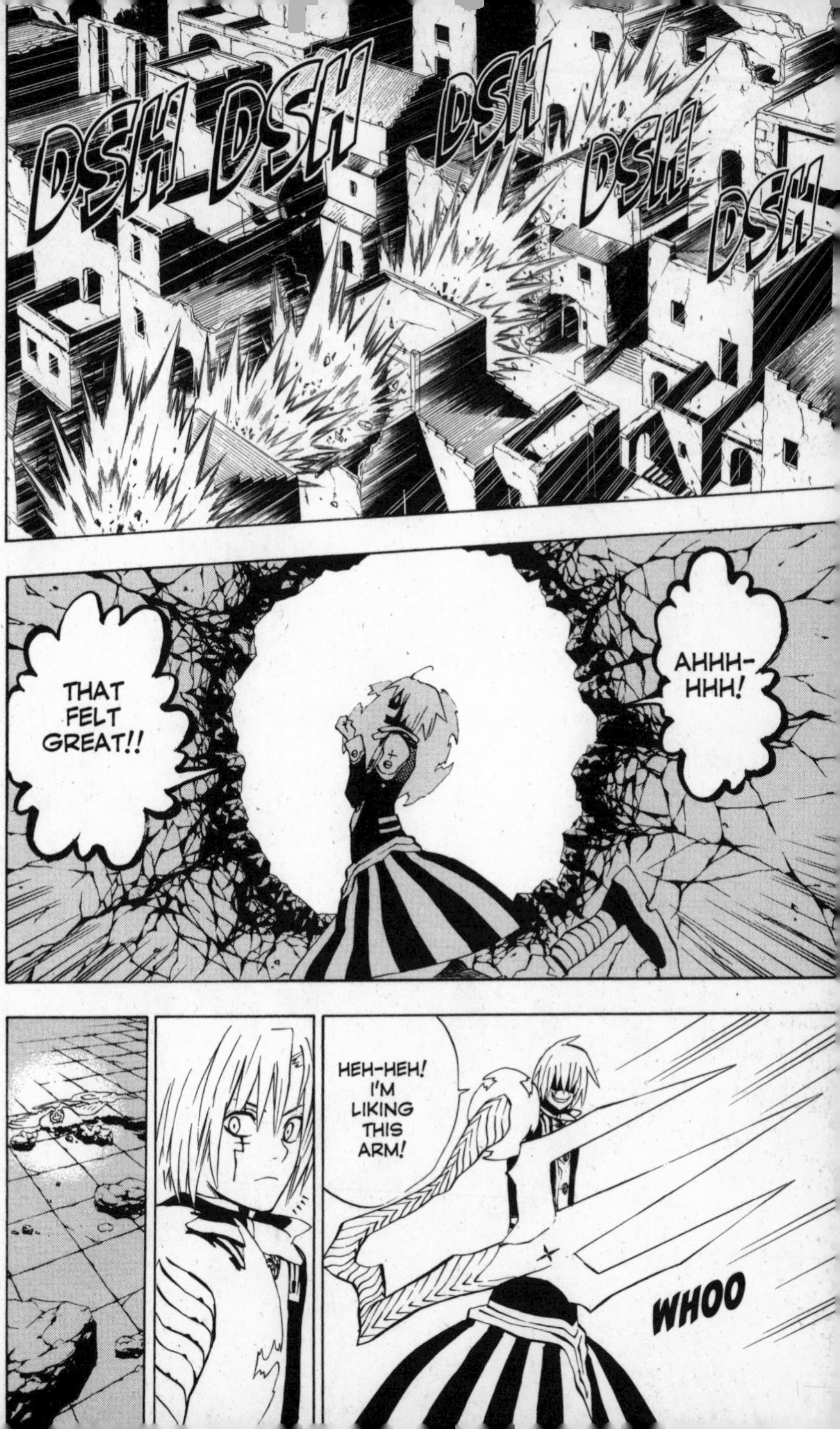
DSH
DSH
DSH
DSH
DSH
AHHH-HHH!
THAT FELT GREAT!!
HEH-HEH! I'M LIKING THIS ARM!
WHOO

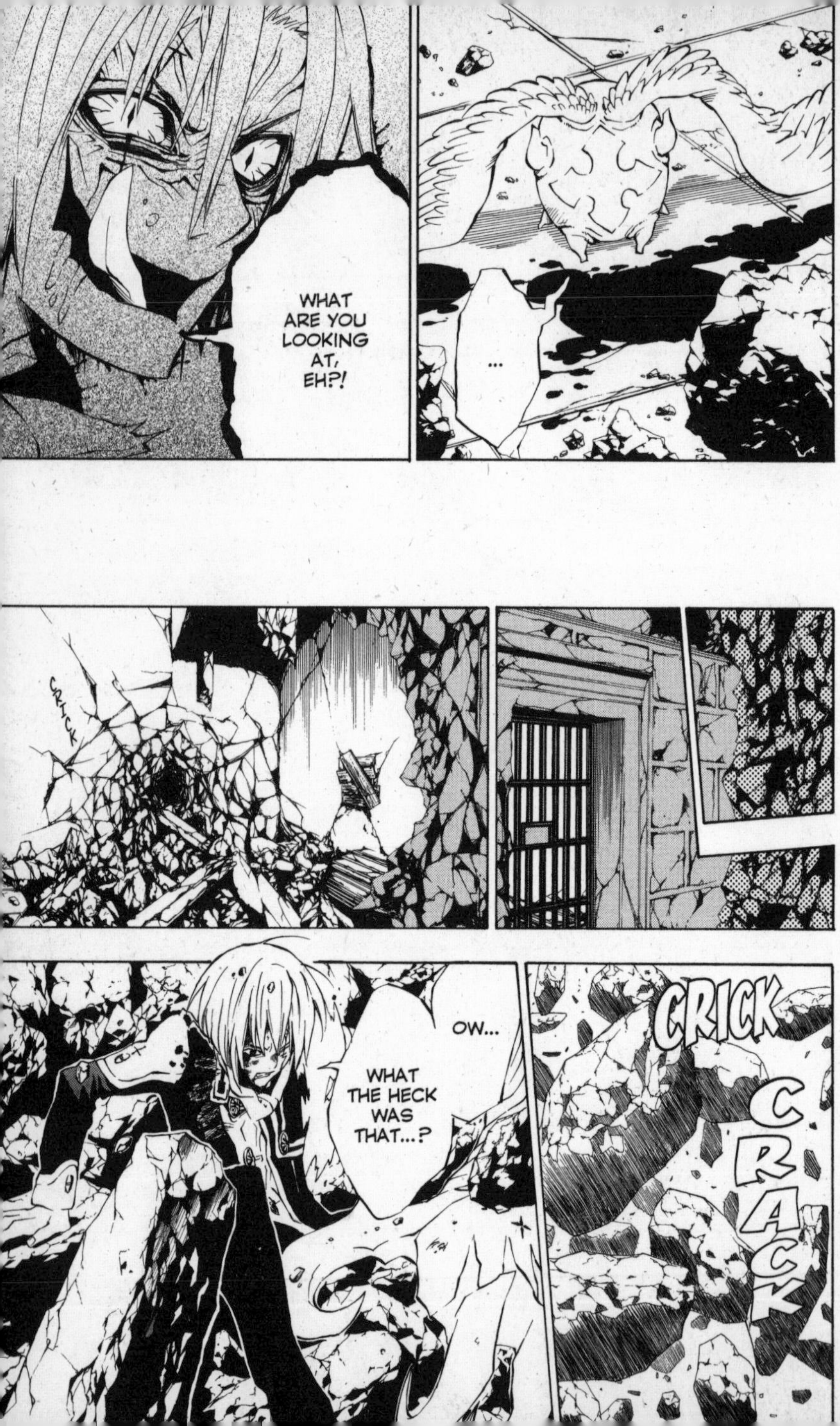
...
WHAT ARE YOU LOOKING AT, EH?!
CRICK
CRICK
CRACK
OW...
WHAT THE HECK WAS THAT...?

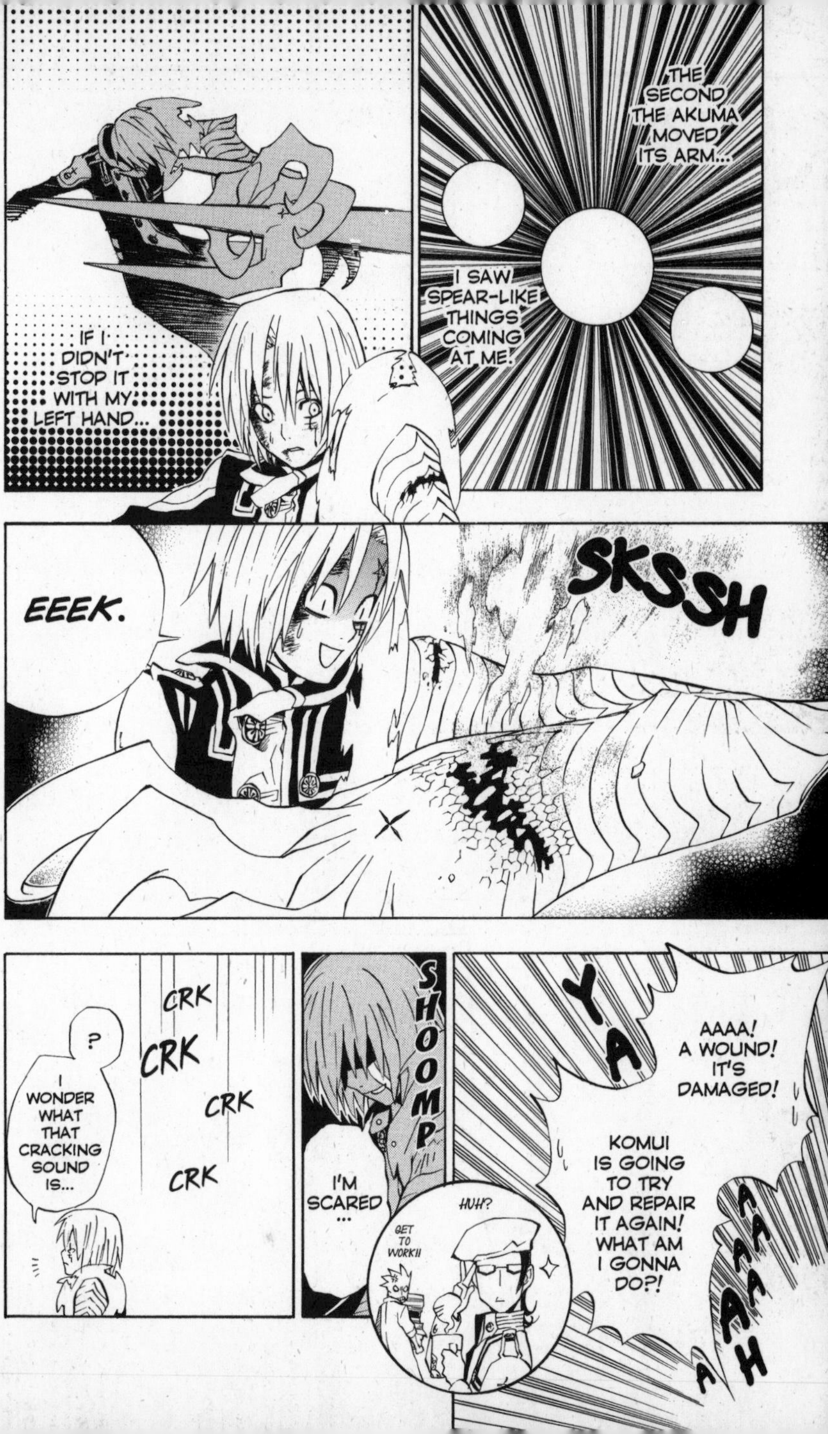
THE SECOND THE AKUMA MOVED ITS ARM...
I SAW SPEAR-LIKE THINGS COMING AT ME.
IF I DIDN'T STOP IT WITH MY LEFT HAND...
SKSSH
EEEK.
YA
AAAA! A WOUND! IT'S DAMAGED!
KOMUI IS GOING TO TRY AND REPAIR IT AGAIN! WHAT AM I GONNA DO?!
AAAAAAH
HUH?
GET TO WORK!!
SHOOMP
I'M SCARED...
CRK
CRK
CRK
CRK
?
I WONDER WHAT THAT CRACKING SOUND IS...

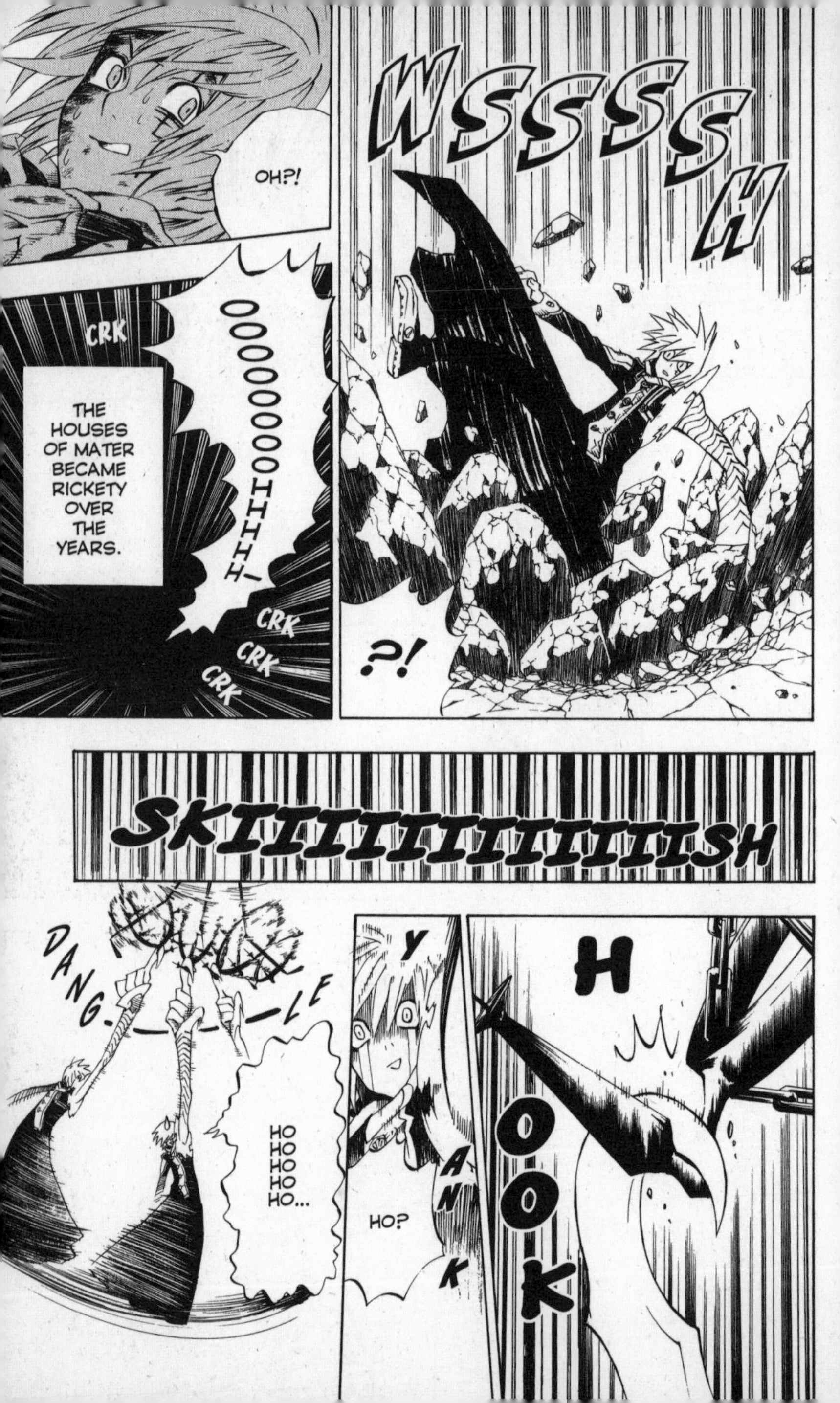
WSSSSH
?!
OH?!
CRK
OOOOOOOOOHHHHH–
THE HOUSES OF MATER BECAME RICKETY OVER THE YEARS.
CRK
CRK
CRK
SKIIIIIIIIIIIIISH
HOOK
YANK
HO?
DANG-LE
HO HO HO HO HO HO...

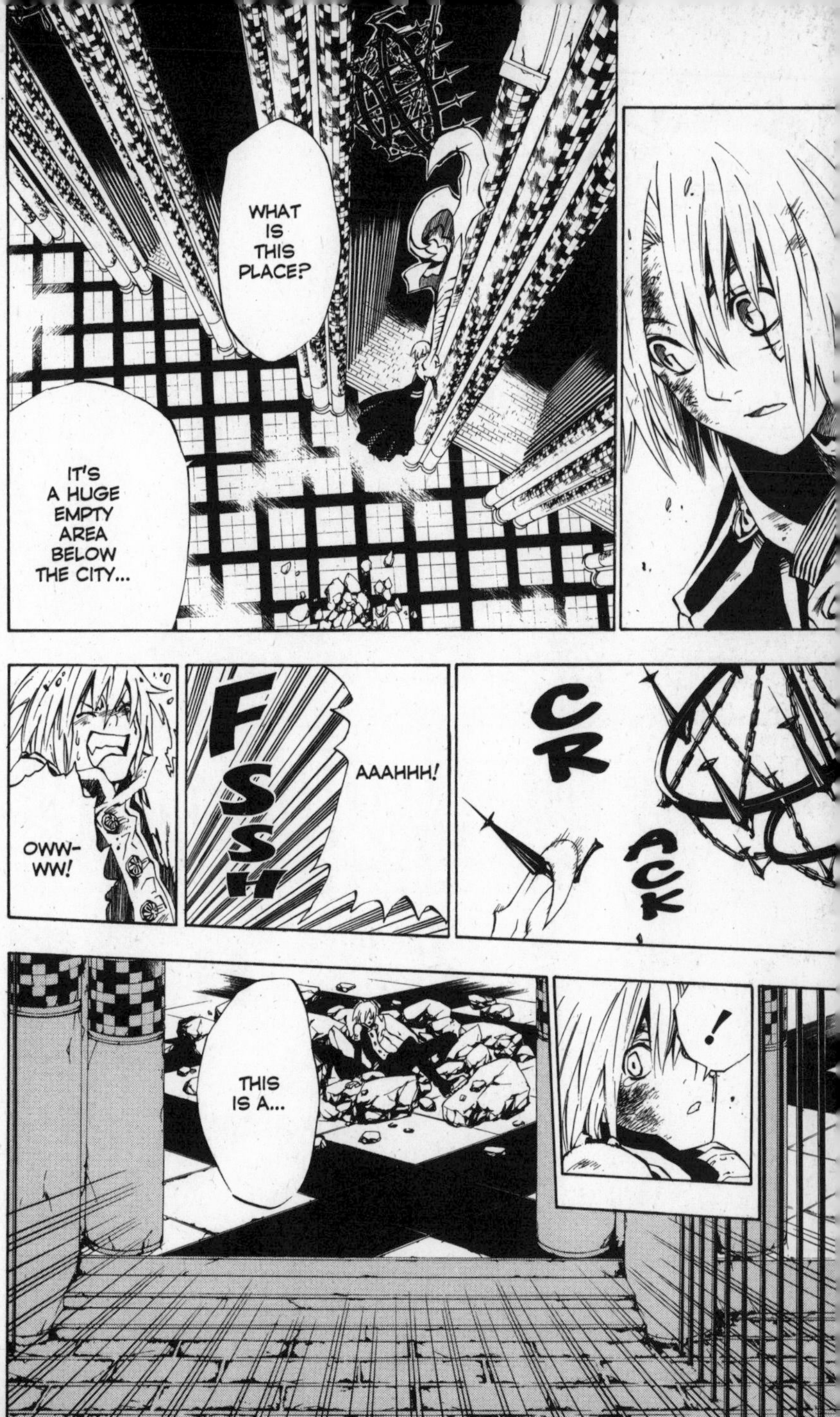
WHAT IS THIS PLACE?
IT'S A HUGE EMPTY AREA BELOW THE CITY...
CRACK
FSSH
AAAHHH!
OWW-WW!
!
THIS IS A...

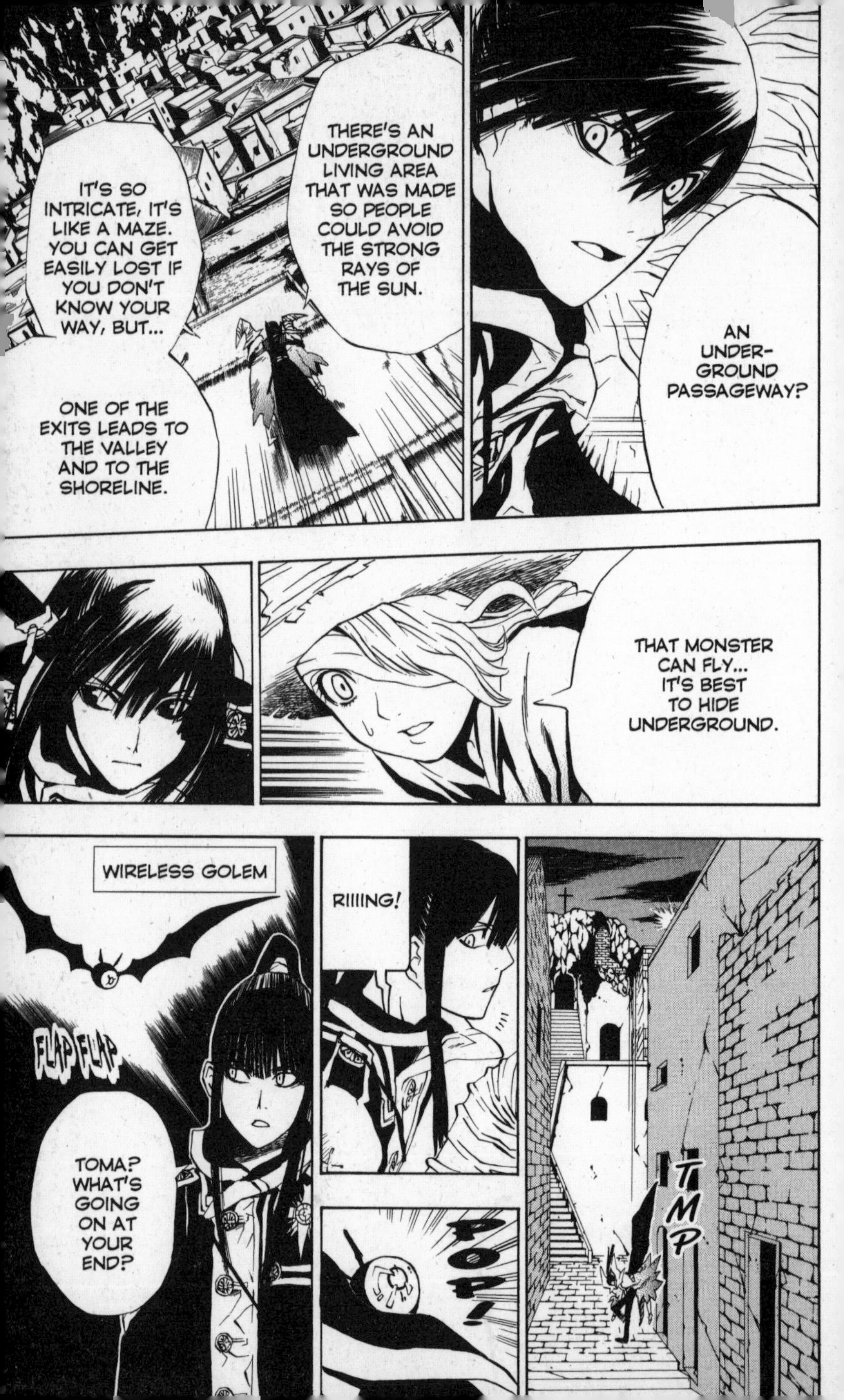
AN UNDER-GROUND PASSAGEWAY?
THERE'S AN UNDERGROUND LIVING AREA THAT WAS MADE SO PEOPLE COULD AVOID THE STRONG RAYS OF THE SUN.
IT'S SO INTRICATE, IT'S LIKE A MAZE. YOU CAN GET EASILY LOST IF YOU DON'T KNOW YOUR WAY, BUT...
ONE OF THE EXITS LEADS TO THE VALLEY AND TO THE SHORELINE.
THAT MONSTER CAN FLY... IT'S BEST TO HIDE UNDERGROUND.
TMP
RIIIING!
POP!
WIRELESS GOLEM
FLAP FLAP
TOMA? WHAT'S GOING ON AT YOUR END?

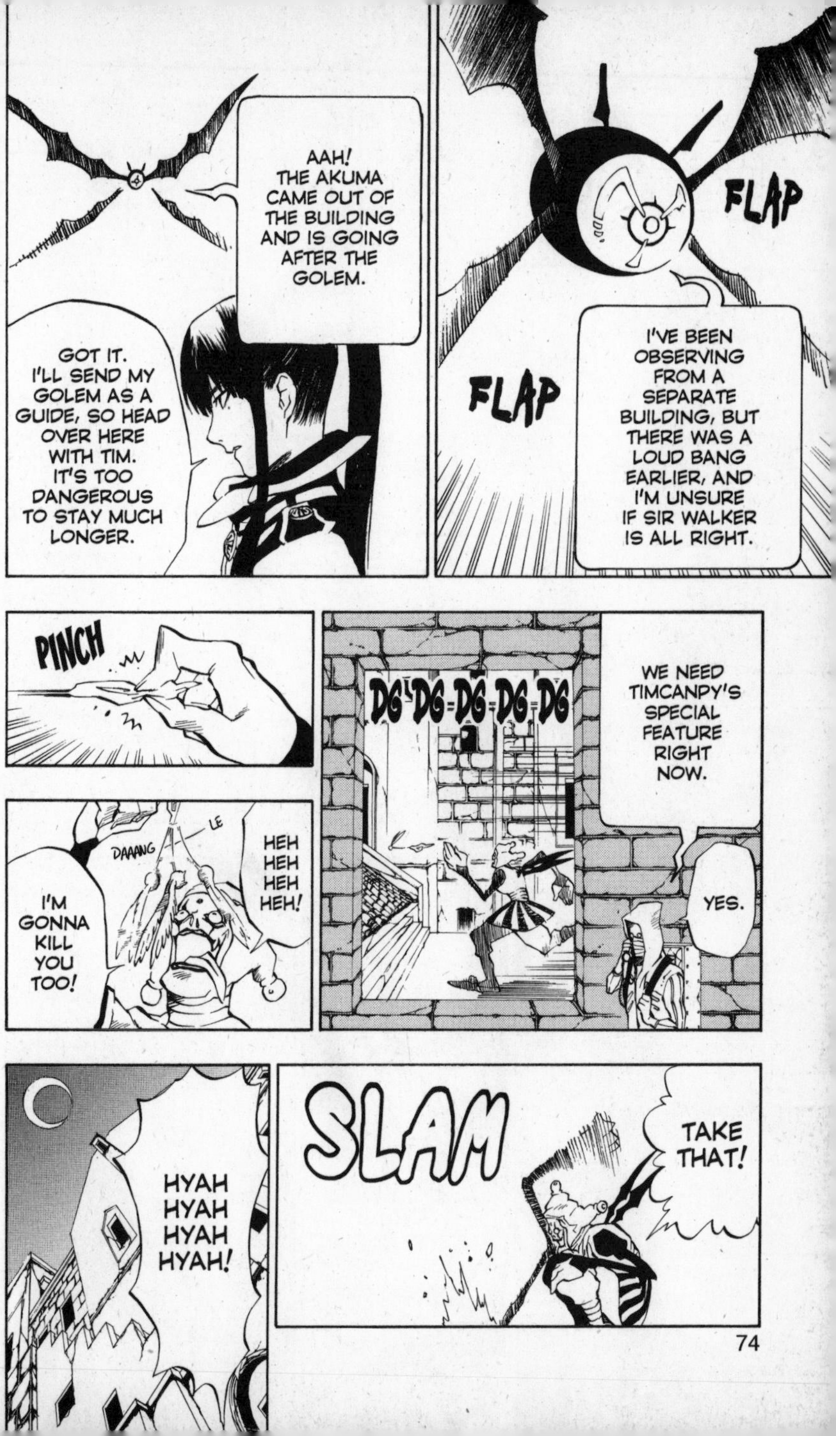
FLAP
I'VE BEEN OBSERVING FROM A SEPARATE BUILDING, BUT THERE WAS A LOUD BANG EARLIER, AND I'M UNSURE IF SIR WALKER IS ALL RIGHT.
FLAP
AAH! THE AKUMA CAME OUT OF THE BUILDING AND IS GOING AFTER THE GOLEM.
GOT IT. I'LL SEND MY GOLEM AS A GUIDE, SO HEAD OVER HERE WITH TIM. IT'S TOO DANGEROUS TO STAY MUCH LONGER.
DG DG DG DG DG
WE NEED TIMCANPY'S SPECIAL FEATURE RIGHT NOW.
YES.
PINCH
HEH HEH HEH HEH!
LE
DAAANG
I'M GONNA KILL YOU TOO!
SLAM
TAKE THAT!
HYAH HYAH HYAH HYAH!

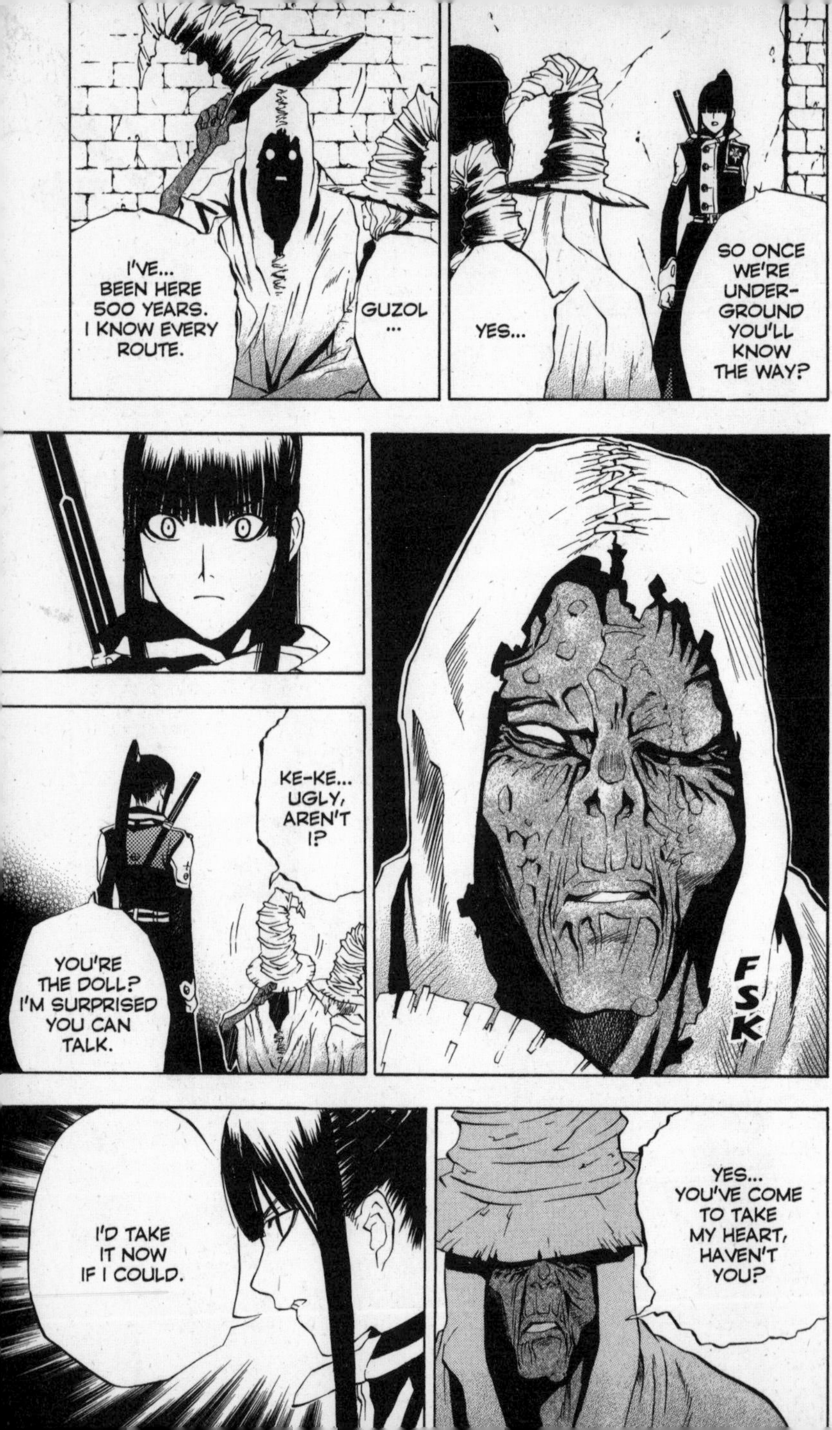
SO ONCE WE'RE UNDER-GROUND YOU'LL KNOW THE WAY?
YES...
GUZOL...
I'VE... BEEN HERE 500 YEARS. I KNOW EVERY ROUTE.
FSK
KE-KE... UGLY, AREN'T I?
YOU'RE THE DOLL? I'M SURPRISED YOU CAN TALK.
YES... YOU'VE COME TO TAKE MY HEART, HAVEN'T YOU?
I'D TAKE IT NOW IF I COULD.

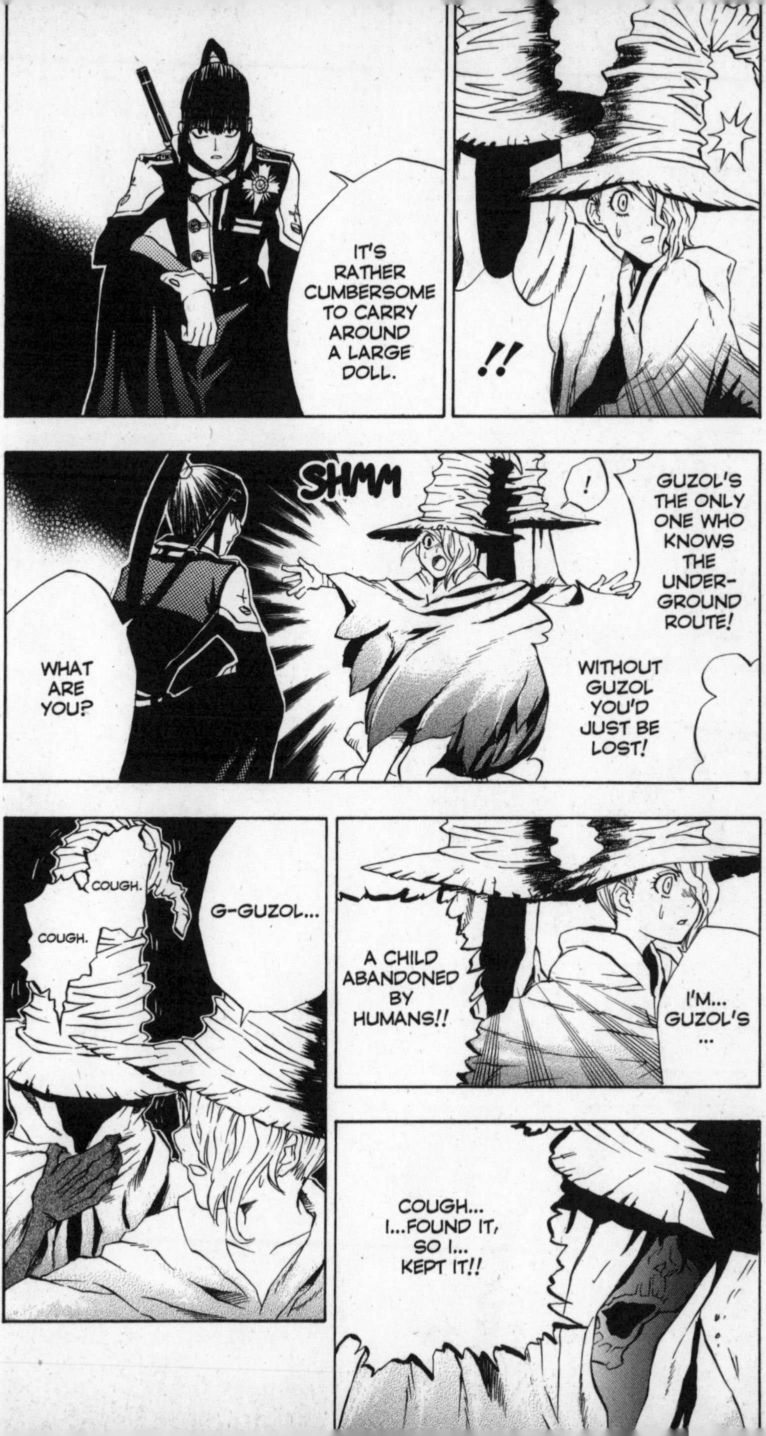
!!
IT'S RATHER CUMBERSOME TO CARRY AROUND A LARGE DOLL.
GUZOL'S THE ONLY ONE WHO KNOWS THE UNDER-GROUND ROUTE!
!
SHMM
WITHOUT GUZOL YOU'D JUST BE LOST!
WHAT ARE YOU?
I'M... GUZOL'S ...
A CHILD ABANDONED BY HUMANS!!
COUGH... I...FOUND IT, SO I... KEPT IT!!
G-GUZOL...
COUGH.
COUGH.

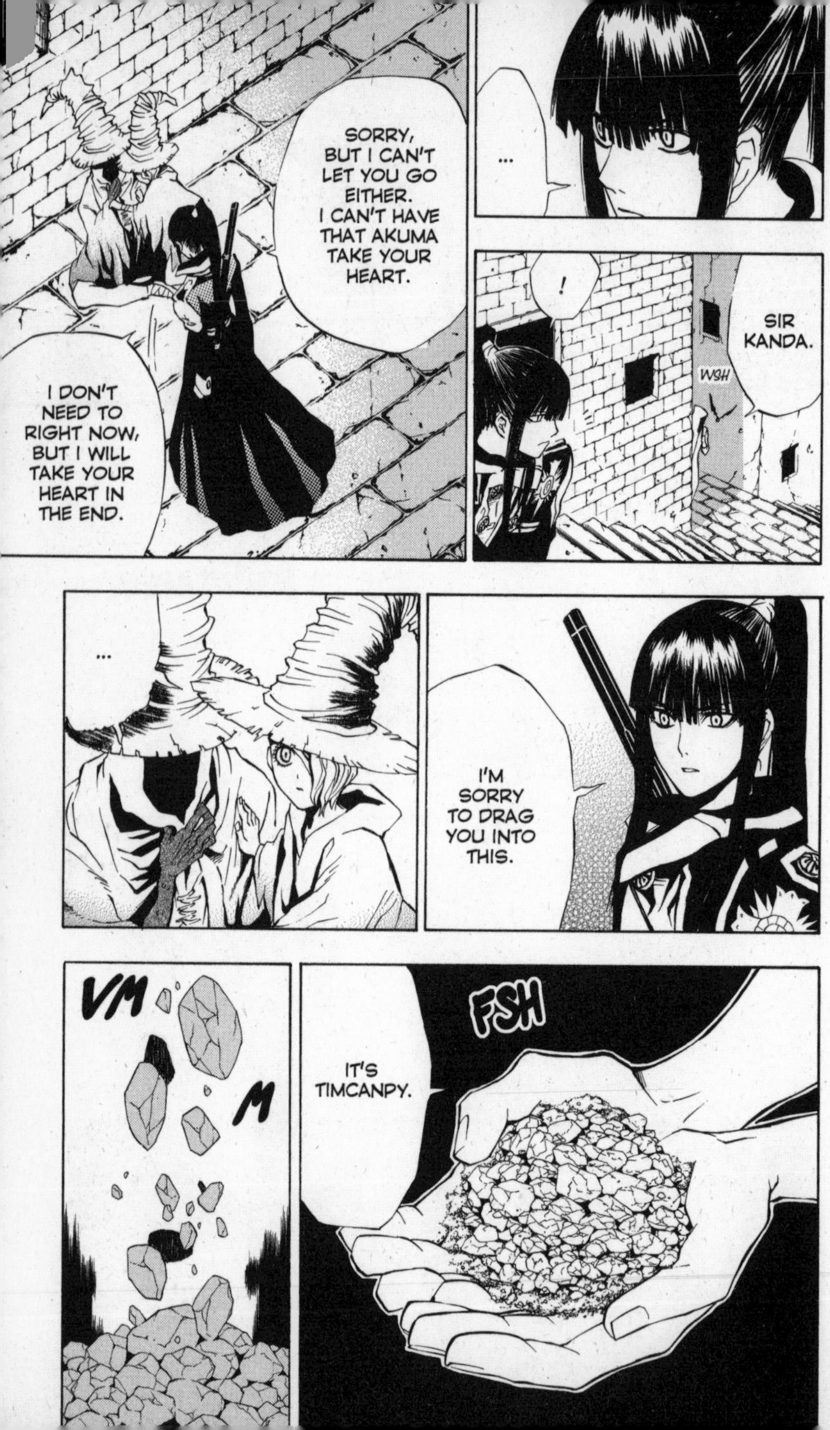
...
!
SIR KANDA.
WSH
SORRY, BUT I CAN'T LET YOU GO EITHER. I CAN'T HAVE THAT AKUMA TAKE YOUR HEART.
I DON'T NEED TO RIGHT NOW, BUT I WILL TAKE YOUR HEART IN THE END.
I'M SORRY TO DRAG YOU INTO THIS.
...
FSH
IT'S TIMCANPY.
VM
M

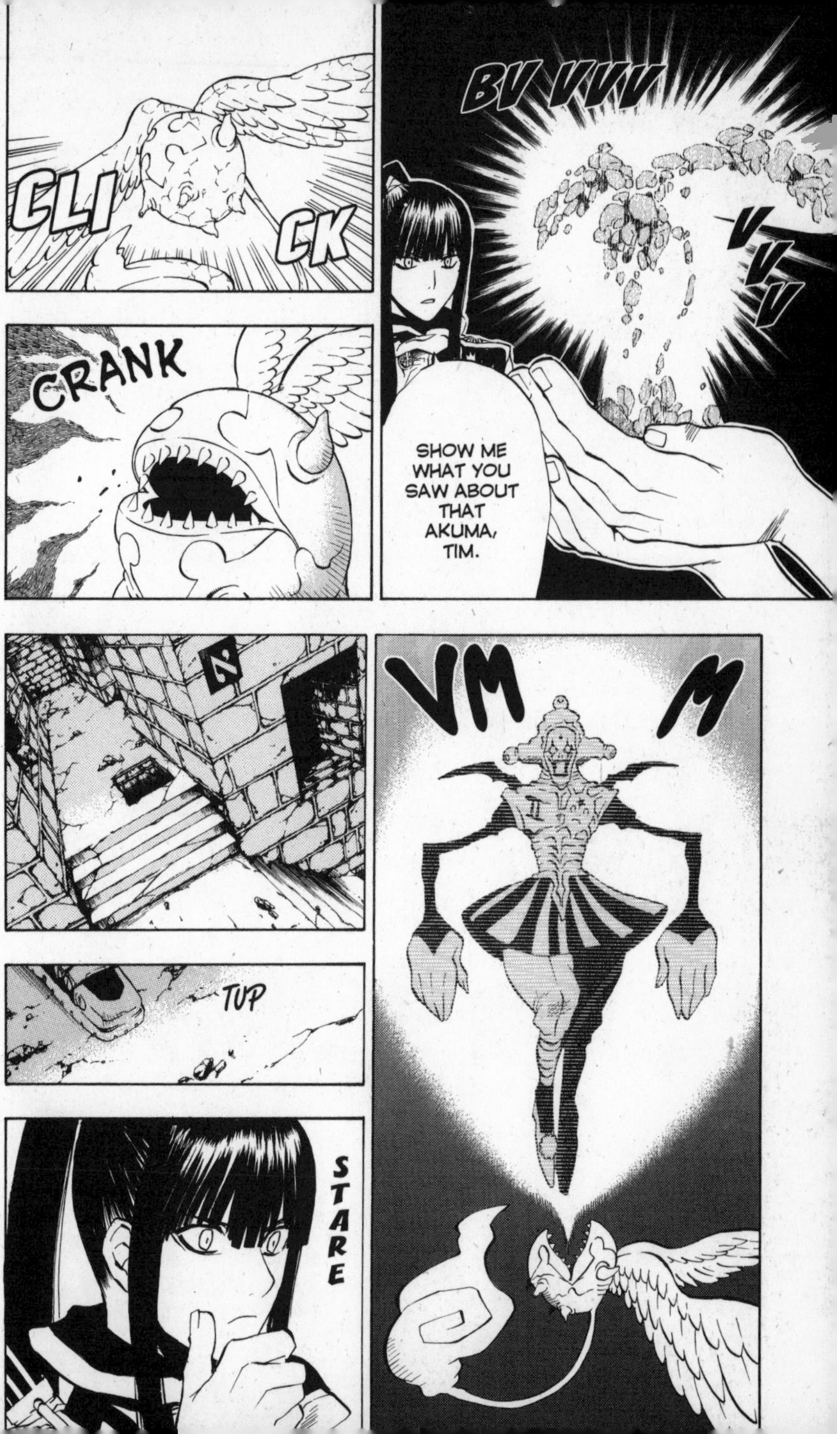
BV VVV
V V V
SHOW ME WHAT YOU SAW ABOUT THAT AKUMA, TIM.
CLI CK
CRANK
VM M
TUP
STARE

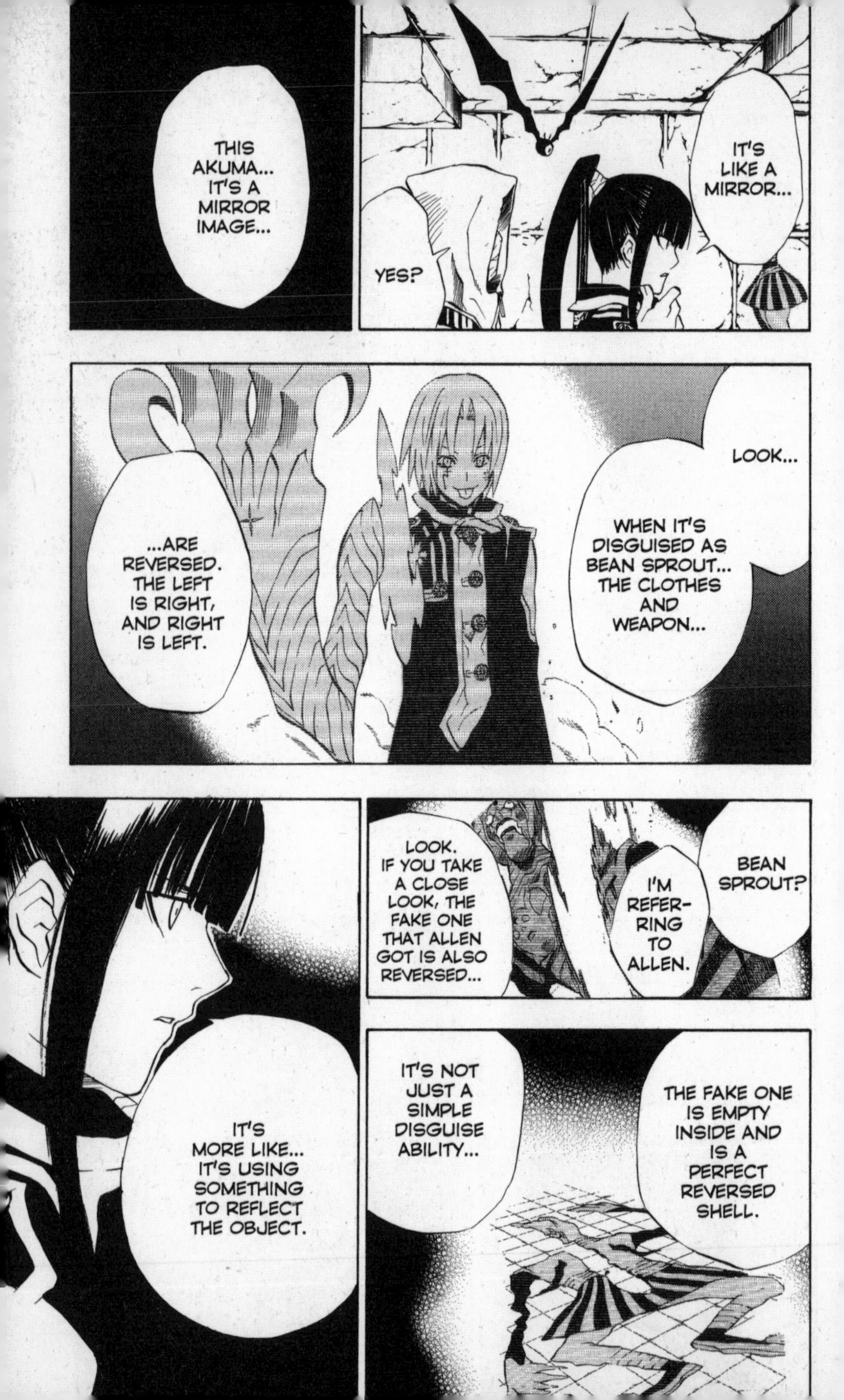
IT'S LIKE A MIRROR...
YES?
THIS AKUMA... IT'S A MIRROR IMAGE...
LOOK... WHEN IT'S DISGUISED AS BEAN SPROUT... THE CLOTHES AND WEAPON...
...ARE REVERSED. THE LEFT IS RIGHT, AND RIGHT IS LEFT.
BEAN SPROUT?
I'M REFER-RING TO ALLEN.
LOOK. IF YOU TAKE A CLOSE LOOK, THE FAKE ONE THAT ALLEN GOT IS ALSO REVERSED...
THE FAKE ONE IS EMPTY INSIDE AND IS A PERFECT REVERSED SHELL.
IT'S NOT JUST A SIMPLE DISGUISE ABILITY...
IT'S MORE LIKE... IT'S USING SOMETHING TO REFLECT THE OBJECT.

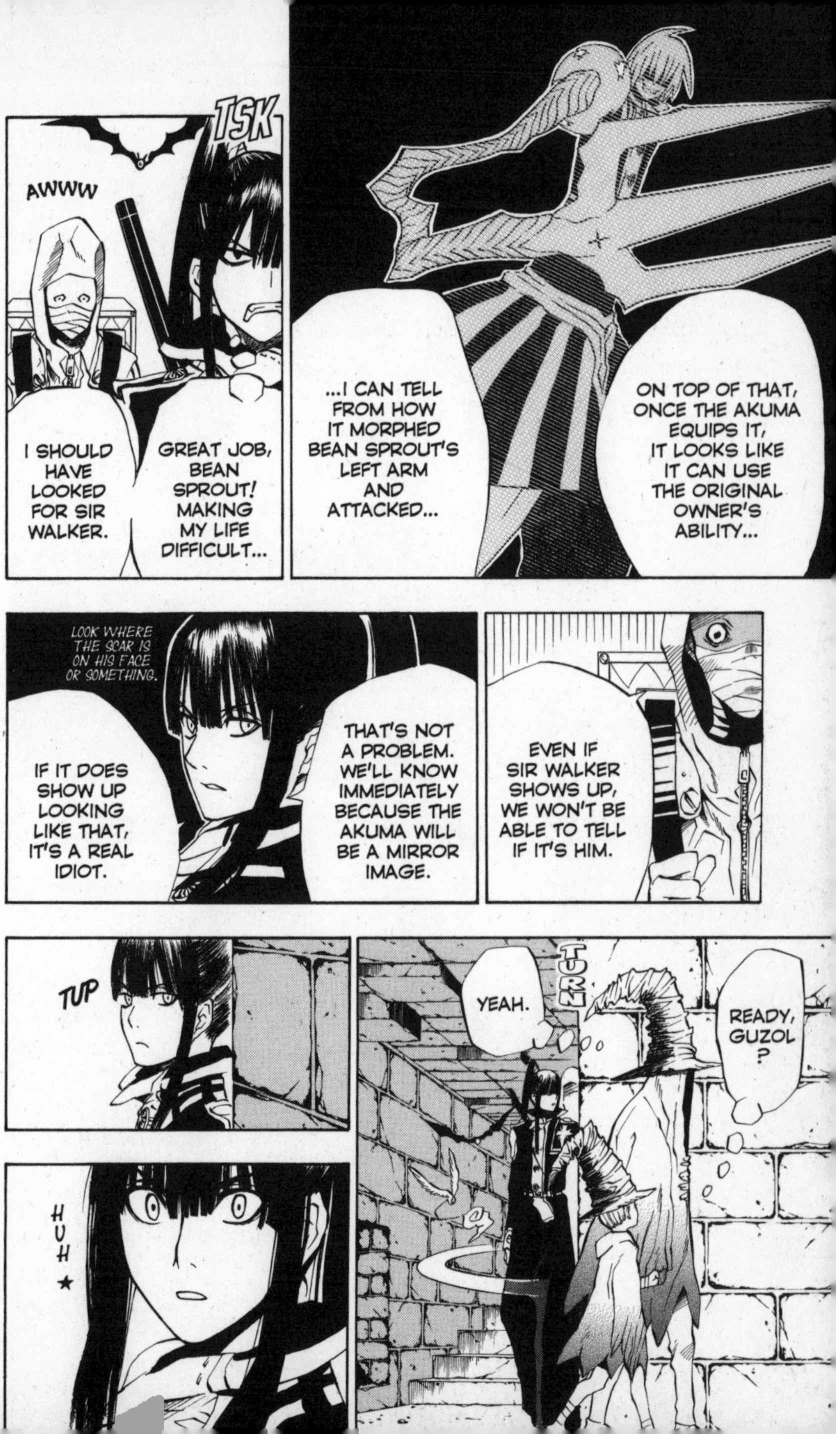
...I CAN TELL FROM HOW IT MORPHED BEAN SPROUT'S LEFT ARM AND ATTACKED...
ON TOP OF THAT, ONCE THE AKUMA EQUIPS IT, IT LOOKS LIKE IT CAN USE THE ORIGINAL OWNER'S ABILITY...
TSK
GREAT JOB, BEAN SPROUT! MAKING MY LIFE DIFFICULT...
AWWW
I SHOULD HAVE LOOKED FOR SIR WALKER.
EVEN IF SIR WALKER SHOWS UP, WE WON'T BE ABLE TO TELL IF IT'S HIM.
THAT'S NOT A PROBLEM. WE'LL KNOW IMMEDIATELY BECAUSE THE AKUMA WILL BE A MIRROR IMAGE.
IF IT DOES SHOW UP LOOKING LIKE THAT, IT'S A REAL IDIOT.
LOOK WHERE THE SCAR IS ON HIS FACE OR SOMETHING.
READY, GUZOL?
TURN
YEAH.
TUP
HUH★

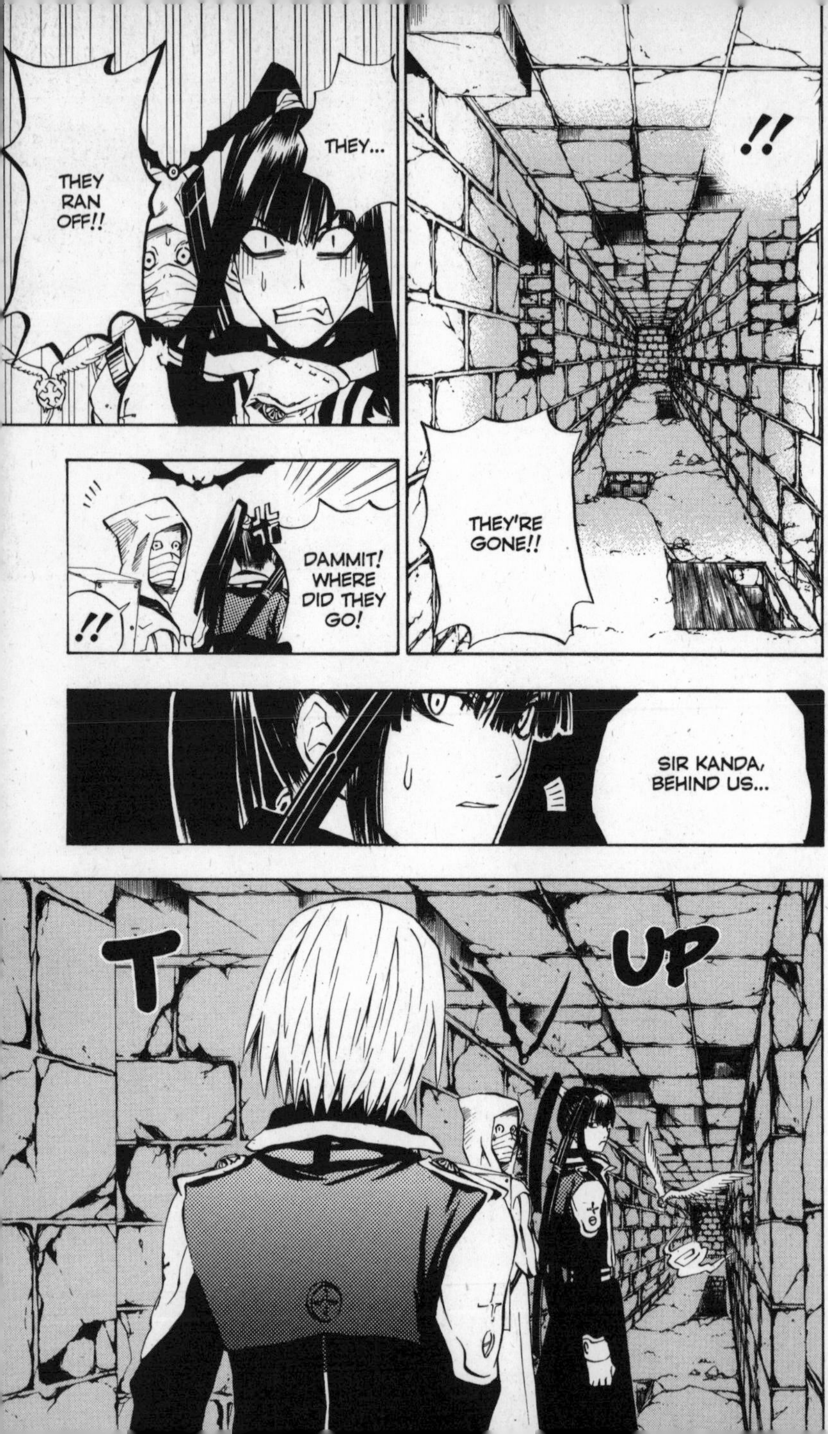
!!
THEY'RE GONE!!
THEY...
THEY RAN OFF!!
DAMMIT! WHERE DID THEY GO!
!!
SIR KANDA, BEHIND US...
T UP

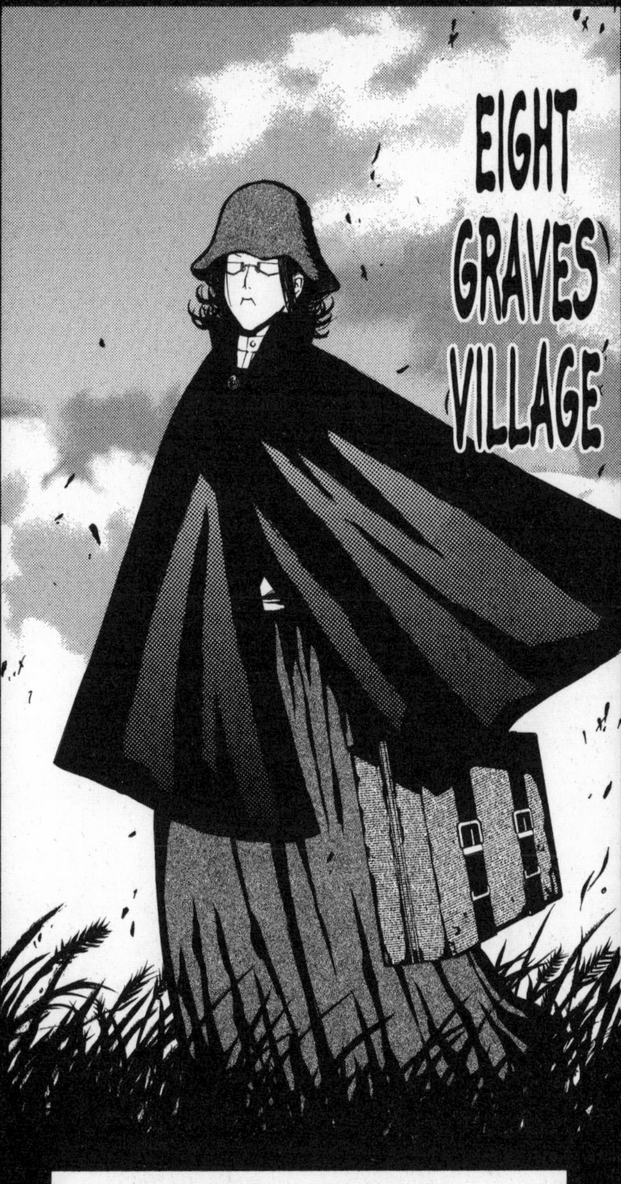
EIGHT GRAVES VILLAGE

KOMUSUKE KINDAICHI

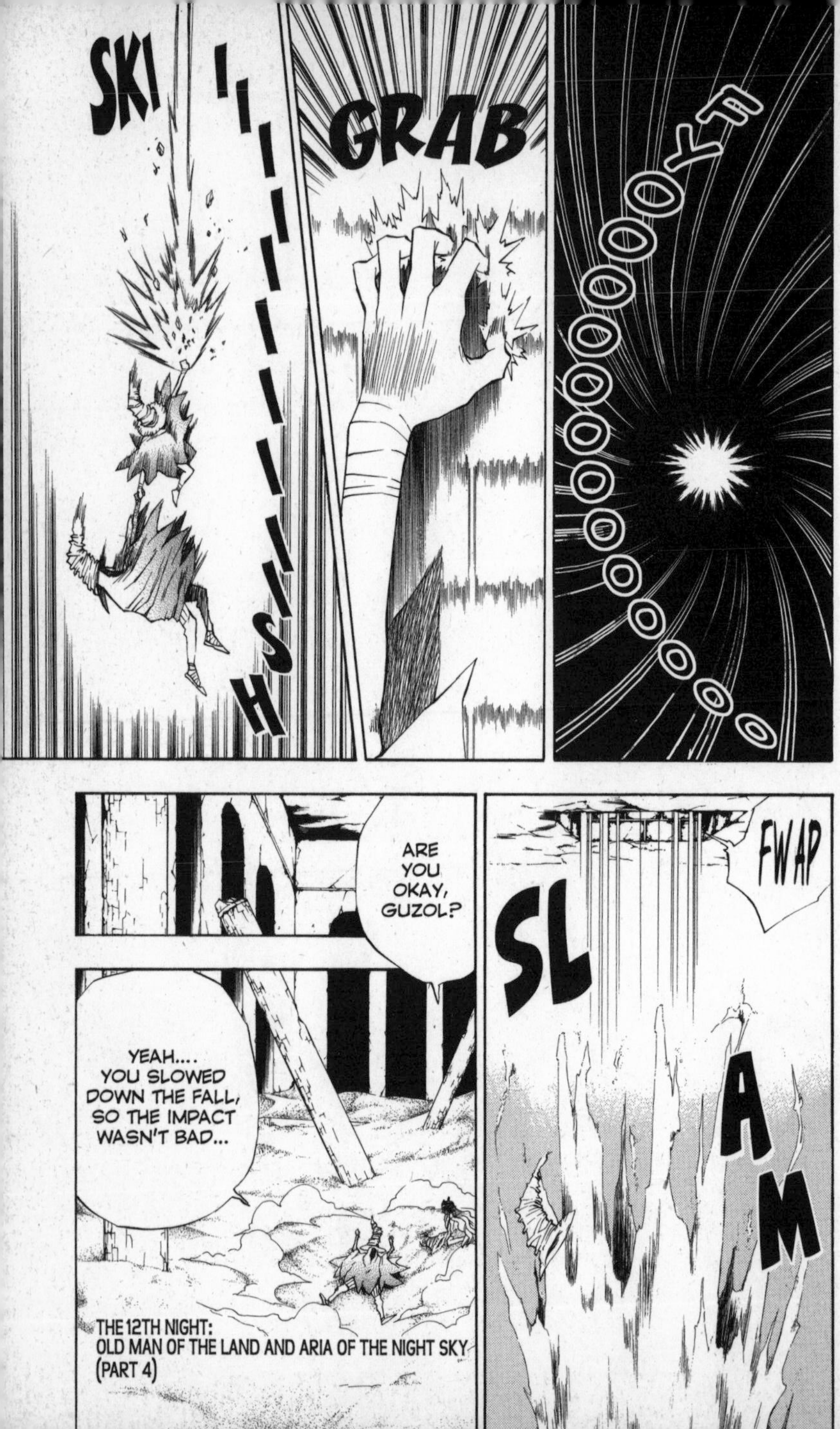
EYOOOOOOOOOOOOOOOOO
GRAB
SKIIIIIIIIISH
FWAP
SLAM
ARE YOU OKAY, GUZOL?
YEAH.... YOU SLOWED DOWN THE FALL, SO THE IMPACT WASN'T BAD...
THE 12TH NIGHT:
OLD MAN OF THE LAND AND ARIA OF THE NIGHT SKY
(PART 4)

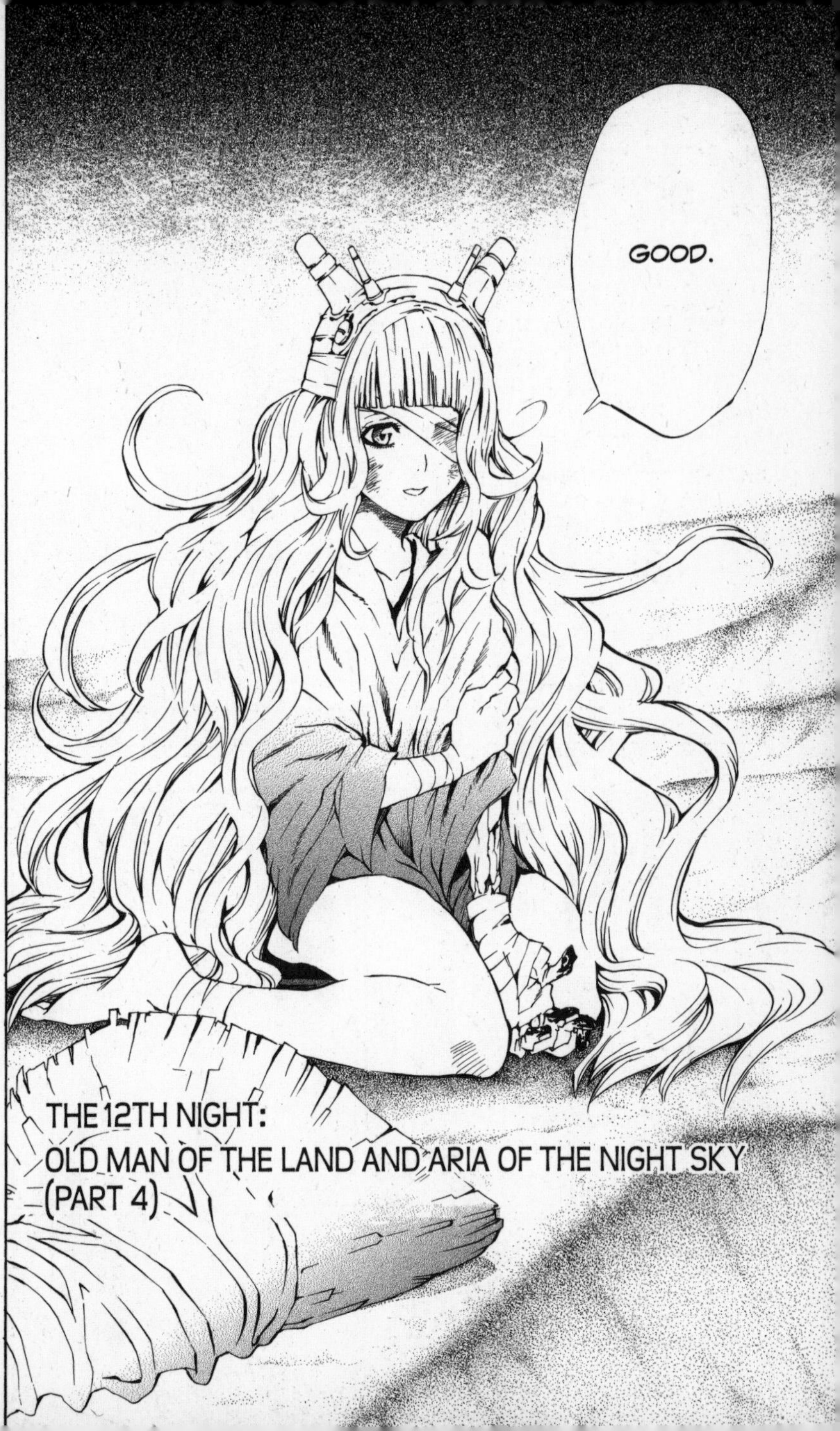
GOOD.

THE 12TH NIGHT:
OLD MAN OF THE LAND AND ARIA OF THE NIGHT SKY (PART 4)

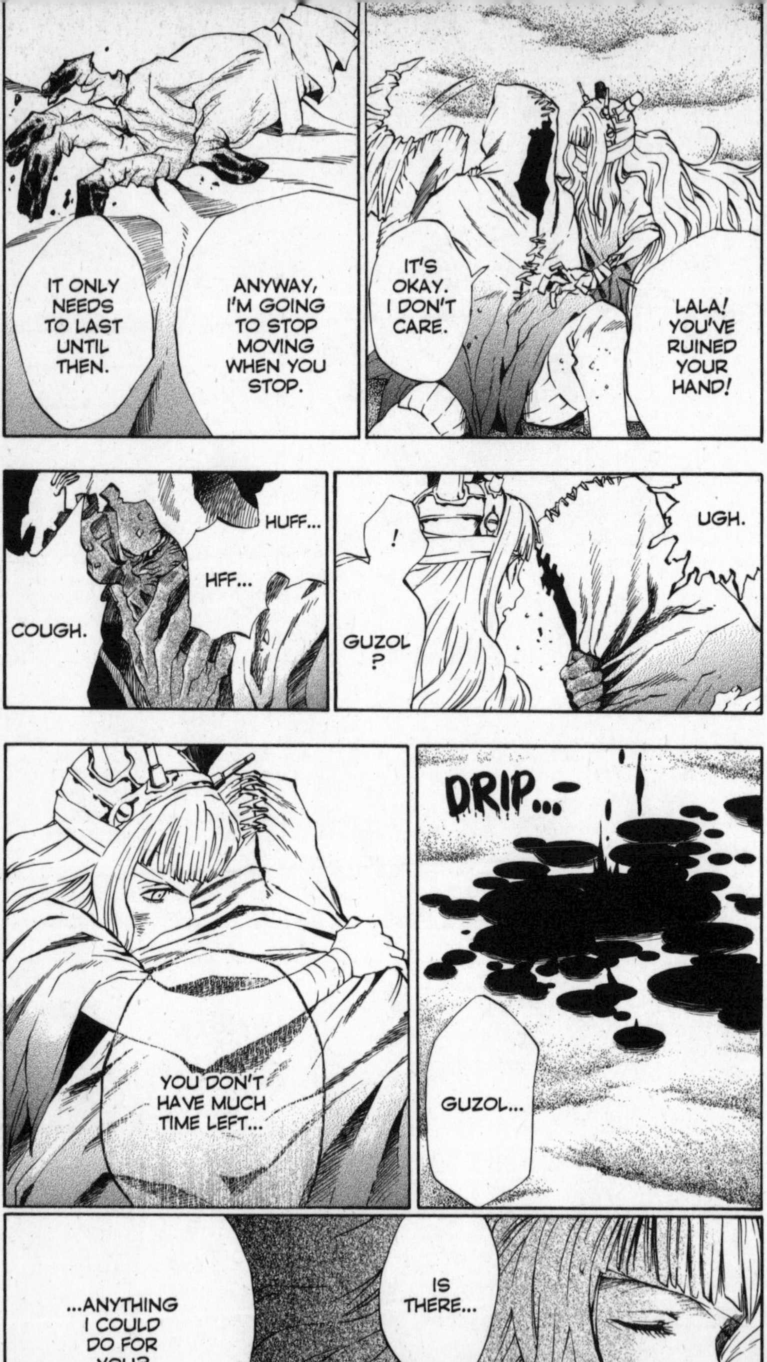
LALA! YOU'VE RUINED YOUR HAND!
IT'S OKAY. I DON'T CARE.
ANYWAY, I'M GOING TO STOP MOVING WHEN YOU STOP.
IT ONLY NEEDS TO LAST UNTIL THEN.
UGH.
!
GUZOL ?
HUFF...
HFF...
COUGH.
DRIP...
GUZOL...
YOU DON'T HAVE MUCH TIME LEFT...
IS THERE...
...ANYTHING I COULD DO FOR YOU?

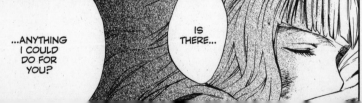

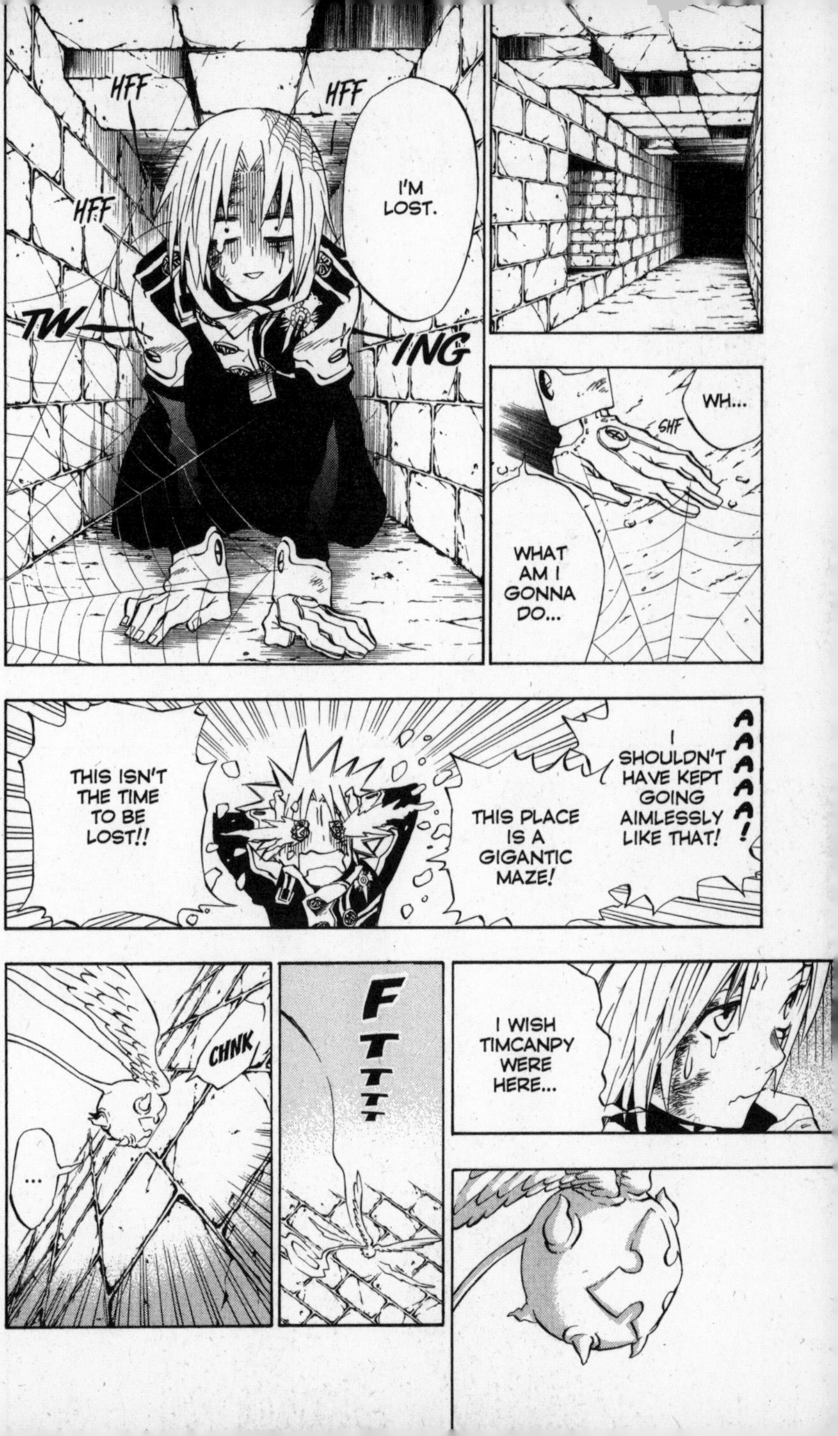
HFF
HFF
I'M LOST.
HFF
TW—
ING
SHF
WH...
WHAT AM I GONNA DO...
THIS ISN'T THE TIME TO BE LOST!!
THIS PLACE IS A GIGANTIC MAZE!
I SHOULDN'T HAVE KEPT GOING AIMLESSLY LIKE THAT!
AAAAAA!
CHNK
...
FTTT
I WISH TIMCANPY WERE HERE...

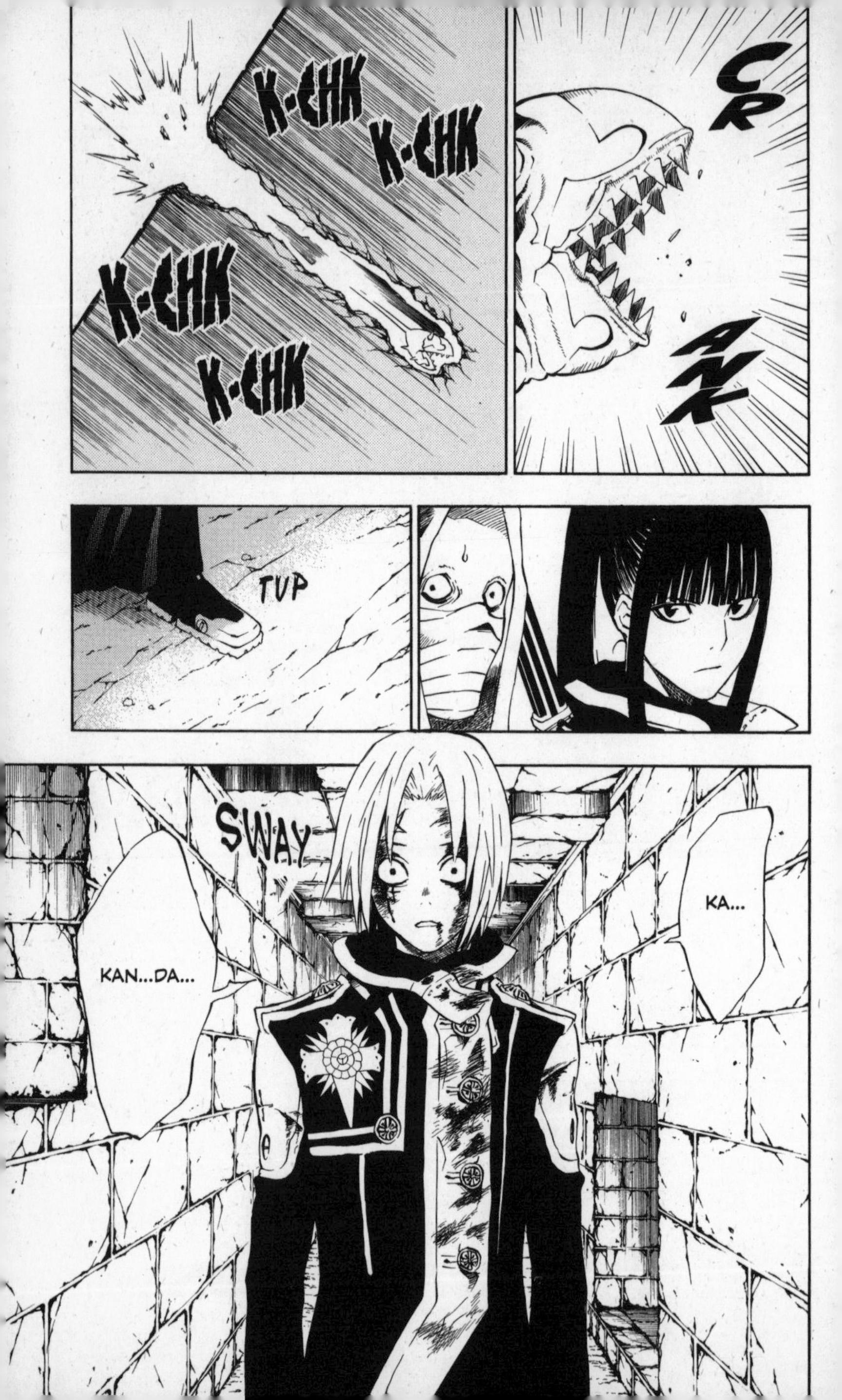
CRANK
K-CHK
K-CHK
K-CHK
K-CHK
TUP
KA...
SWAY
KAN...DA...

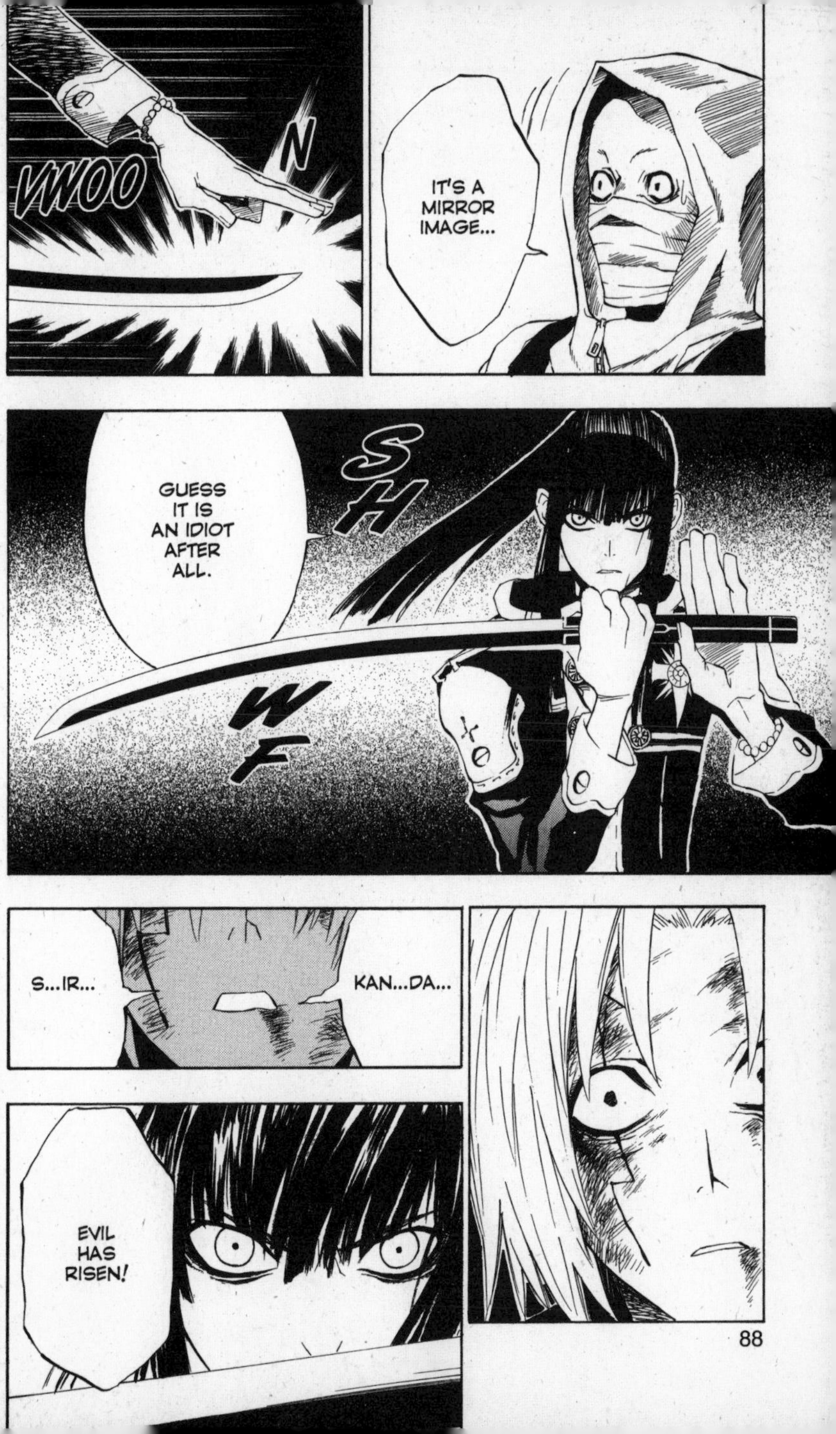
IT'S A MIRROR IMAGE...
VWOO
N
SHWF
GUESS IT IS AN IDIOT AFTER ALL.
KAN...DA...
S...IR...
EVIL HAS RISEN!

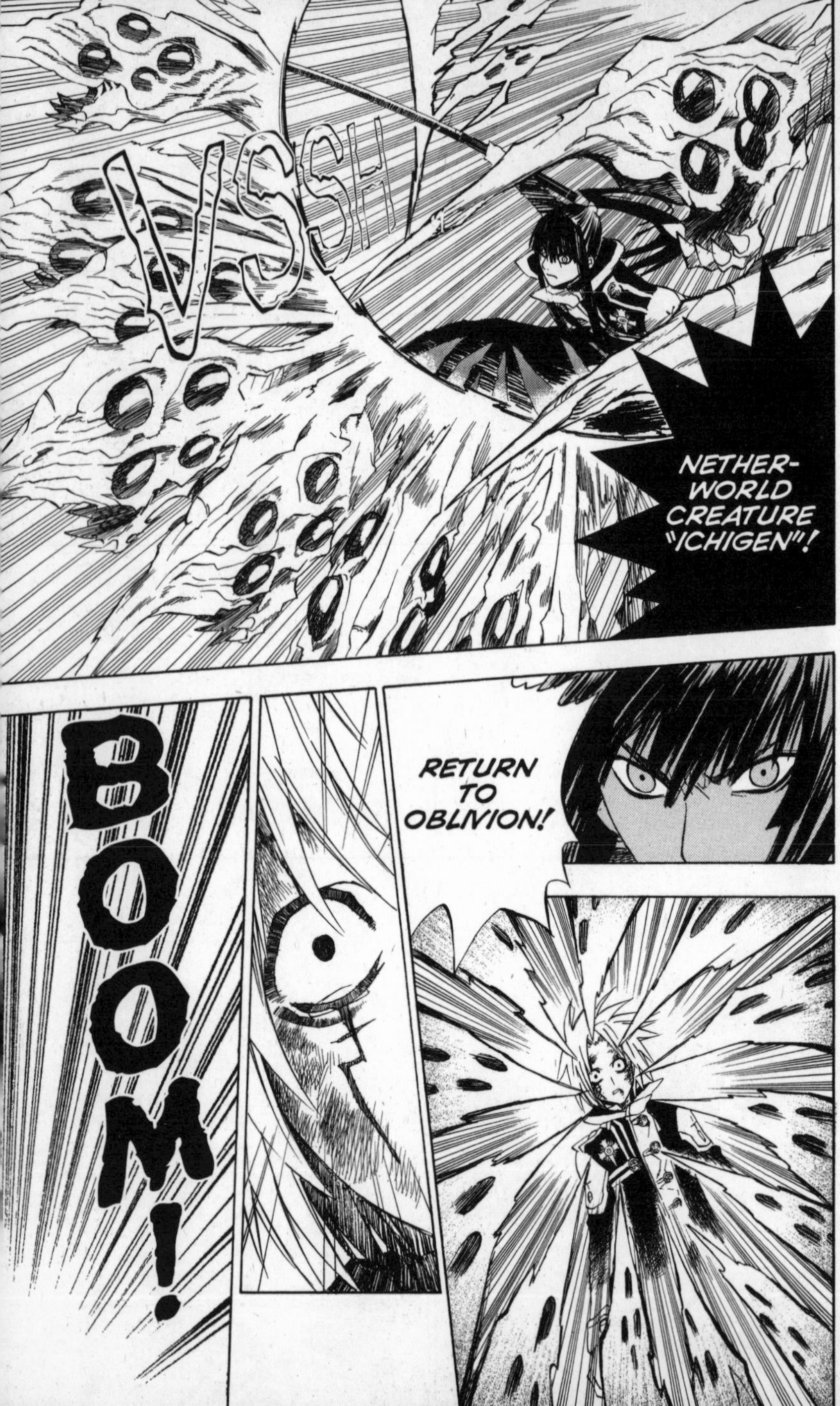
VSSH
NETHER-WORLD CREATURE "ICHIGEN"!
RETURN TO OBLIVION!
BOOM!

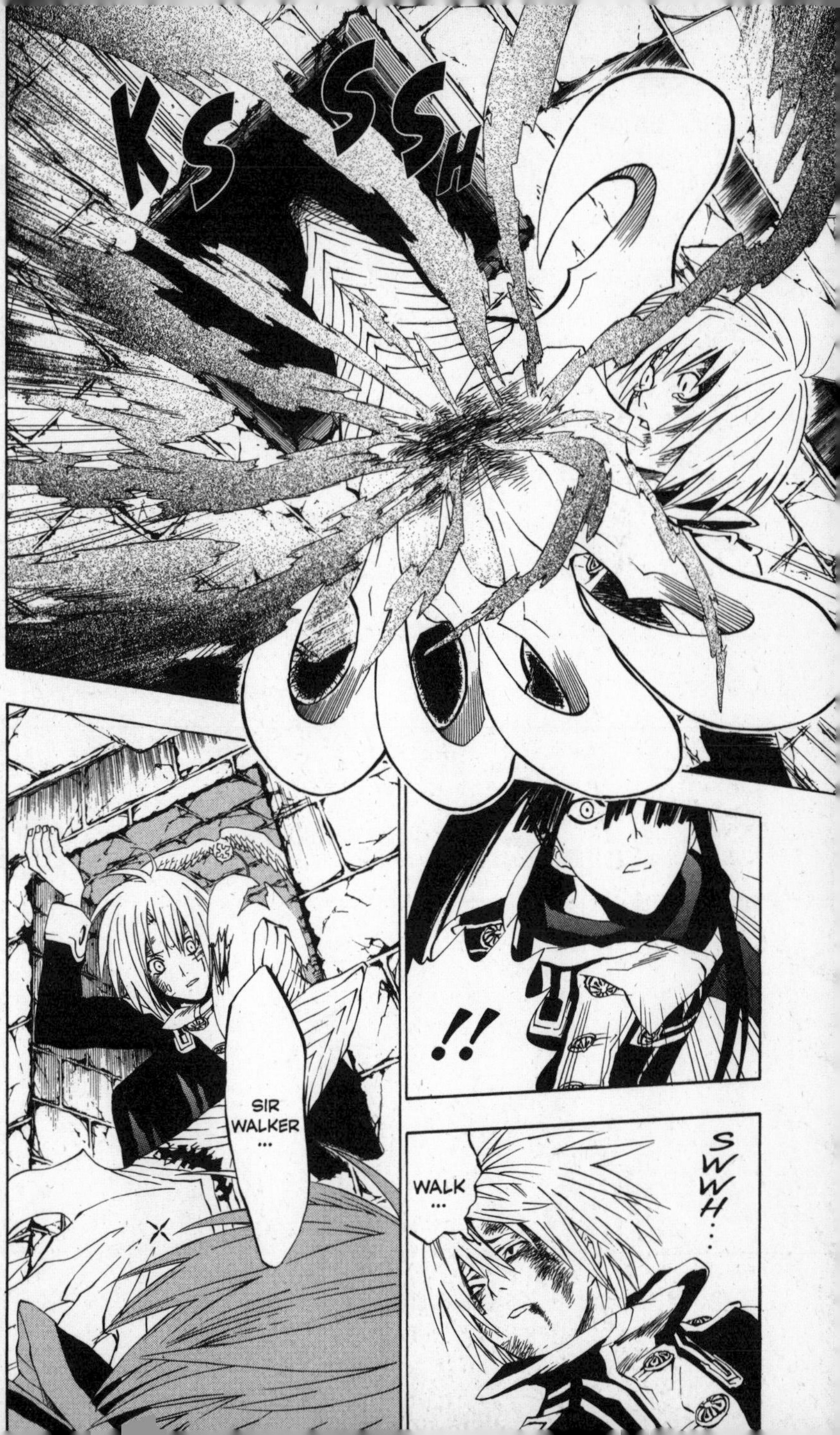
KSSSH
!!
SIR WALKER...
WALK...
SWWH...

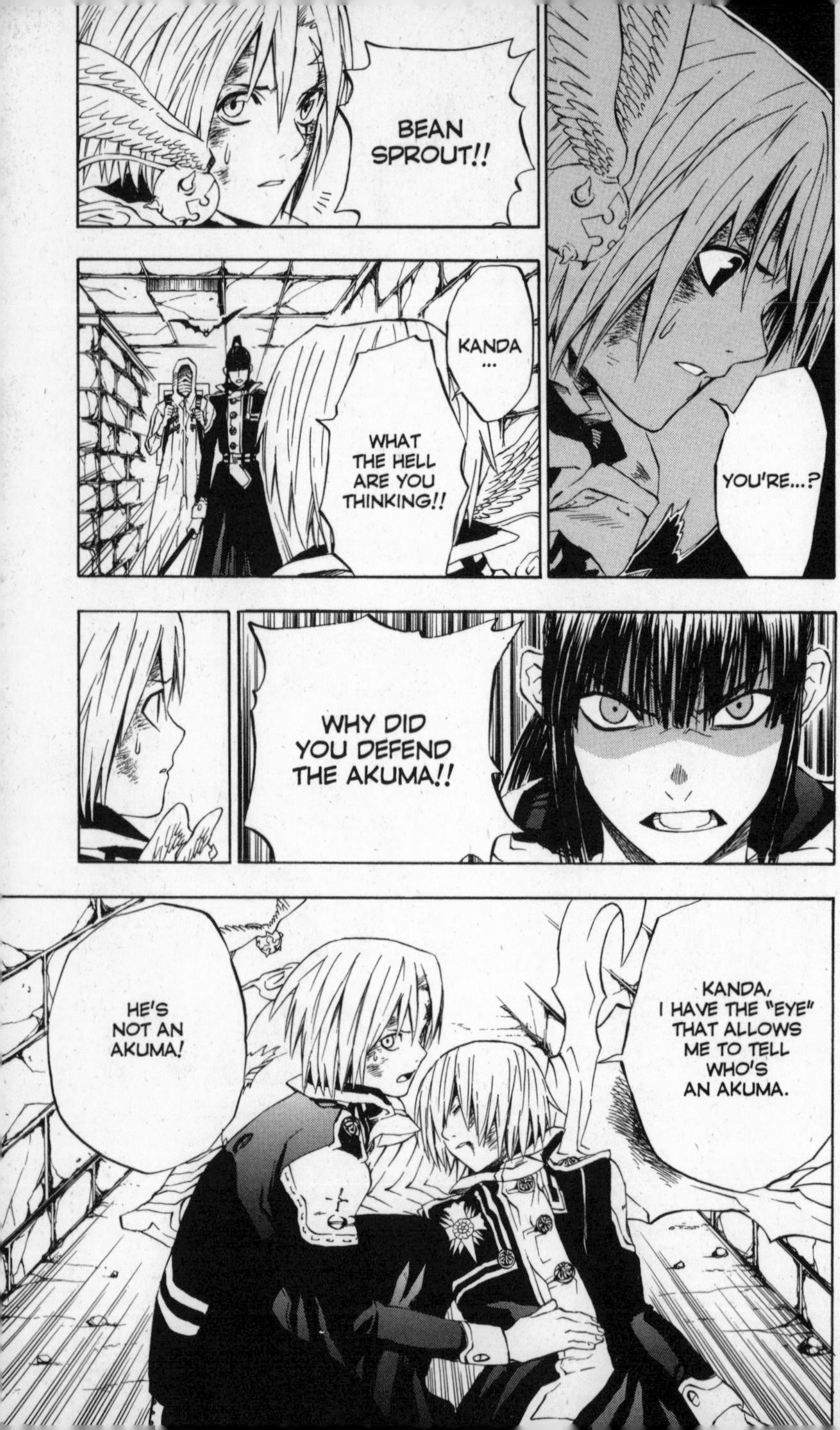
YOU'RE...?
BEAN SPROUT!!
KANDA...
WHAT THE HELL ARE YOU THINKING!!
WHY DID YOU DEFEND THE AKUMA!!
KANDA, I HAVE THE "EYE" THAT ALLOWS ME TO TELL WHO'S AN AKUMA.
HE'S NOT AN AKUMA!

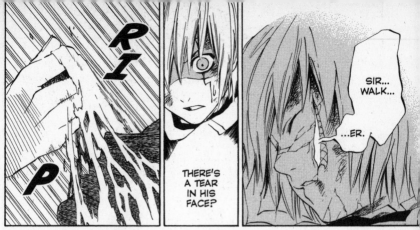

RIP

THERE'S A TEAR IN HIS FACE?

SIR... WALK... ...ER.

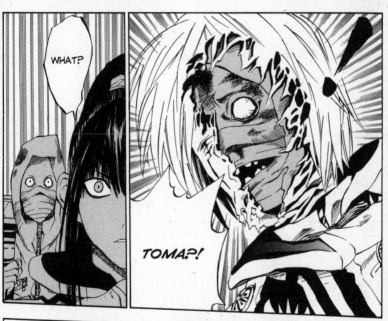

WHAT?

TOMA?!

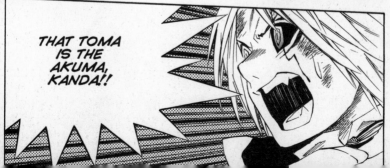

THAT TOMA IS THE AKUMA, KANDA!!

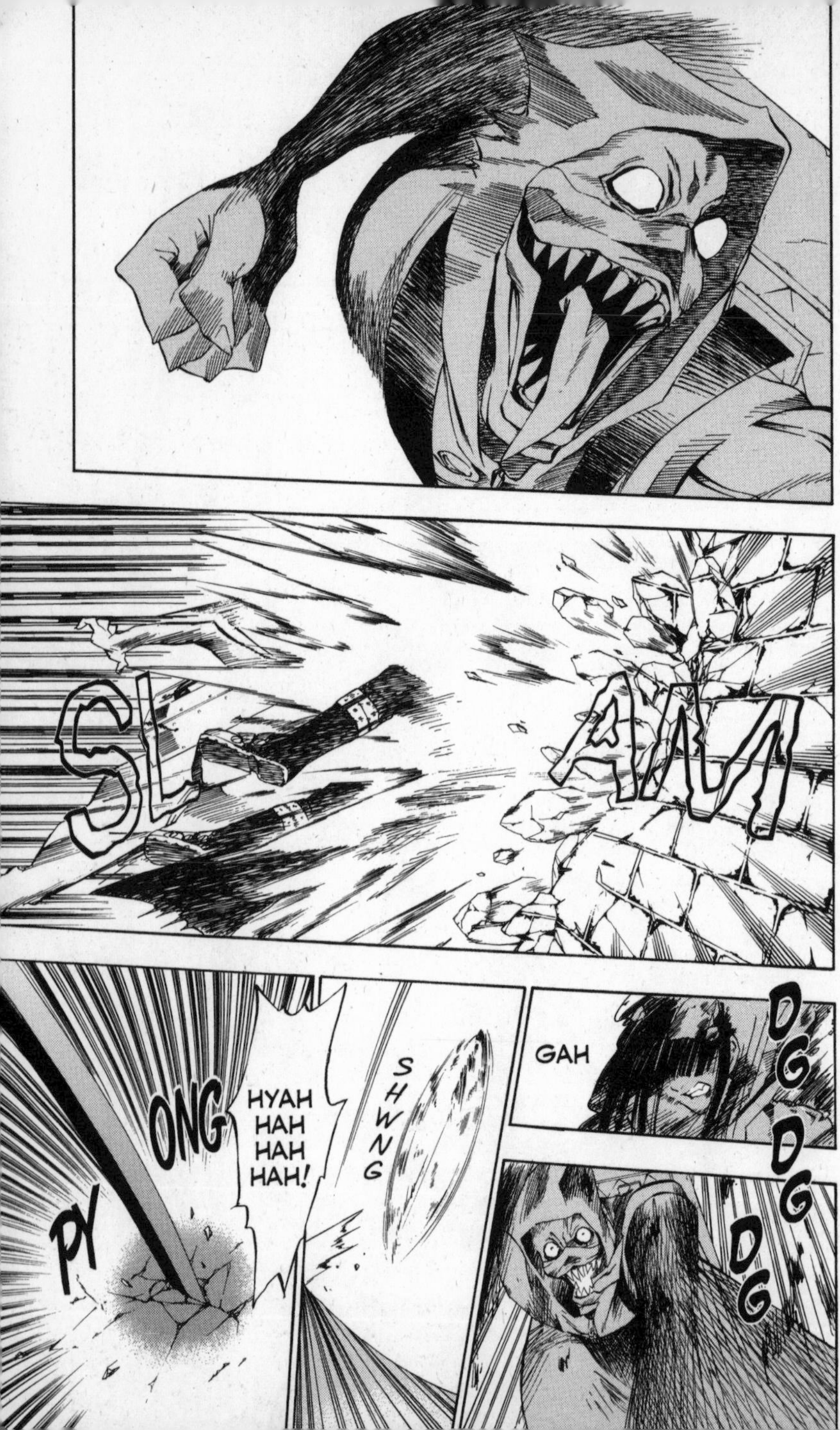
SLAM
GAH
DG DG DG
DG DG
SHWNG
HYAH HAH HAH HAH!
PYONG

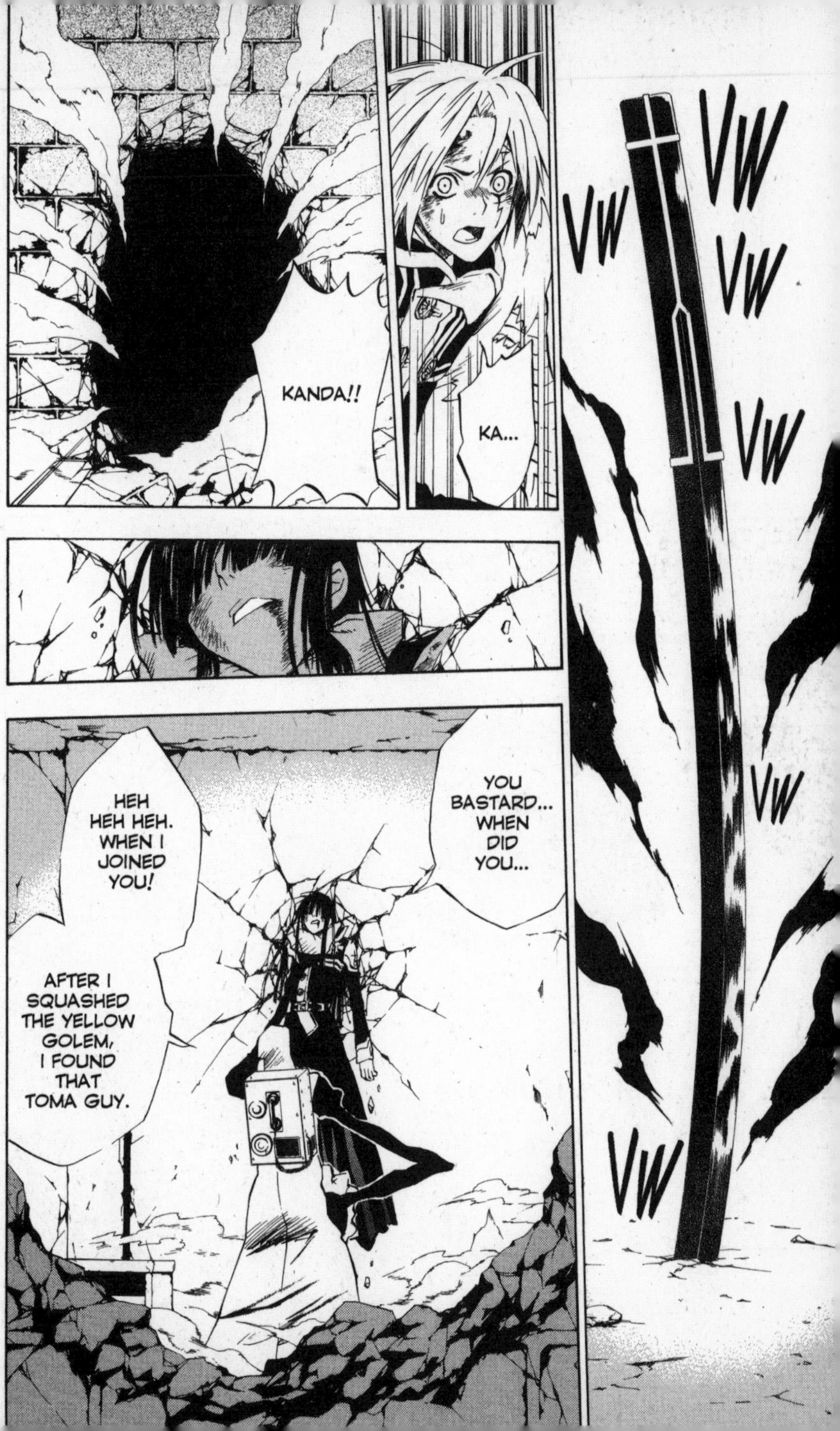
VW
VW
VW
VW
VW
VW
KA...
KANDA!!
YOU BASTARD... WHEN DID YOU...
HEH HEH HEH. WHEN I JOINED YOU!
AFTER I SQUASHED THE YELLOW GOLEM, I FOUND THAT TOMA GUY.

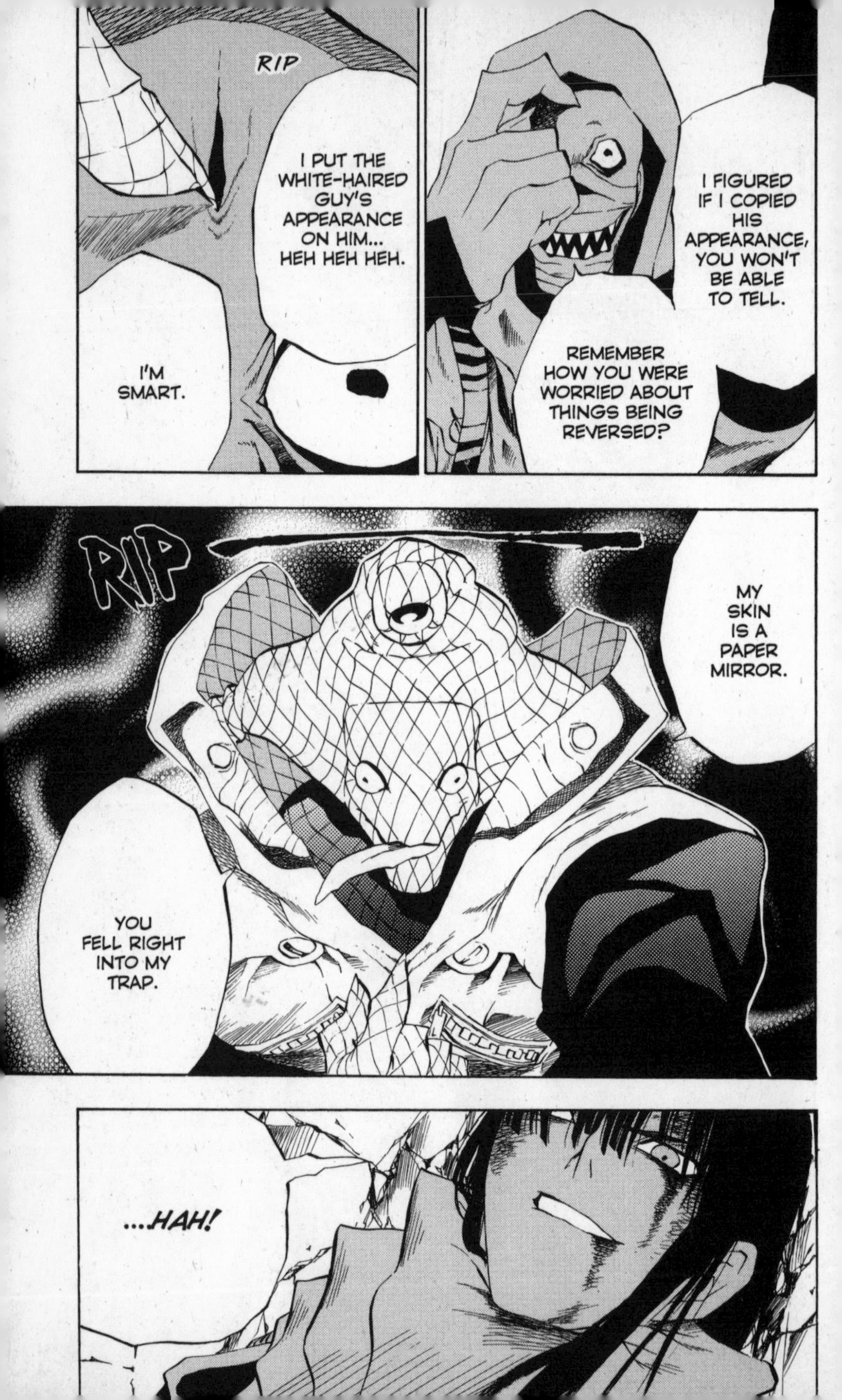
I FIGURED IF I COPIED HIS APPEARANCE, YOU WON'T BE ABLE TO TELL.
REMEMBER HOW YOU WERE WORRIED ABOUT THINGS BEING REVERSED?
RIP
I PUT THE WHITE-HAIRED GUY'S APPEARANCE ON HIM... HEH HEH HEH.
I'M SMART.
RIP
MY SKIN IS A PAPER MIRROR.
YOU FELL RIGHT INTO MY TRAP.
...HAH!

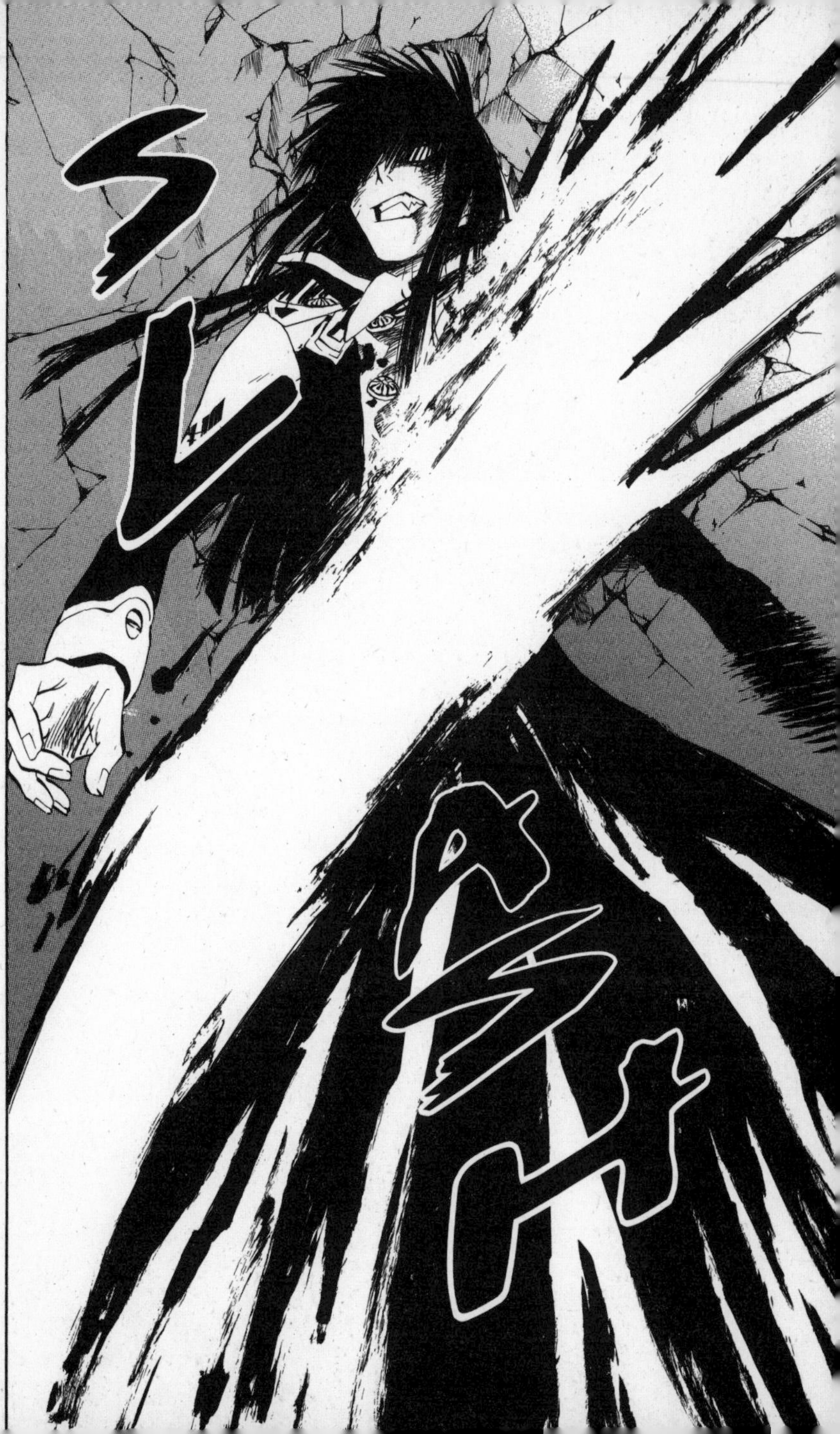
SLASH

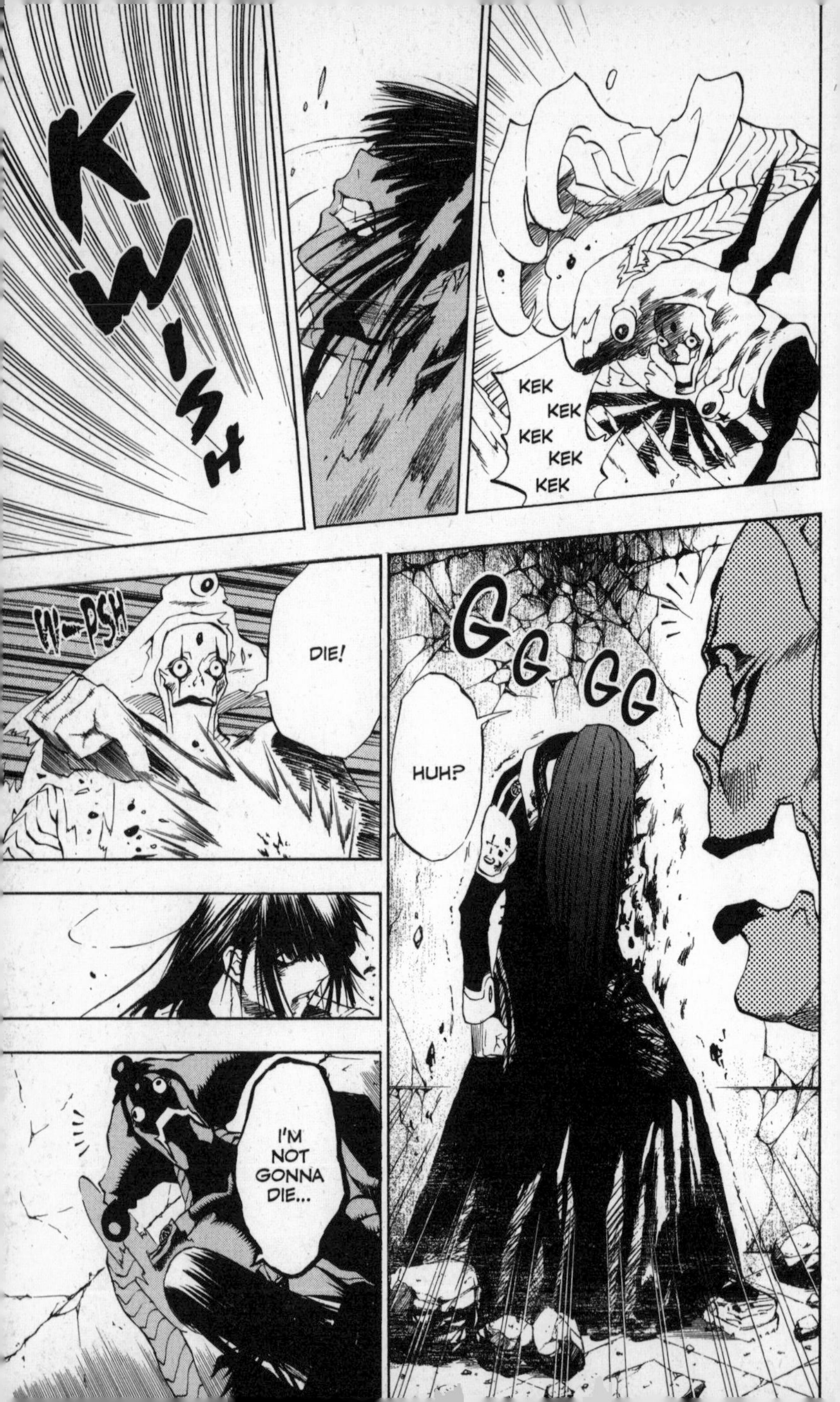
KEK KEK KEK KEK KEK
KWISH
GGGG
HUH?
W-PSH
DIE!
I'M NOT GONNA DIE...

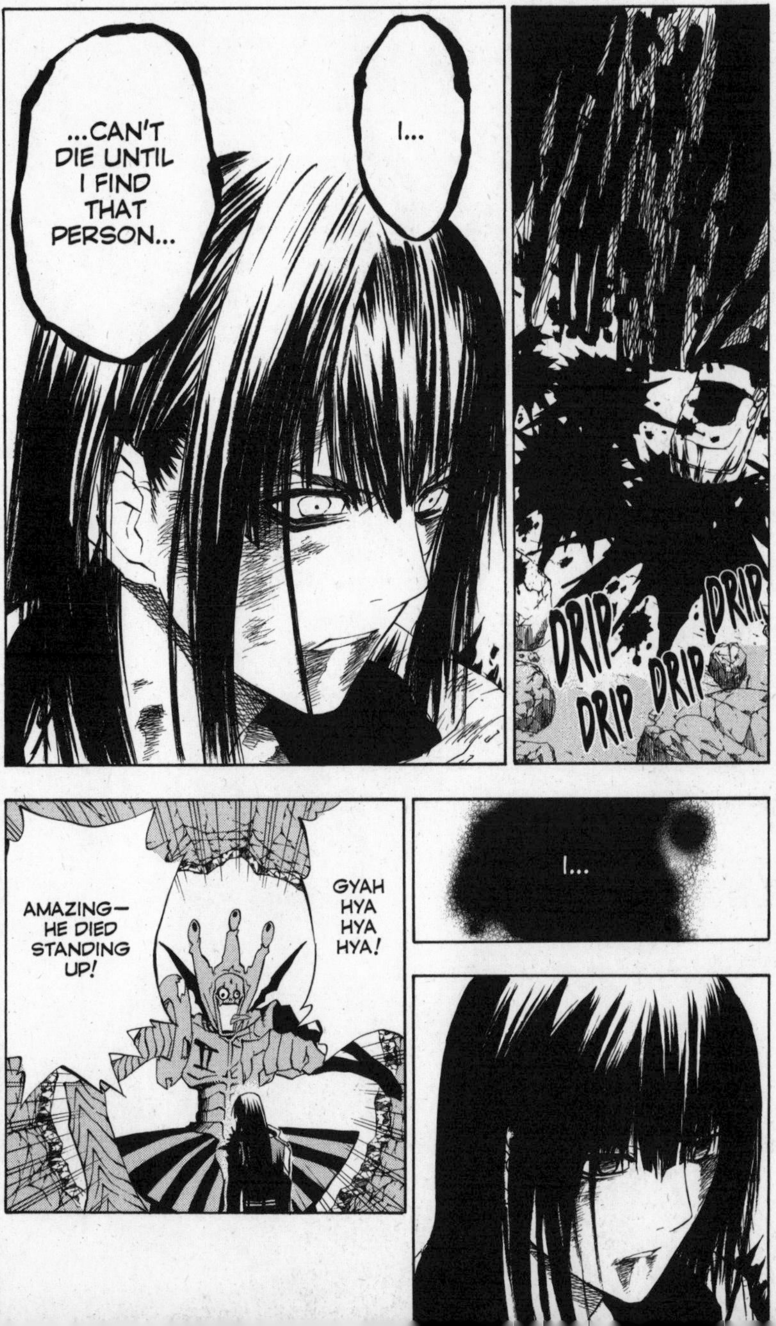
DRIP
DRIP
DRIP
DRIP
I...
...CAN'T DIE UNTIL I FIND THAT PERSON...
I...
GYAH HYA HYA HYA!
AMAZING— HE DIED STANDING UP!

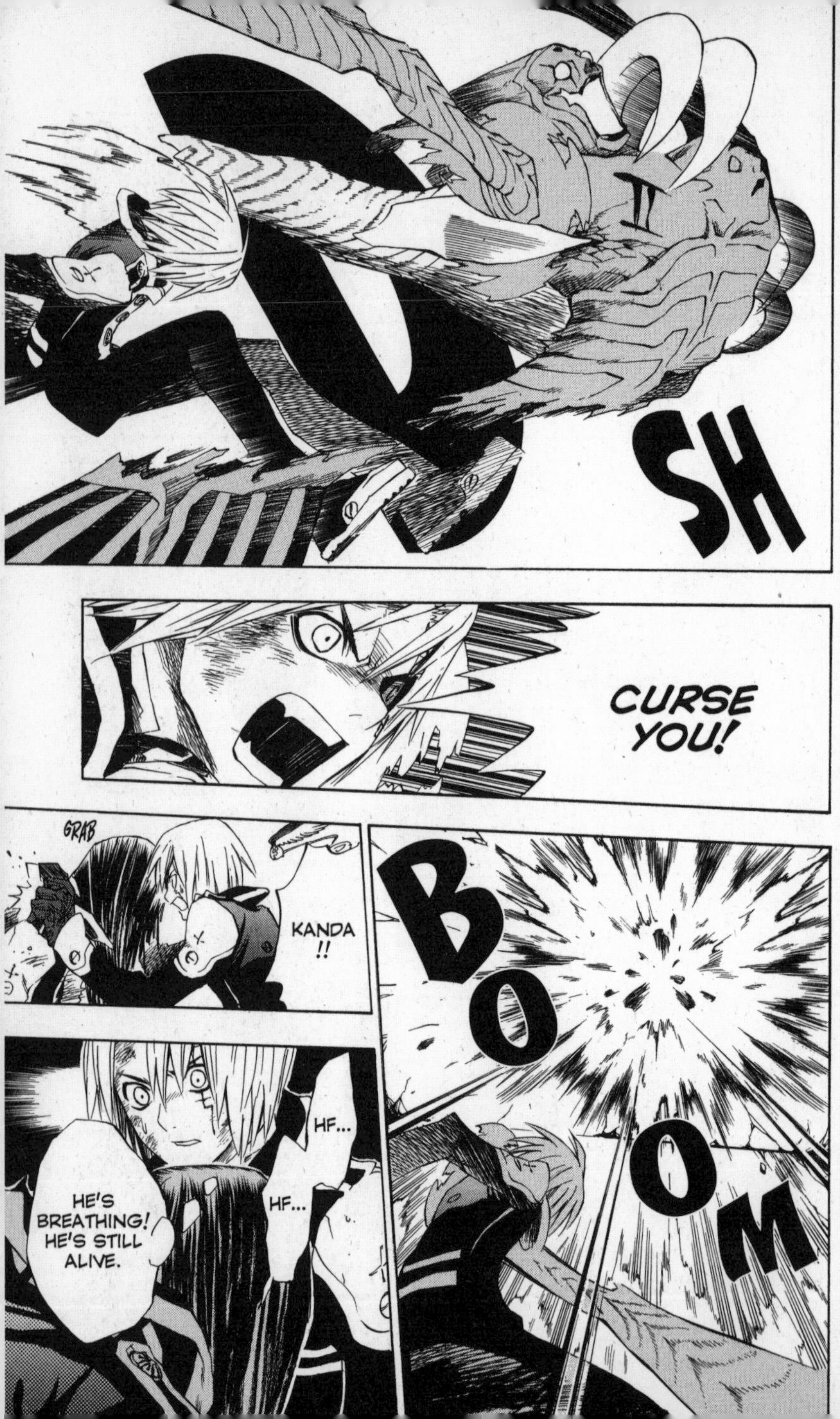
SH
CURSE YOU!
BOOM
GRAB
KANDA !!
HF...
HF...
HE'S BREATHING! HE'S STILL ALIVE.

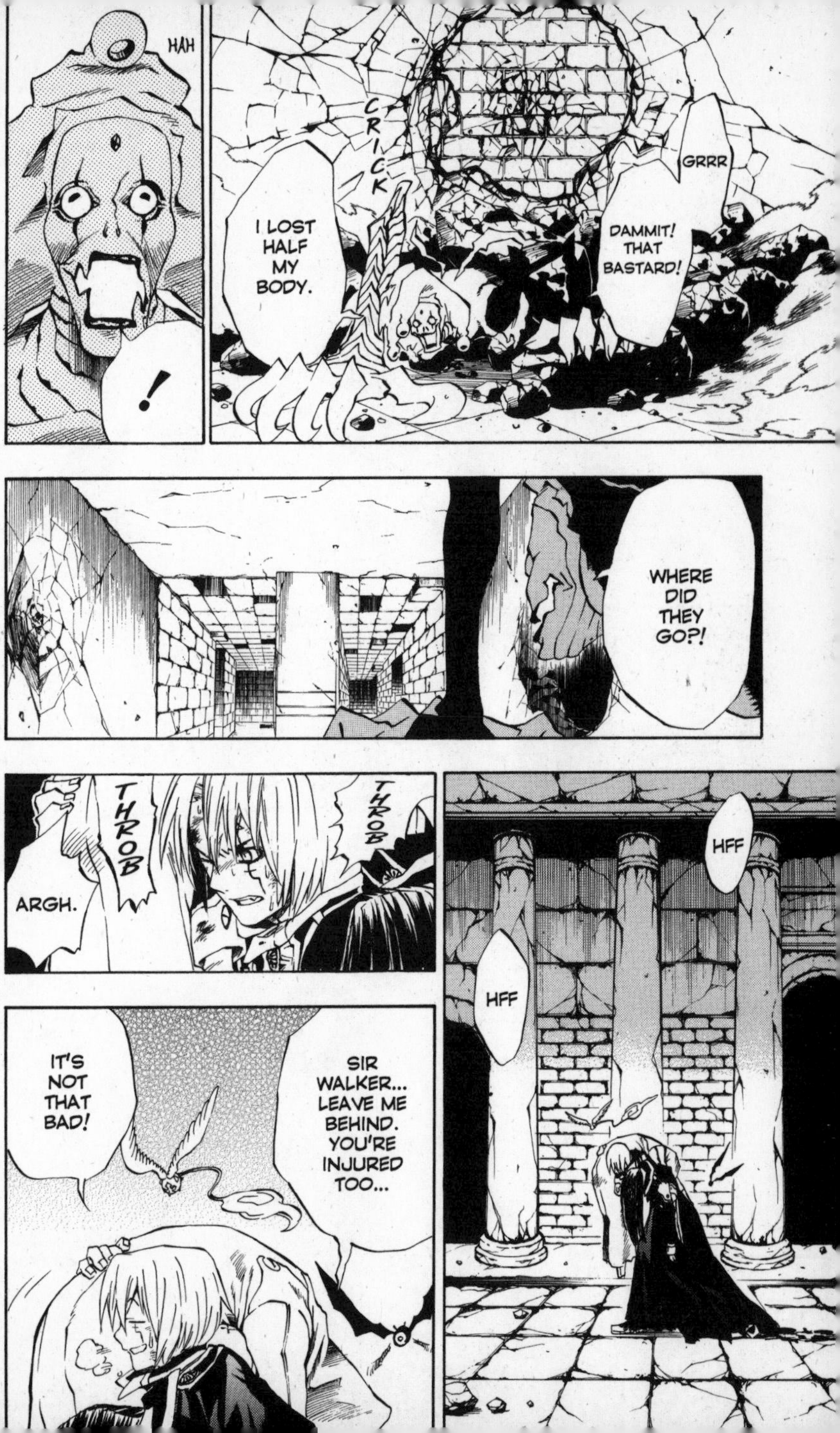
GRRR
DAMMIT! THAT BASTARD!
CRICK
I LOST HALF MY BODY.
HAH
!
WHERE DID THEY GO?!
HFF
HFF
THROB
THROB
ARGH.
SIR WALKER... LEAVE ME BEHIND. YOU'RE INJURED TOO...
IT'S NOT THAT BAD!

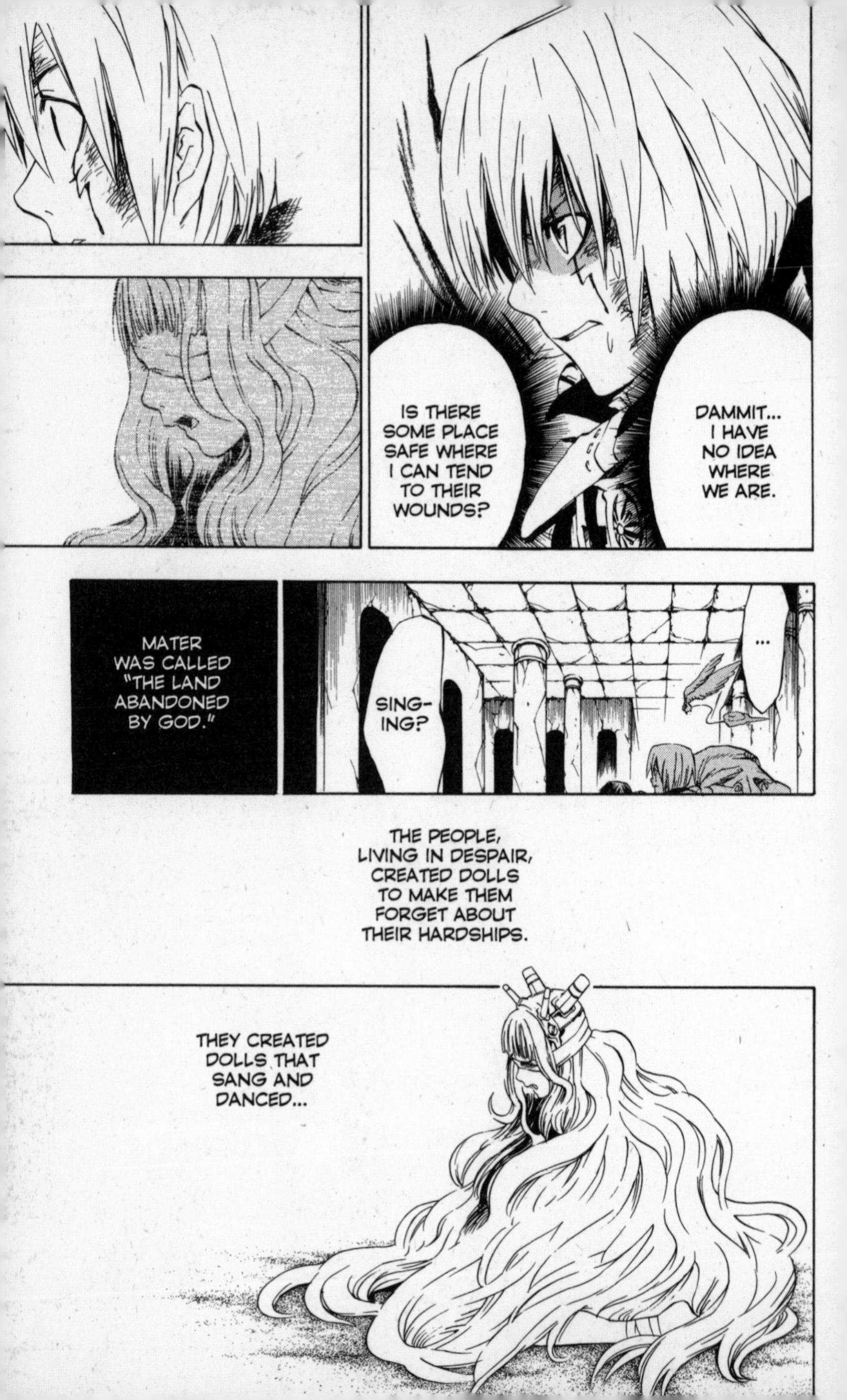
DAMMIT... I HAVE NO IDEA WHERE WE ARE.
IS THERE SOME PLACE SAFE WHERE I CAN TEND TO THEIR WOUNDS?
...
SING-ING?
MATER WAS CALLED "THE LAND ABANDONED BY GOD."
THE PEOPLE, LIVING IN DESPAIR, CREATED DOLLS TO MAKE THEM FORGET ABOUT THEIR HARDSHIPS.
THEY CREATED DOLLS THAT SANG AND DANCED...

SUPER 4 STRIP COMIC ACT

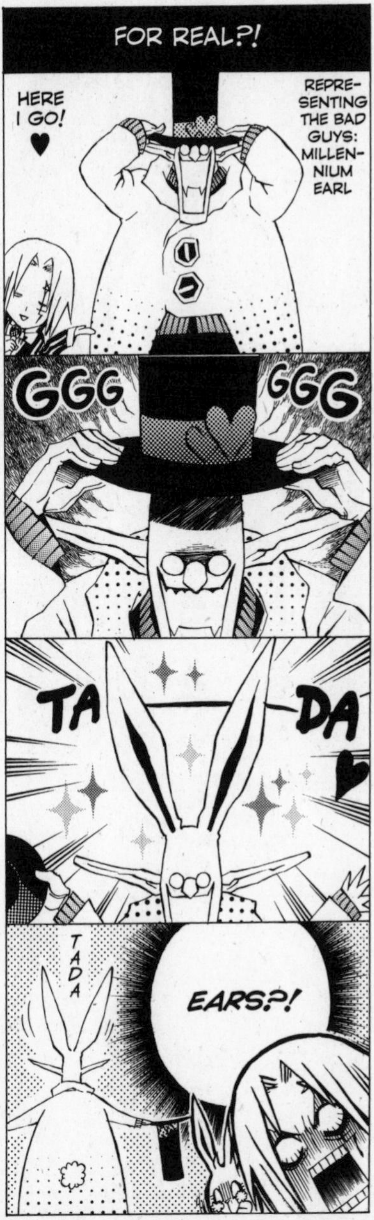
FOR REAL?!
REPRESENTING THE BAD GUYS: MILLENNIUM EARL
HERE I GO! ♥
GGG
GGG
TA
DA ♥
EARS?!
TADA

THE 13TH NIGHT: OLD MAN OF THE LAND AND ARIA OF THE NIGHT SKY (PART 5)

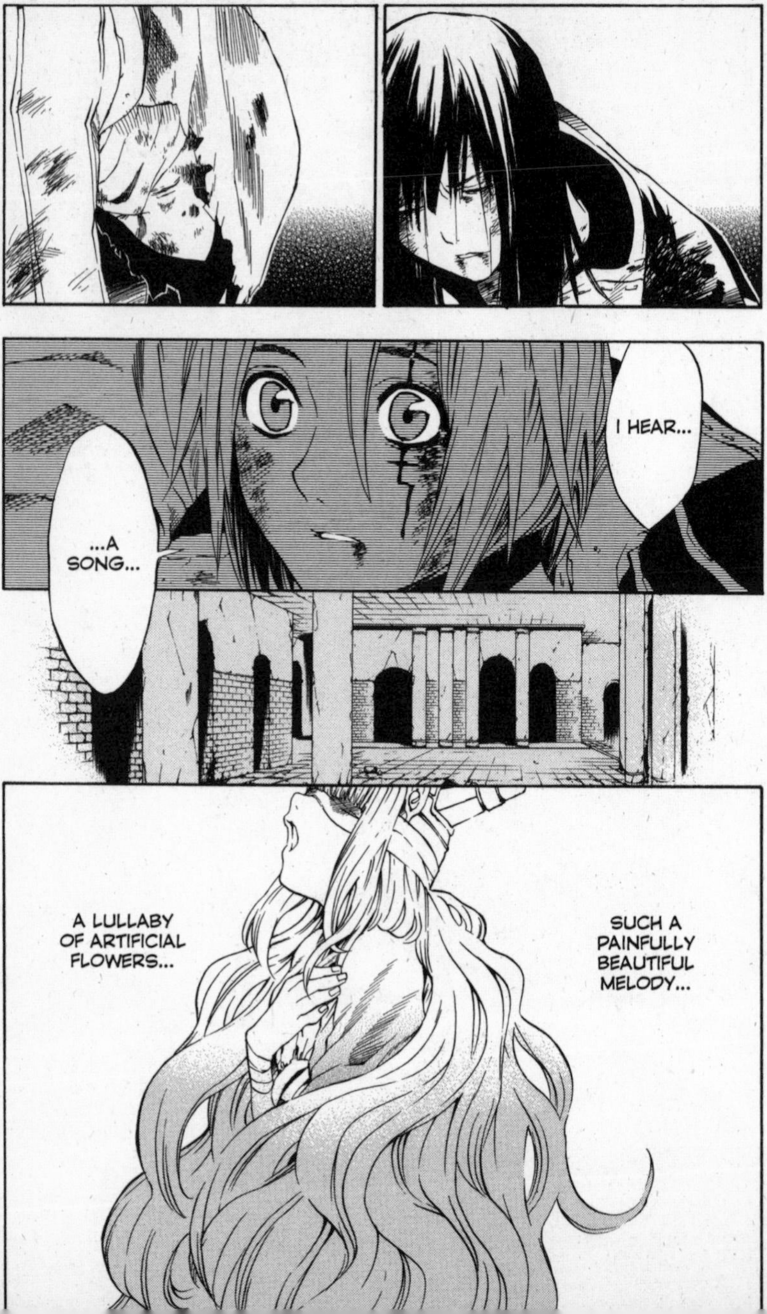
I HEAR...
...A SONG...
SUCH A PAINFULLY BEAUTIFUL MELODY...
A LULLABY OF ARTIFICIAL FLOWERS...

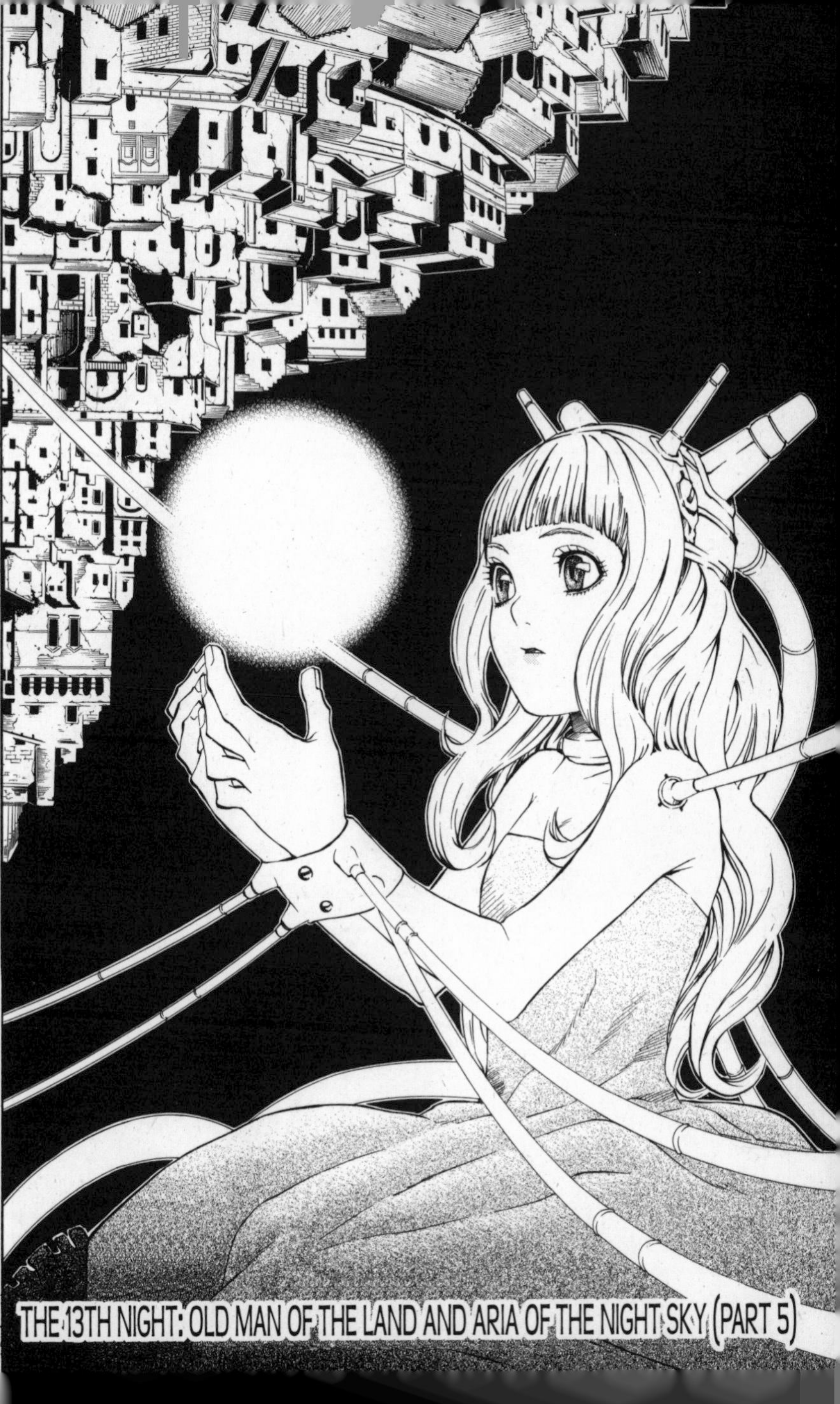
THE 13TH NIGHT: OLD MAN OF THE LAND AND ARIA OF THE NIGHT SKY (PART 5)

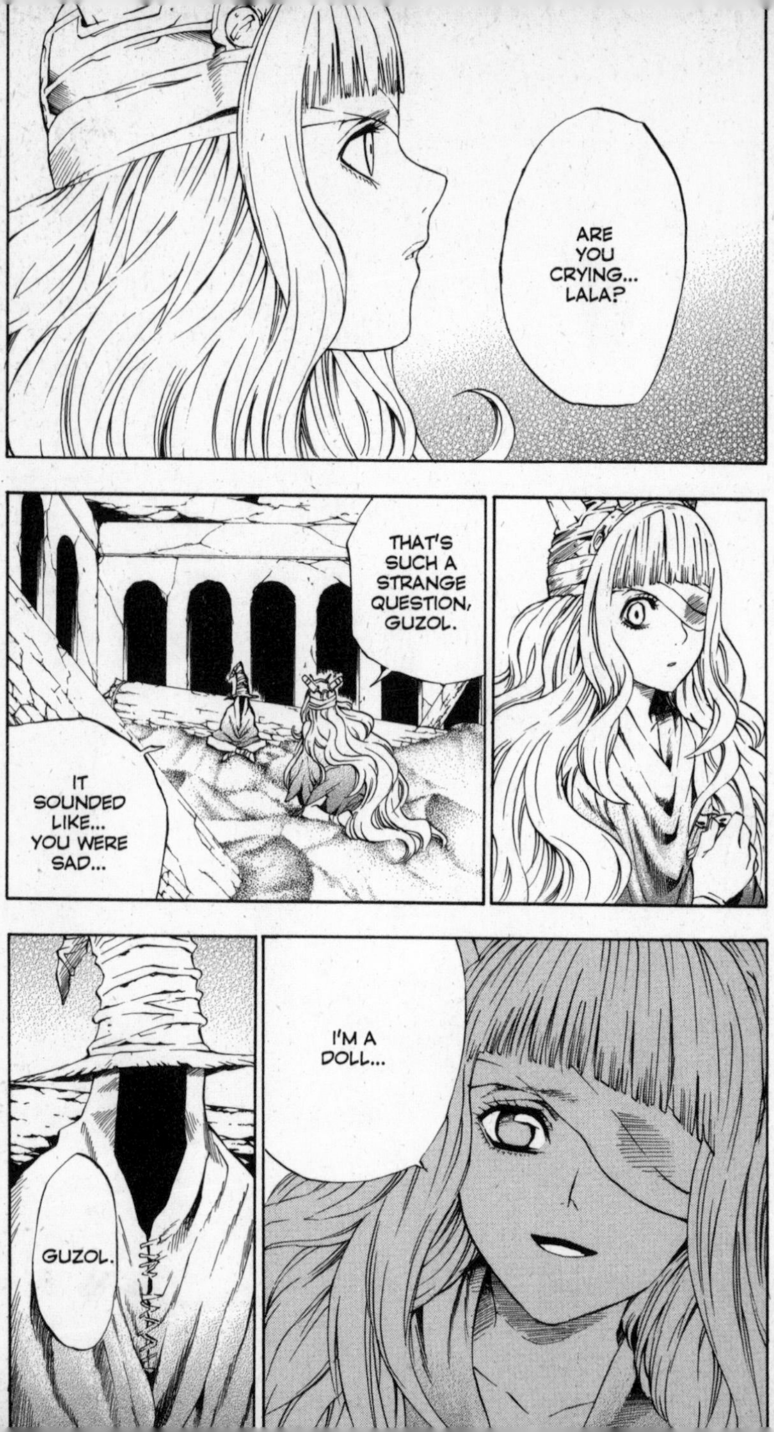
ARE YOU CRYING... LALA?
THAT'S SUCH A STRANGE QUESTION, GUZOL.
IT SOUNDED LIKE... YOU WERE SAD...
GUZOL.
I'M A DOLL...

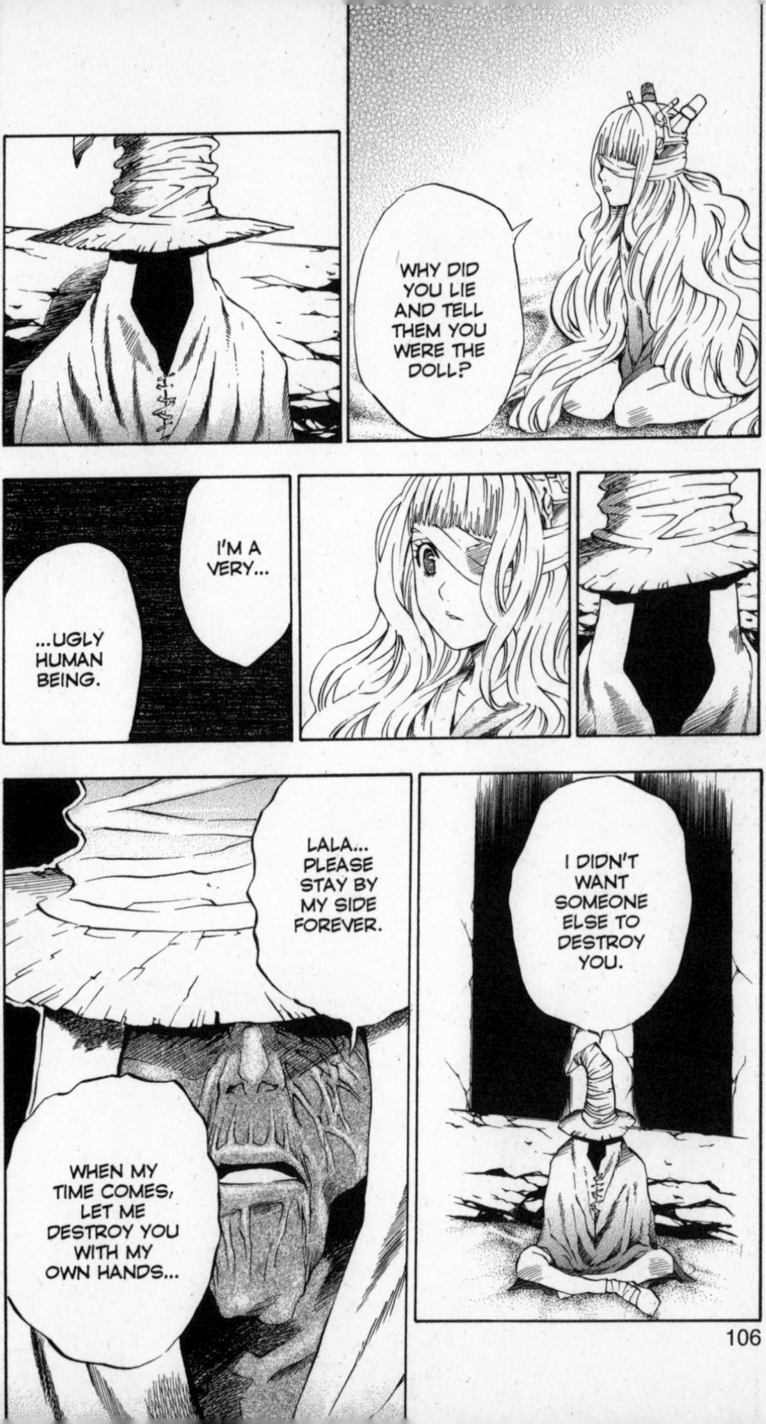
WHY DID YOU LIE AND TELL THEM YOU WERE THE DOLL?
I'M A VERY...
...UGLY HUMAN BEING.
I DIDN'T WANT SOMEONE ELSE TO DESTROY YOU.
LALA... PLEASE STAY BY MY SIDE FOREVER.
WHEN MY TIME COMES, LET ME DESTROY YOU WITH MY OWN HANDS...

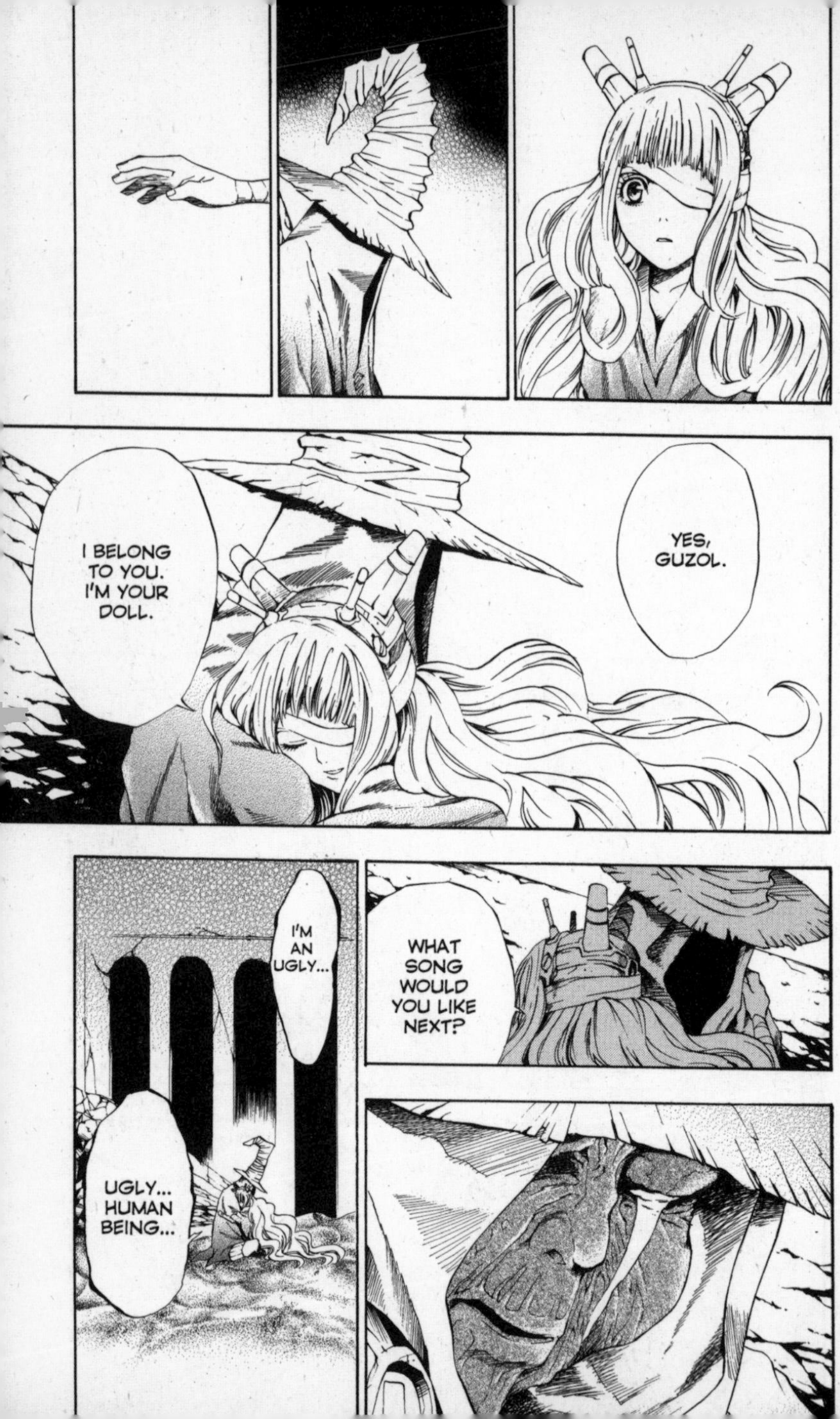
YES, GUZOL.
I BELONG TO YOU. I'M YOUR DOLL.
WHAT SONG WOULD YOU LIKE NEXT?
I'M AN UGLY...
UGLY... HUMAN BEING...

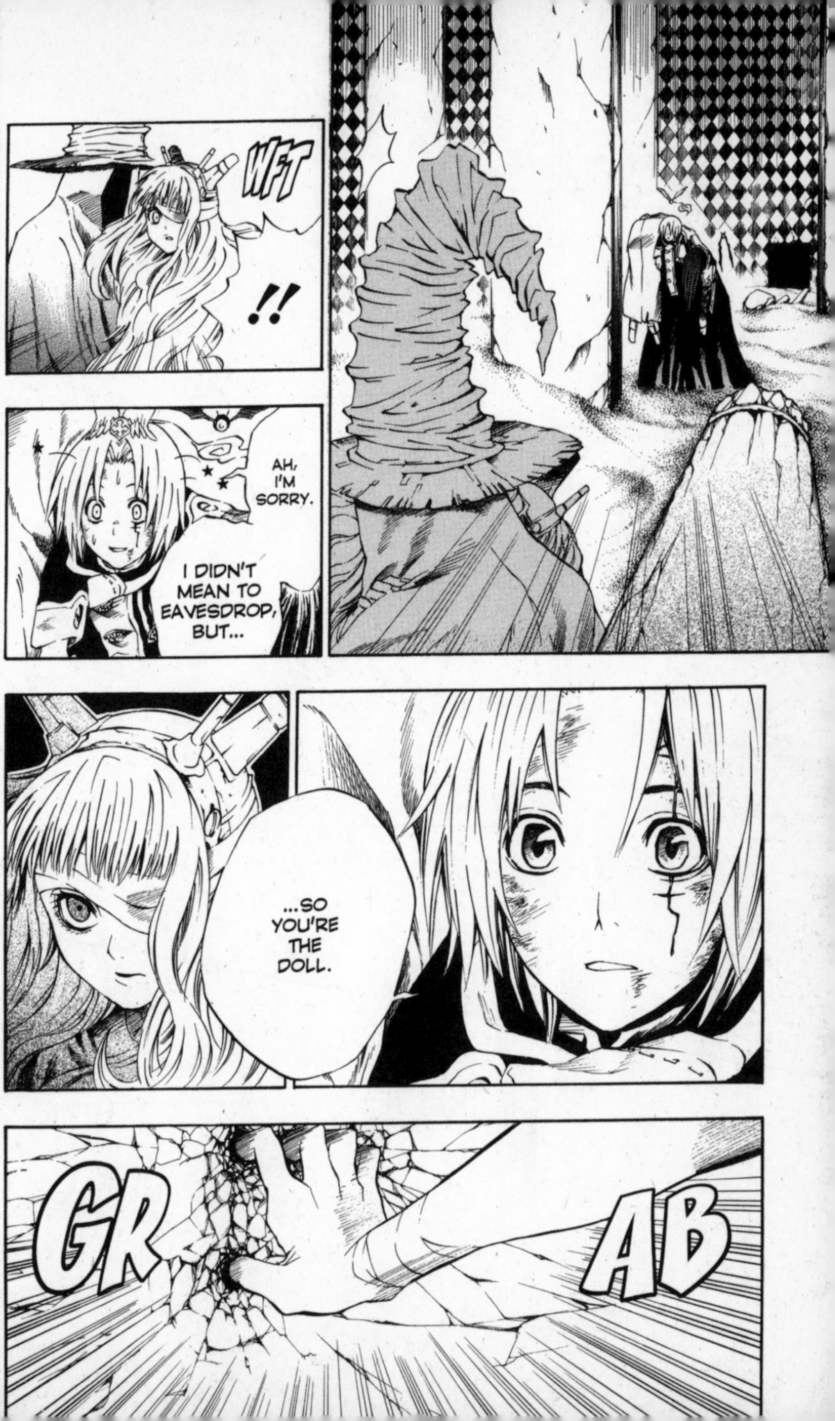
WFT
!!
AH, I'M SORRY.
I DIDN'T MEAN TO EAVESDROP, BUT...
...SO YOU'RE THE DOLL.
GR AB

READ THIS WAY

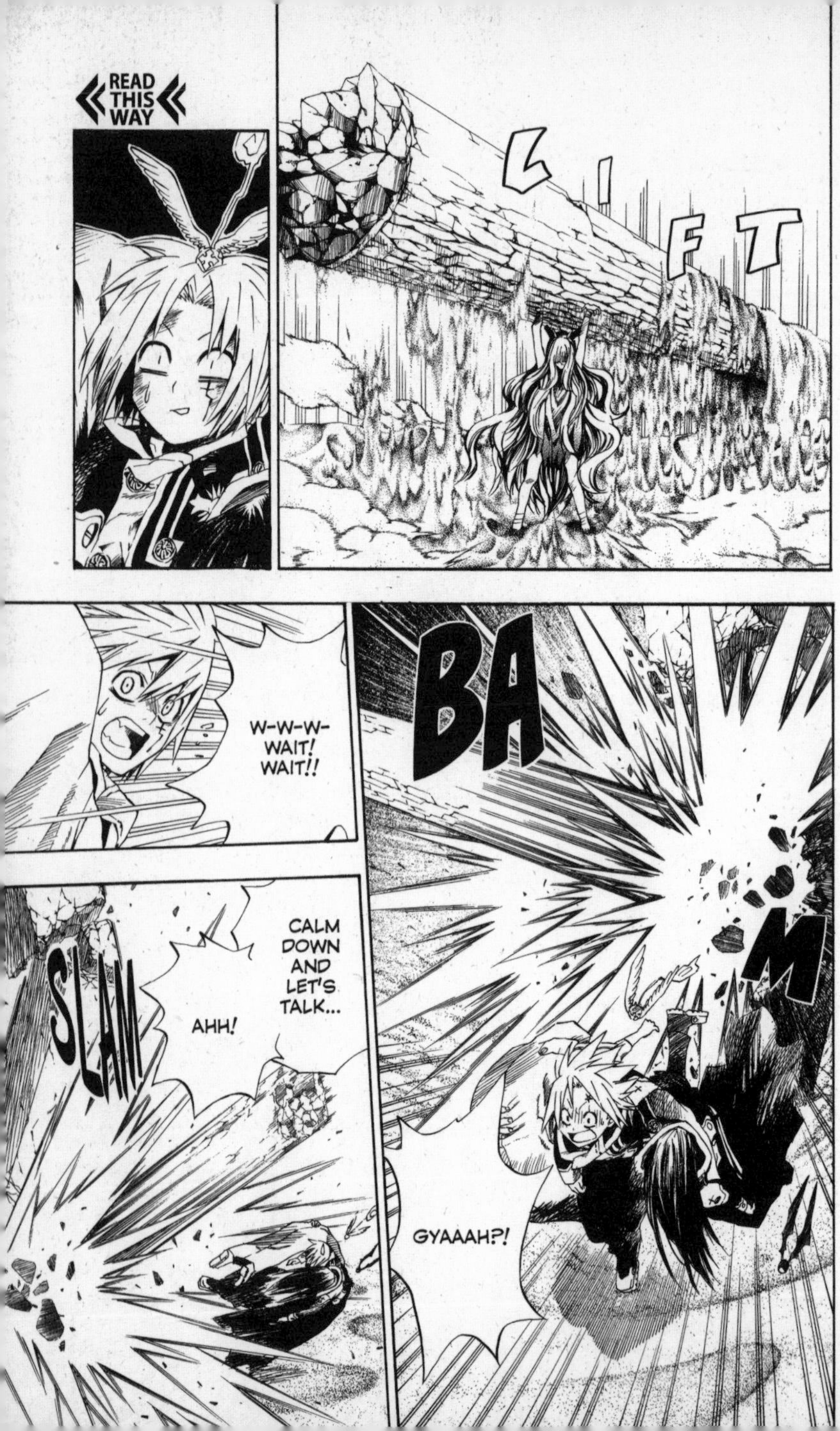
LIFT
BAM
GYAAAH?!
W-W-W-WAIT! WAIT!!
CALM DOWN AND LET'S TALK...
AHH!
SLAM

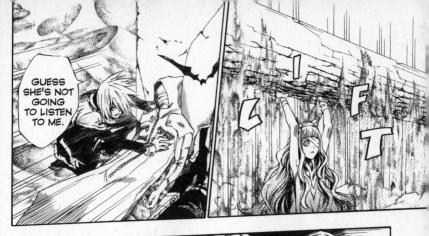

GUESS SHE'S NOT GOING TO LISTEN TO ME.

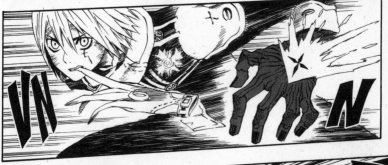

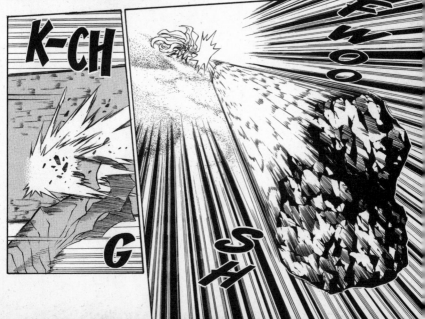

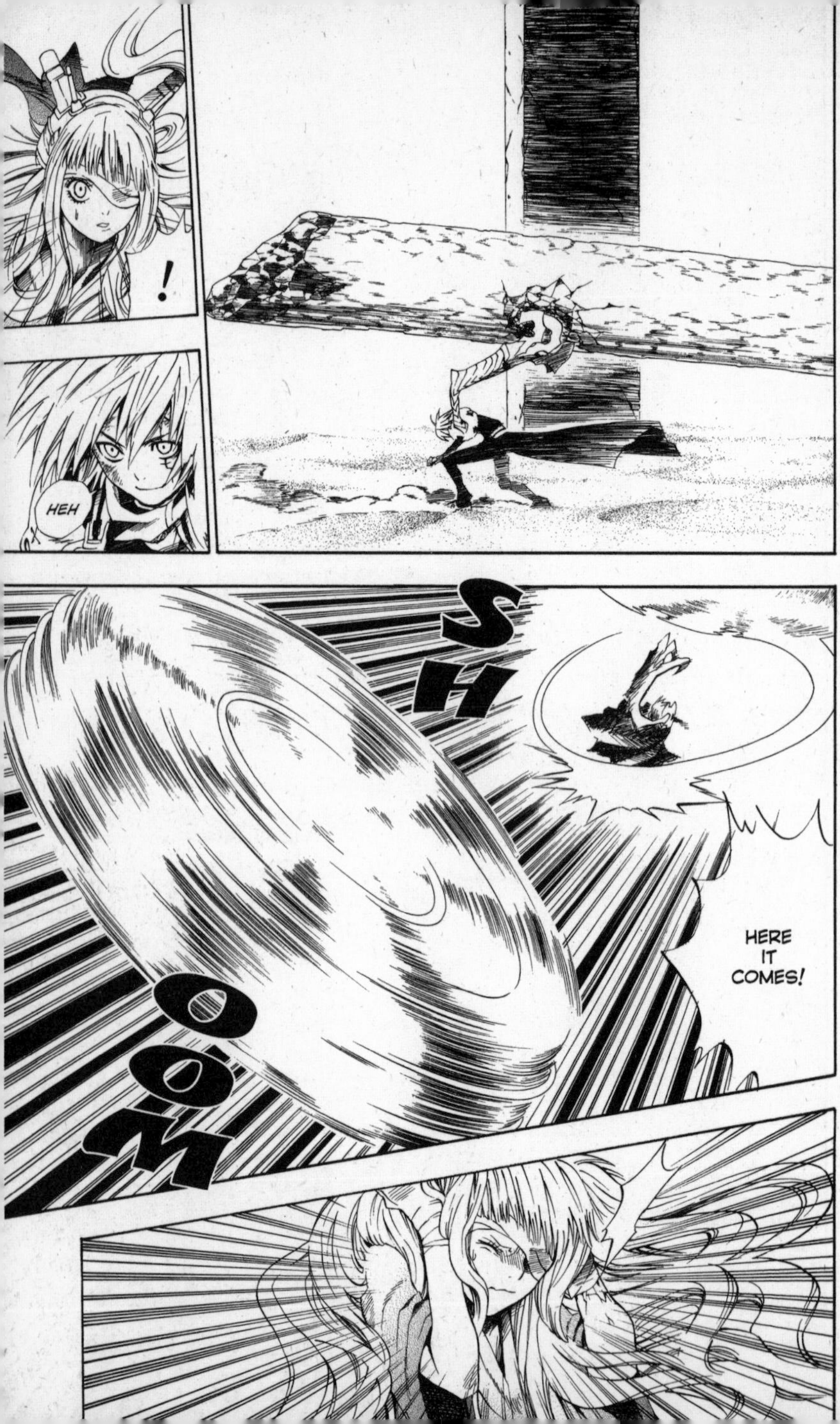
!
HEH
HERE IT COMES!
SHOOM

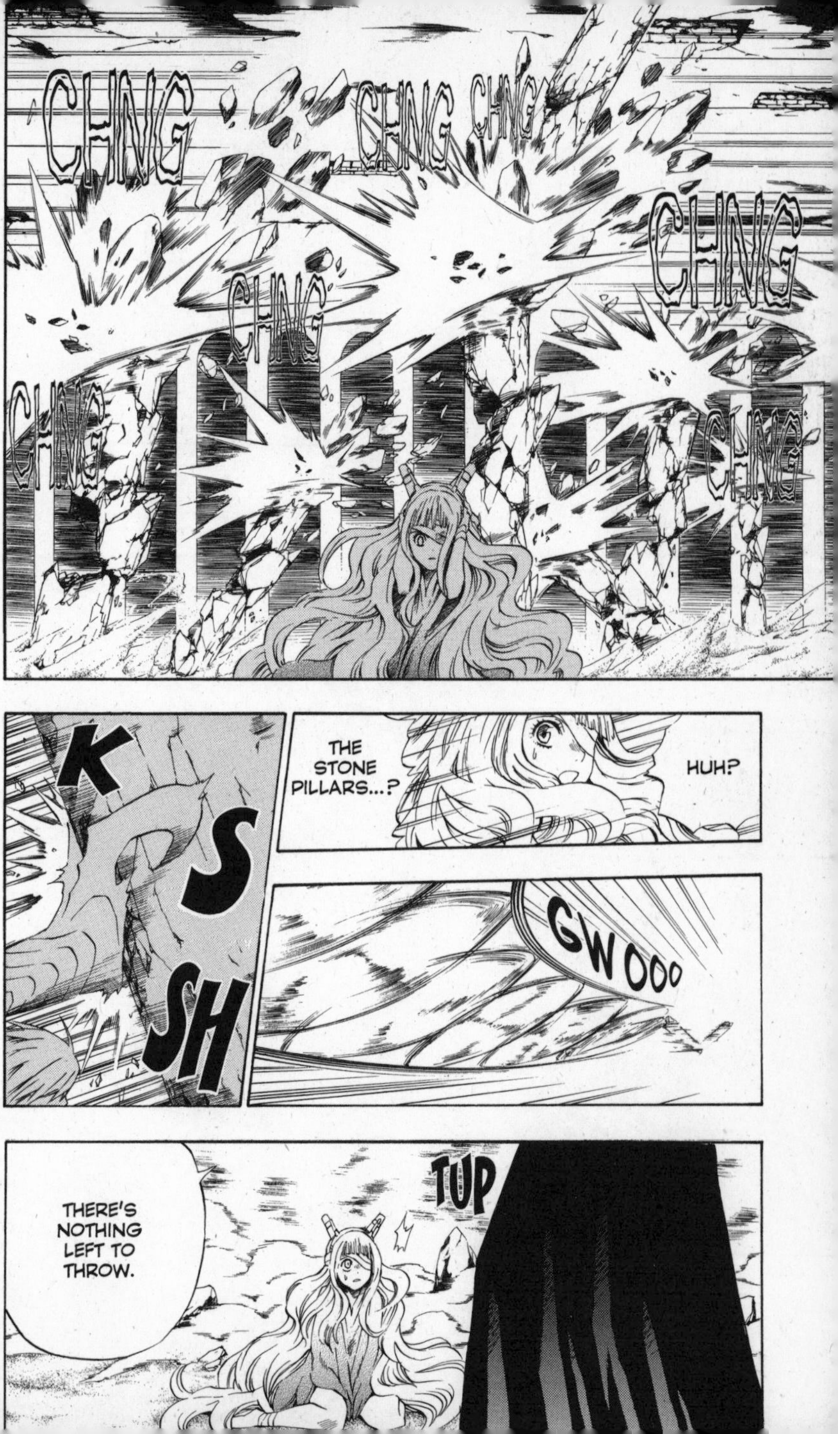
CHING
CHING
CHING
CHING
CHING
CHING
CHING
HUH?
THE STONE PILLARS...?
KSSH
GWOOO
TUP
THERE'S NOTHING LEFT TO THROW.

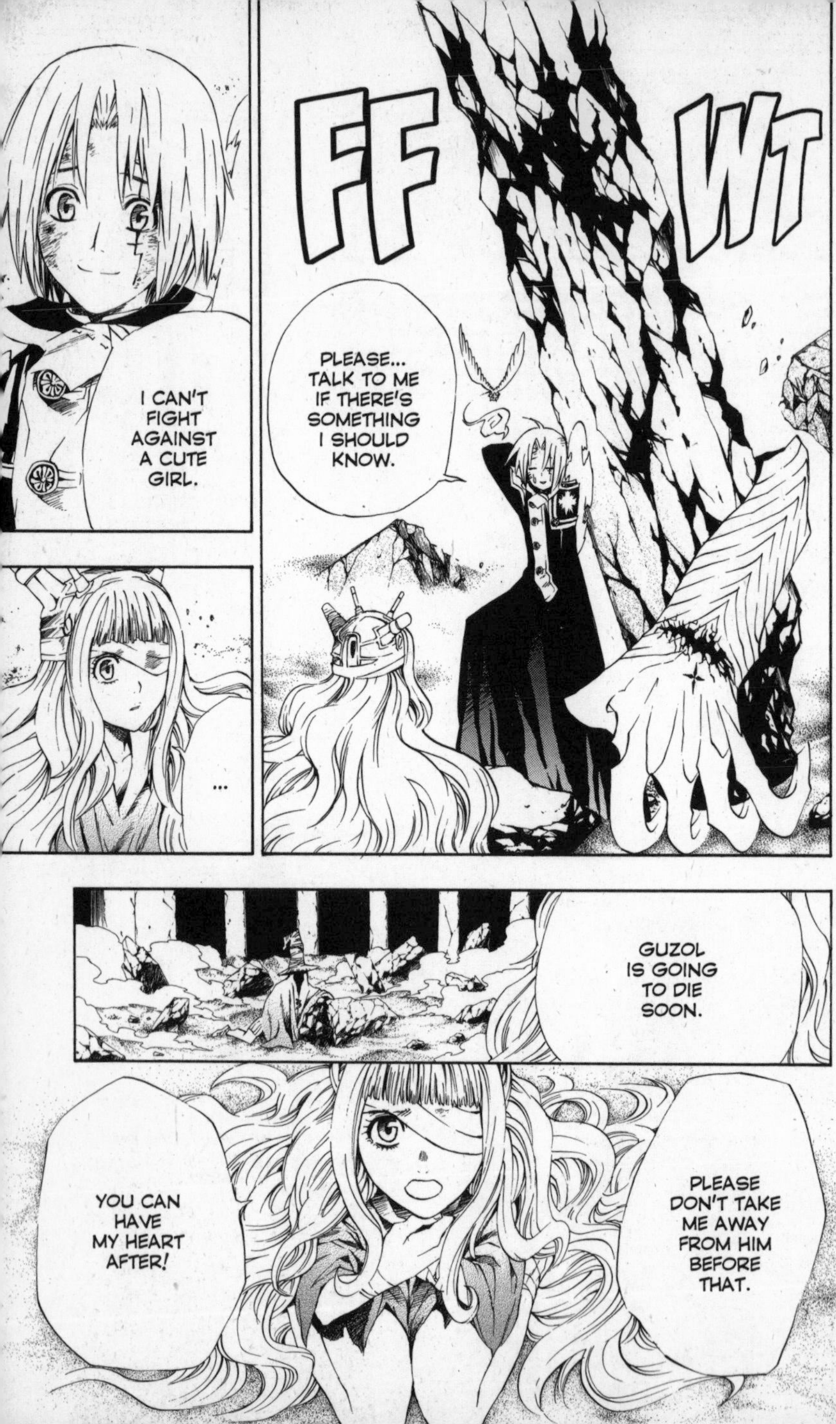
FFWT
PLEASE... TALK TO ME IF THERE'S SOMETHING I SHOULD KNOW.
I CAN'T FIGHT AGAINST A CUTE GIRL.
...
GUZOL IS GOING TO DIE SOON.
PLEASE DON'T TAKE ME AWAY FROM HIM BEFORE THAT.
YOU CAN HAVE MY HEART AFTER!

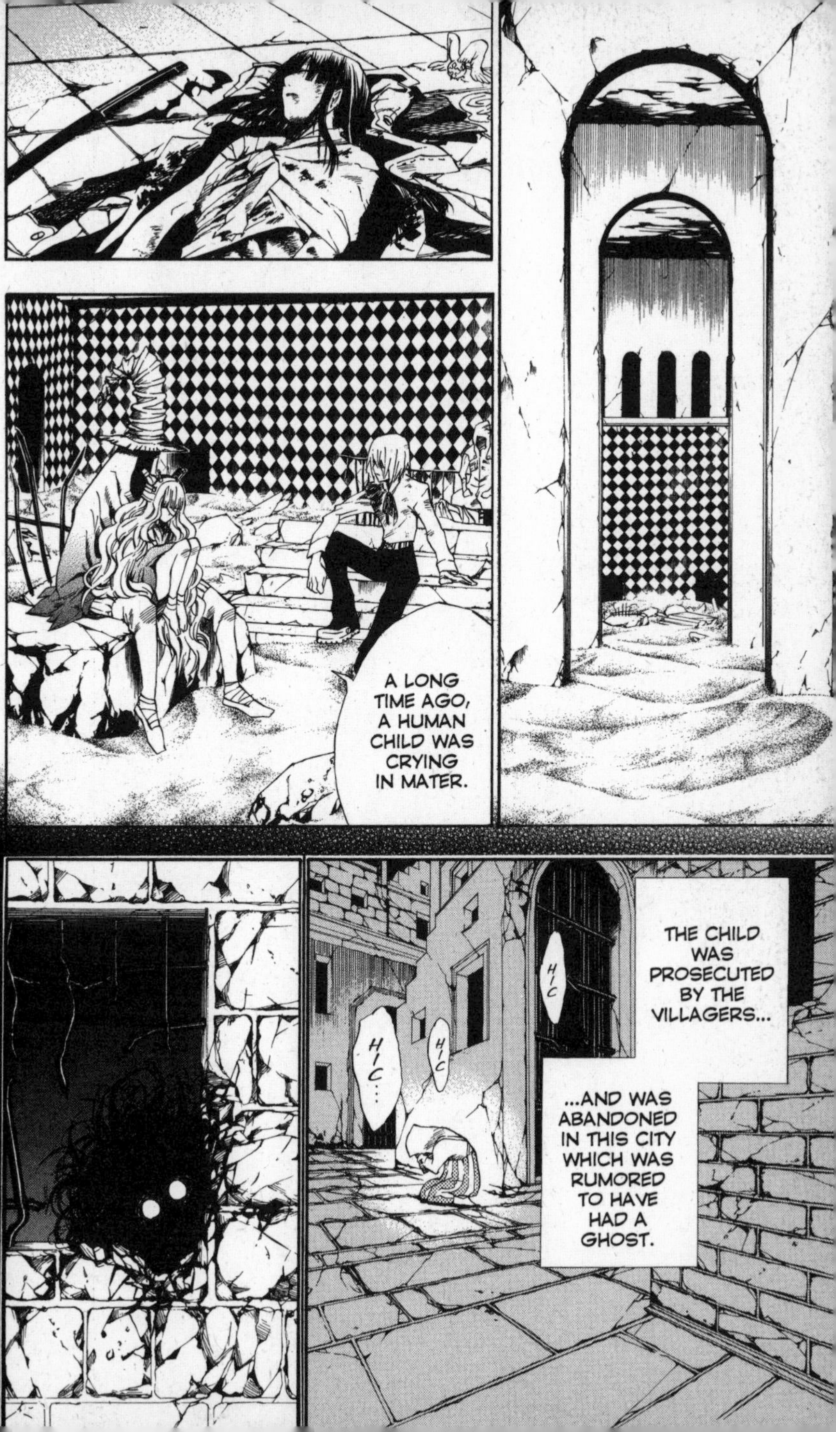
A LONG TIME AGO, A HUMAN CHILD WAS CRYING IN MATER.
THE CHILD WAS PROSECUTED BY THE VILLAGERS...
HIC
HIC
HIC...
...AND WAS ABANDONED IN THIS CITY WHICH WAS RUMORED TO HAVE HAD A GHOST.

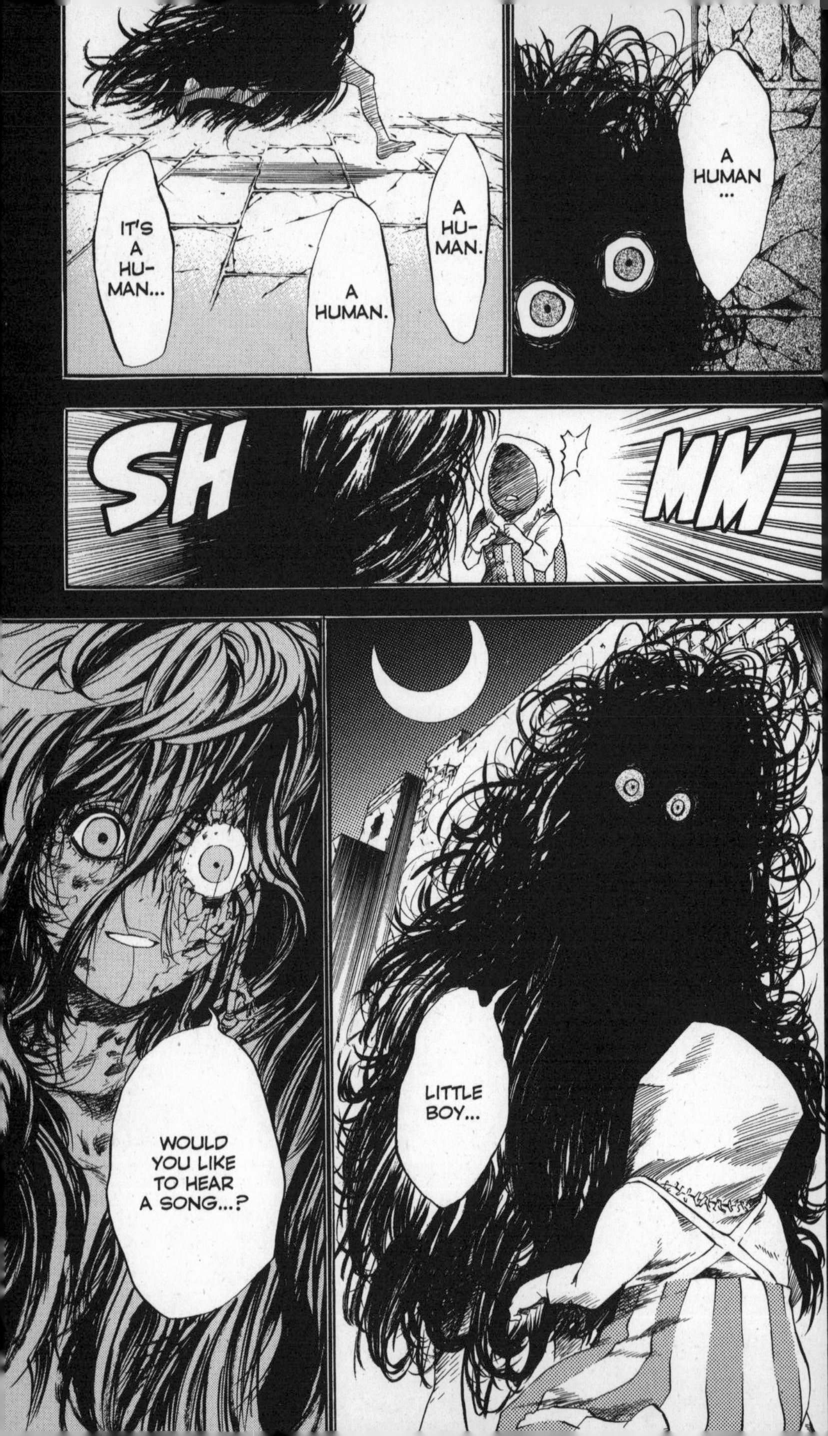
A HUMAN ...
A HU-MAN.
A HUMAN.
IT'S A HU-MAN...
SH MM
LITTLE BOY...
WOULD YOU LIKE TO HEAR A SONG...?

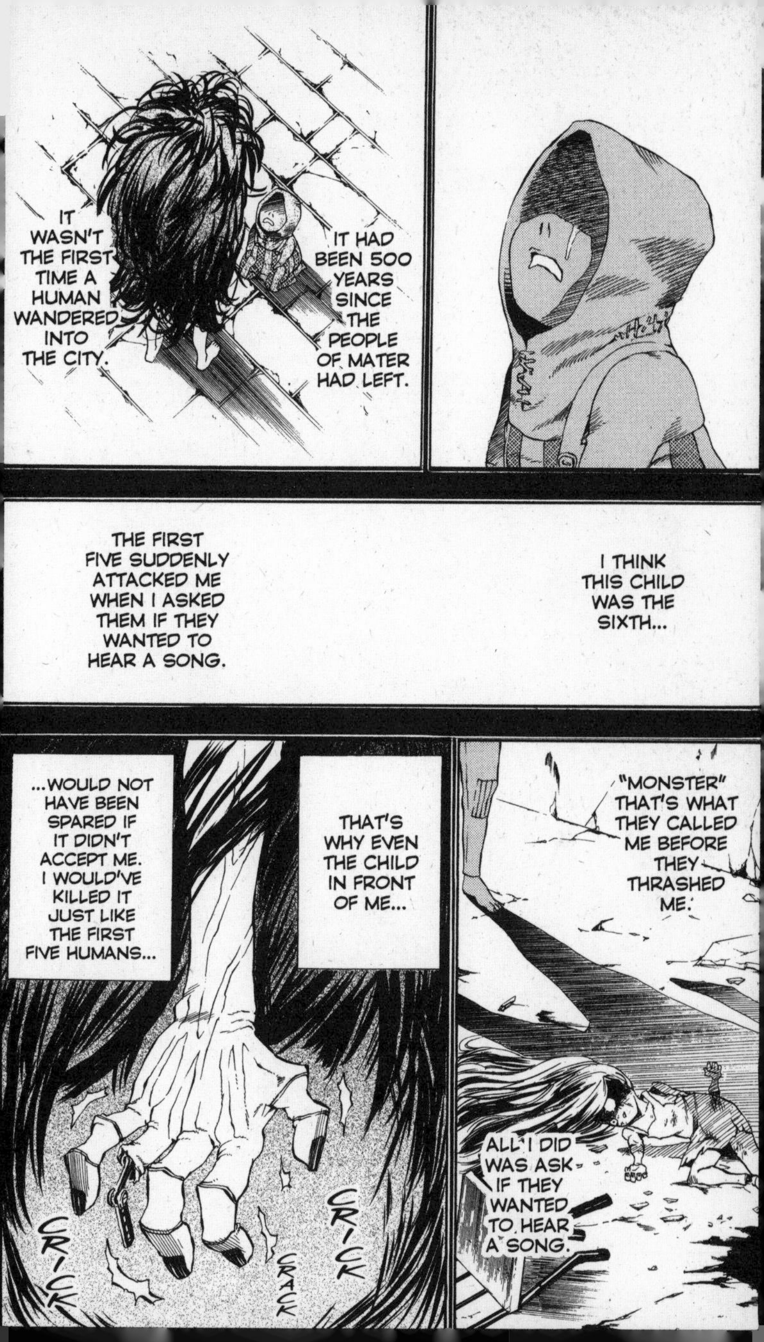
IT HAD BEEN 500 YEARS SINCE THE PEOPLE OF MATER HAD LEFT.
IT WASN'T THE FIRST TIME A HUMAN WANDERED INTO THE CITY.
I THINK THIS CHILD WAS THE SIXTH...
THE FIRST FIVE SUDDENLY ATTACKED ME WHEN I ASKED THEM IF THEY WANTED TO HEAR A SONG.
"MONSTER" THAT'S WHAT THEY CALLED ME BEFORE THEY THRASHED ME.
ALL I DID WAS ASK IF THEY WANTED TO HEAR A SONG.
THAT'S WHY EVEN THE CHILD IN FRONT OF ME...
...WOULD NOT HAVE BEEN SPARED IF IT DIDN'T ACCEPT ME. I WOULD'VE KILLED IT JUST LIKE THE FIRST FIVE HUMANS...
CRICK
CRACK
CRICK

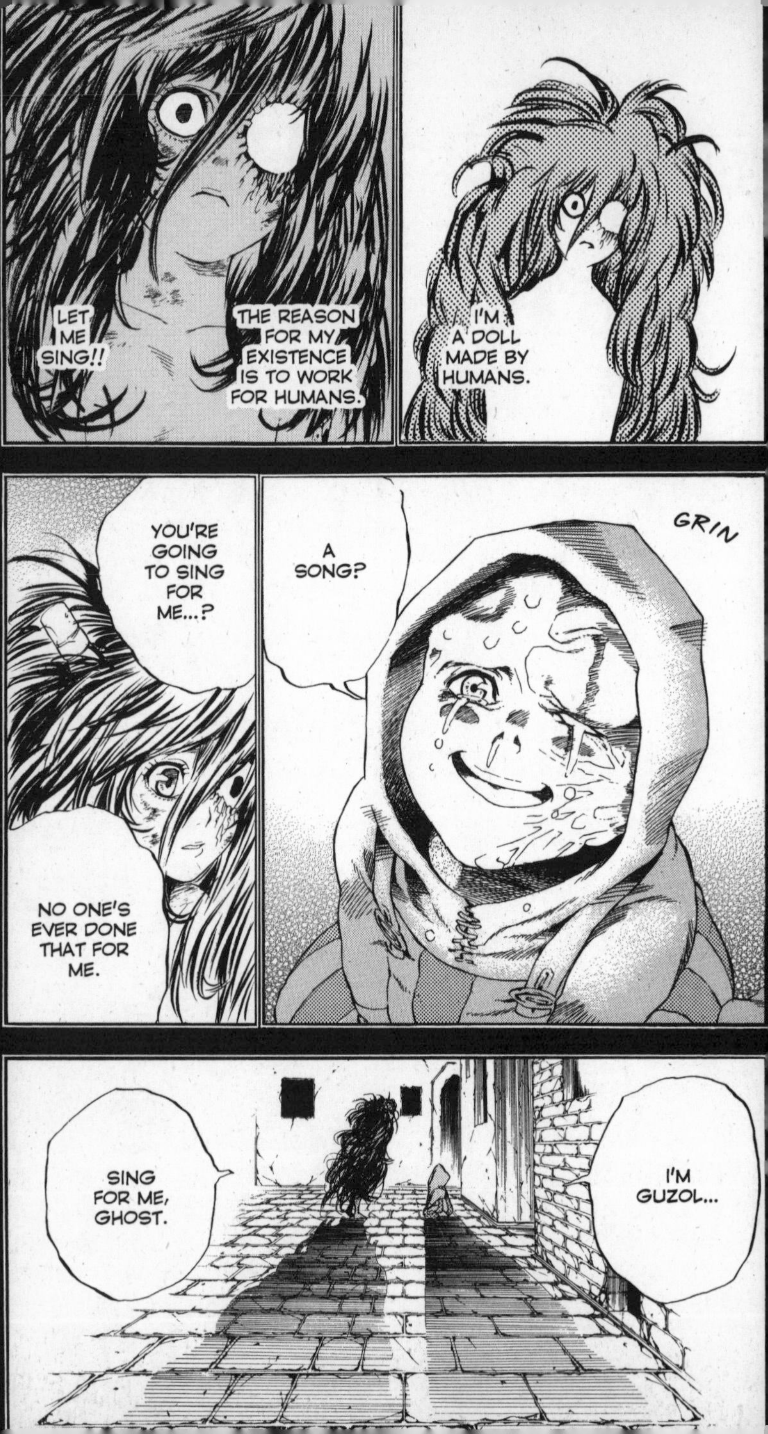
I'M A DOLL MADE BY HUMANS.
THE REASON FOR MY EXISTENCE IS TO WORK FOR HUMANS.
LET ME SING!!
GRIN
A SONG?
YOU'RE GOING TO SING FOR ME...?
NO ONE'S EVER DONE THAT FOR ME.
I'M GUZOL...
SING FOR ME, GHOST.

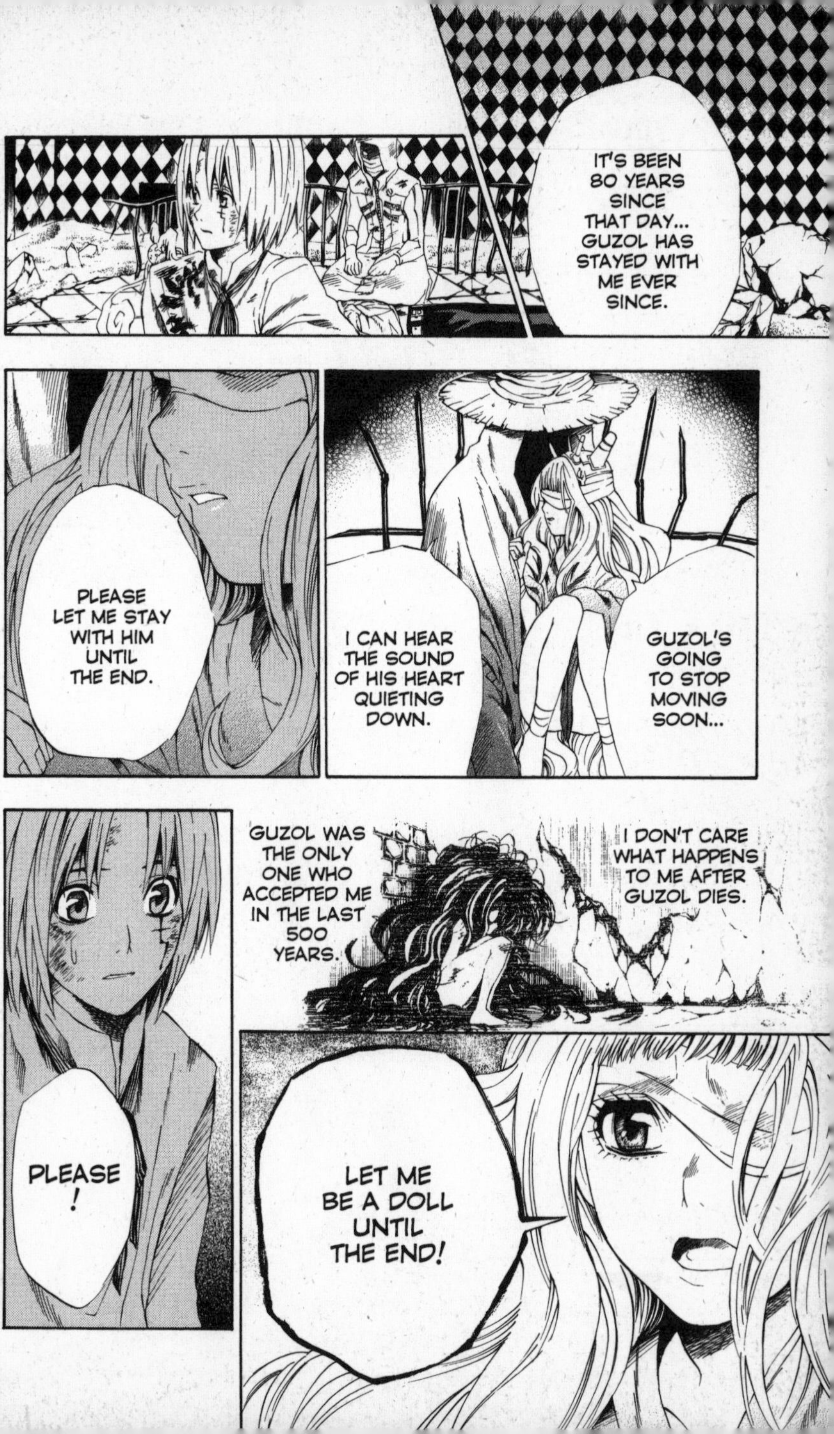
IT'S BEEN 80 YEARS SINCE THAT DAY... GUZOL HAS STAYED WITH ME EVER SINCE.
GUZOL'S GOING TO STOP MOVING SOON...
I CAN HEAR THE SOUND OF HIS HEART QUIETING DOWN.
PLEASE LET ME STAY WITH HIM UNTIL THE END.
I DON'T CARE WHAT HAPPENS TO ME AFTER GUZOL DIES.
GUZOL WAS THE ONLY ONE WHO ACCEPTED ME IN THE LAST 500 YEARS.
LET ME BE A DOLL UNTIL THE END!
PLEASE!

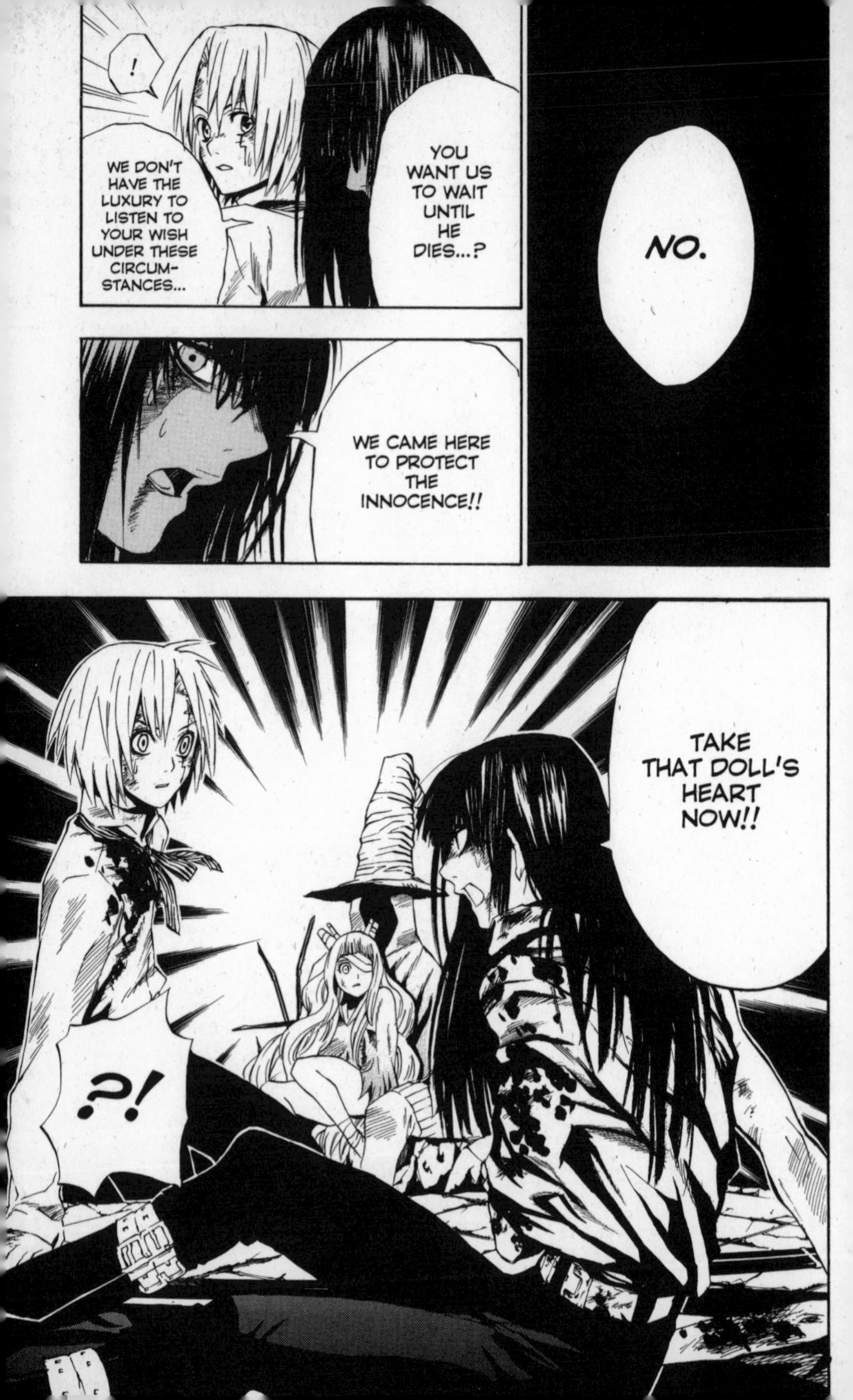
NO.
!
YOU WANT US TO WAIT UNTIL HE DIES...?
WE DON'T HAVE THE LUXURY TO LISTEN TO YOUR WISH UNDER THESE CIRCUM-STANCES...
WE CAME HERE TO PROTECT THE INNOCENCE!!
TAKE THAT DOLL'S HEART NOW!!
?!

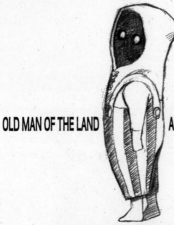

OLD MAN OF THE LAND ♫ **AND ARIA OF THE NIGHT SKY**

I LOOSELY BASED THIS STORY ON THE
NOH PLAY CALLED "KOI NO OMONI"
(THE HEAVY BURDEN OF LOVE).
IT'S ABOUT AN OLD MAN WHO FALLS
IN LOVE WITH A YOUNG MAIDEN. I GOT
GUZOL'S NAME FROM "KLINGSOR'S
MAGIC GARDEN" FROM WAGNER'S OPERA
"PARSIFAL." LALA IS A SONGSTRESS;
HENCE, LALA.

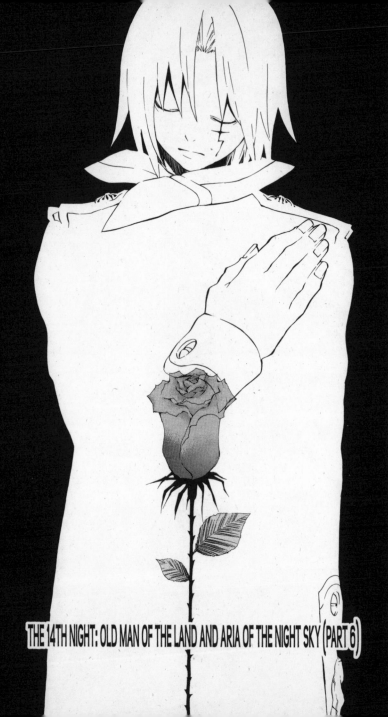

THE 14TH NIGHT: OLD MAN OF THE LAND AND ARIA OF THE NIGHT SKY (PART 6)

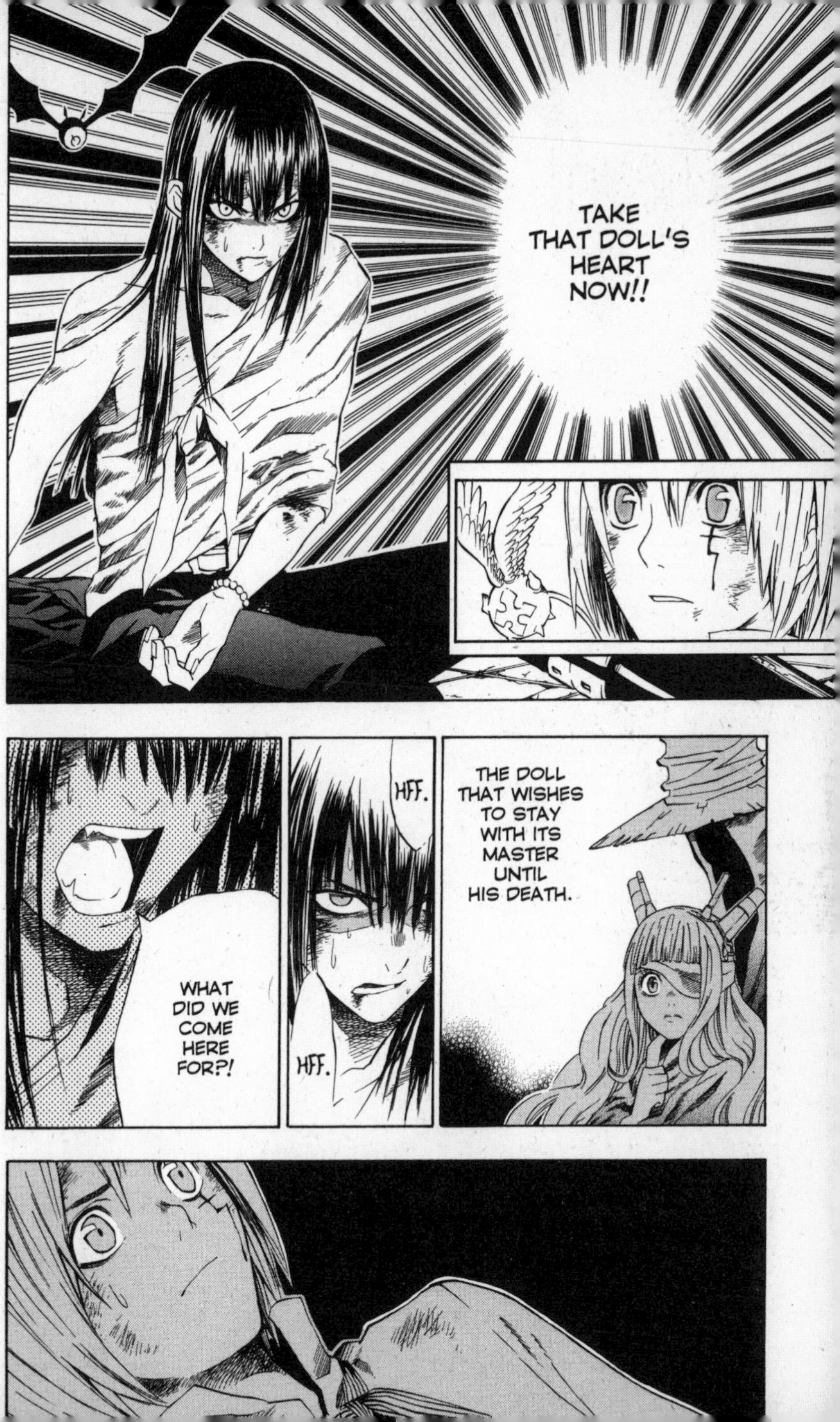
TAKE THAT DOLL'S HEART NOW!!
THE DOLL THAT WISHES TO STAY WITH ITS MASTER UNTIL HIS DEATH.
HFF.
HFF.
WHAT DID WE COME HERE FOR?!

READ THIS WAY

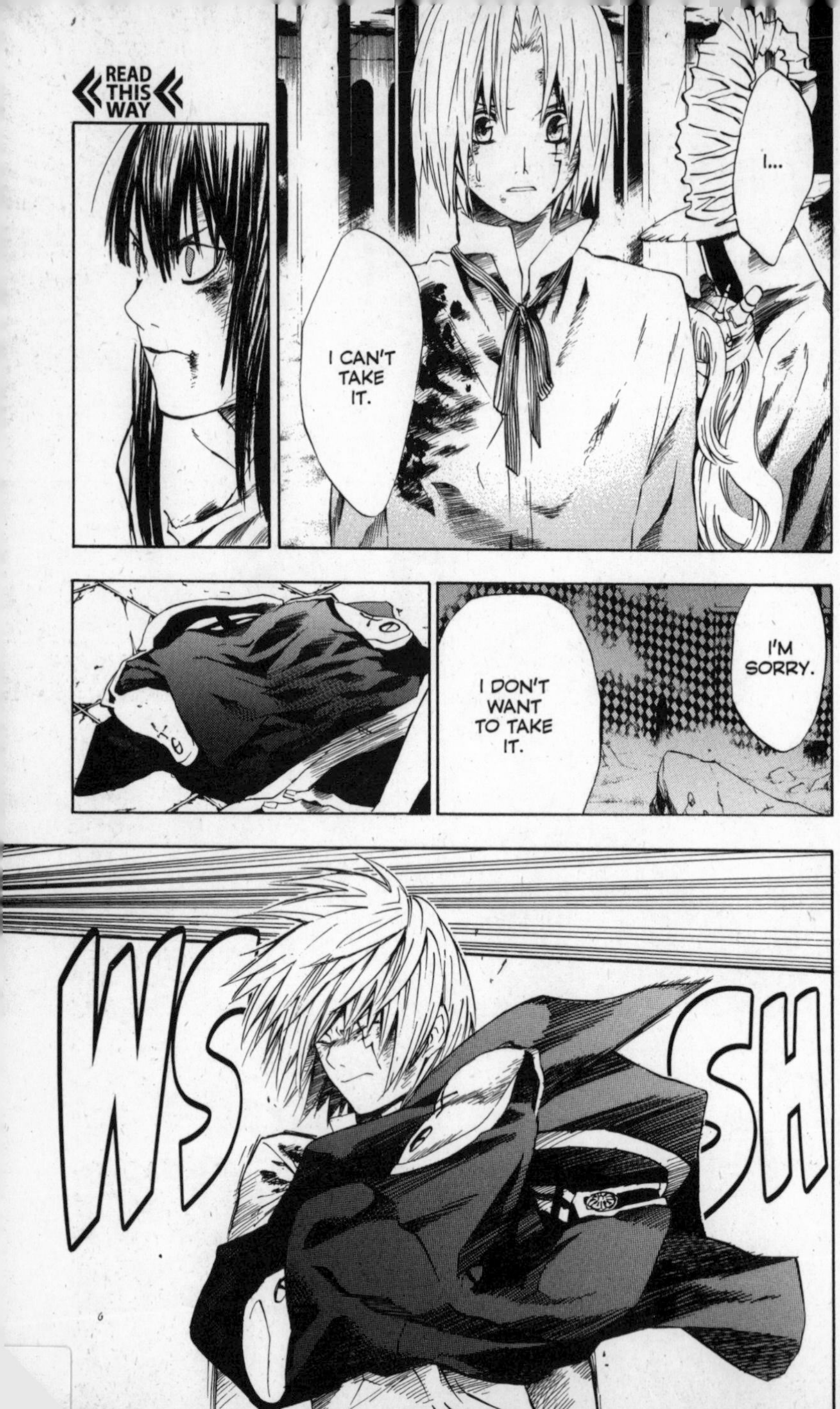
I...
I CAN'T TAKE IT.
I'M SORRY.
I DON'T WANT TO TAKE IT.
WS
SH

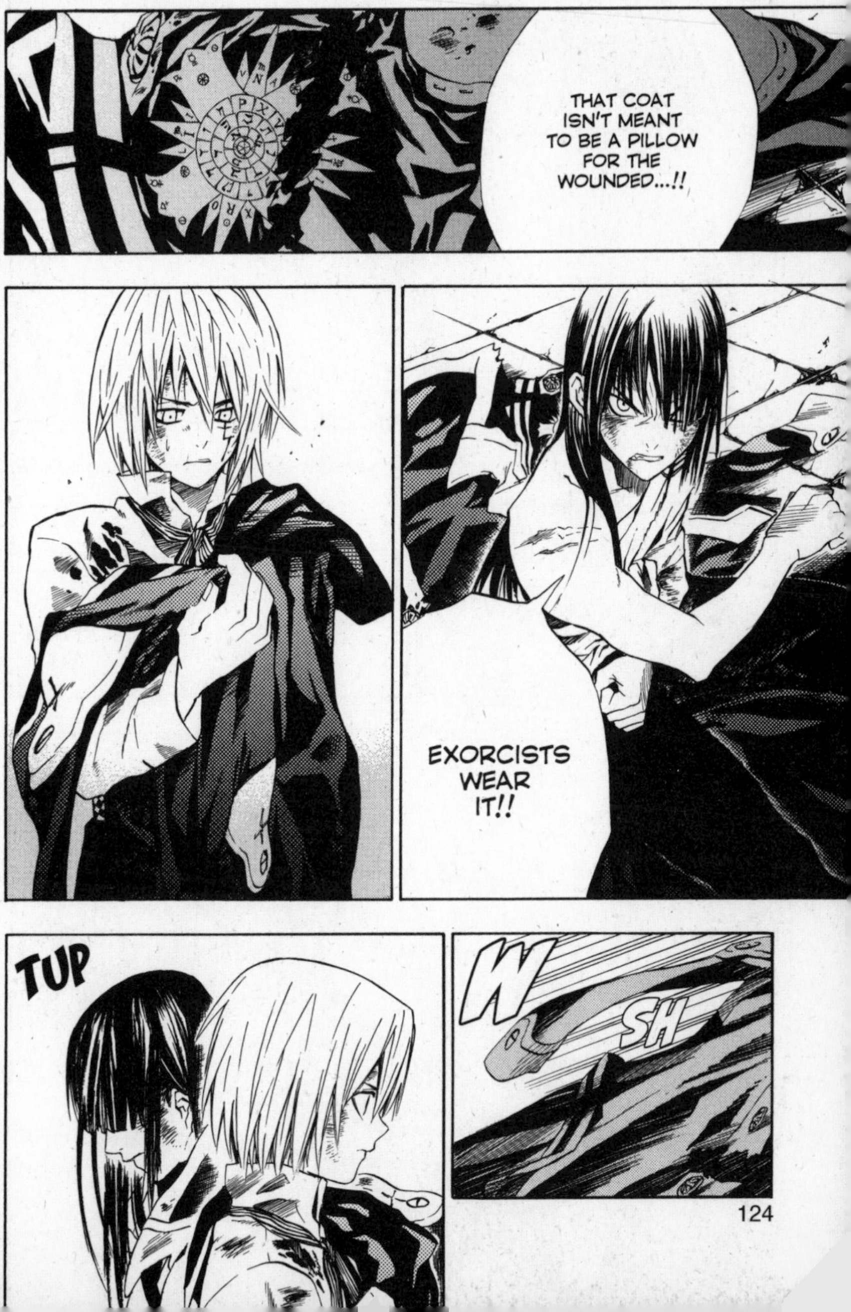
THAT COAT ISN'T MEANT TO BE A PILLOW FOR THE WOUNDED...!!
EXORCISTS WEAR IT!!
WSH
TUP

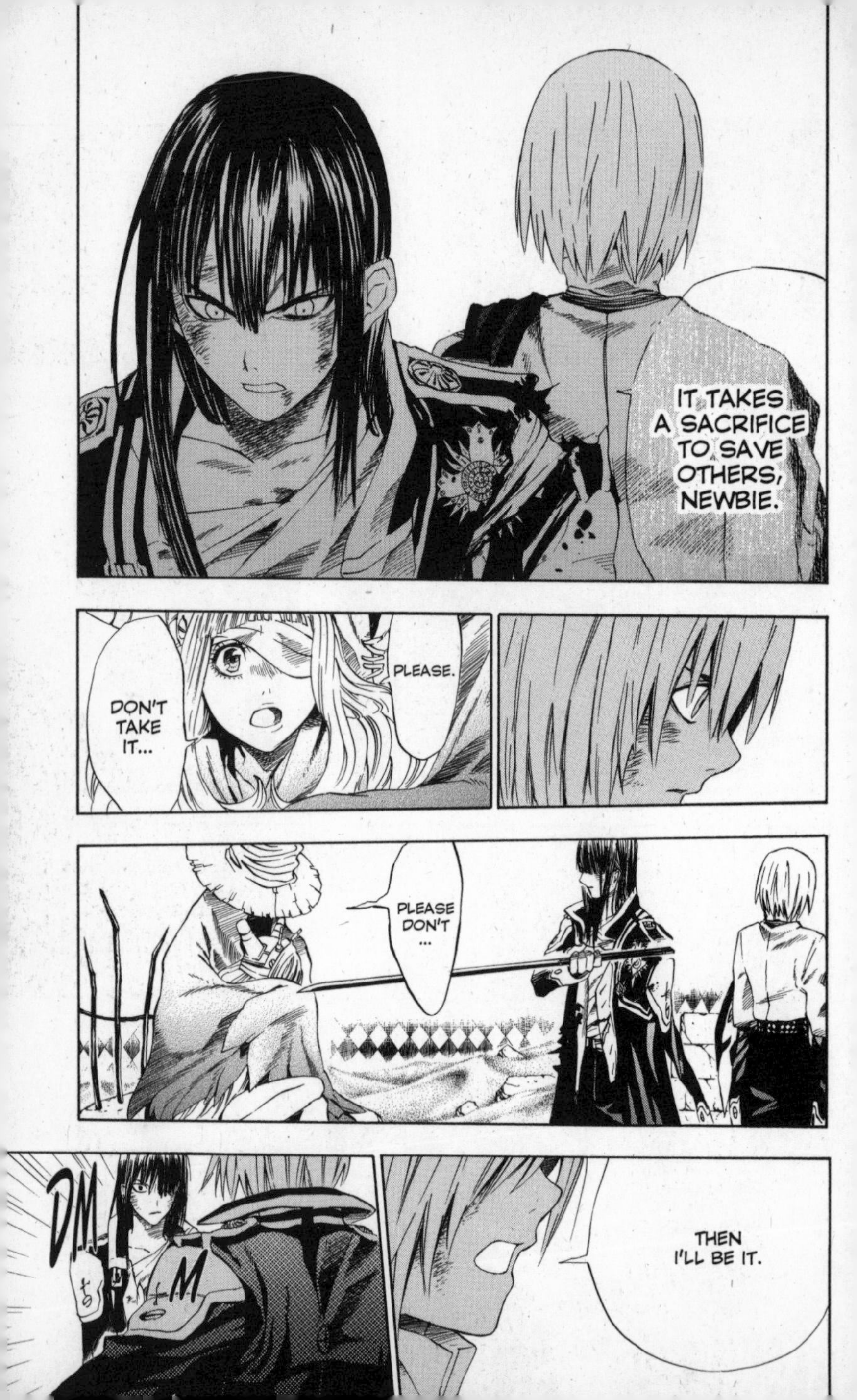
IT TAKES A SACRIFICE TO SAVE OTHERS, NEWBIE.
DON'T TAKE IT...
PLEASE.
PLEASE DON'T ...
THEN I'LL BE IT.
DM M

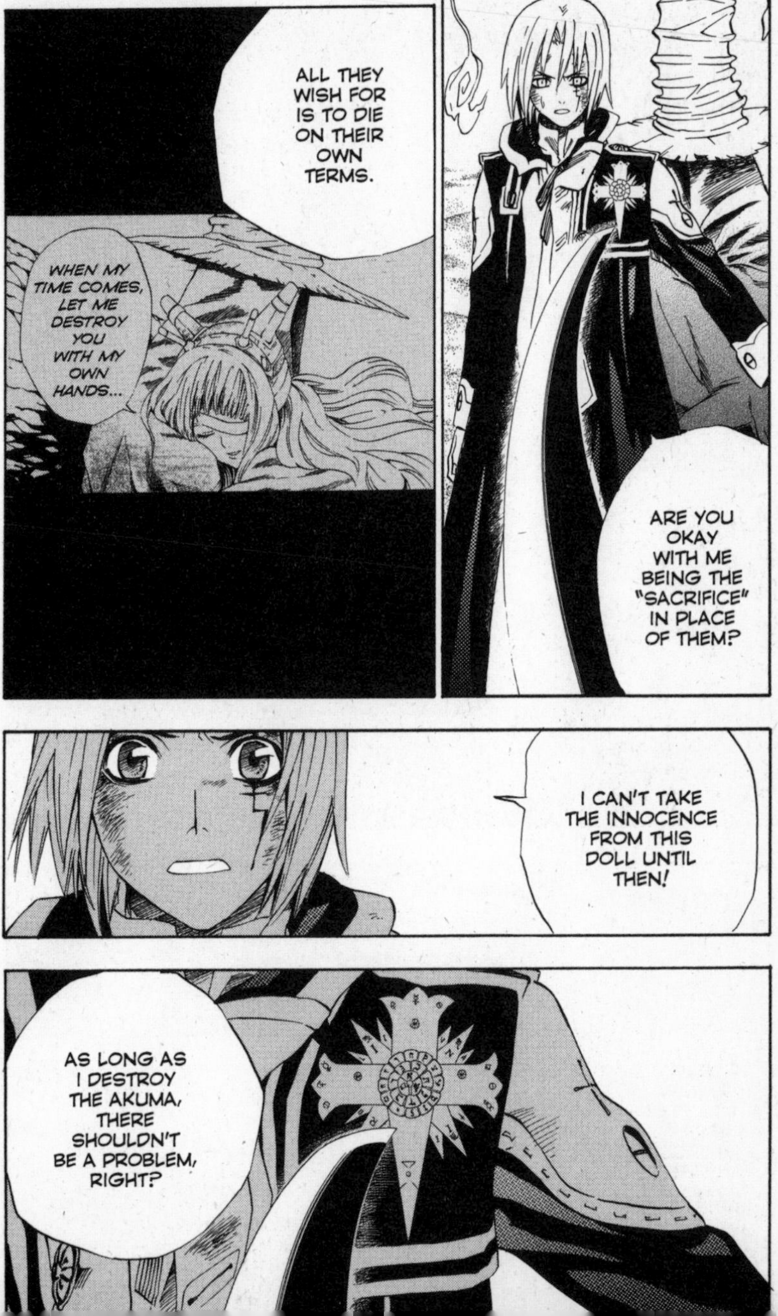
ARE YOU OKAY WITH ME BEING THE "SACRIFICE" IN PLACE OF THEM?
ALL THEY WISH FOR IS TO DIE ON THEIR OWN TERMS.
WHEN MY TIME COMES, LET ME DESTROY YOU WITH MY OWN HANDS...
I CAN'T TAKE THE INNOCENCE FROM THIS DOLL UNTIL THEN!
AS LONG AS I DESTROY THE AKUMA, THERE SHOULDN'T BE A PROBLEM, RIGHT?

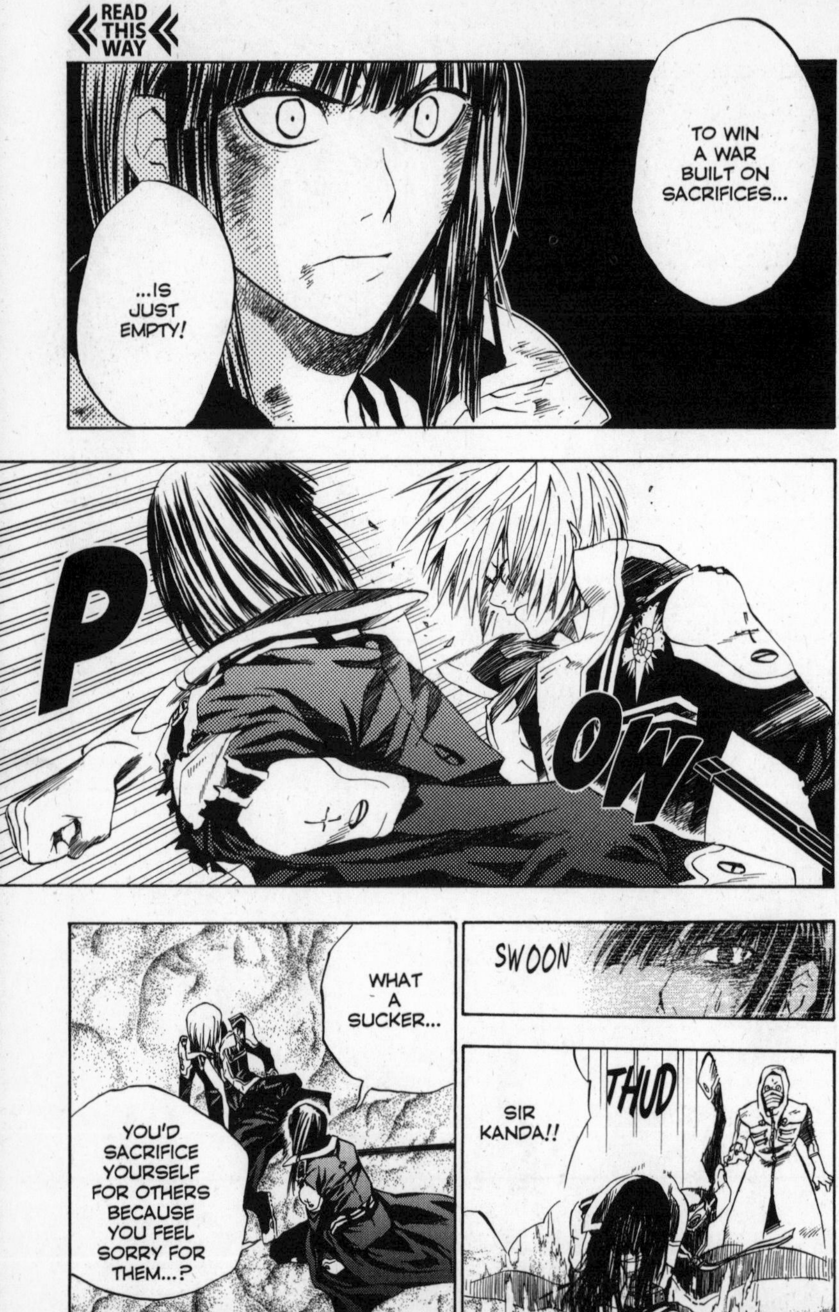
READ THIS WAY
TO WIN A WAR BUILT ON SACRIFICES...
...IS JUST EMPTY!
POW
SWOON
THUD
SIR KANDA!!
WHAT A SUCKER...
YOU'D SACRIFICE YOURSELF FOR OTHERS BECAUSE YOU FEEL SORRY FOR THEM...?

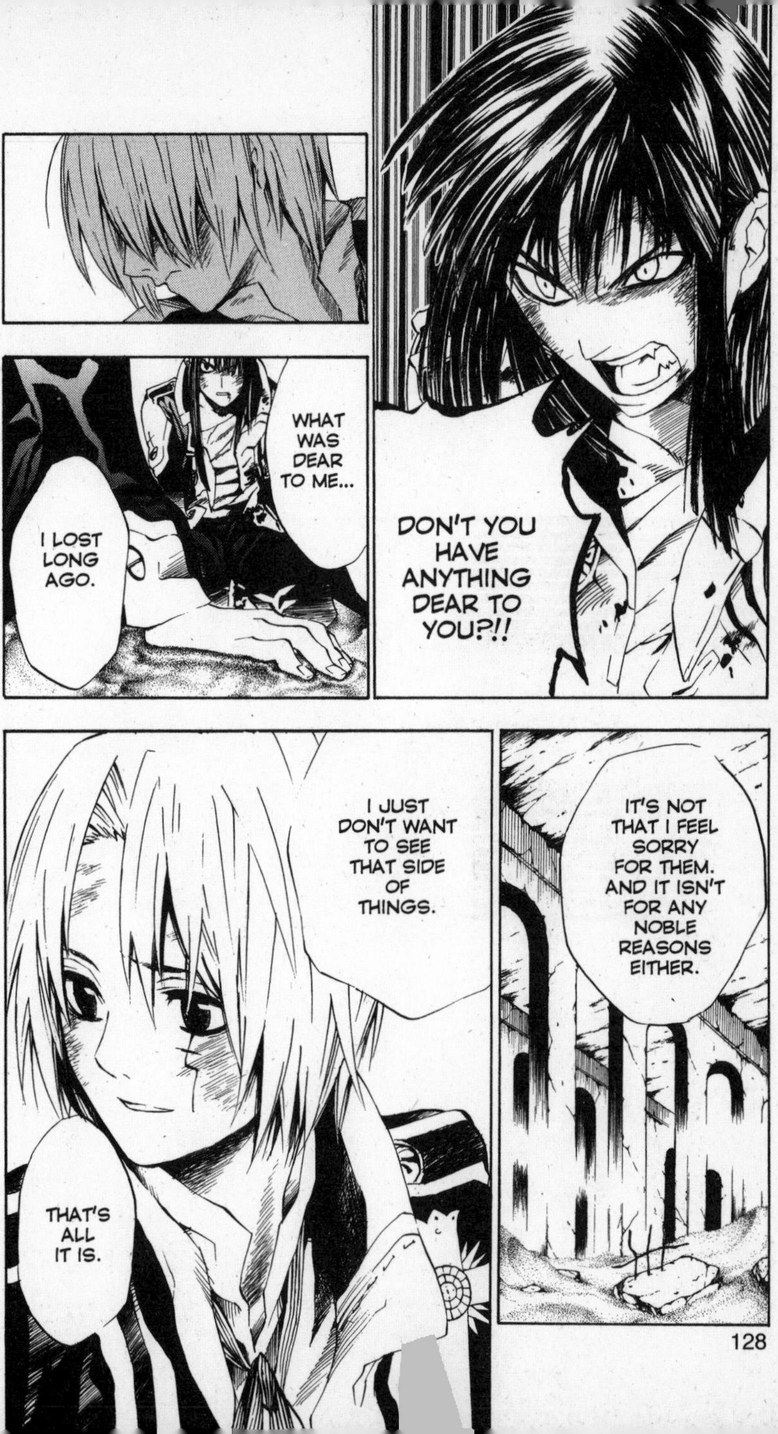
DON'T YOU HAVE ANYTHING DEAR TO YOU?!!
WHAT WAS DEAR TO ME...
I LOST LONG AGO.
IT'S NOT THAT I FEEL SORRY FOR THEM. AND IT ISN'T FOR ANY NOBLE REASONS EITHER.
I JUST DON'T WANT TO SEE THAT SIDE OF THINGS.
THAT'S ALL IT IS.

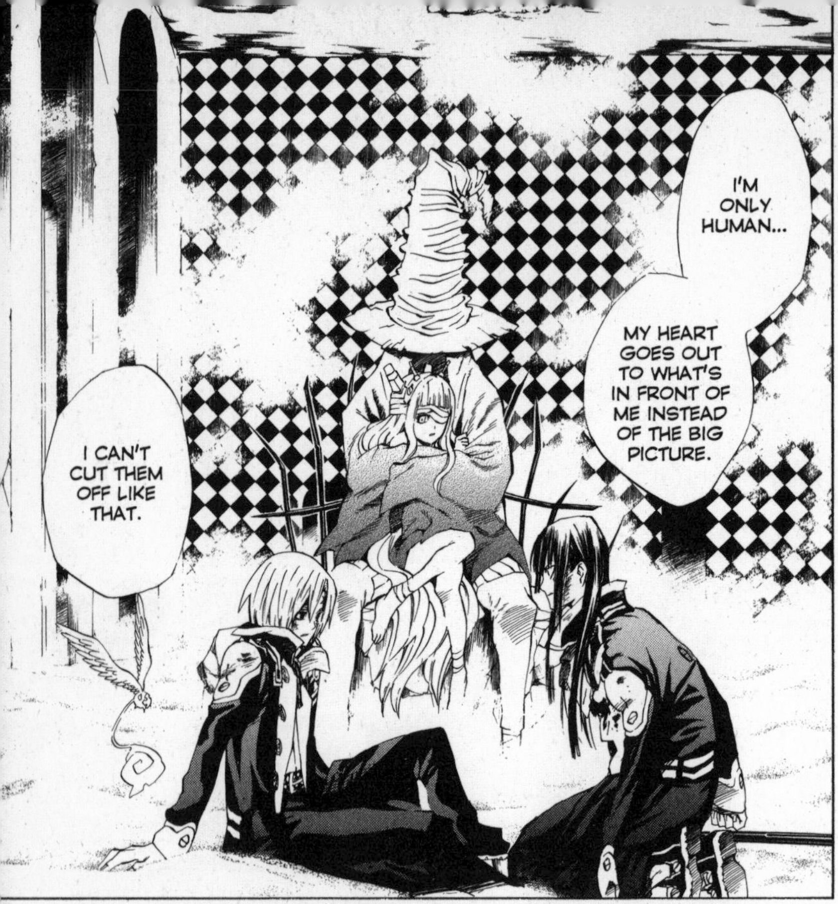
I'M ONLY HUMAN...
MY HEART GOES OUT TO WHAT'S IN FRONT OF ME INSTEAD OF THE BIG PICTURE.
I CAN'T CUT THEM OFF LIKE THAT.

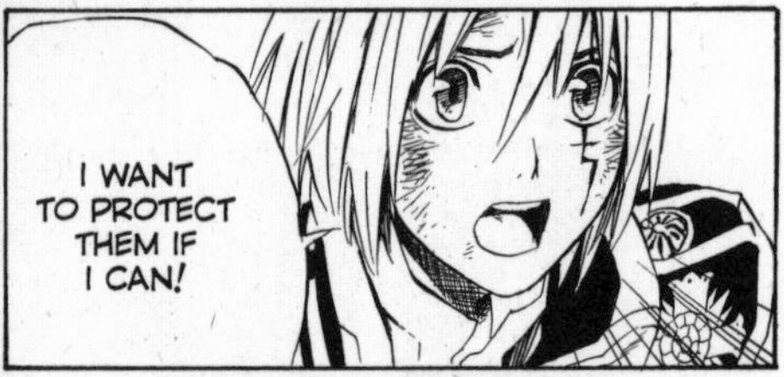
I WANT TO PROTECT THEM IF I CAN!

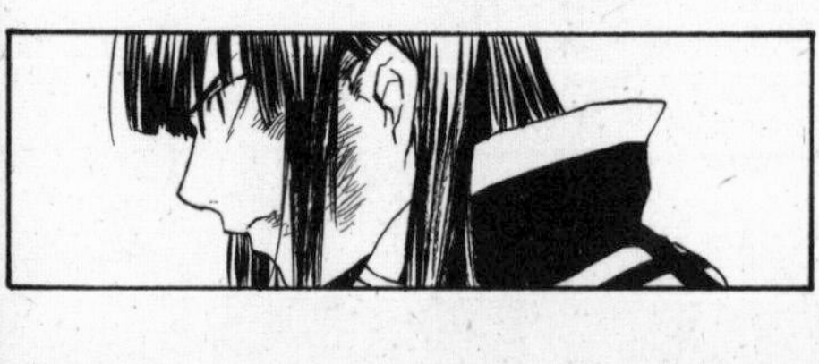

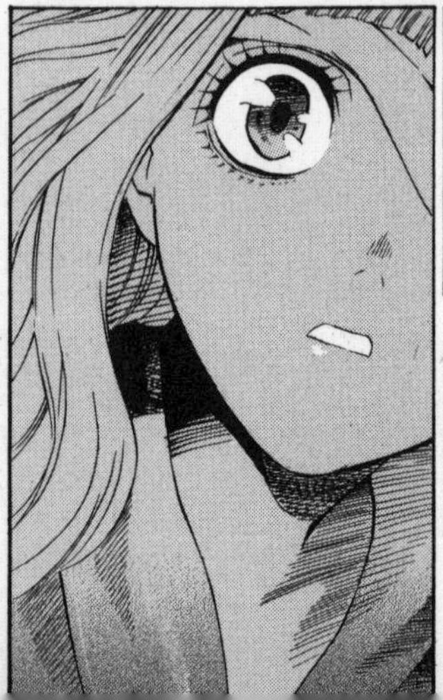

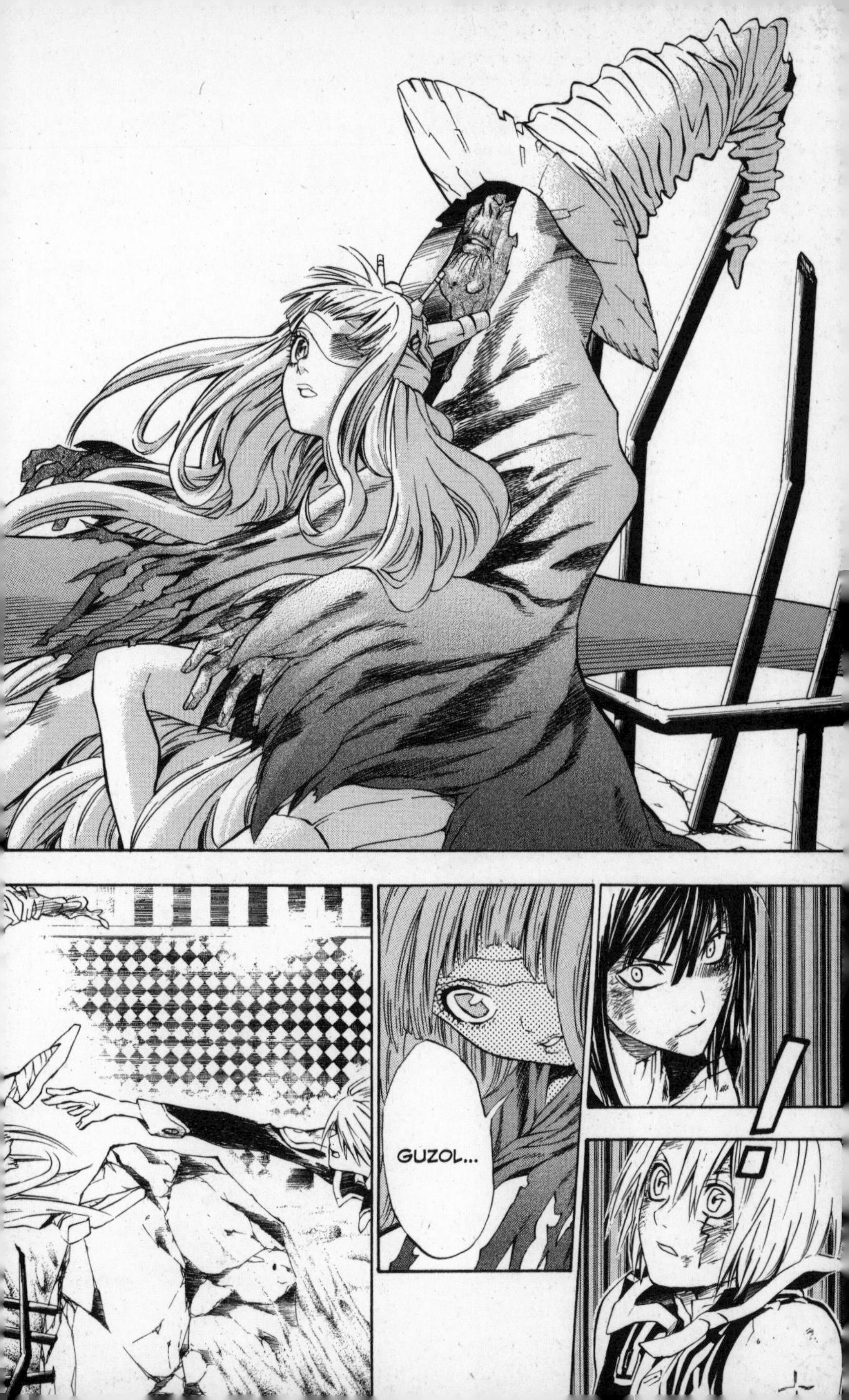
GUZOL...

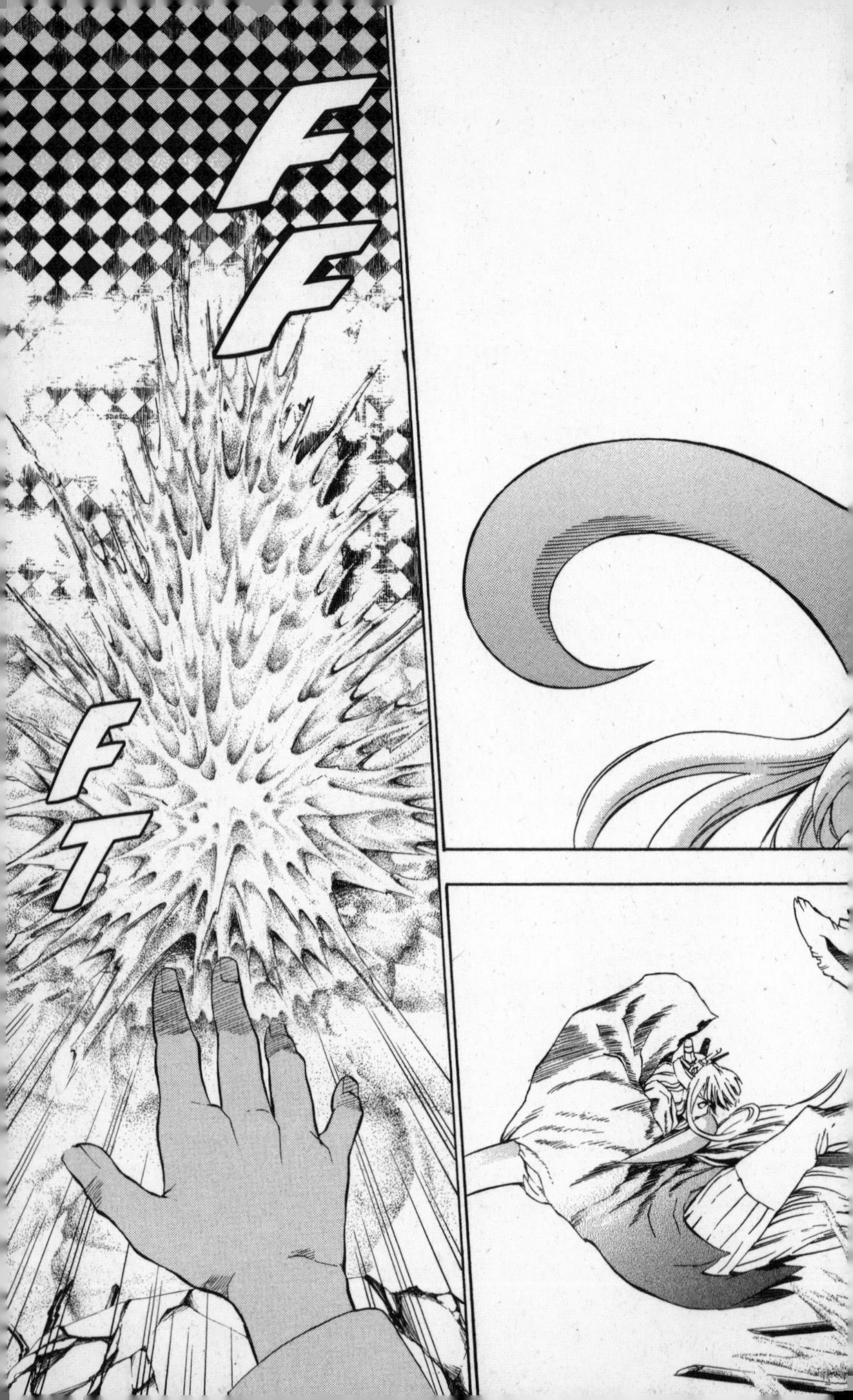
FF
FT

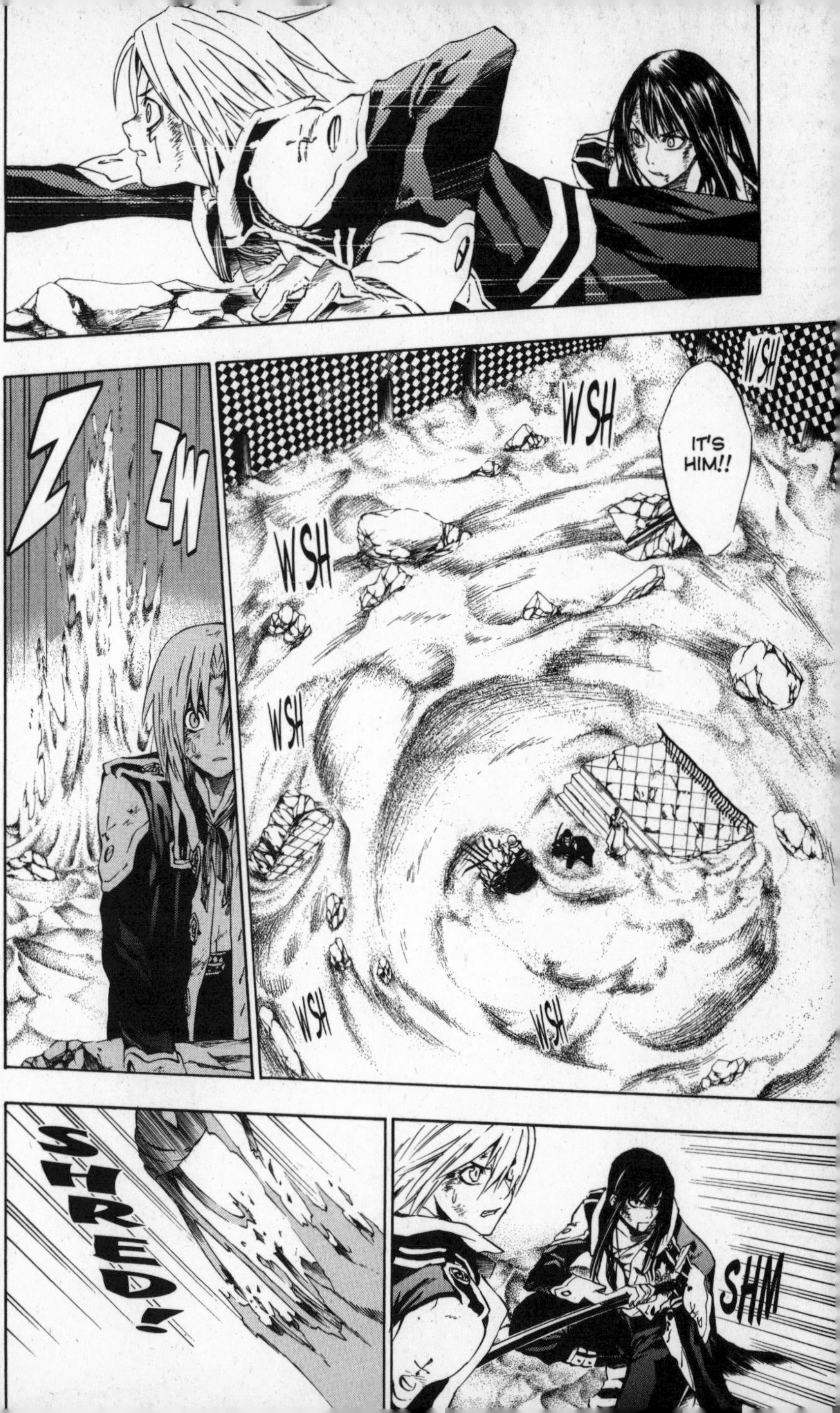
WSH
IT'S HIM!!
WSH
WSH
WSH
WSH
WSH
Z
ZW
SHM
SHRED!

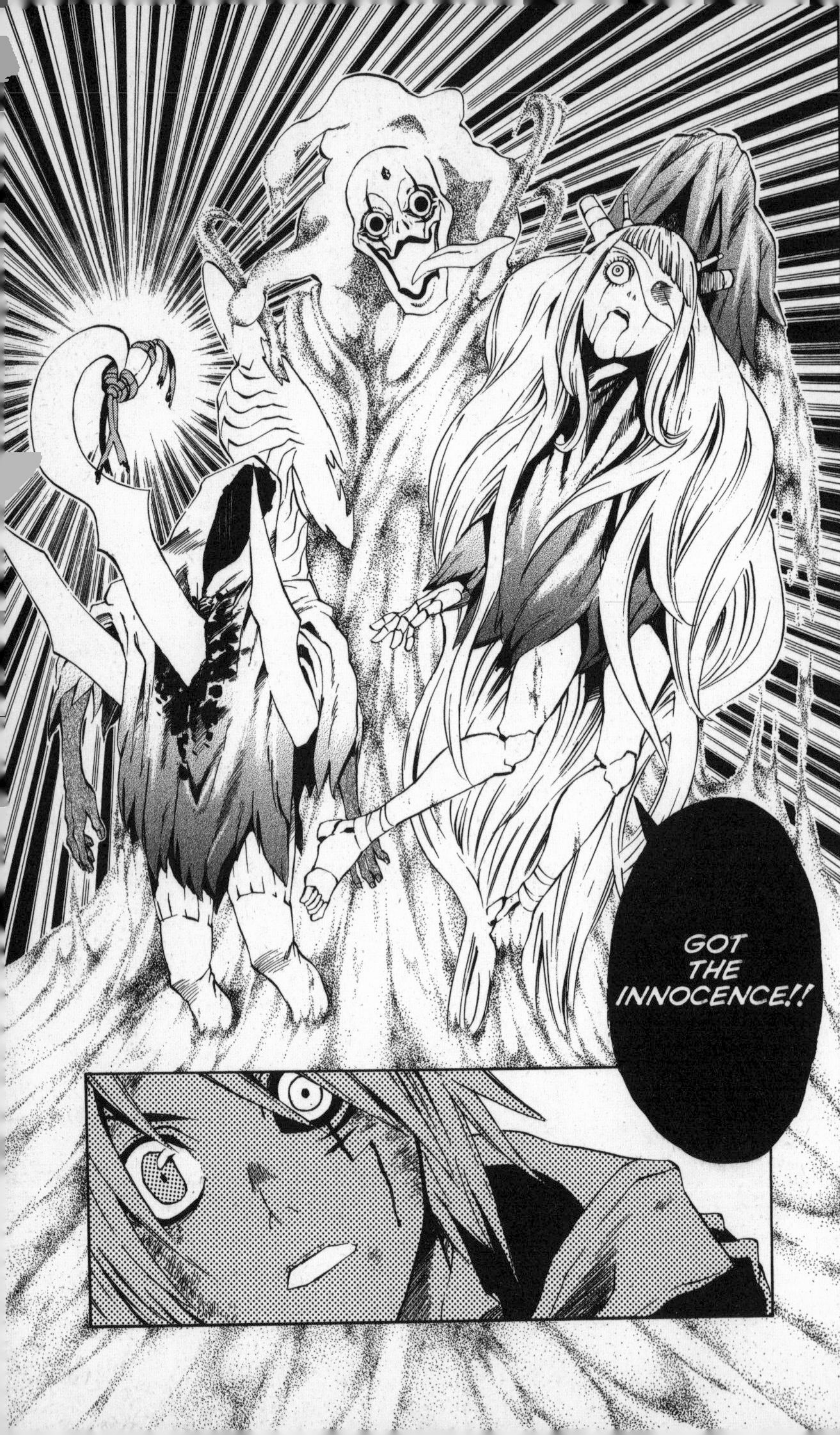
GOT THE INNOCENCE!!

THUD
LA...
LA-LA...
OOZE
LA-LA...
OOOH—
VNN
VNN
VNN
SO THIS IS AN INNOCENCE.
KWSH

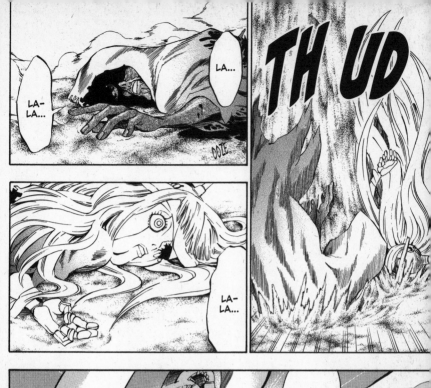

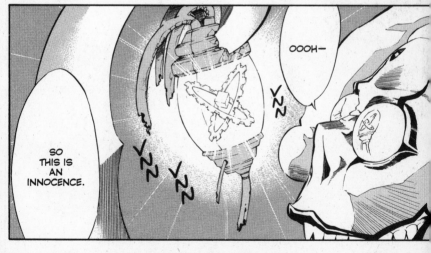

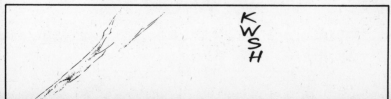

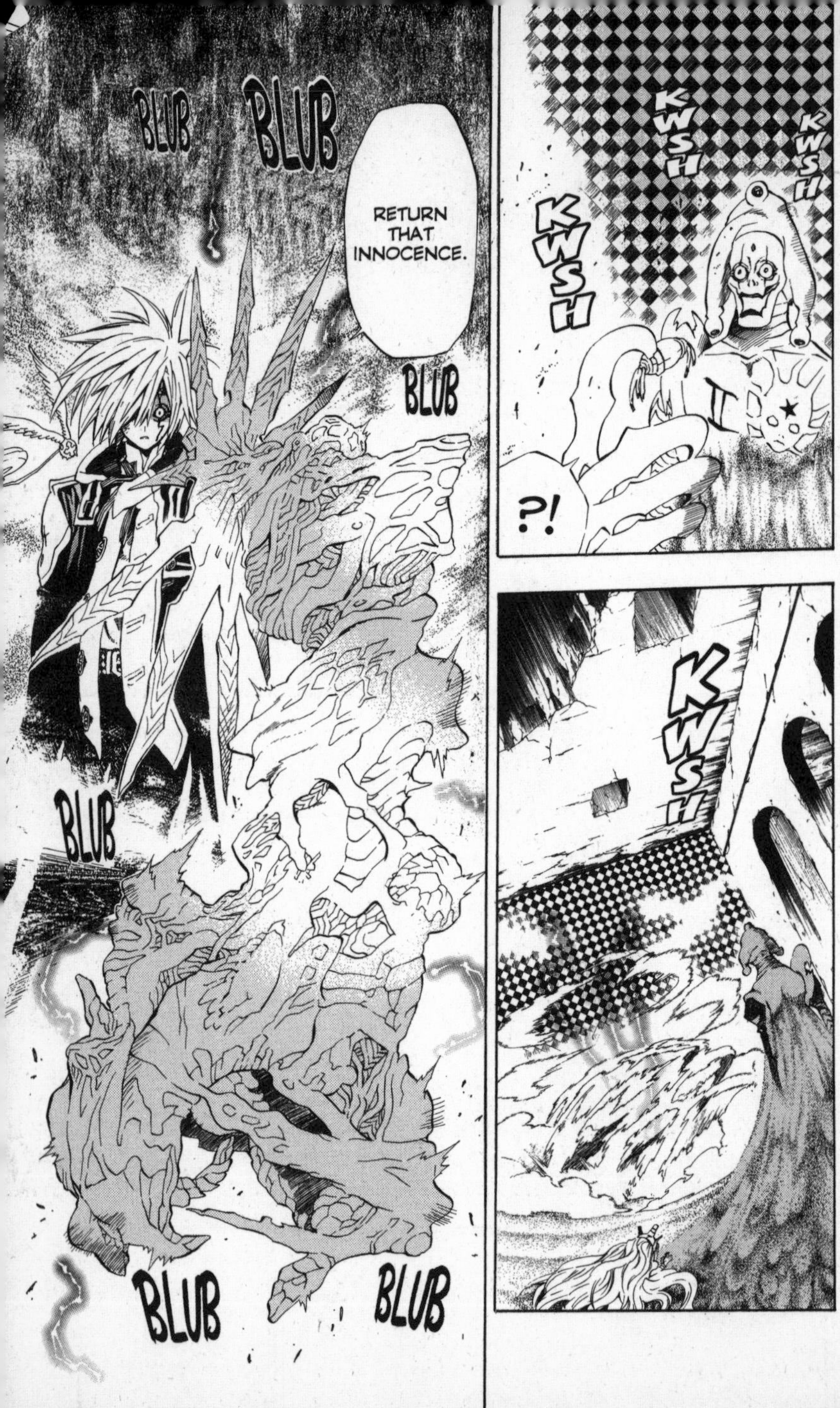
KWSH
KWSH
KWSH
?!
KWSH
BLUB
BLUB
RETURN THAT INNOCENCE.
BLUB
BLUB
BLUB
BLUB

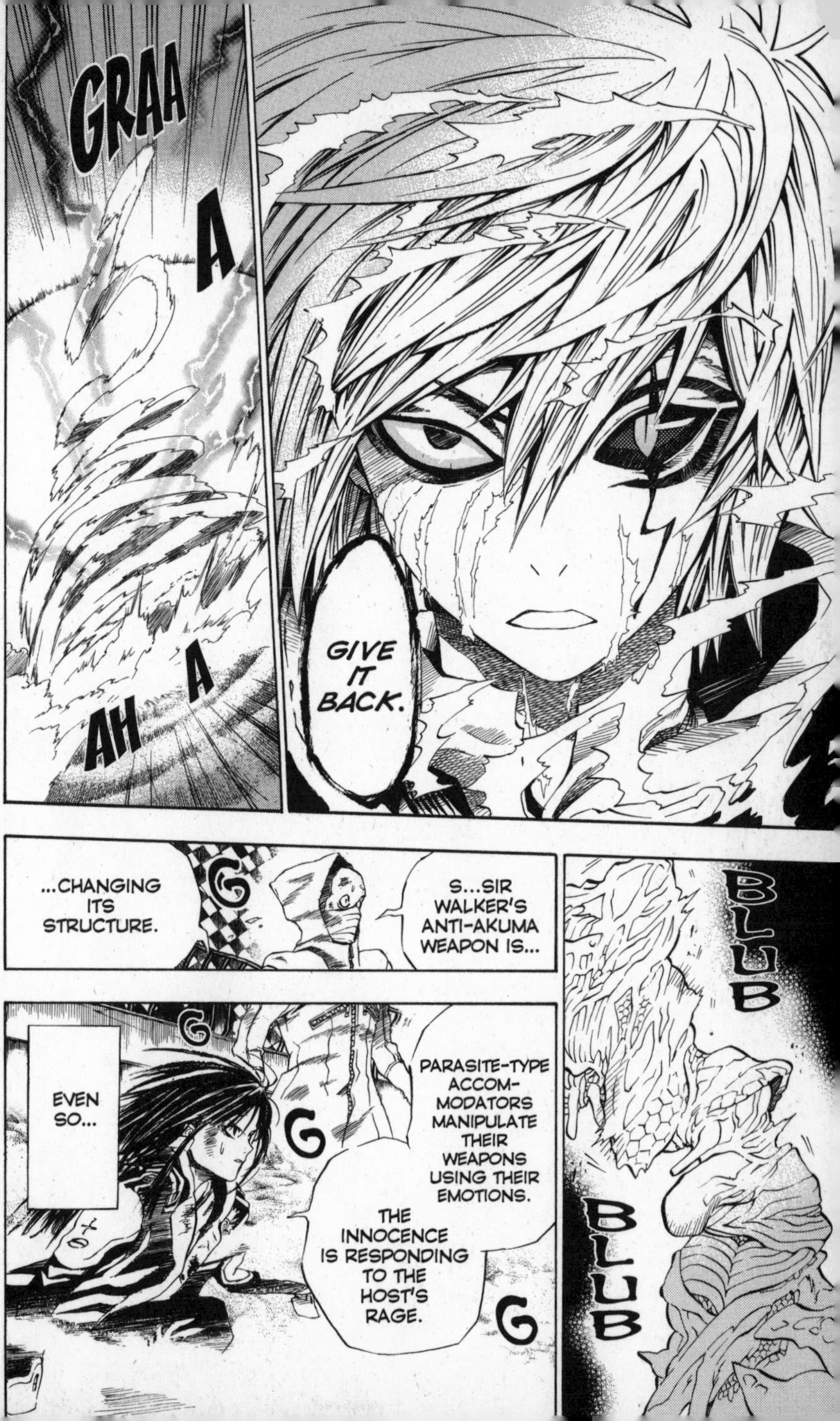
GIVE IT BACK.
GRAA A A AH
BLUB BLUB
S...SIR WALKER'S ANTI-AKUMA WEAPON IS...
...CHANGING ITS STRUCTURE.
G
G
PARASITE-TYPE ACCOM-MODATORS MANIPULATE THEIR WEAPONS USING THEIR EMOTIONS.
THE INNOCENCE IS RESPONDING TO THE HOST'S RAGE.
G
EVEN SO...
G

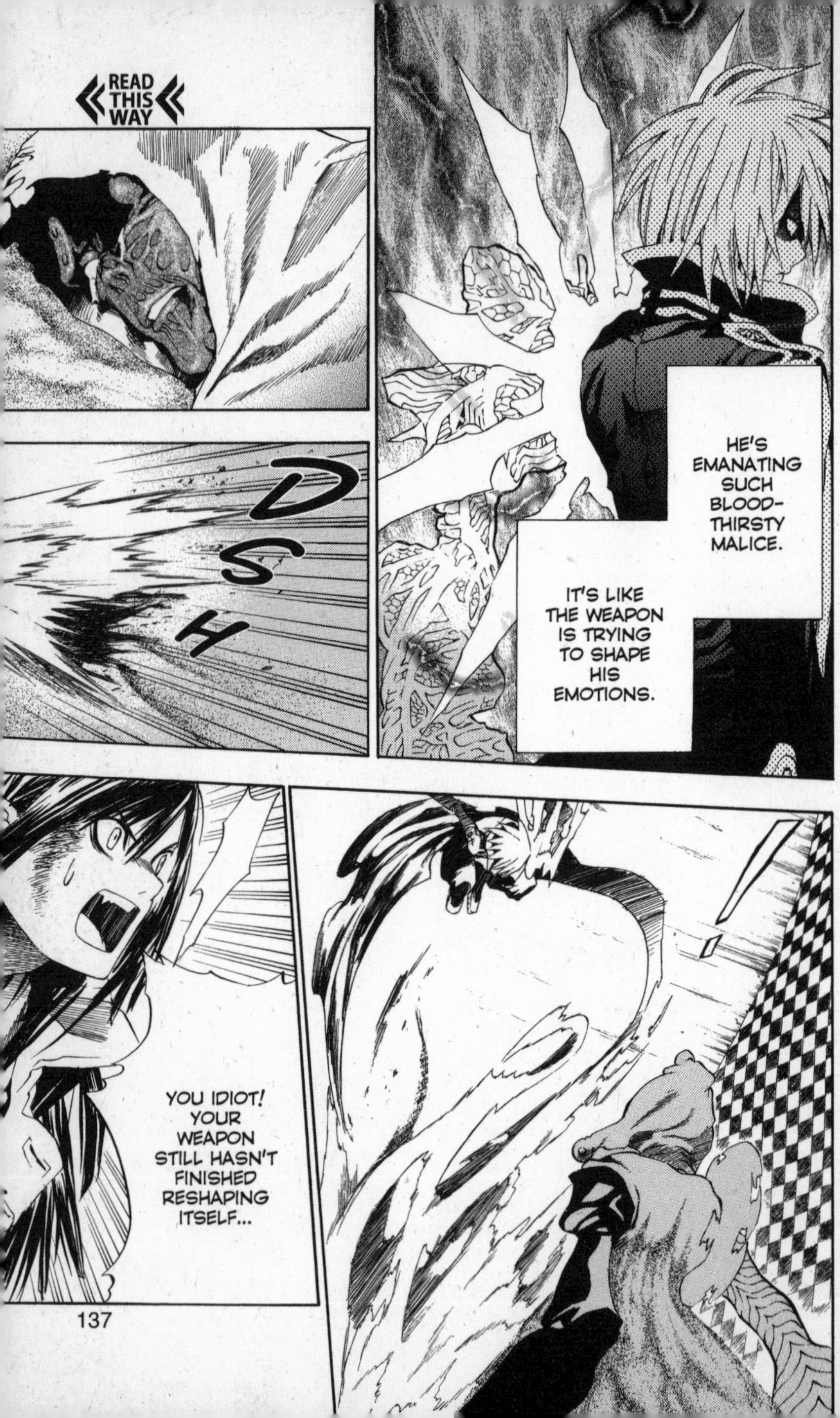
READ THIS WAY
HE'S EMANATING SUCH BLOOD-THIRSTY MALICE.
IT'S LIKE THE WEAPON IS TRYING TO SHAPE HIS EMOTIONS.
DSH
!
YOU IDIOT! YOUR WEAPON STILL HASN'T FINISHED RESHAPING ITSELF...

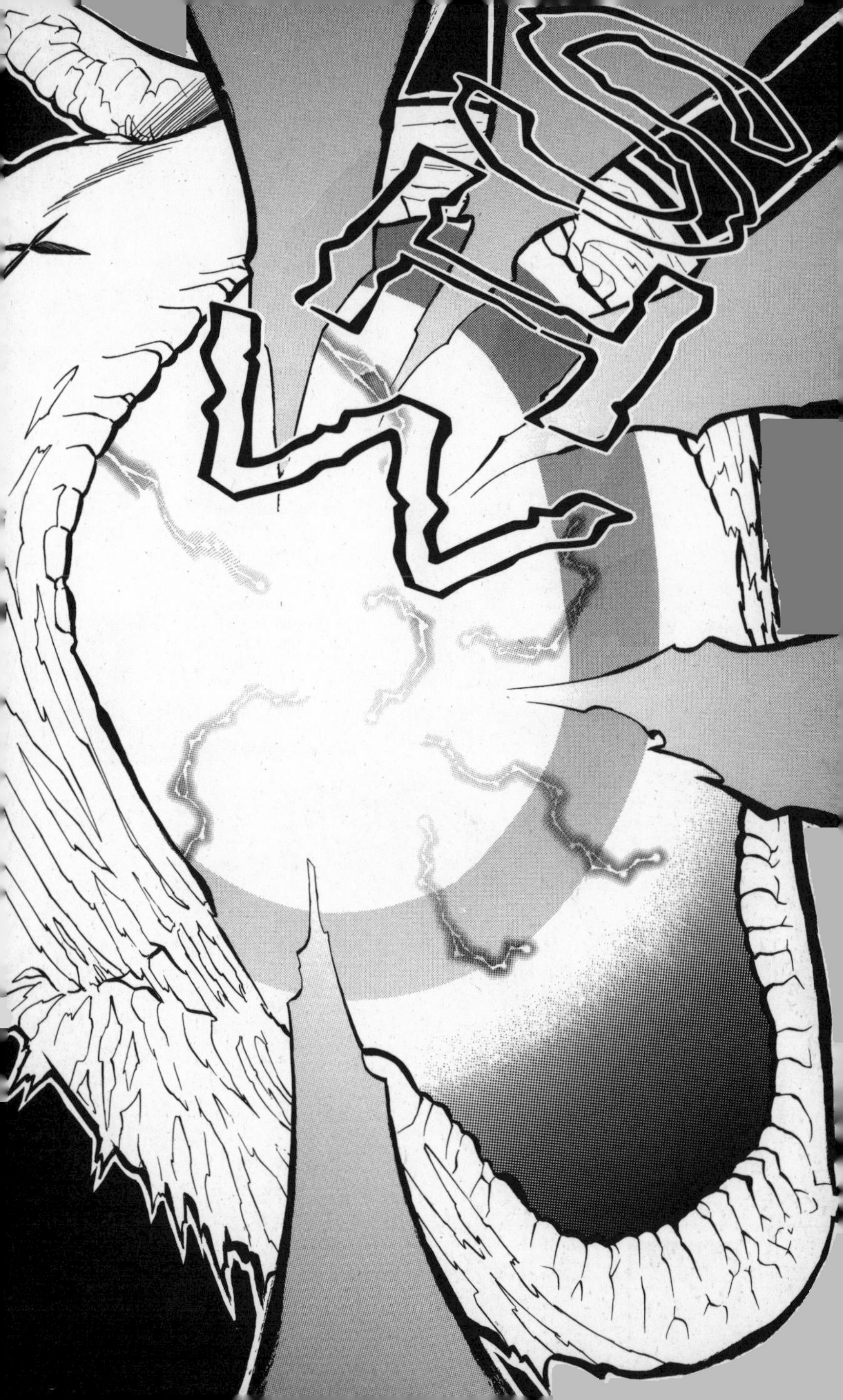

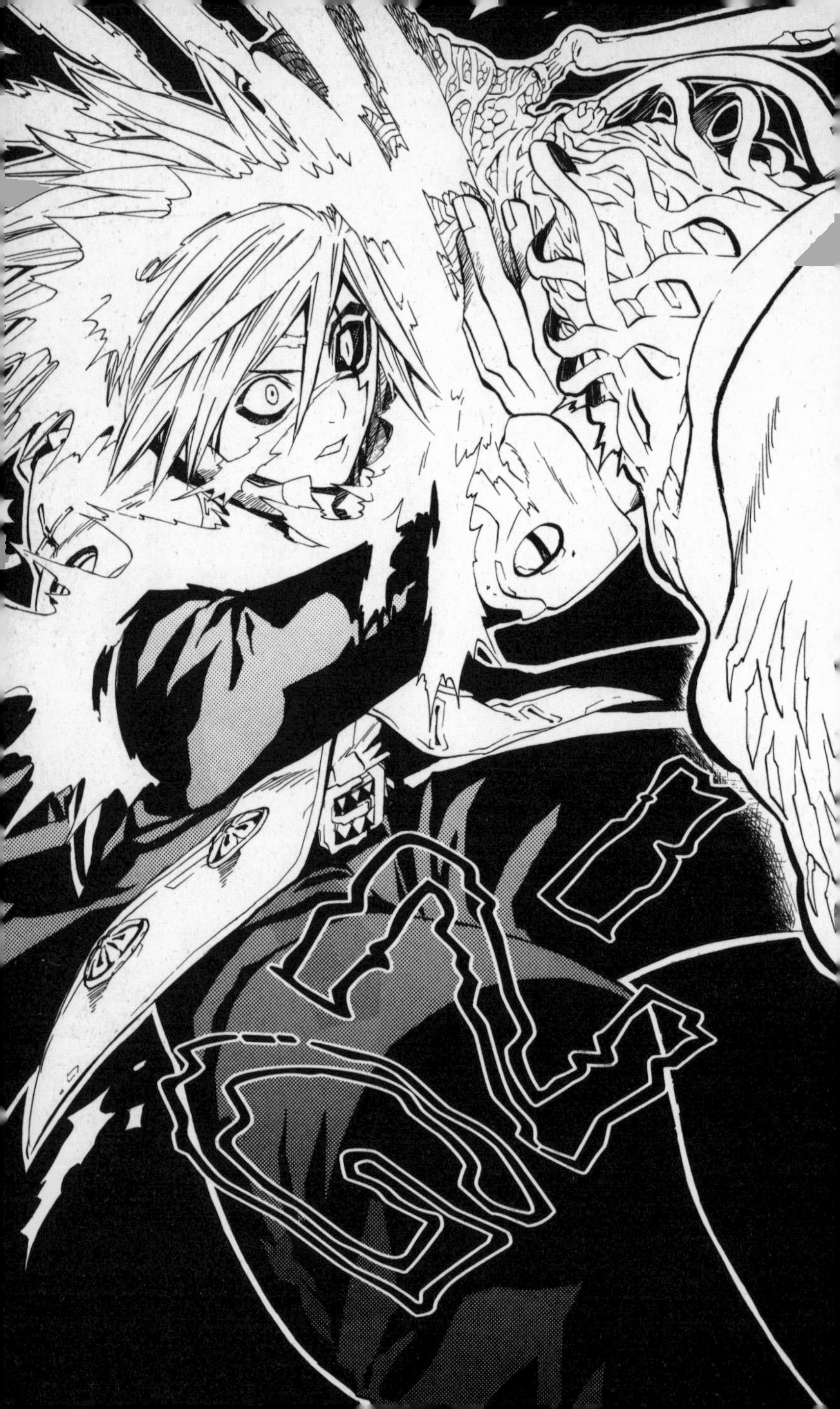

GRAND OPENING!!

READER'S SECTION

KOMUI'S EXPERIMENT ROOM

STARTING NEXT VOLUME—

WE WILL OPEN A READER'S SECTION!

WE'RE GOING TO START OFF WITH THE TWO SECTIONS BELOW!

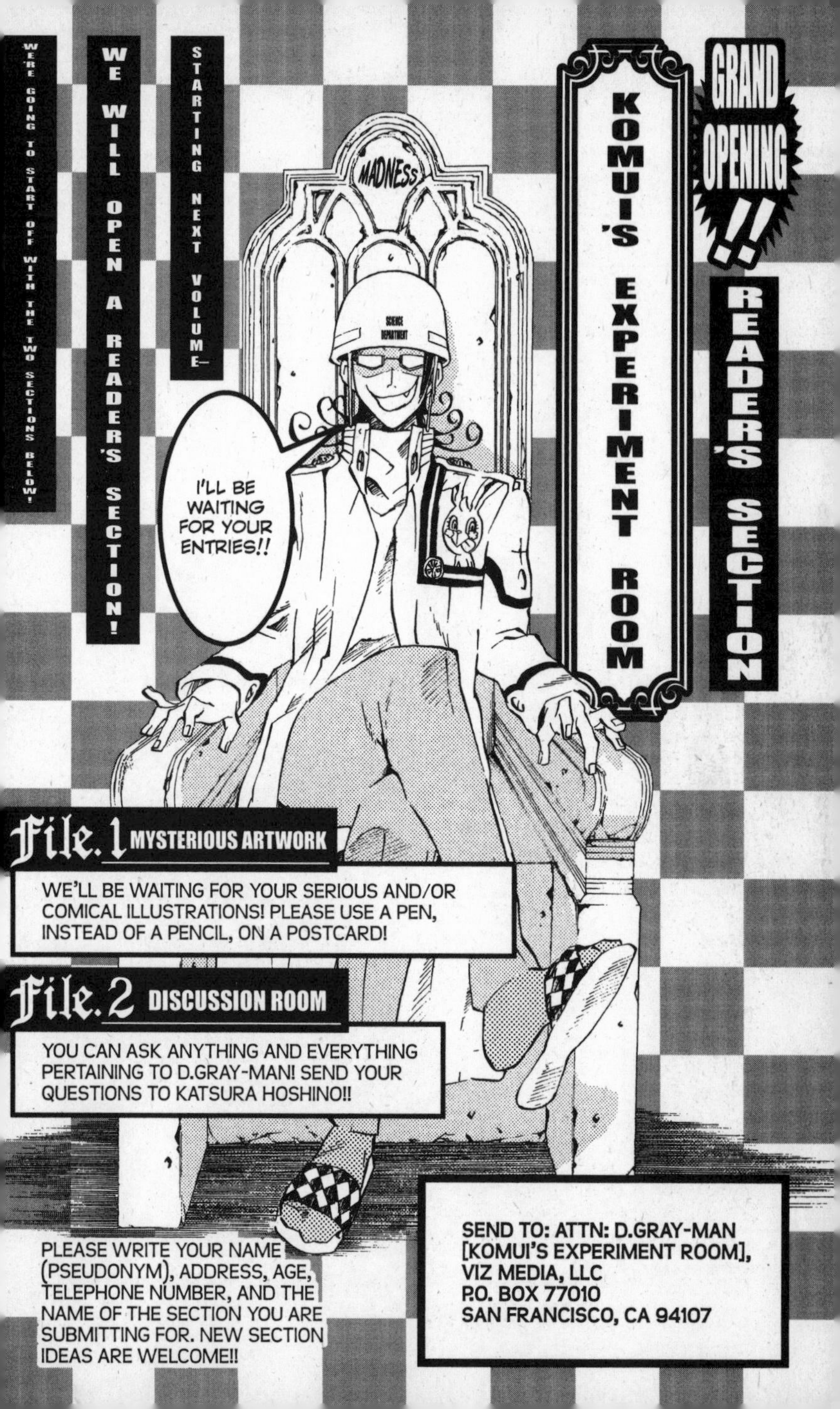
MADNESS
SCIENCE DEPARTMENT
I'LL BE WAITING FOR YOUR ENTRIES!!

File. 1 MYSTERIOUS ARTWORK

WE'LL BE WAITING FOR YOUR SERIOUS AND/OR COMICAL ILLUSTRATIONS! PLEASE USE A PEN, INSTEAD OF A PENCIL, ON A POSTCARD!

File. 2 DISCUSSION ROOM

YOU CAN ASK ANYTHING AND EVERYTHING PERTAINING TO D.GRAY-MAN! SEND YOUR QUESTIONS TO KATSURA HOSHINO!!

PLEASE WRITE YOUR NAME (PSEUDONYM), ADDRESS, AGE, TELEPHONE NUMBER, AND THE NAME OF THE SECTION YOU ARE SUBMITTING FOR. NEW SECTION IDEAS ARE WELCOME!!

SEND TO: ATTN: D.GRAY-MAN [KOMUI'S EXPERIMENT ROOM], VIZ MEDIA, LLC
P.O. BOX 77010
SAN FRANCISCO, CA 94107

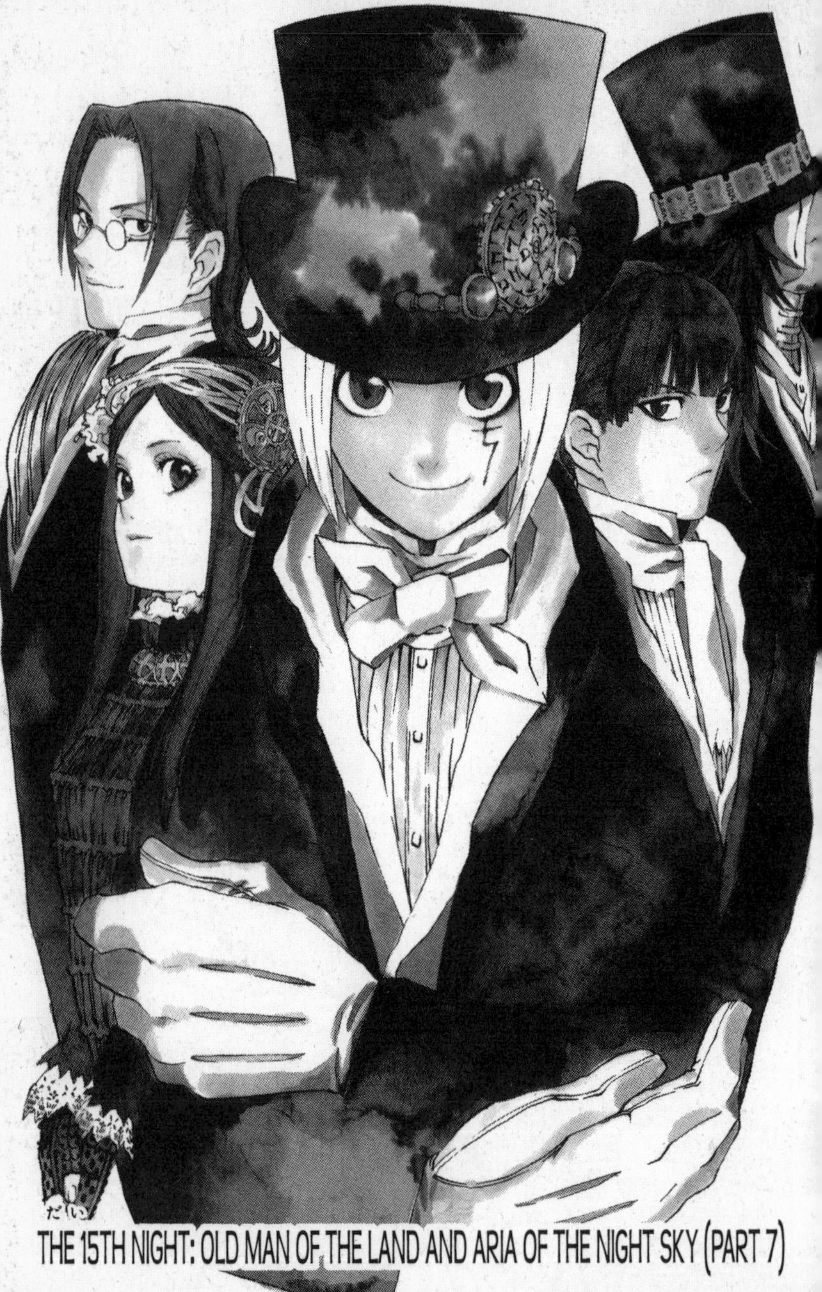

THE 15TH NIGHT: OLD MAN OF THE LAND AND ARIA OF THE NIGHT SKY (PART 7)

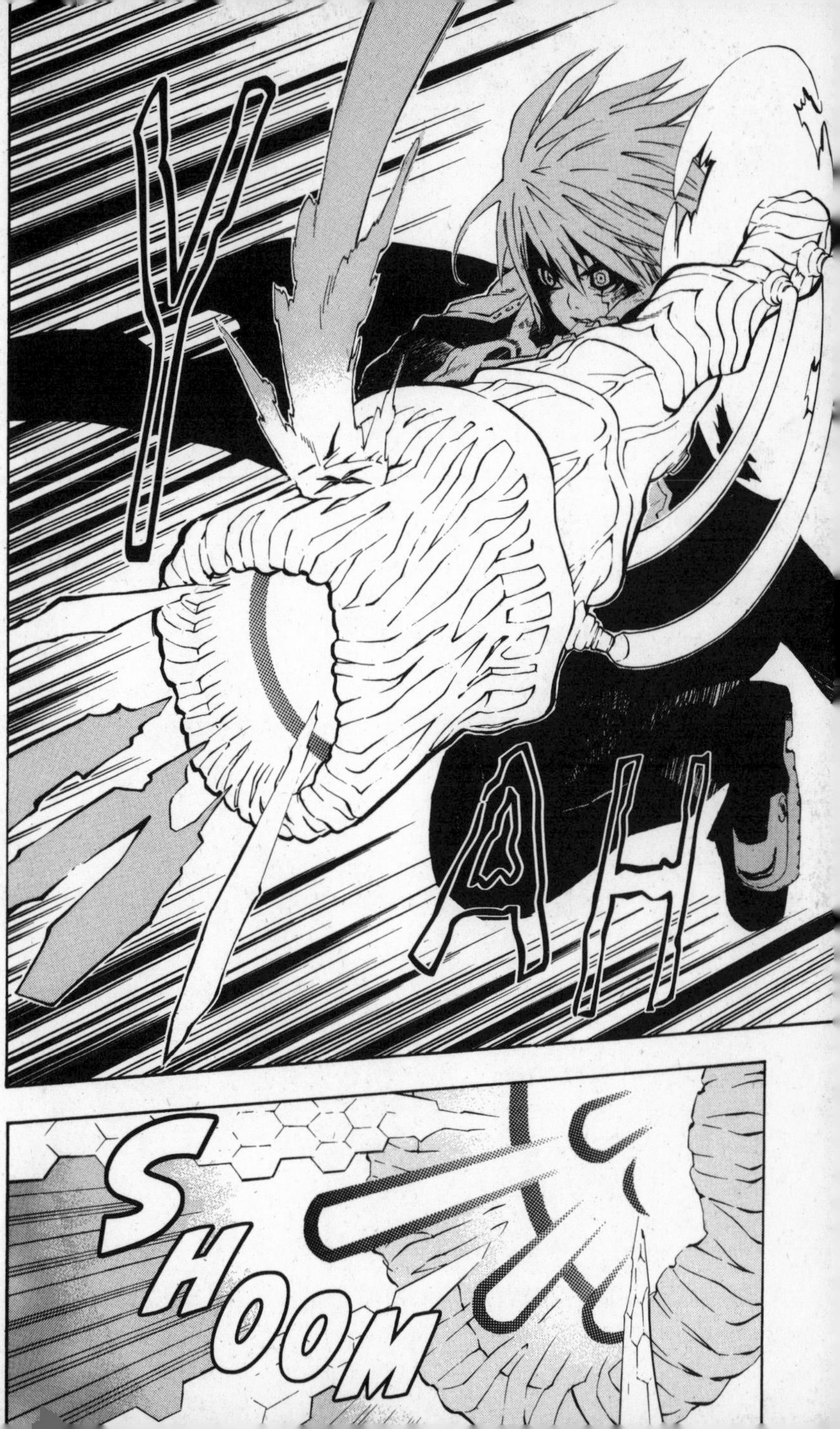
YAH
SHOOM

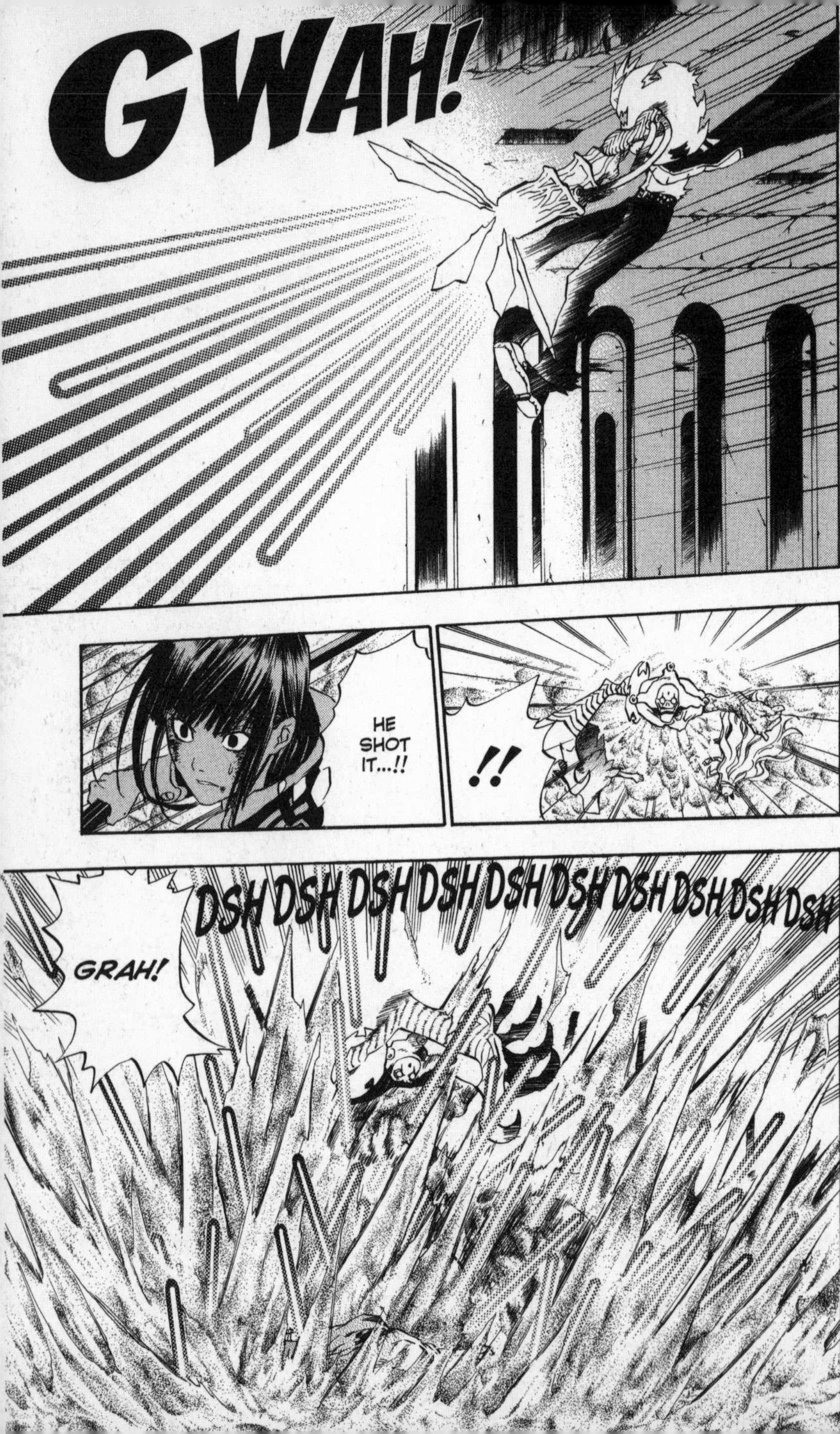
GWAH!
!!
HE SHOT IT...!!
DSH DSH DSH DSH DSH DSH DSH DSH DSH DSH
GRAH!

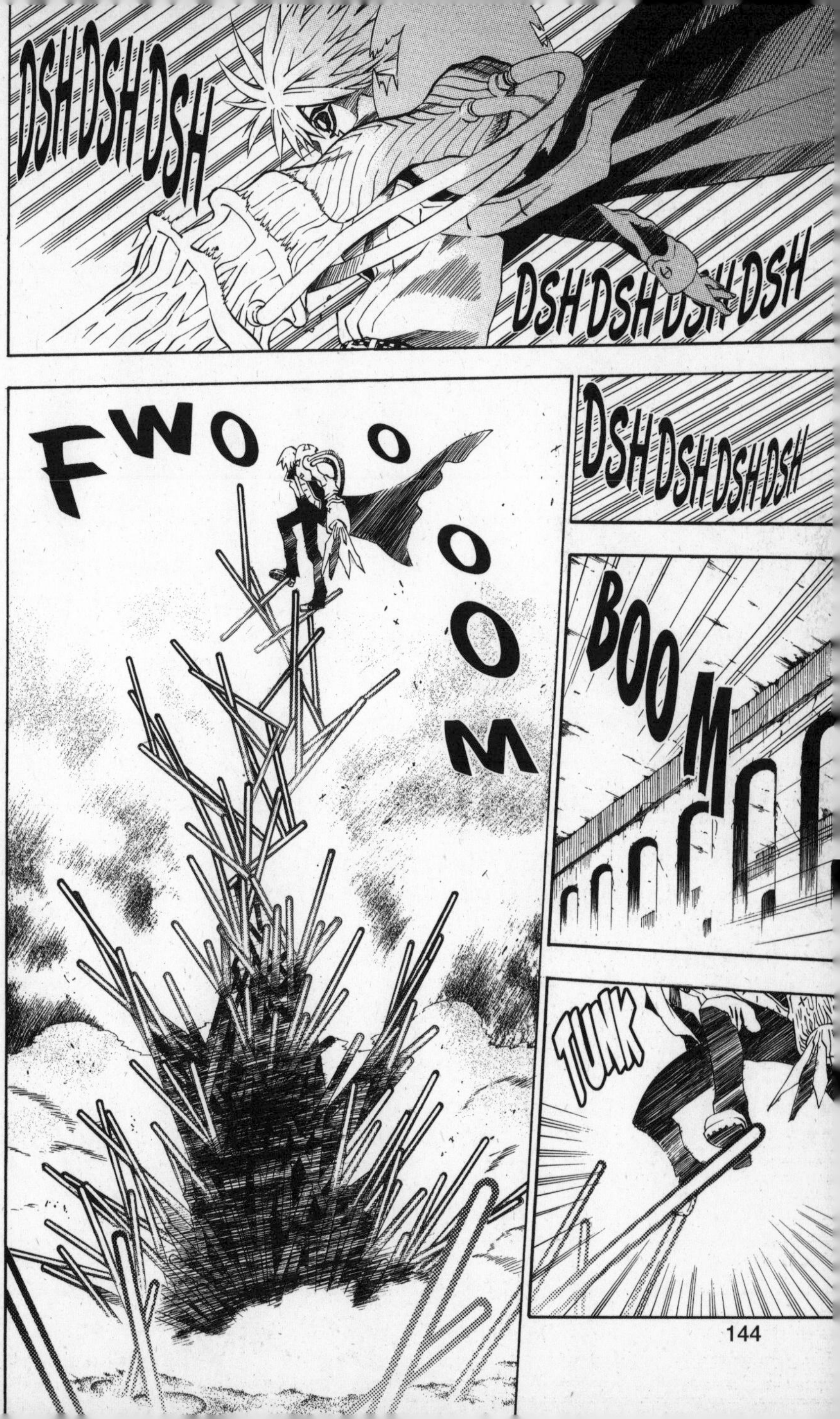
DSH DSH DSH DSH
DSH DSH DSH
DSH DSH DSH DSH
BOOM
TUNK
FWOOOOM

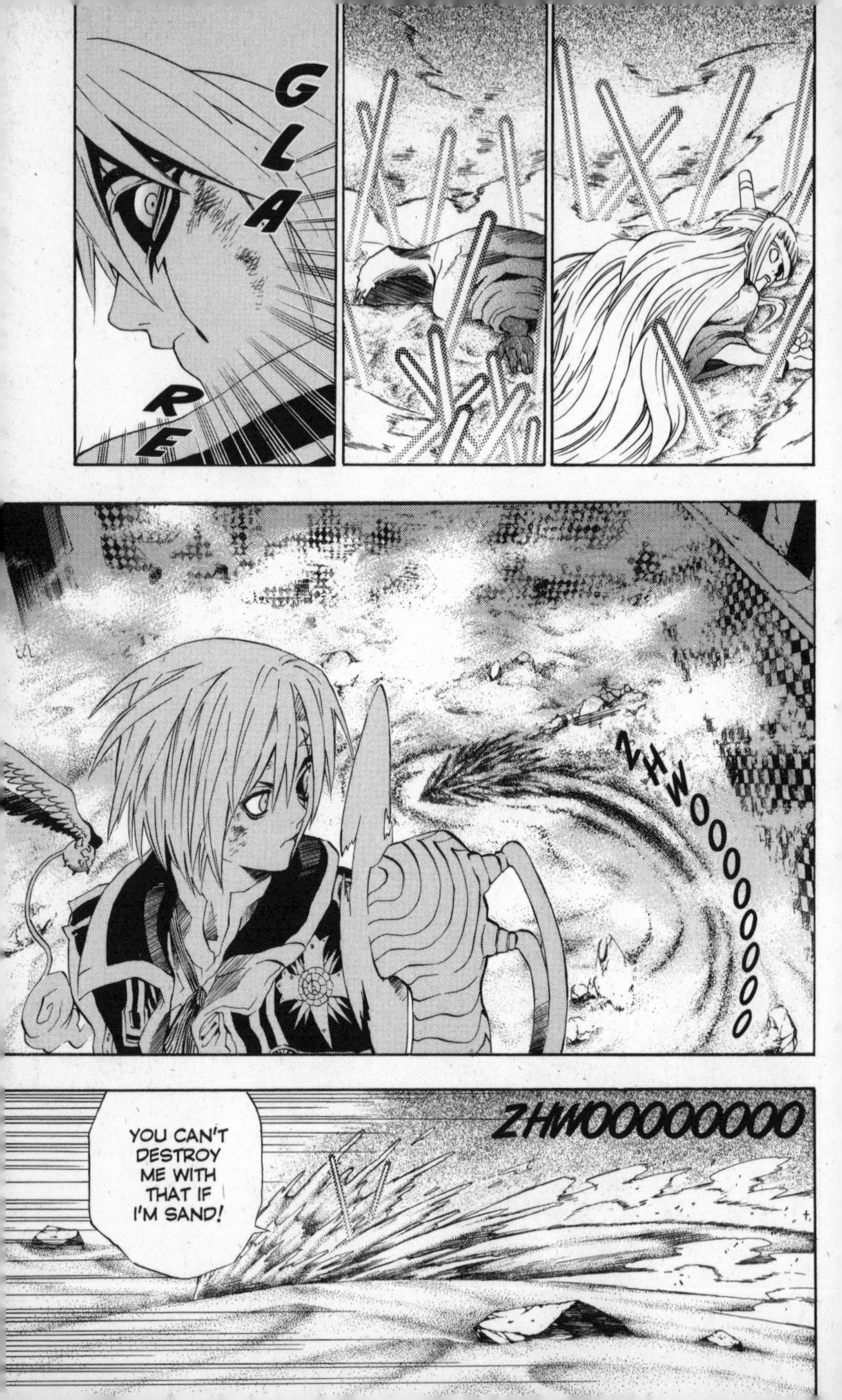
GLARE
ZHWOOOOOOOOO
ZHWOOOOOOOOO
YOU CAN'T DESTROY ME WITH THAT IF I'M SAND!

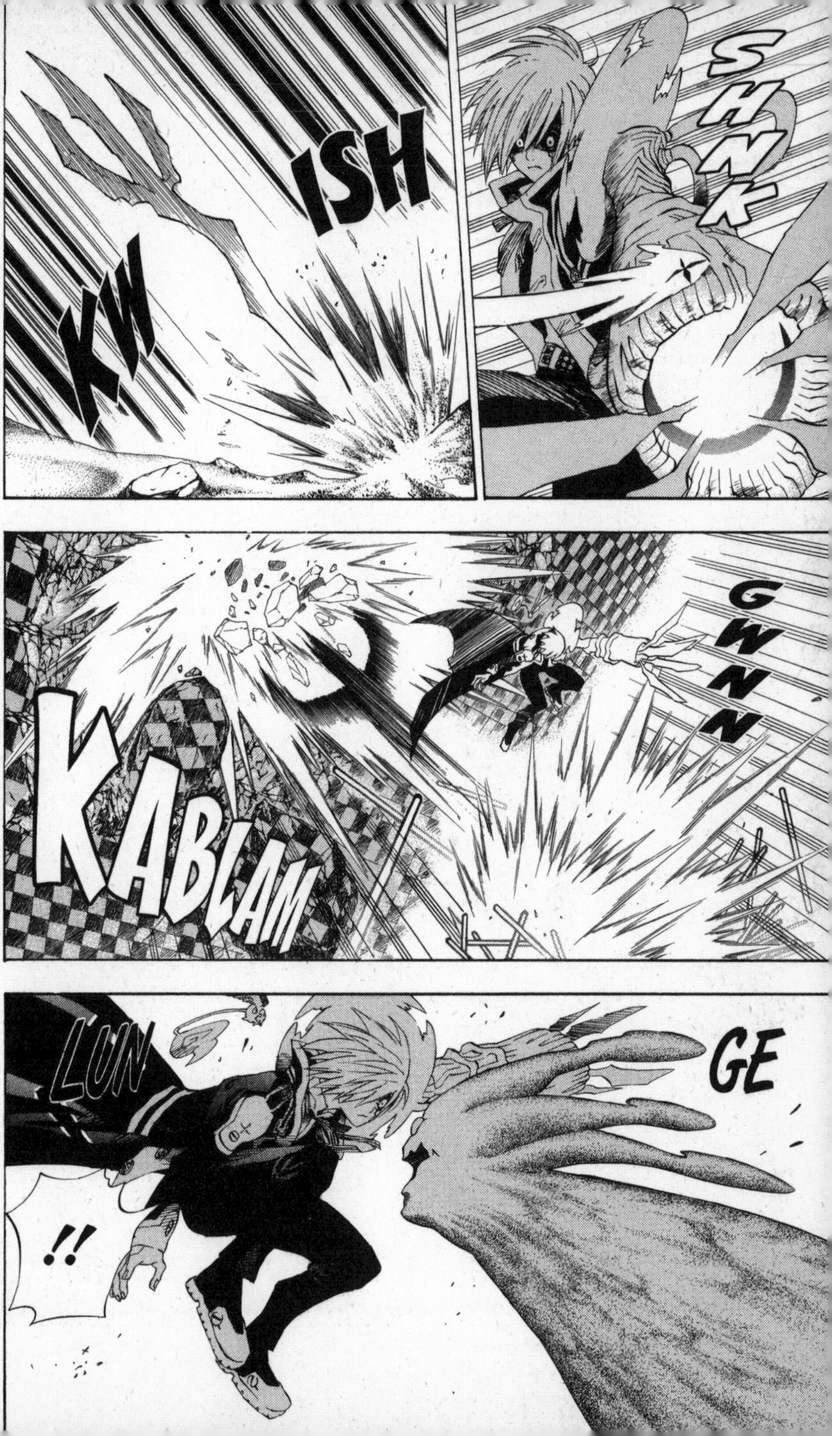
SHNK
KW
ISH
GWNNN
KABLAM
GE
LUN
!!

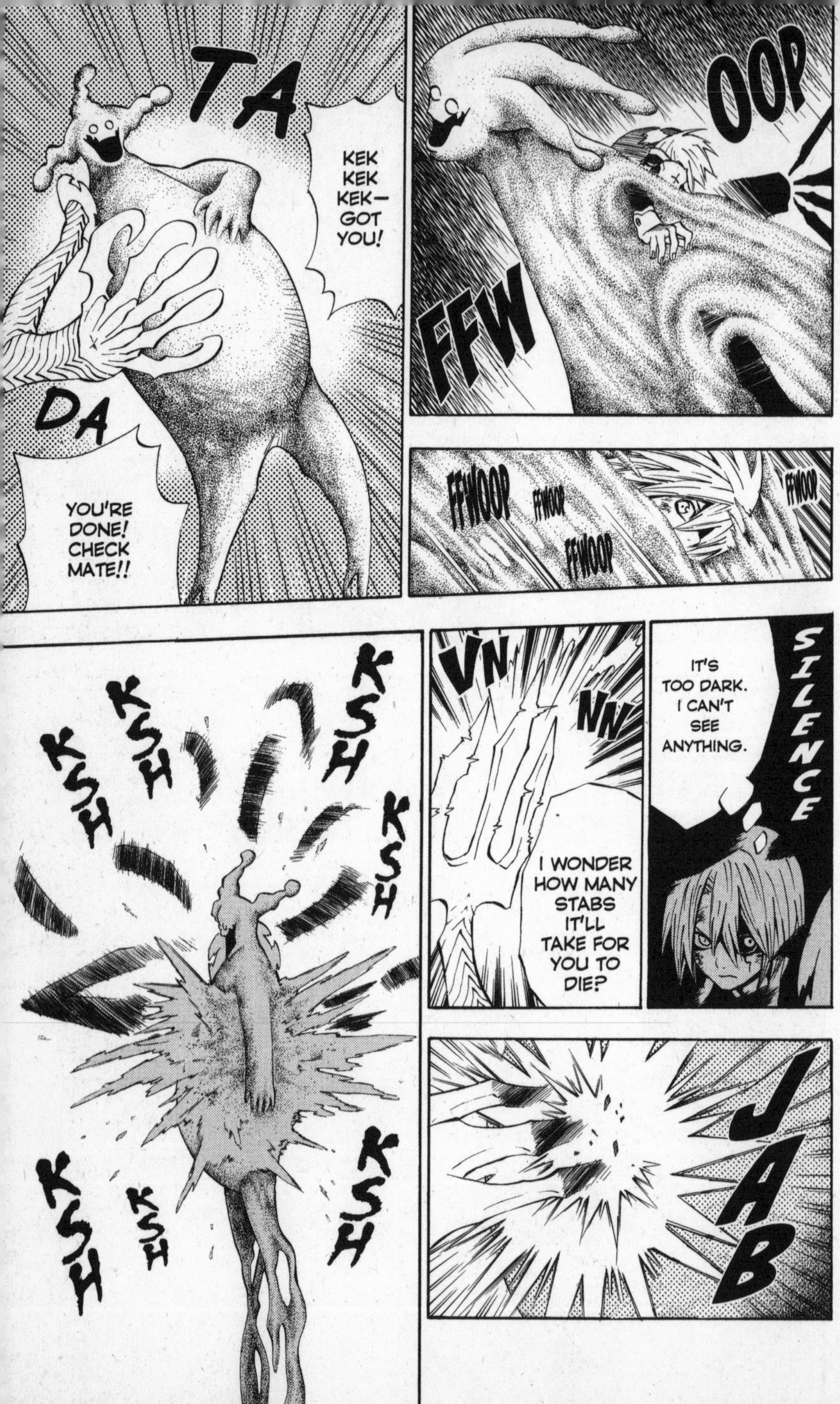
OOP
FFW
FFWOOP
FFWOOP
FFWOOP
FFWOOP
TA
KEK KEK KEK— GOT YOU!
DA
YOU'RE DONE! CHECK MATE!!
SILENCE
IT'S TOO DARK. I CAN'T SEE ANYTHING.
VNNN
I WONDER HOW MANY STABS IT'LL TAKE FOR YOU TO DIE?
JAB
KSH
KSH
KSH
KSH
KSH
KSH
KSH
KSH

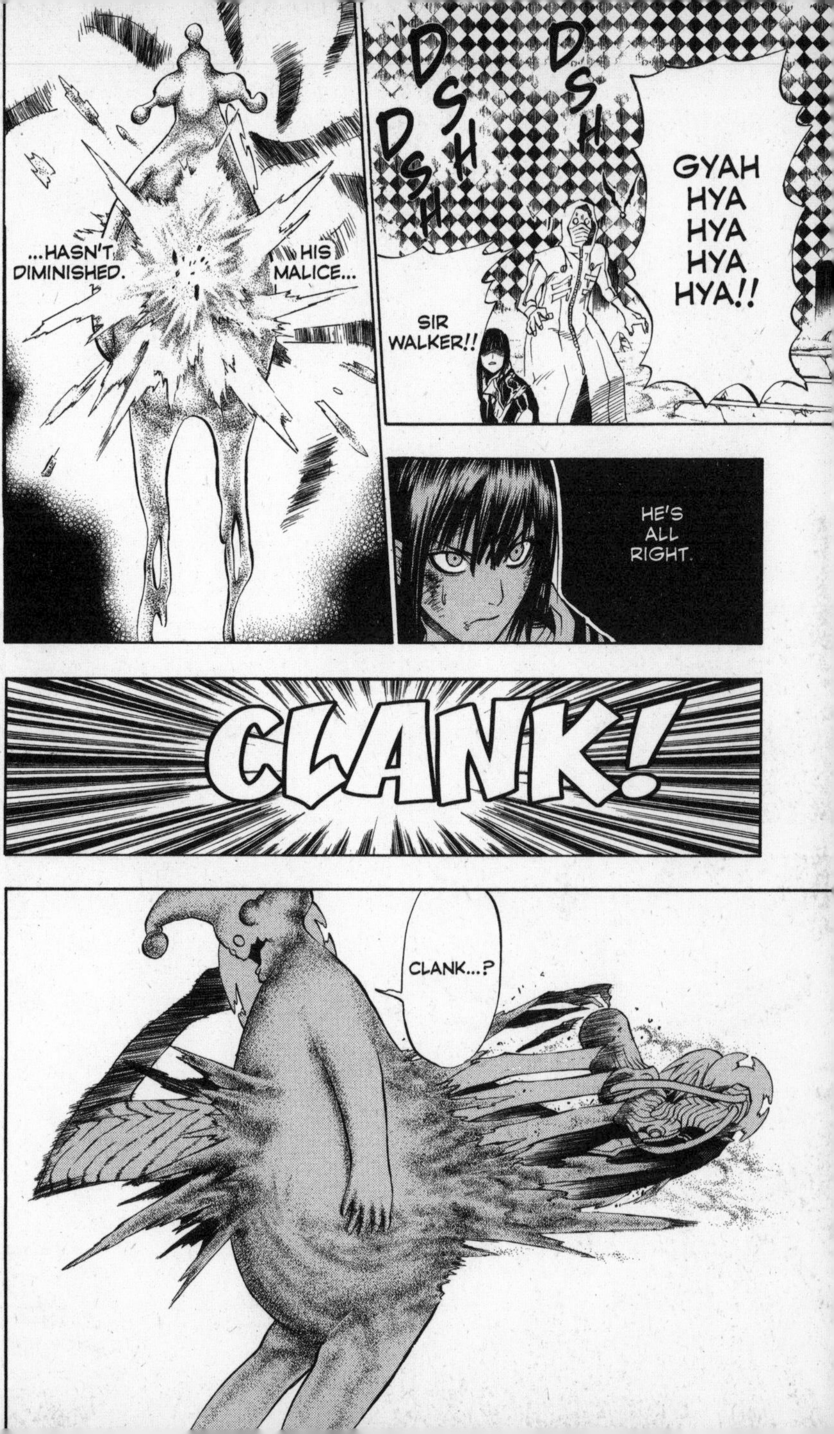
DSH DSH DSH
GYAH HYA HYA HYA HYA!!
SIR WALKER!!
HE'S ALL RIGHT.
HIS MALICE...
...HASN'T DIMINISHED.
CLANK!
CLANK...?

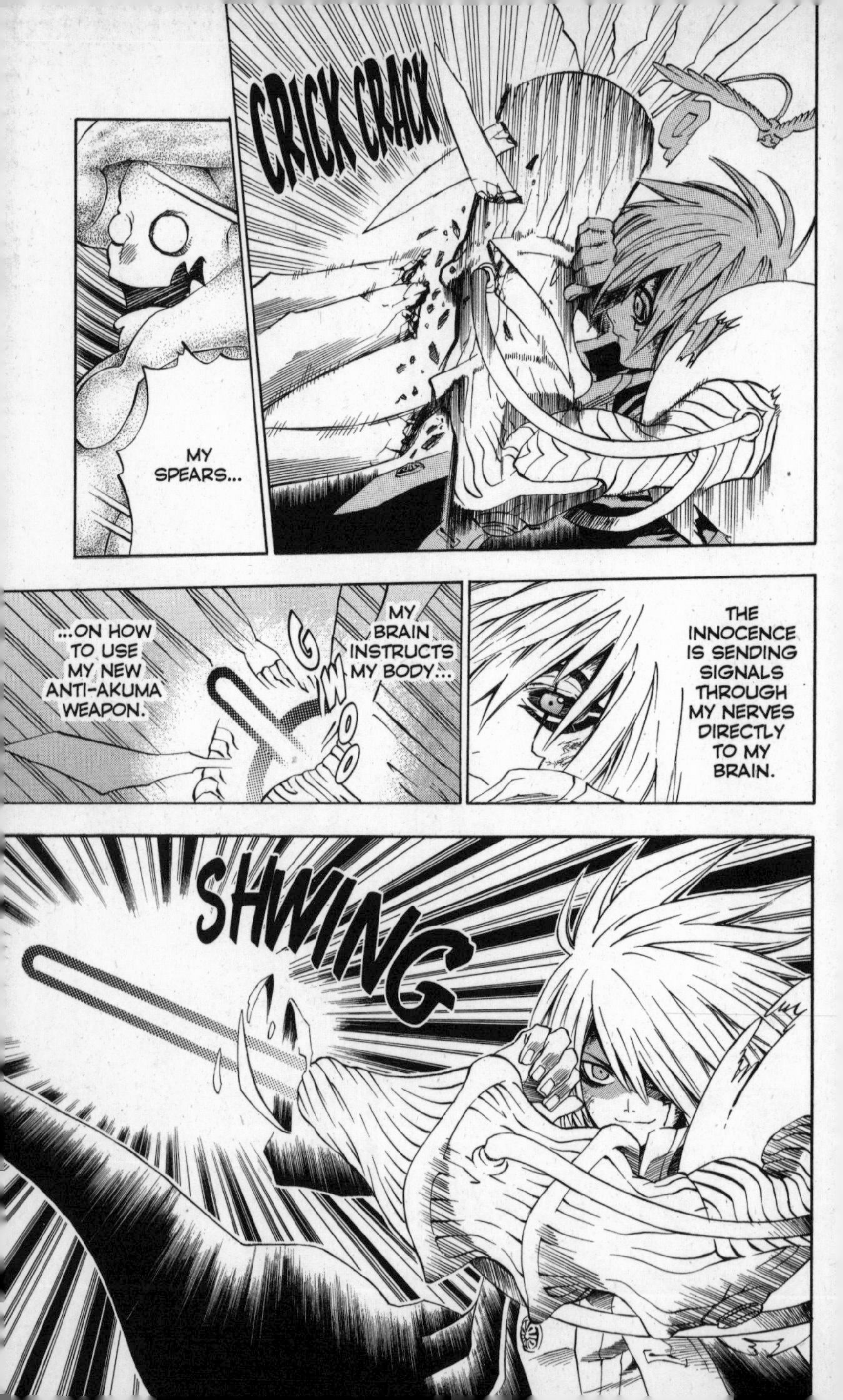
CRICK CRACK
MY SPEARS...
THE INNOCENCE IS SENDING SIGNALS THROUGH MY NERVES DIRECTLY TO MY BRAIN.
MY BRAIN INSTRUCTS MY BODY...
...ON HOW TO USE MY NEW ANTI-AKUMA WEAPON.
SHWING

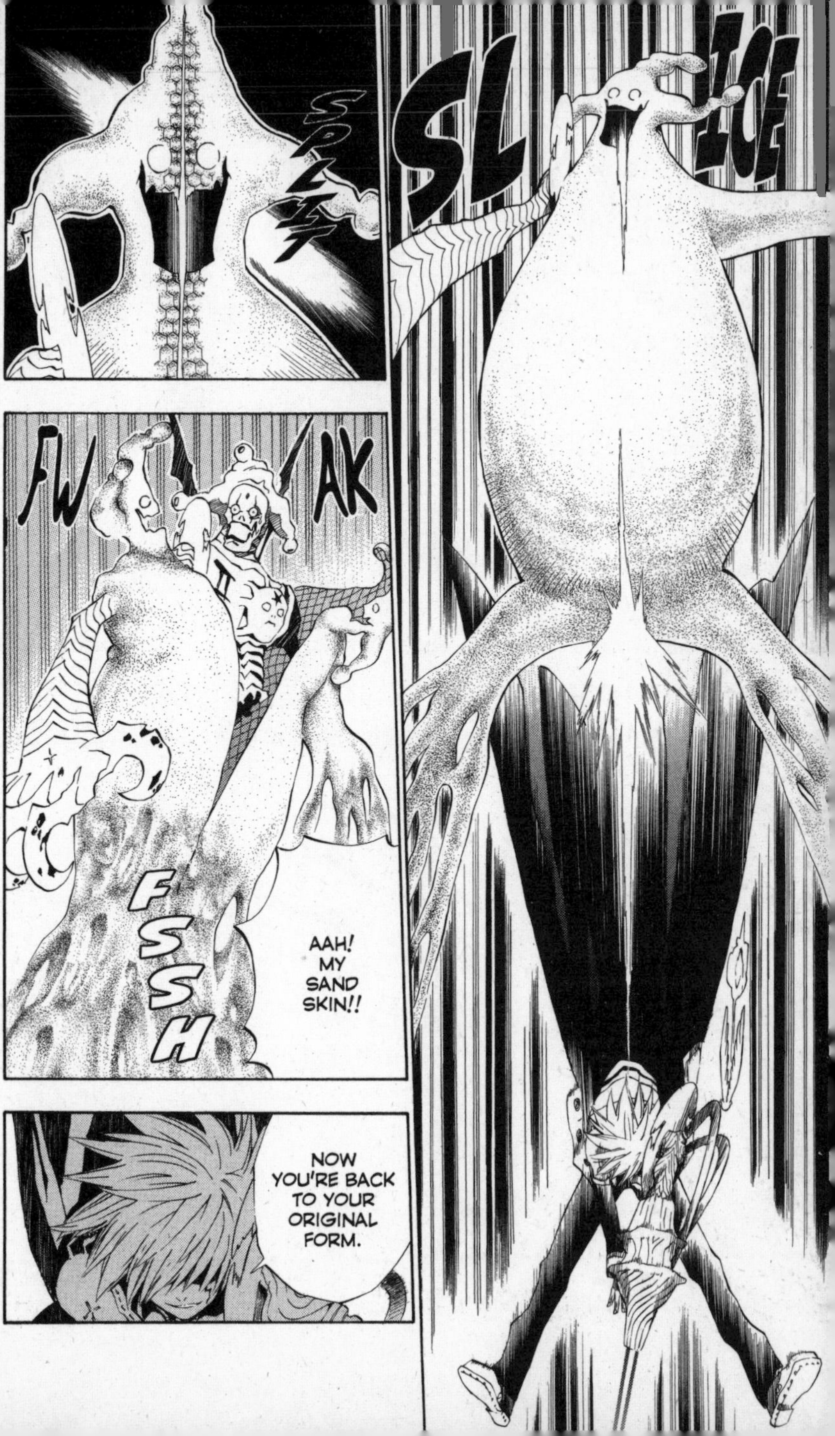
SLICE
SPLIT
FWAK
FSSH
AAH! MY SAND SKIN!!
NOW YOU'RE BACK TO YOUR ORIGINAL FORM.

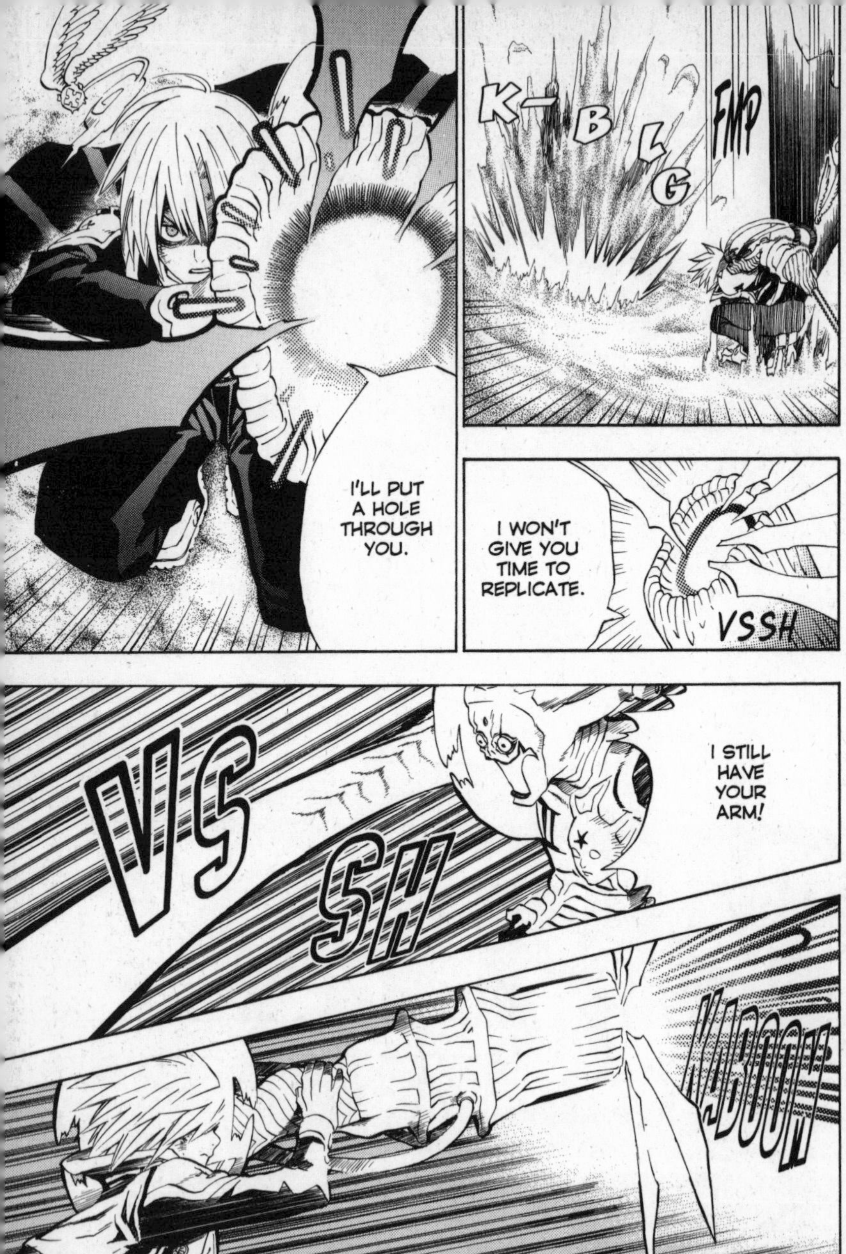
K-BLG
FMP
I WON'T GIVE YOU TIME TO REPLICATE.
VSSH
I'LL PUT A HOLE THROUGH YOU.
I STILL HAVE YOUR ARM!
VSSH
KABOOM

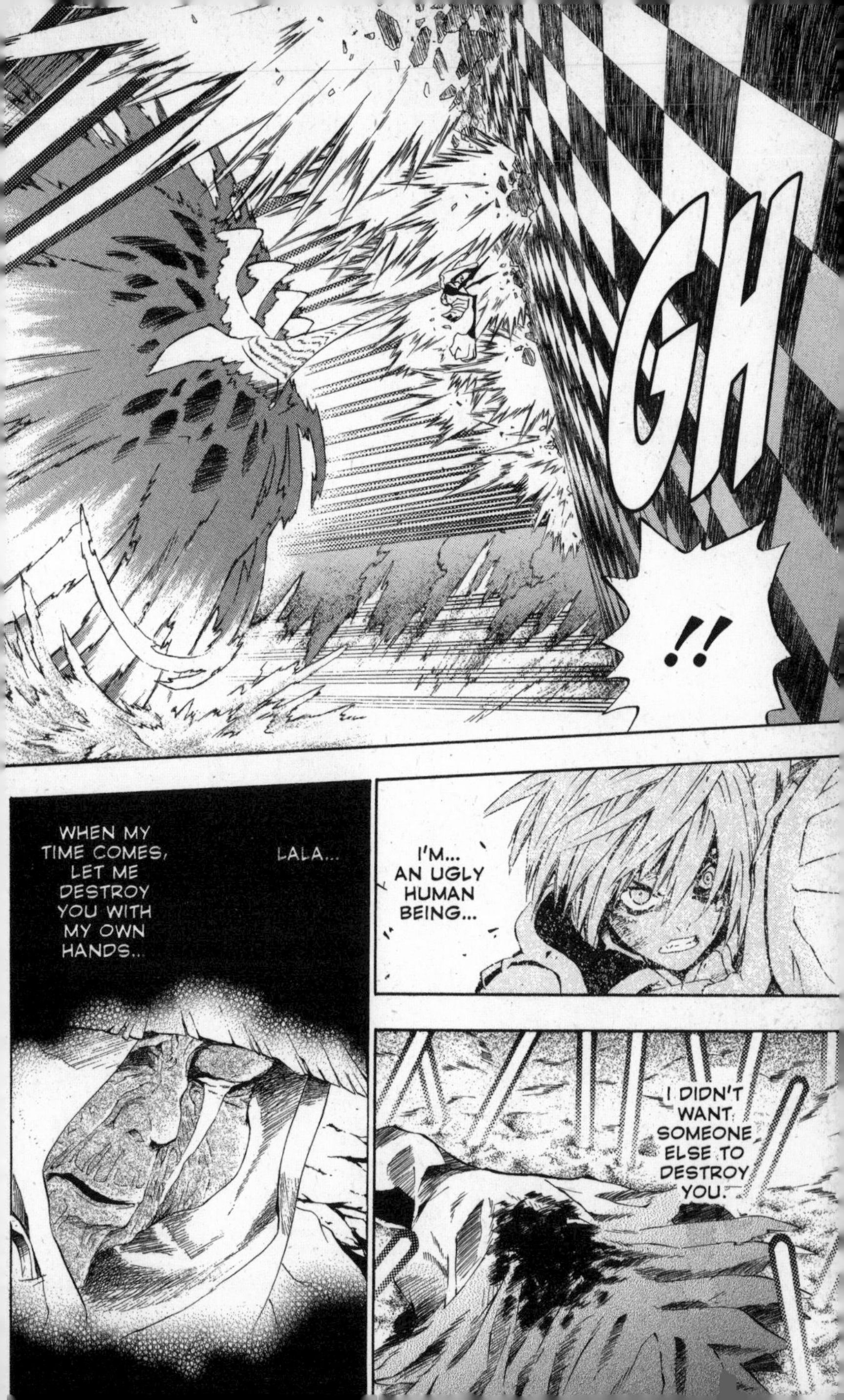
GH
!!
I'M... AN UGLY HUMAN BEING...
I DIDN'T WANT SOMEONE ELSE TO DESTROY YOU.
LALA...
WHEN MY TIME COMES, LET ME DESTROY YOU WITH MY OWN HANDS..

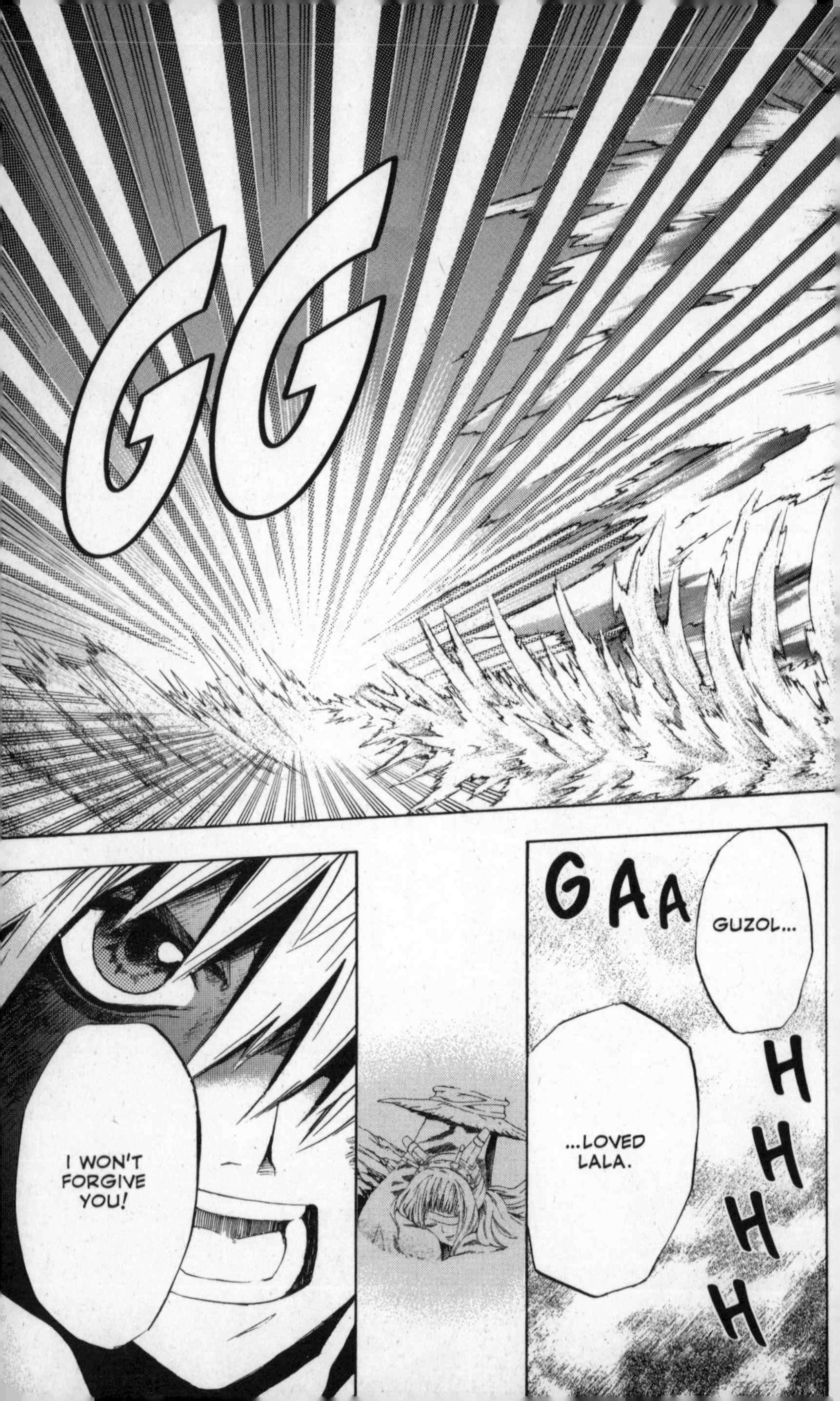
GG
GUZOL...
...LOVED LALA.
GAAHHHH
I WON'T FORGIVE YOU!

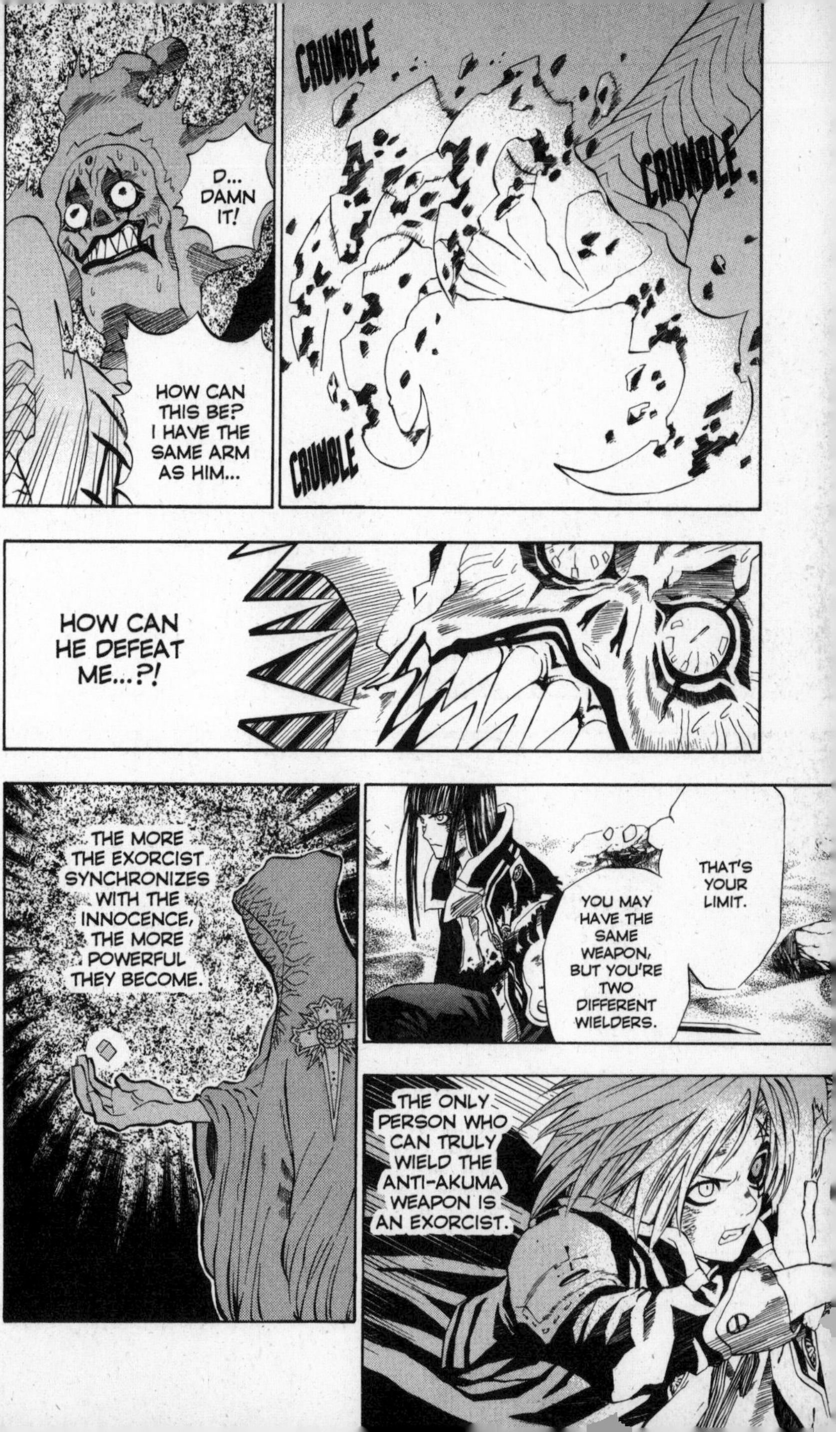
CRUMBLE
CRUMBLE
CRUMBLE
D... DAMN IT!
HOW CAN THIS BE? I HAVE THE SAME ARM AS HIM...
HOW CAN HE DEFEAT ME...?!
THAT'S YOUR LIMIT.
YOU MAY HAVE THE SAME WEAPON, BUT YOU'RE TWO DIFFERENT WIELDERS.
THE ONLY PERSON WHO CAN TRULY WIELD THE ANTI-AKUMA WEAPON IS AN EXORCIST.
THE MORE THE EXORCIST SYNCHRONIZES WITH THE INNOCENCE, THE MORE POWERFUL THEY BECOME.

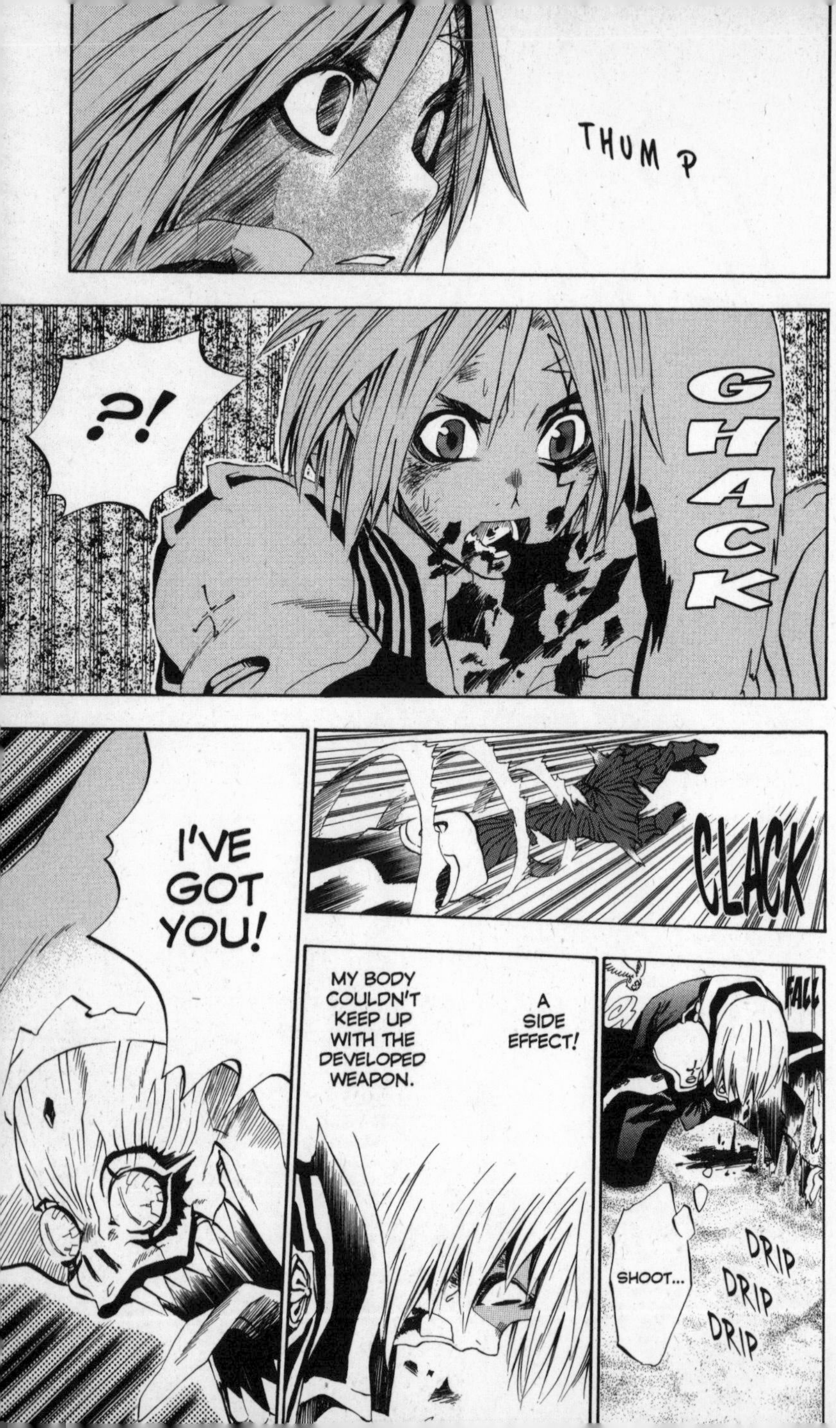
THUMP
?!
GHACK
CLACK
FALL
SHOOT...
DRIP
DRIP
DRIP
MY BODY COULDN'T KEEP UP WITH THE DEVELOPED WEAPON.
A SIDE EFFECT!
I'VE GOT YOU!

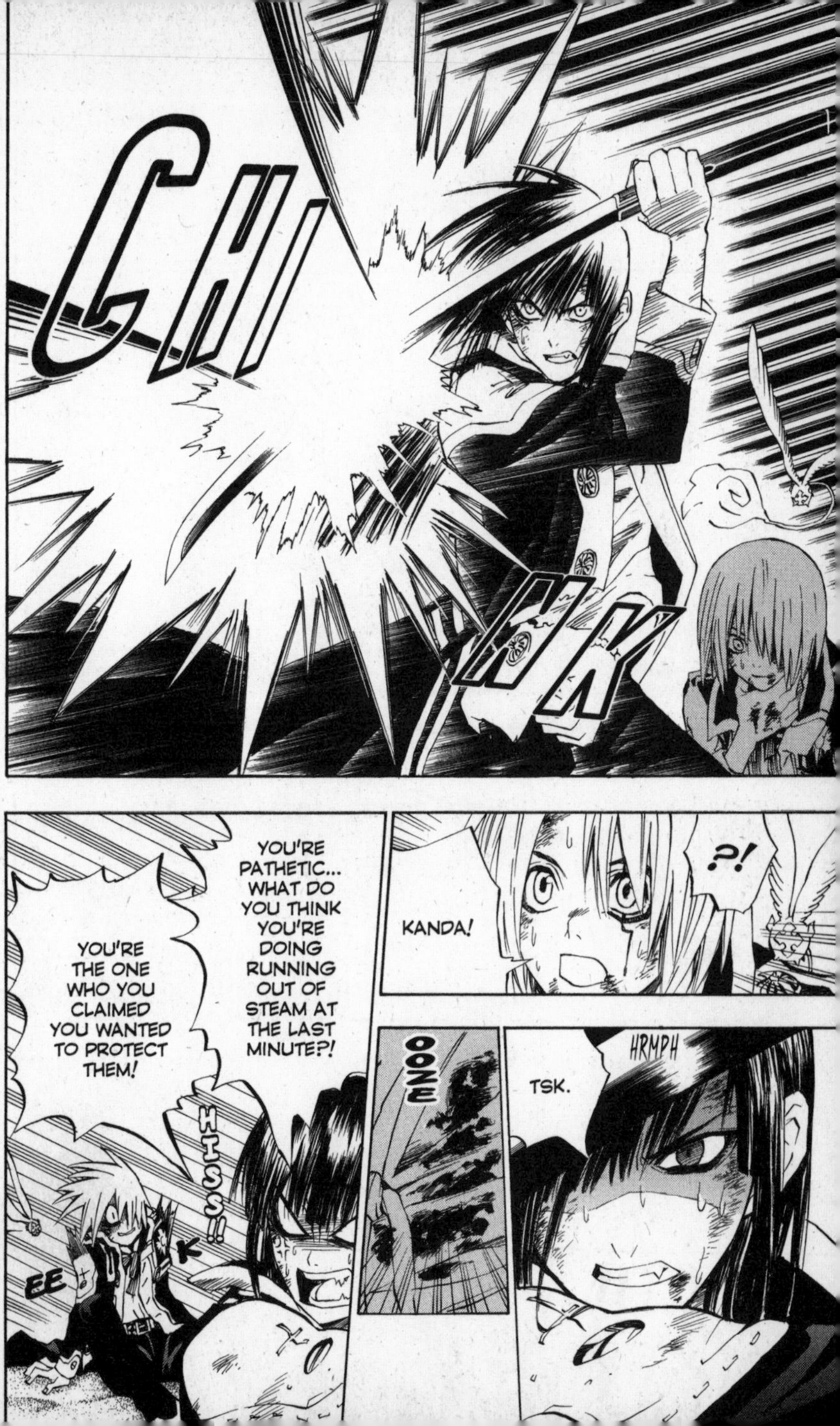
CHINK
?!
KANDA!
HRMPH
TSK.
OOZE
YOU'RE PATHETIC... WHAT DO YOU THINK YOU'RE DOING RUNNING OUT OF STEAM AT THE LAST MINUTE?!
YOU'RE THE ONE WHO YOU CLAIMED YOU WANTED TO PROTECT THEM!
HISS!!
K
EE

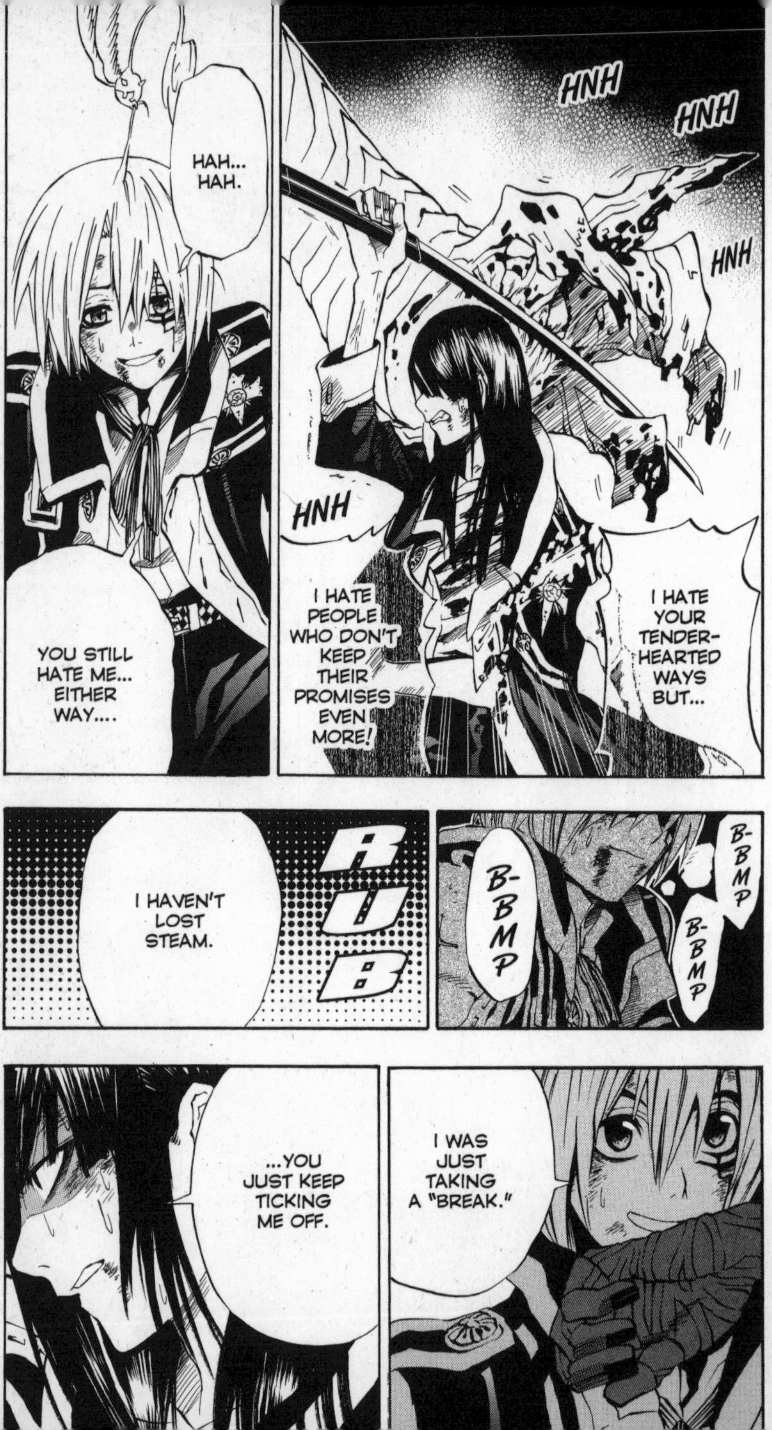
HNH
HNH
HNH
HNH
I HATE YOUR TENDER-HEARTED WAYS BUT...
I HATE PEOPLE WHO DON'T KEEP THEIR PROMISES EVEN MORE!
HAH... HAH.
YOU STILL HATE ME... EITHER WAY....
B-BMP
B-BMP
B-BMP
RUB
I HAVEN'T LOST STEAM.
I WAS JUST TAKING A "BREAK."
...YOU JUST KEEP TICKING ME OFF.

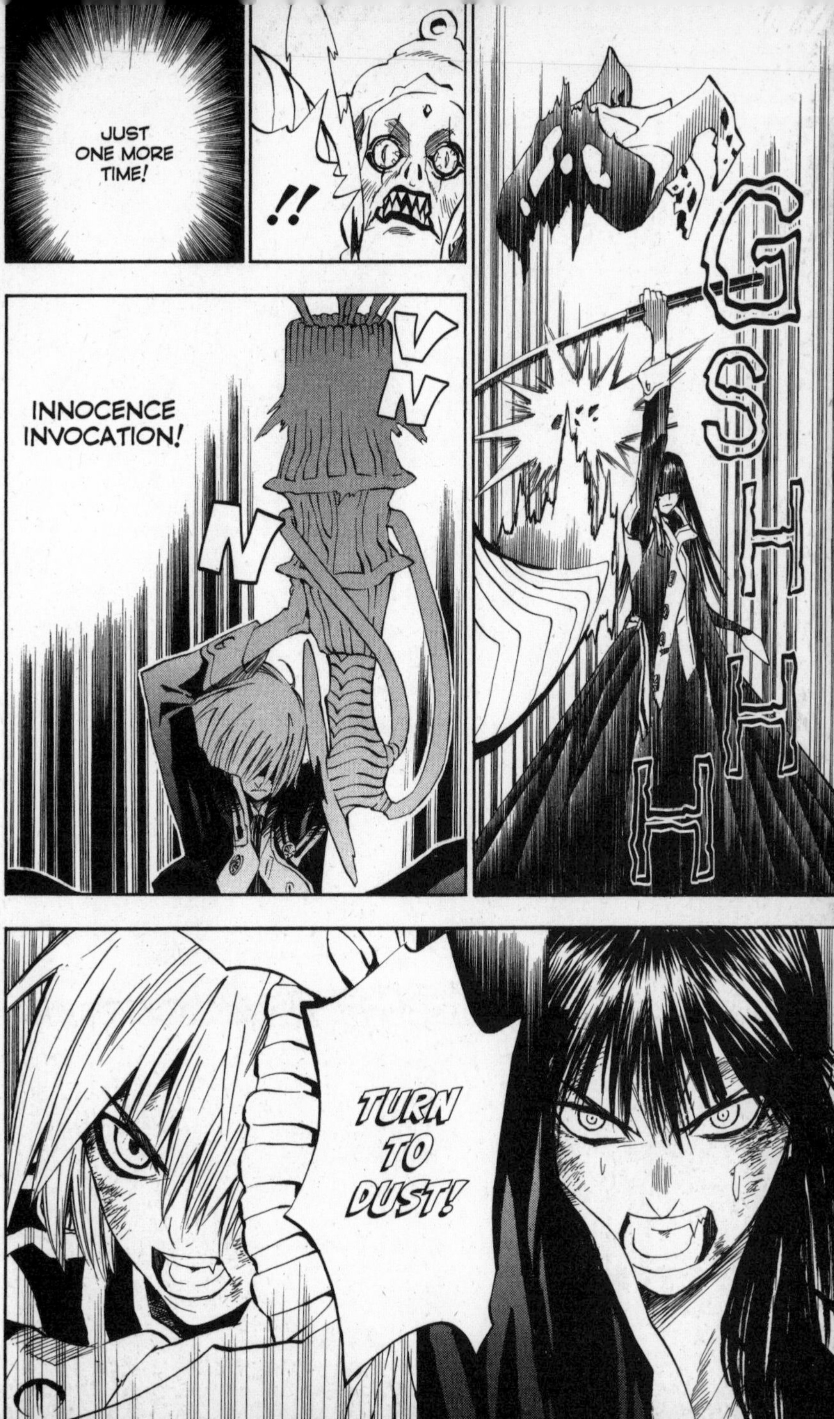
GSHHHH
!!
JUST ONE MORE TIME!
INNOCENCE INVOCATION!
VNN
TURN TO DUST!

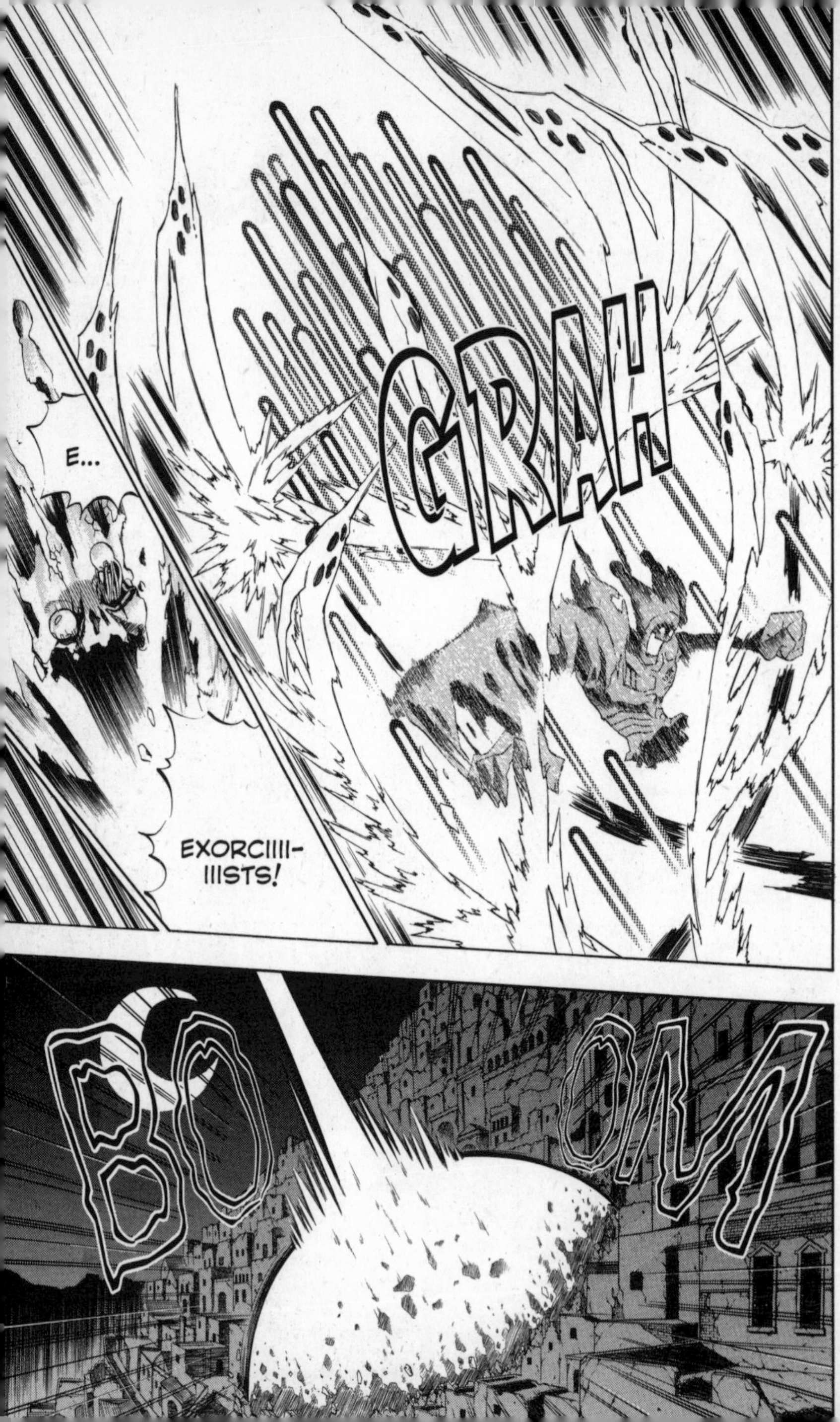
GRAH
E...
EXORCIIIII-
IIISTS!
BOOM

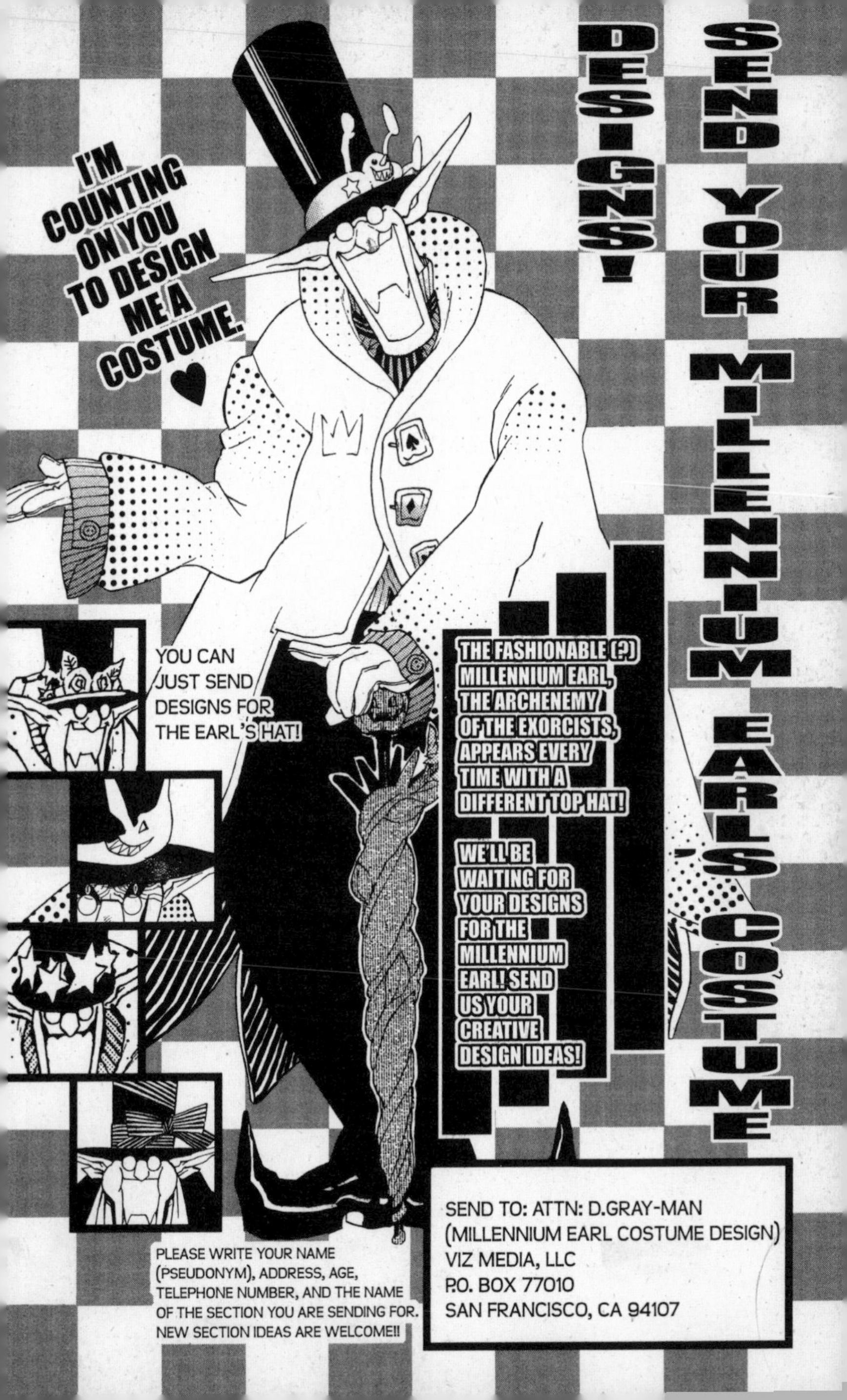
SEND YOUR MILLENNIUM EARL'S COSTUME DESIGNS!
I'M COUNTING ON YOU TO DESIGN ME A COSTUME. ♥
THE FASHIONABLE (?) MILLENNIUM EARL, THE ARCHENEMY OF THE EXORCISTS, APPEARS EVERY TIME WITH A DIFFERENT TOP HAT!
WE'LL BE WAITING FOR YOUR DESIGNS FOR THE MILLENNIUM EARL! SEND US YOUR CREATIVE DESIGN IDEAS!
YOU CAN JUST SEND DESIGNS FOR THE EARL'S HAT!
SEND TO: ATTN: D.GRAY-MAN
(MILLENNIUM EARL COSTUME DESIGN)
VIZ MEDIA, LLC
P.O. BOX 77010
SAN FRANCISCO, CA 94107
PLEASE WRITE YOUR NAME (PSEUDONYM), ADDRESS, AGE, TELEPHONE NUMBER, AND THE NAME OF THE SECTION YOU ARE SENDING FOR. NEW SECTION IDEAS ARE WELCOME!!

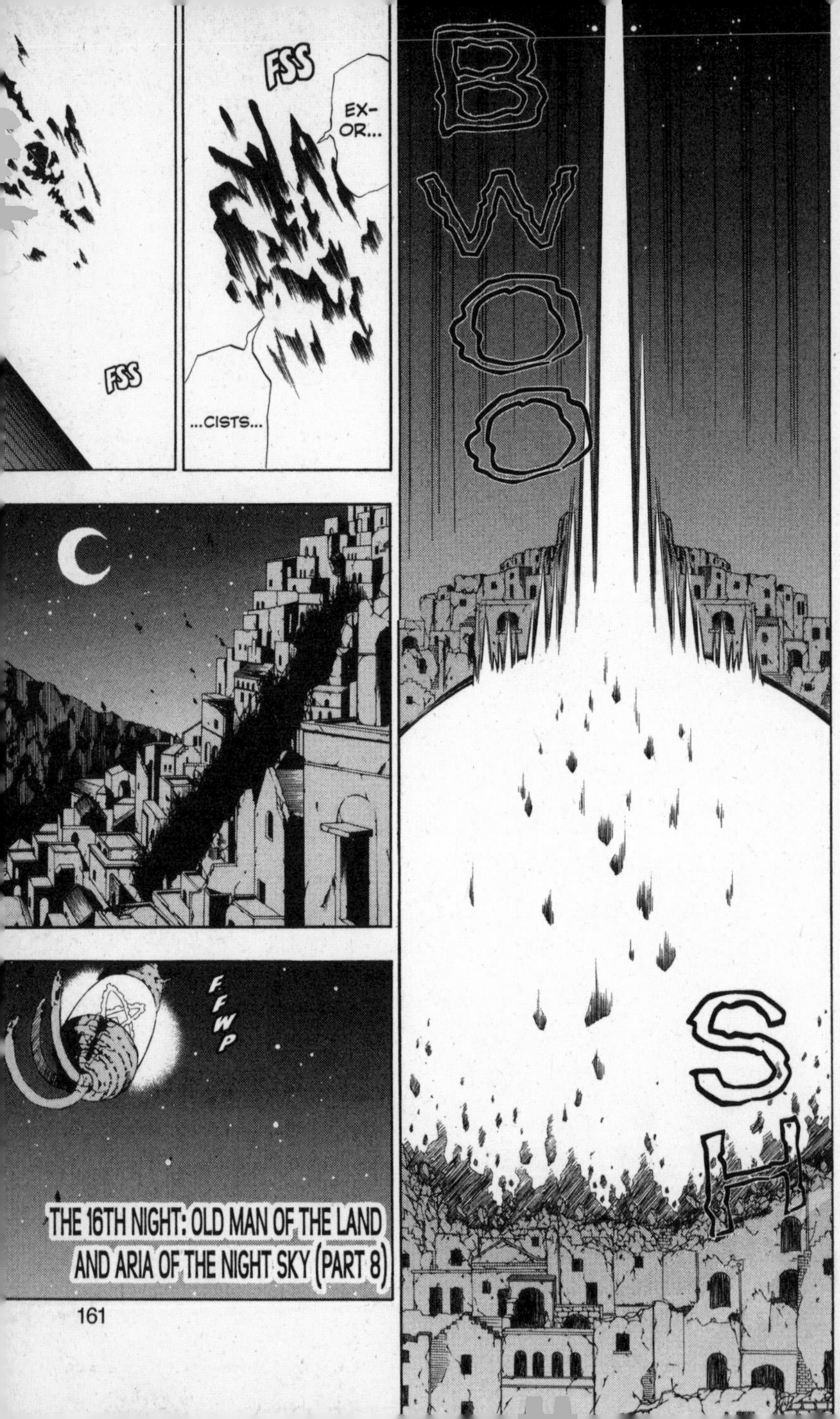
BWOOSH
FSS
EX-OR...
...CISTS...
FSS
FFWP
THE 16TH NIGHT: OLD MAN OF THE LAND AND ARIA OF THE NIGHT SKY (PART 8)

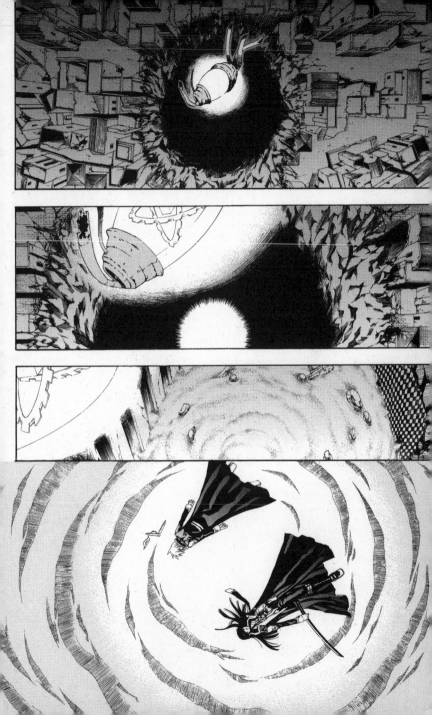

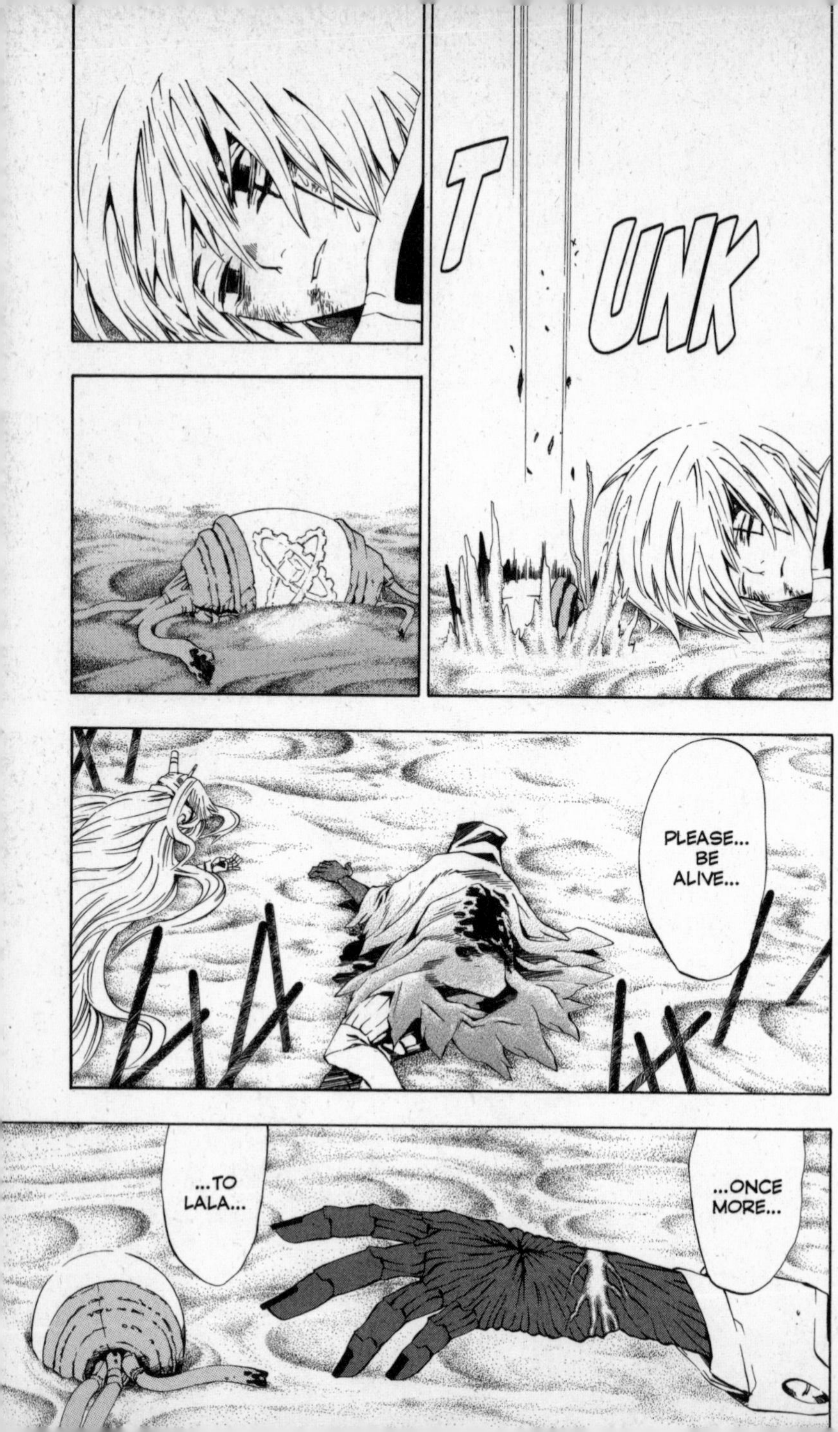
TUNK
PLEASE... BE ALIVE...
...ONCE MORE...
...TO LALA...

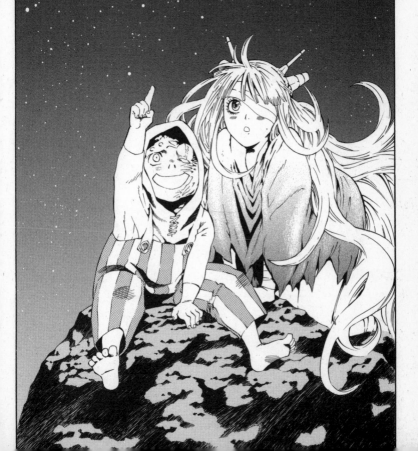

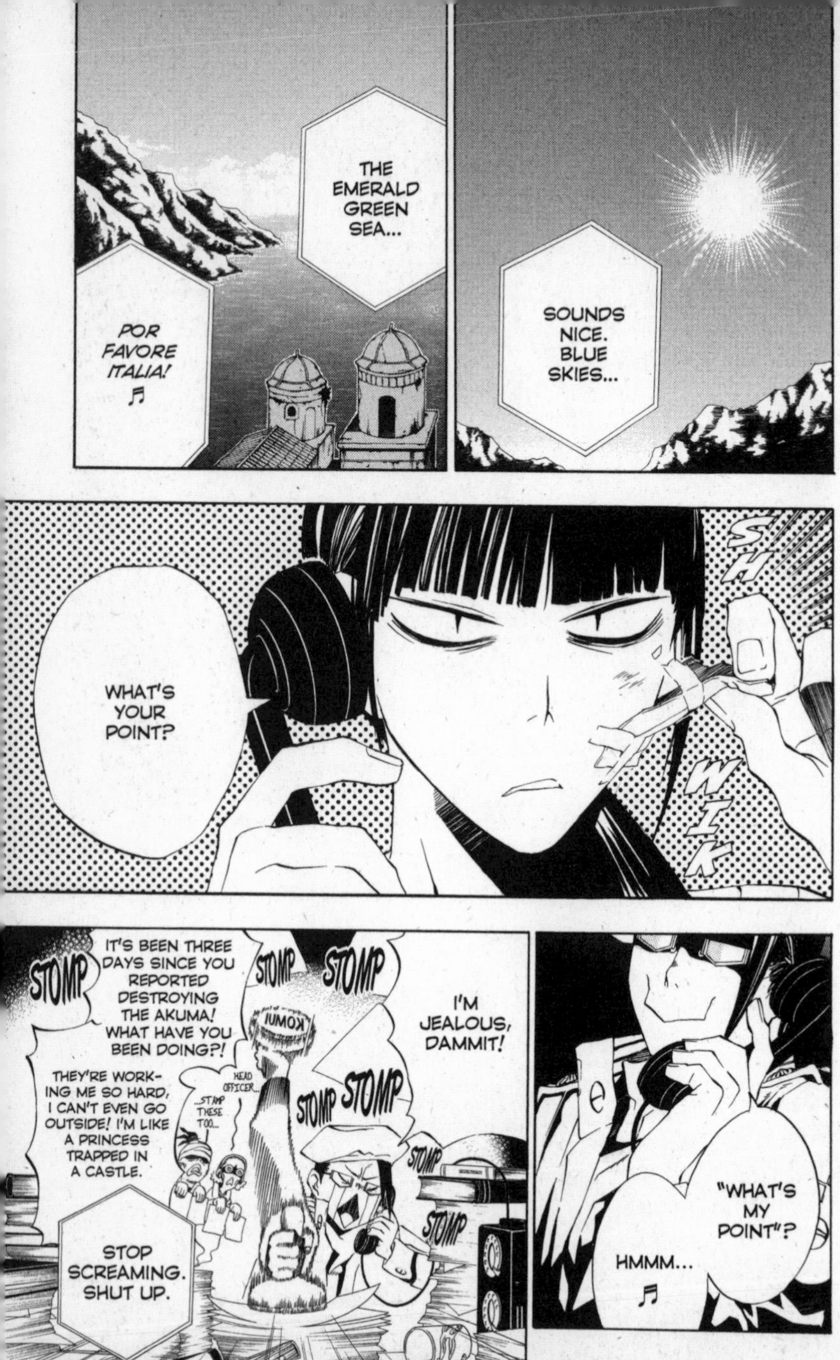
SOUNDS NICE. BLUE SKIES...
THE EMERALD GREEN SEA...
POR FAVORE ITALIA! ♫
SH
WIK
WHAT'S YOUR POINT?
"WHAT'S MY POINT"?
HMMM... ♫
I'M JEALOUS, DAMMIT!
STOMP
STOMP
IT'S BEEN THREE DAYS SINCE YOU REPORTED DESTROYING THE AKUMA! WHAT HAVE YOU BEEN DOING?!
STOMP
KOMUI
STOMP
STOMP
HEAD OFFICER...
...STAMP THESE TOO...
THEY'RE WORKING ME SO HARD, I CAN'T EVEN GO OUTSIDE! I'M LIKE A PRINCESS TRAPPED IN A CASTLE.
STOMP
STOMP
STOP SCREAMING. SHUT UP.

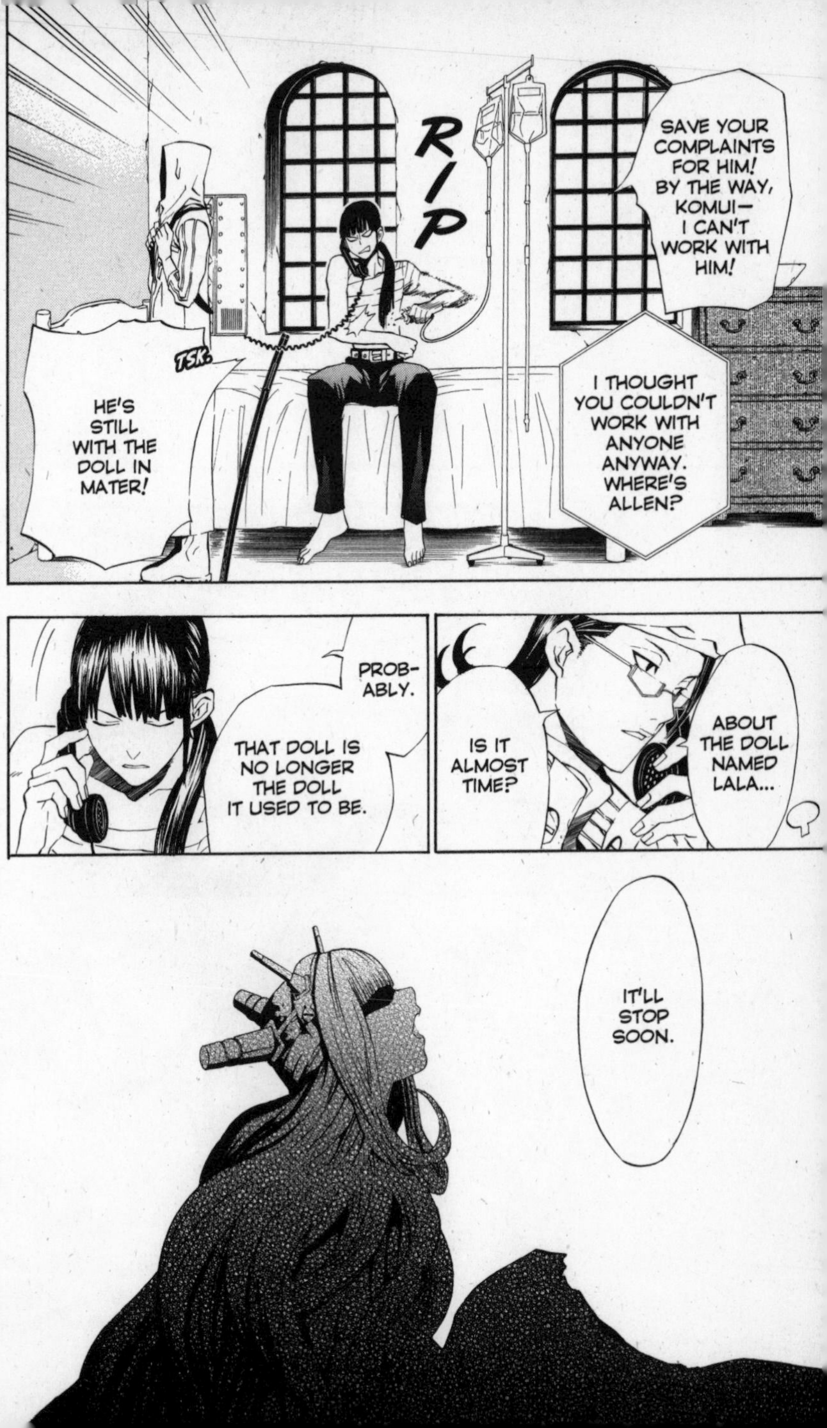
SAVE YOUR COMPLAINTS FOR HIM! BY THE WAY, KOMUI— I CAN'T WORK WITH HIM!
RIP
I THOUGHT YOU COULDN'T WORK WITH ANYONE ANYWAY. WHERE'S ALLEN?
TSK.
HE'S STILL WITH THE DOLL IN MATER!
ABOUT THE DOLL NAMED LALA...
IS IT ALMOST TIME?
PROB-ABLY.
THAT DOLL IS NO LONGER THE DOLL IT USED TO BE.
IT'LL STOP SOON.

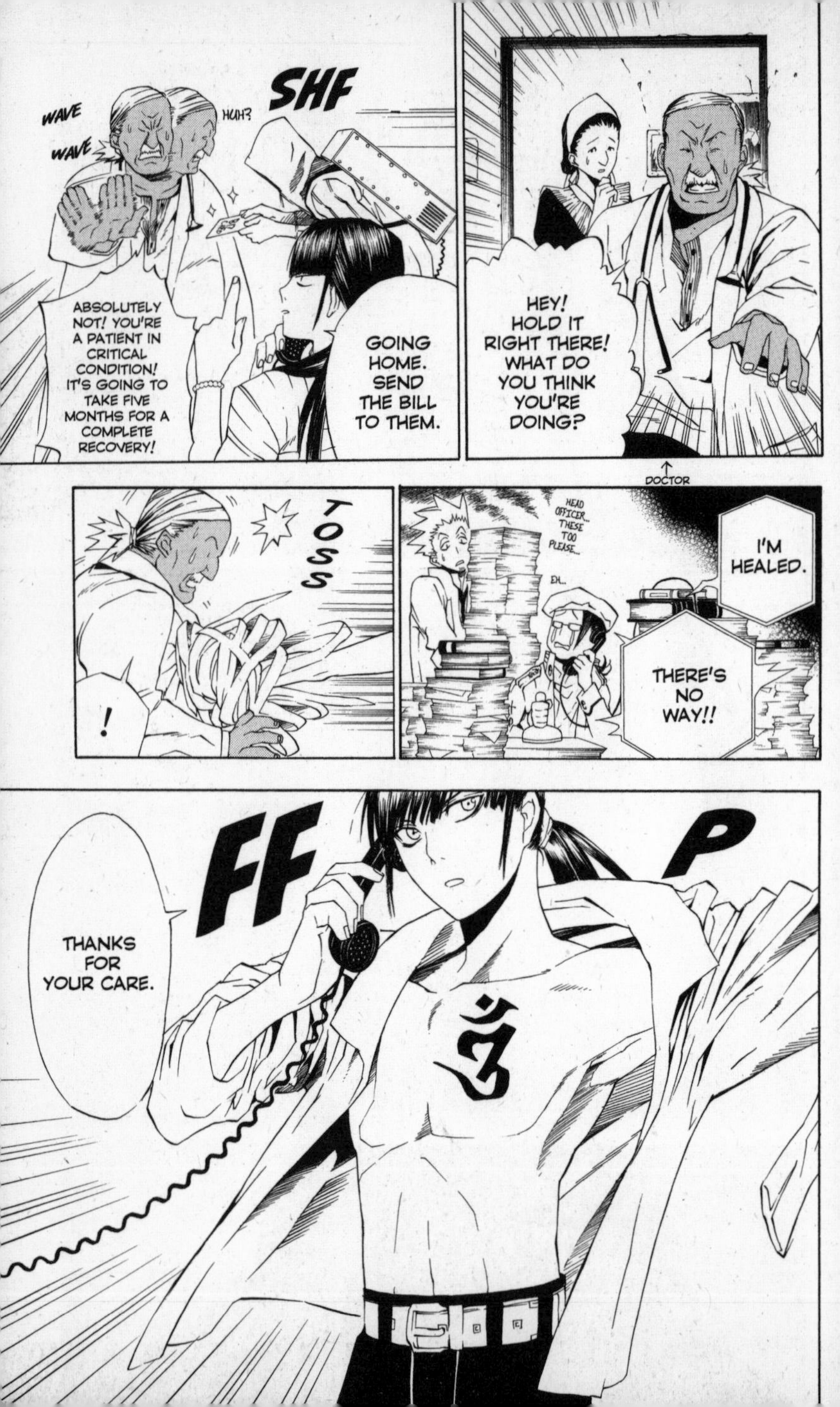
HEY! HOLD IT RIGHT THERE! WHAT DO YOU THINK YOU'RE DOING?
DOCTOR
SHF
GOING HOME. SEND THE BILL TO THEM.
HUH?
WAVE
WAVE
ABSOLUTELY NOT! YOU'RE A PATIENT IN CRITICAL CONDITION! IT'S GOING TO TAKE FIVE MONTHS FOR A COMPLETE RECOVERY!
HEAD OFFICER... THESE TOO PLEASE...
EH...
I'M HEALED.
THERE'S NO WAY!!
TOSS
!
FF
P
THANKS FOR YOUR CARE.

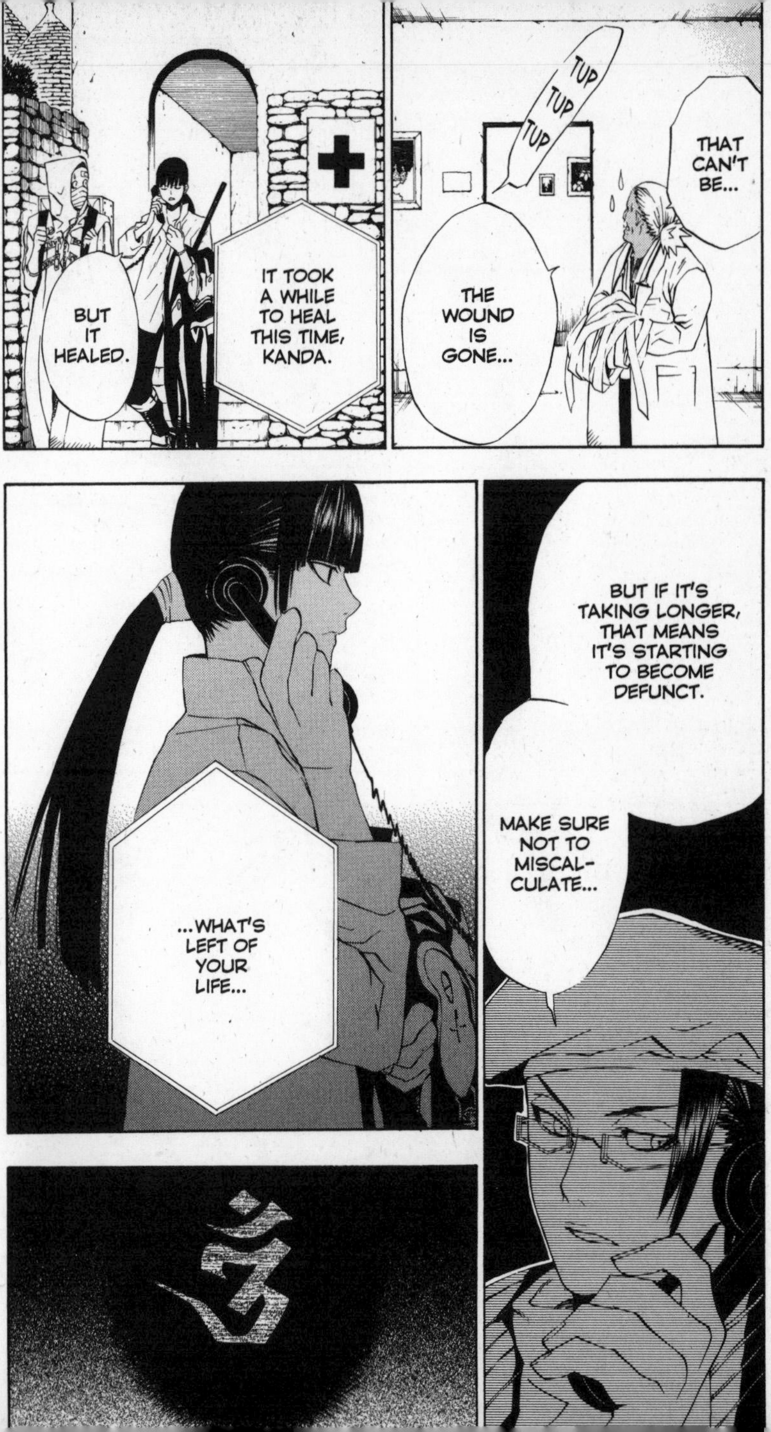
THAT CAN'T BE...
TUP TUP TUP
THE WOUND IS GONE...
IT TOOK A WHILE TO HEAL THIS TIME, KANDA.
BUT IT HEALED.
BUT IF IT'S TAKING LONGER, THAT MEANS IT'S STARTING TO BECOME DEFUNCT.
MAKE SURE NOT TO MISCAL-CULATE...
...WHAT'S LEFT OF YOUR LIFE...

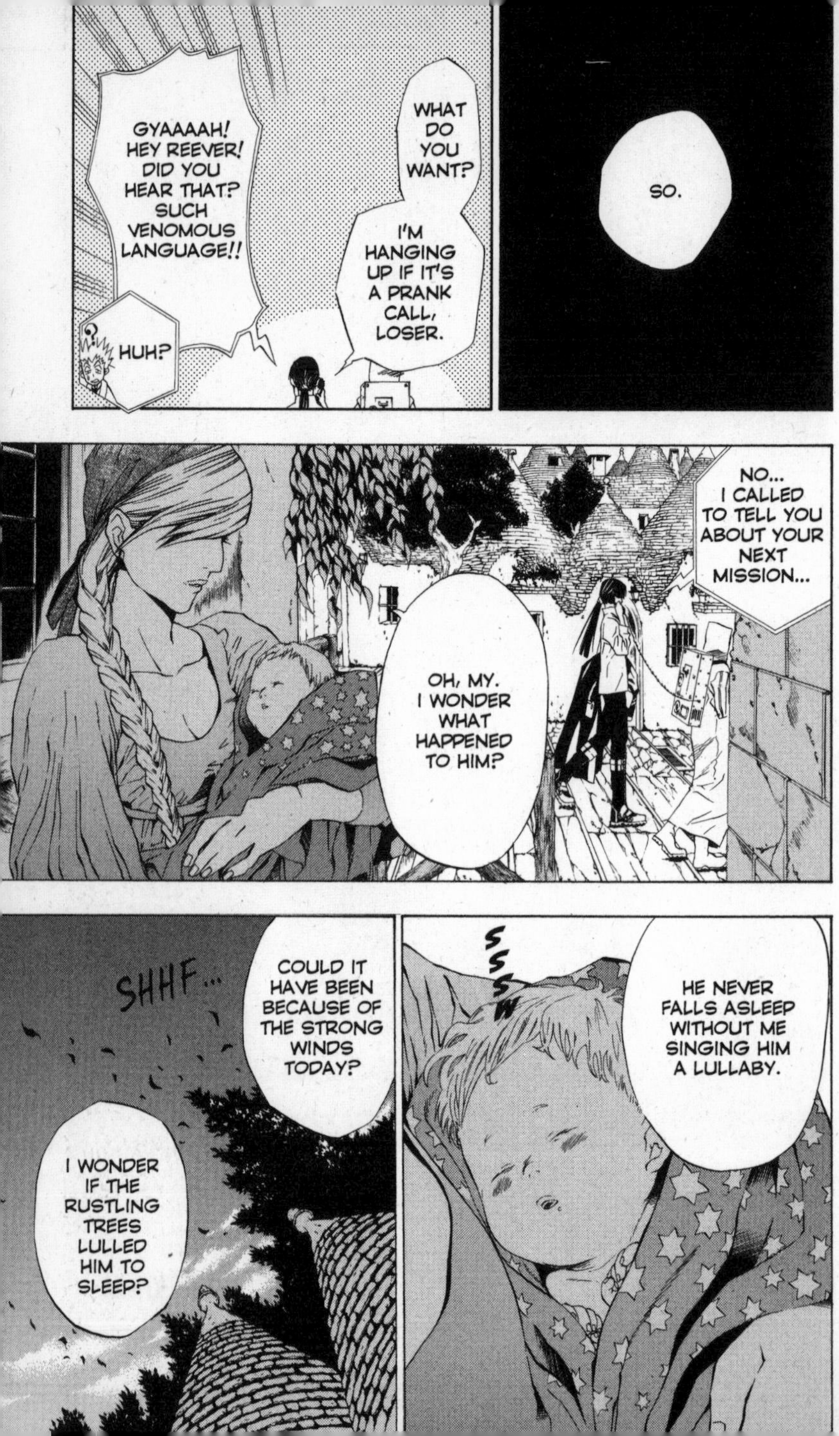
SO.
WHAT DO YOU WANT?
I'M HANGING UP IF IT'S A PRANK CALL, LOSER.
GYAAAAH! HEY REEVER! DID YOU HEAR THAT? SUCH VENOMOUS LANGUAGE!!
HUH?
NO... I CALLED TO TELL YOU ABOUT YOUR NEXT MISSION...
OH, MY. I WONDER WHAT HAPPENED TO HIM?
SSSS
HE NEVER FALLS ASLEEP WITHOUT ME SINGING HIM A LULLABY.
COULD IT HAVE BEEN BECAUSE OF THE STRONG WINDS TODAY?
SHHF...
I WONDER IF THE RUSTLING TREES LULLED HIM TO SLEEP?

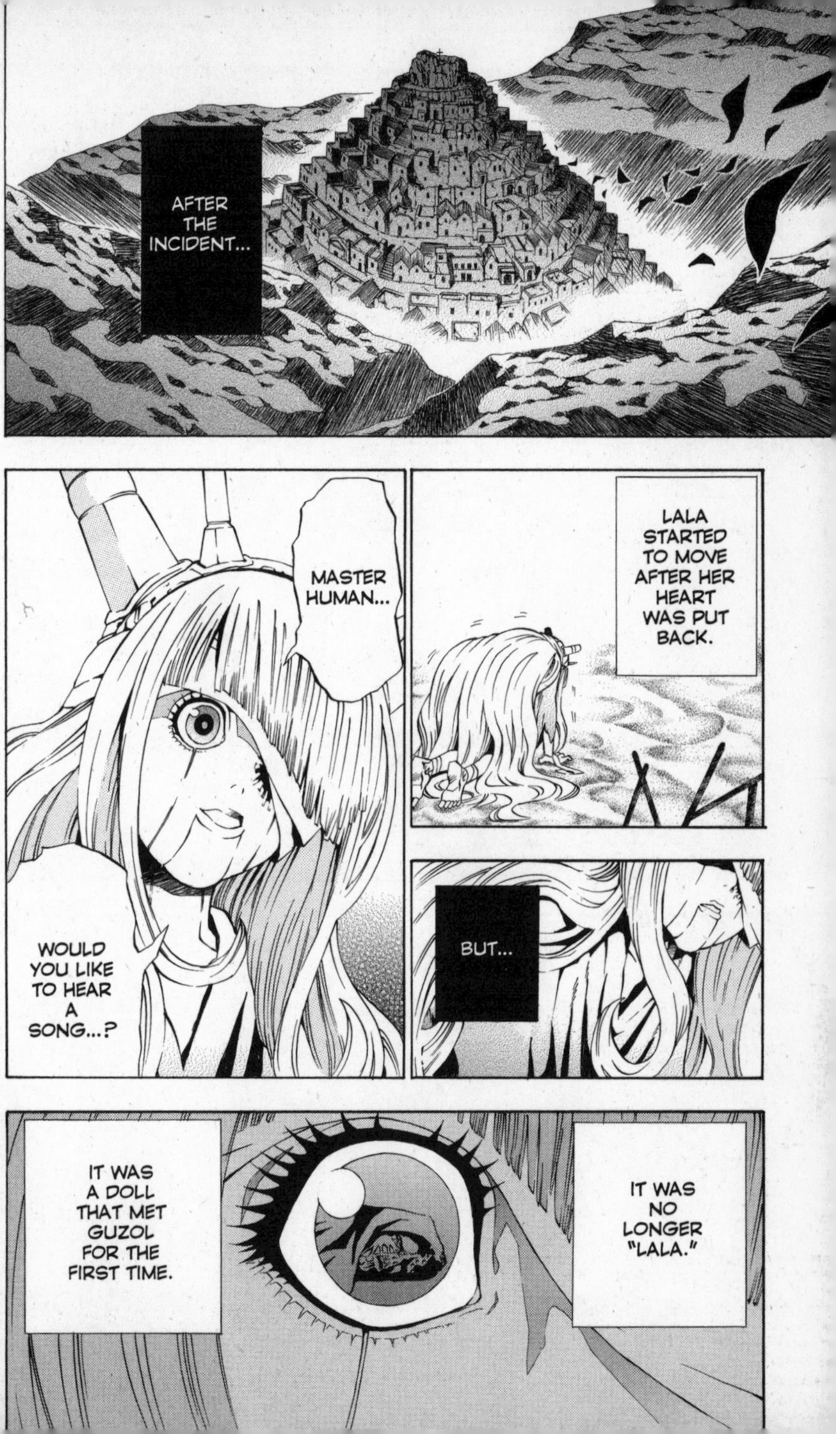
AFTER THE INCIDENT...
LALA STARTED TO MOVE AFTER HER HEART WAS PUT BACK.
BUT...
MASTER HUMAN...
WOULD YOU LIKE TO HEAR A SONG...?
IT WAS NO LONGER "LALA."
IT WAS A DOLL THAT MET GUZOL FOR THE FIRST TIME.

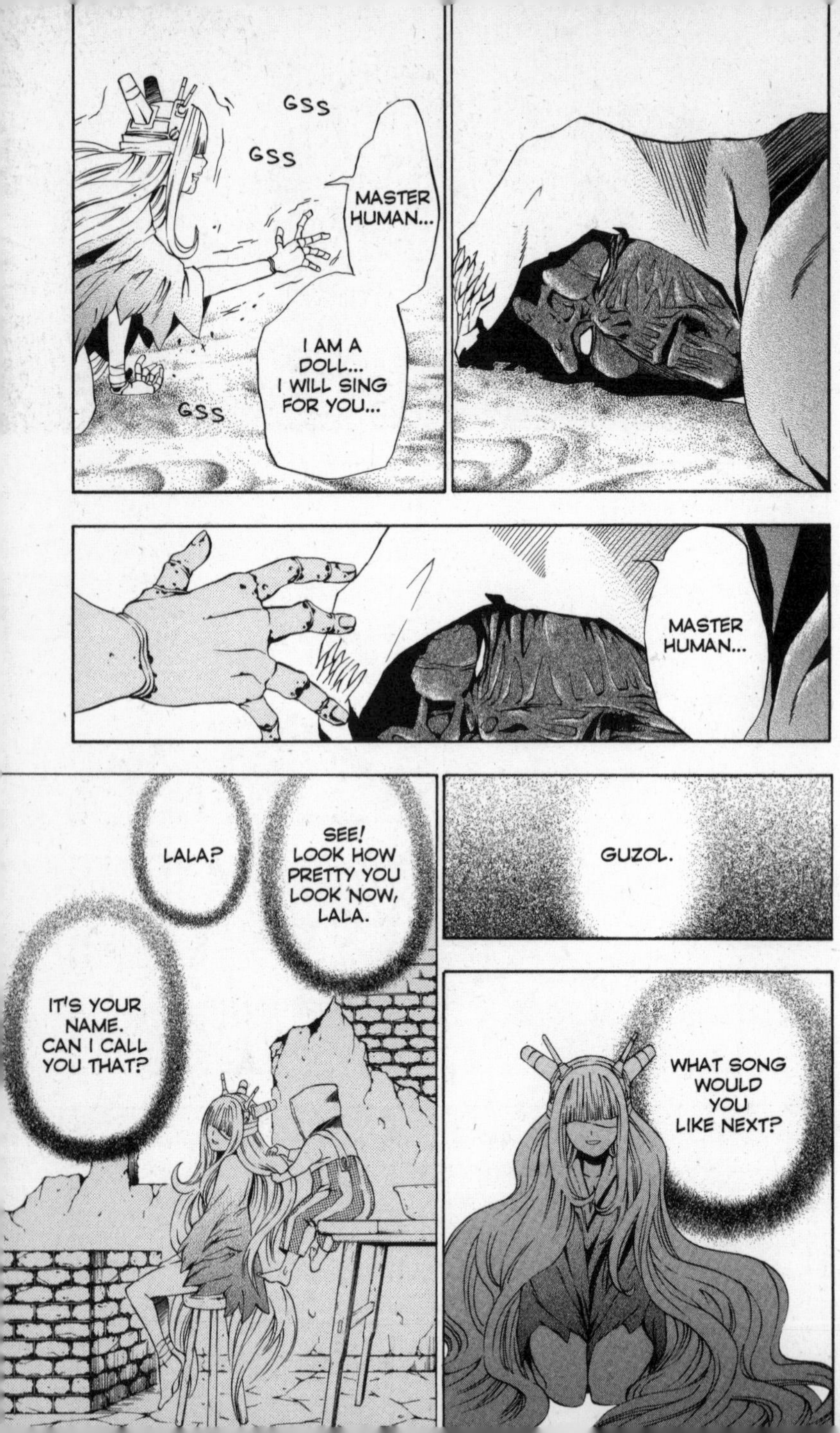
GSS
GSS
MASTER HUMAN...
I AM A DOLL... I WILL SING FOR YOU...
GSS
MASTER HUMAN...
GUZOL.
WHAT SONG WOULD YOU LIKE NEXT?
SEE! LOOK HOW PRETTY YOU LOOK NOW, LALA.
LALA?
IT'S YOUR NAME. CAN I CALL YOU THAT?

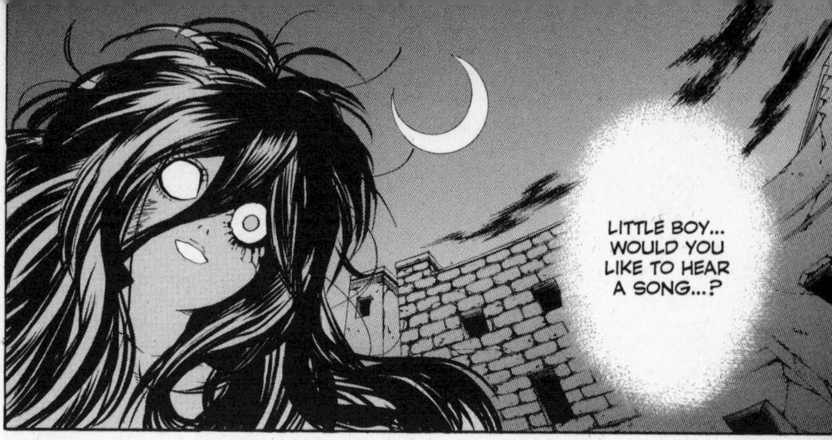
LITTLE BOY... WOULD YOU LIKE TO HEAR A SONG...?

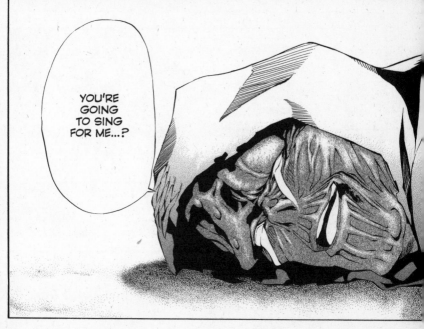

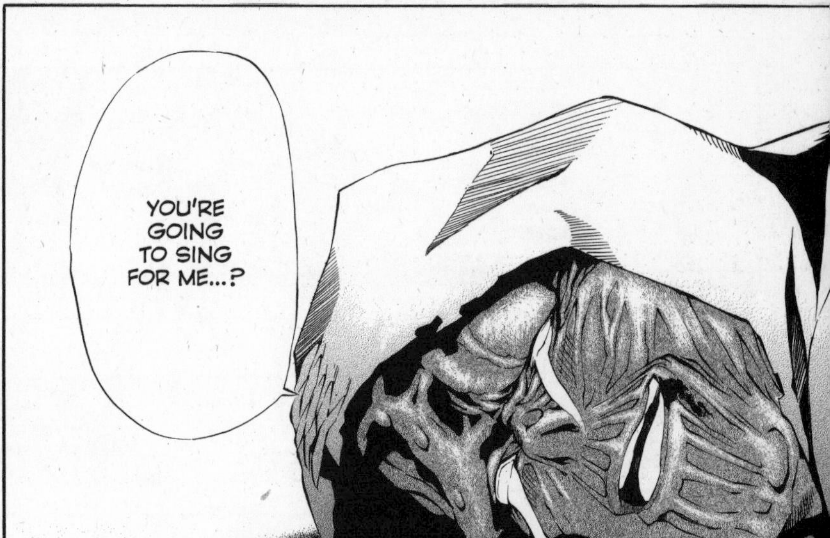
YOU'RE GOING TO SING FOR ME...?

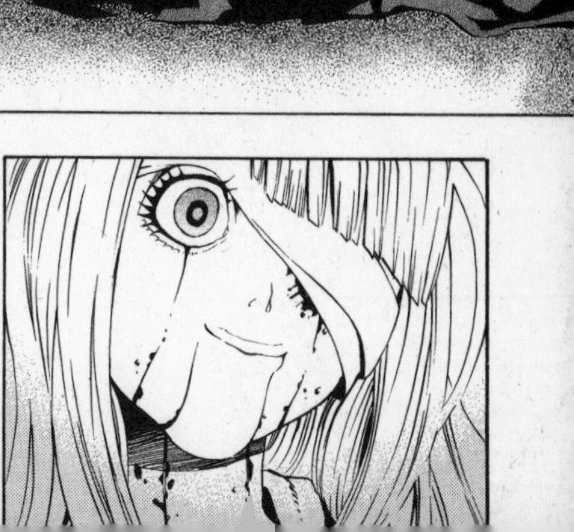

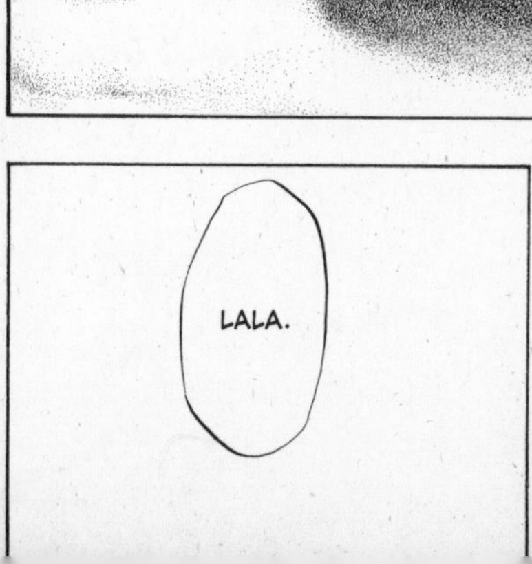
LALA.

READ THIS WAY

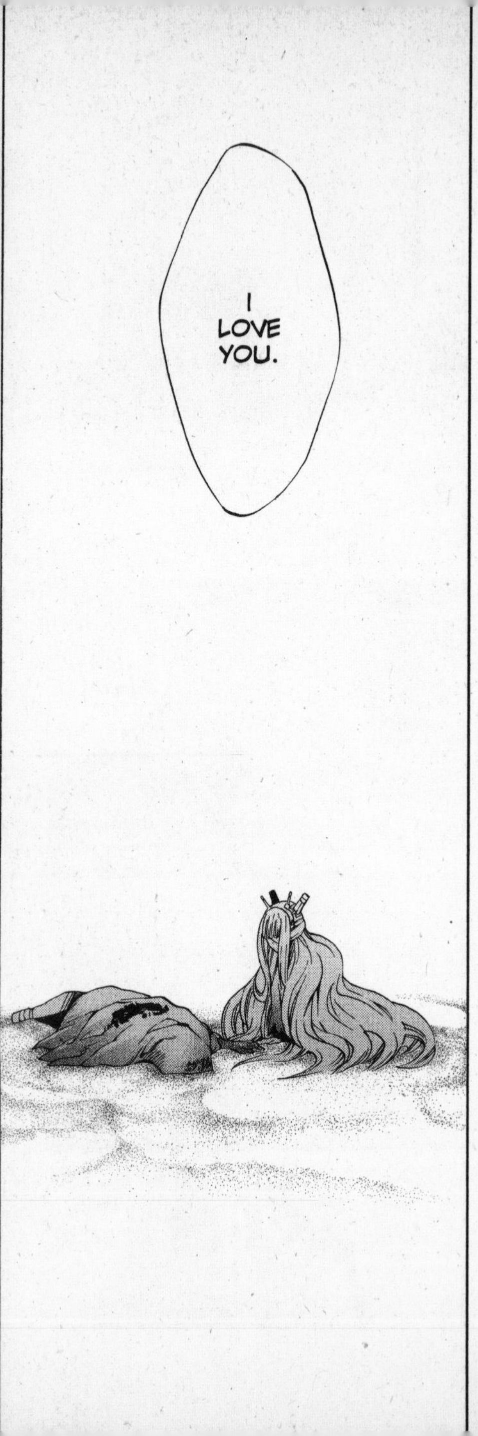
I LOVE YOU.

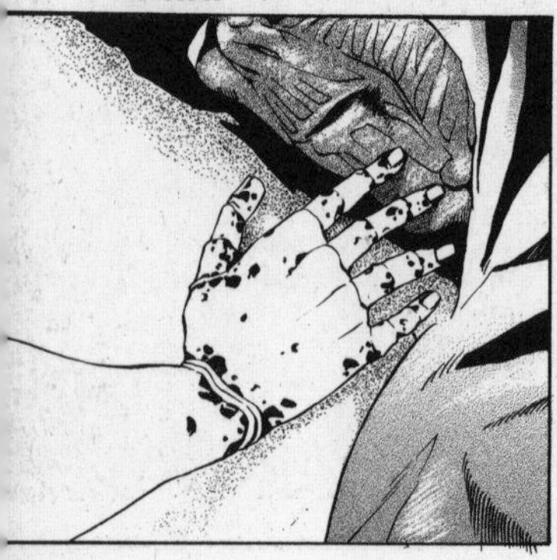

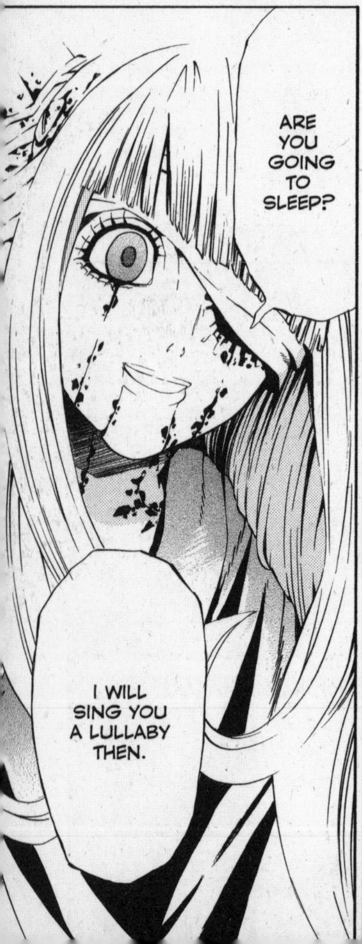
ARE YOU GOING TO SLEEP?
I WILL SING YOU A LULLABY THEN.

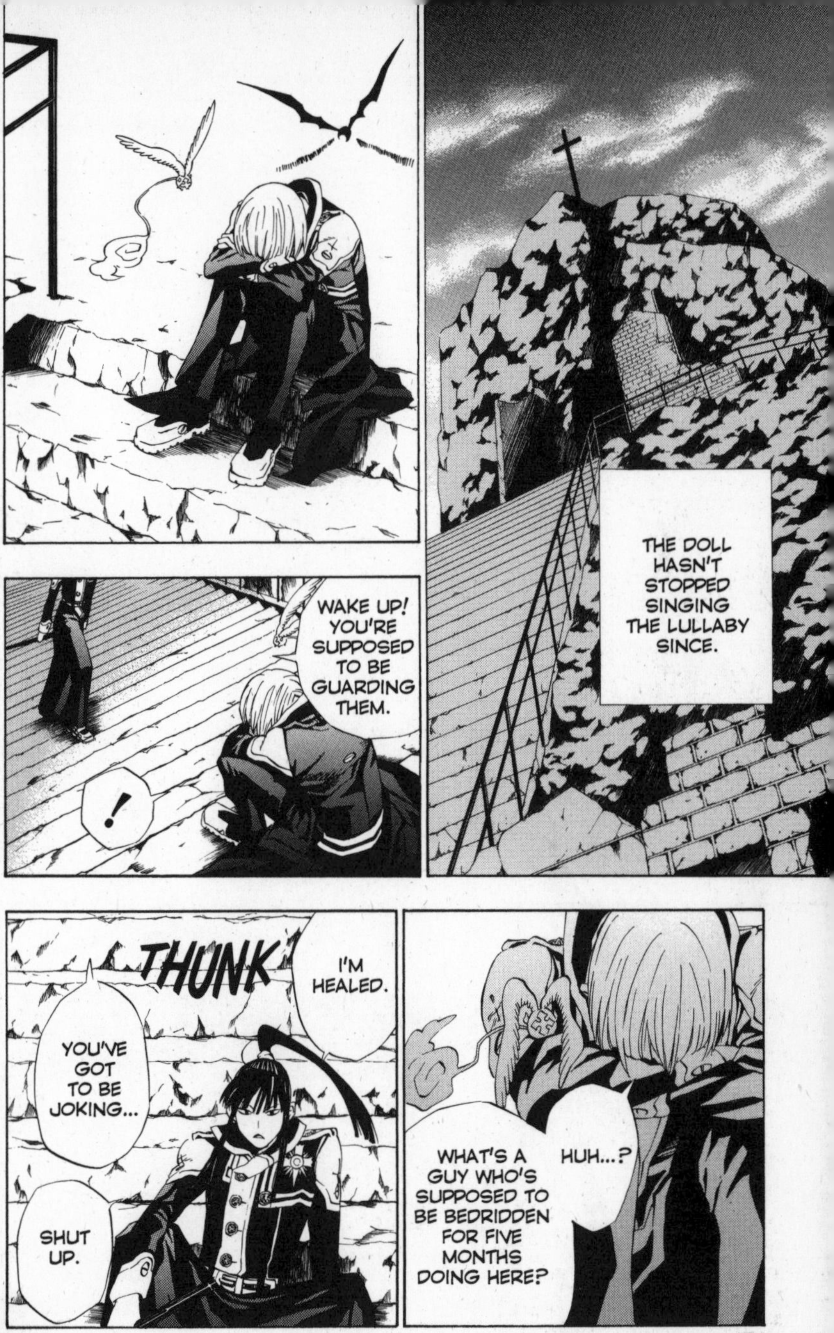
THE DOLL HASN'T STOPPED SINGING THE LULLABY SINCE.
WAKE UP! YOU'RE SUPPOSED TO BE GUARDING THEM.
!
HUH...?
WHAT'S A GUY WHO'S SUPPOSED TO BE BEDRIDDEN FOR FIVE MONTHS DOING HERE?
I'M HEALED.
THUNK
YOU'VE GOT TO BE JOKING...
SHUT UP.

READ THIS WAY

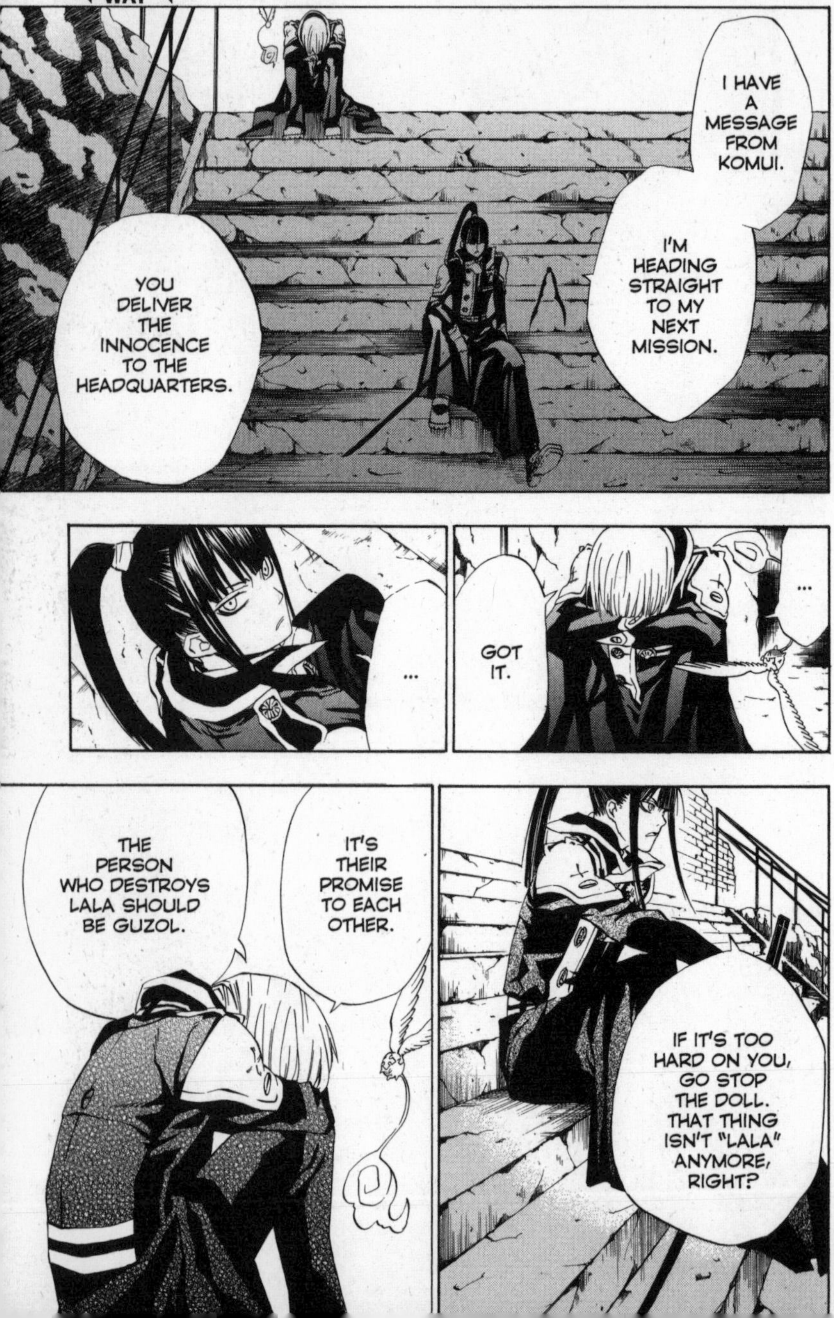
I HAVE A MESSAGE FROM KOMUI.
I'M HEADING STRAIGHT TO MY NEXT MISSION.
YOU DELIVER THE INNOCENCE TO THE HEADQUARTERS.
...
GOT IT.
...
IF IT'S TOO HARD ON YOU, GO STOP THE DOLL. THAT THING ISN'T "LALA" ANYMORE, RIGHT?
IT'S THEIR PROMISE TO EACH OTHER.
THE PERSON WHO DESTROYS LALA SHOULD BE GUZOL.

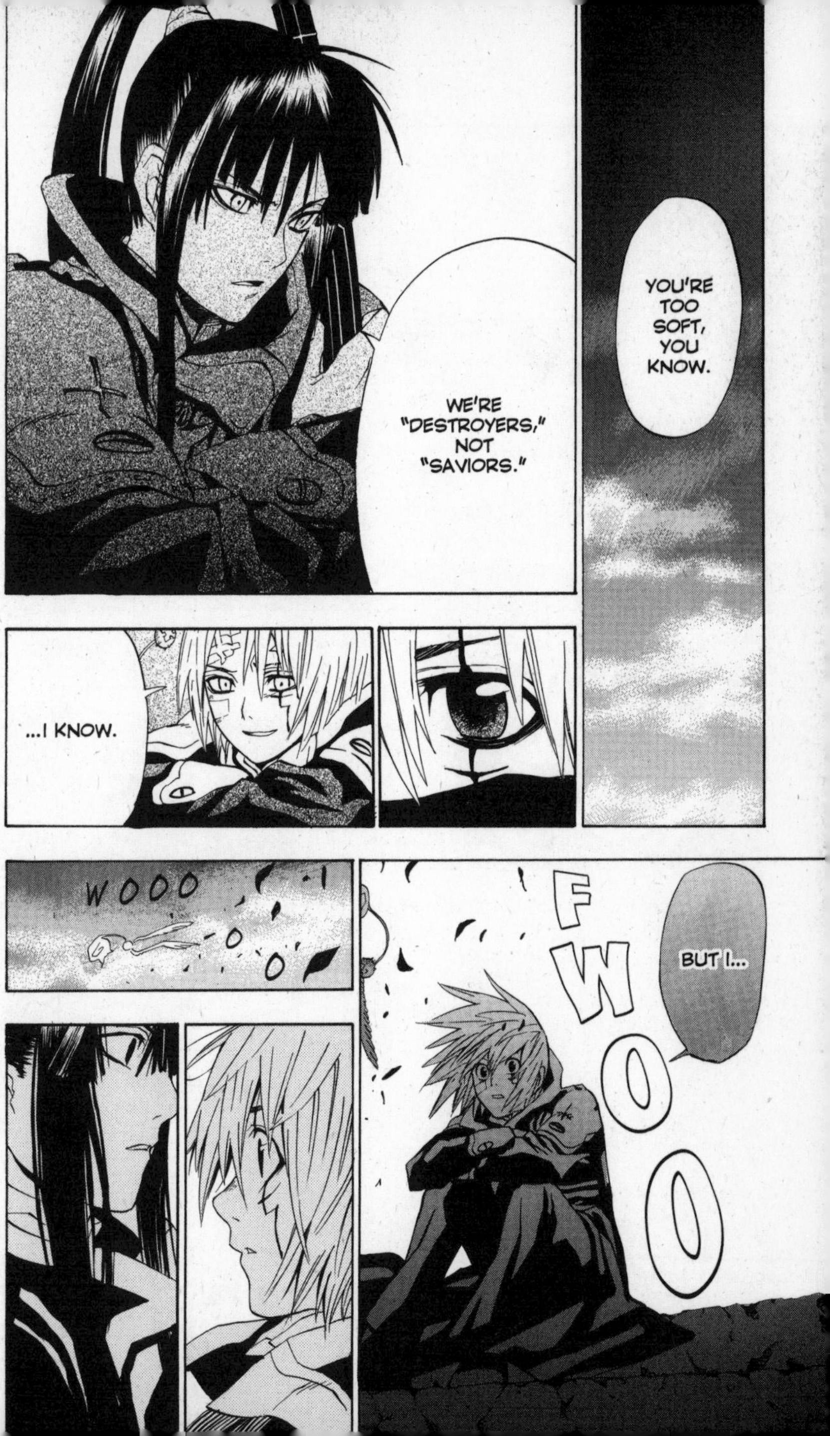
YOU'RE TOO SOFT, YOU KNOW.
WE'RE "DESTROYERS," NOT "SAVIORS."
...I KNOW.
FWOOO
BUT I...
WOOO-O-O

READ THIS WAY

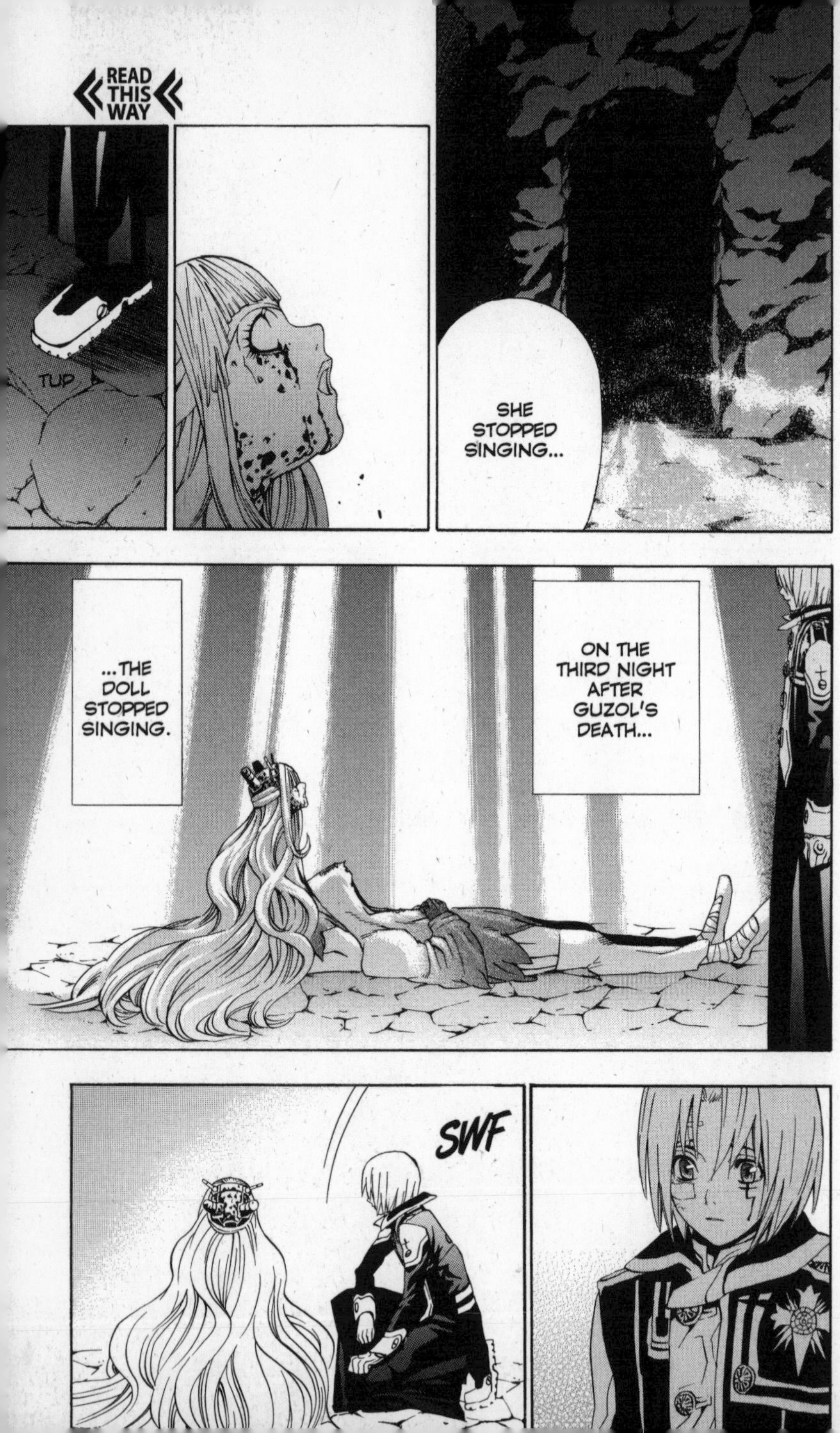

SHE STOPPED SINGING...
TUP
ON THE THIRD NIGHT AFTER GUZOL'S DEATH...
...THE DOLL STOPPED SINGING.
SWF

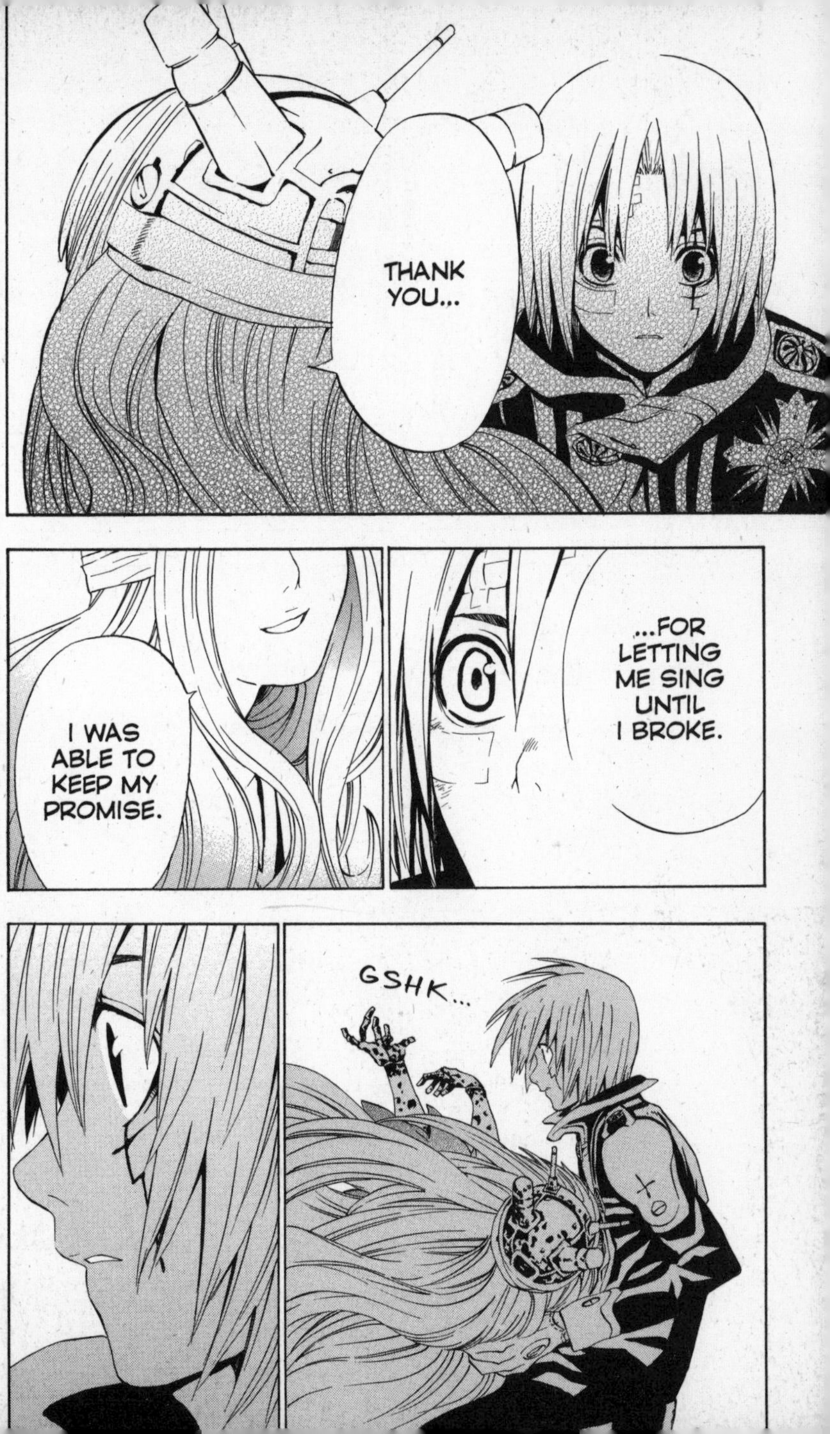
THANK YOU...
...FOR LETTING ME SING UNTIL I BROKE.
I WAS ABLE TO KEEP MY PROMISE.
GSHK...

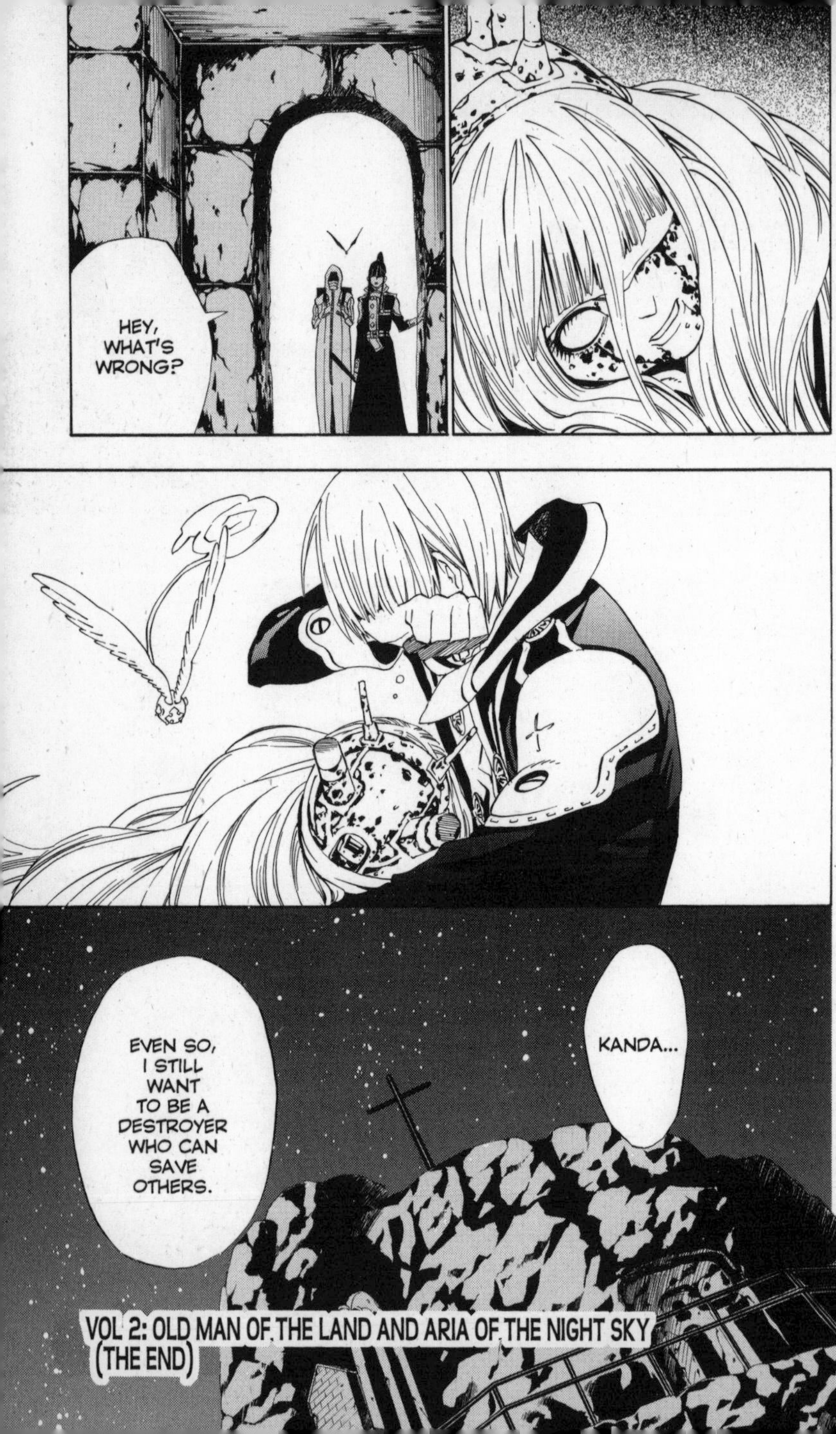
HEY, WHAT'S WRONG?
KANDA...
EVEN SO, I STILL WANT TO BE A DESTROYER WHO CAN SAVE OTHERS.
VOL 2: OLD MAN OF THE LAND AND ARIA OF THE NIGHT SKY (THE END)

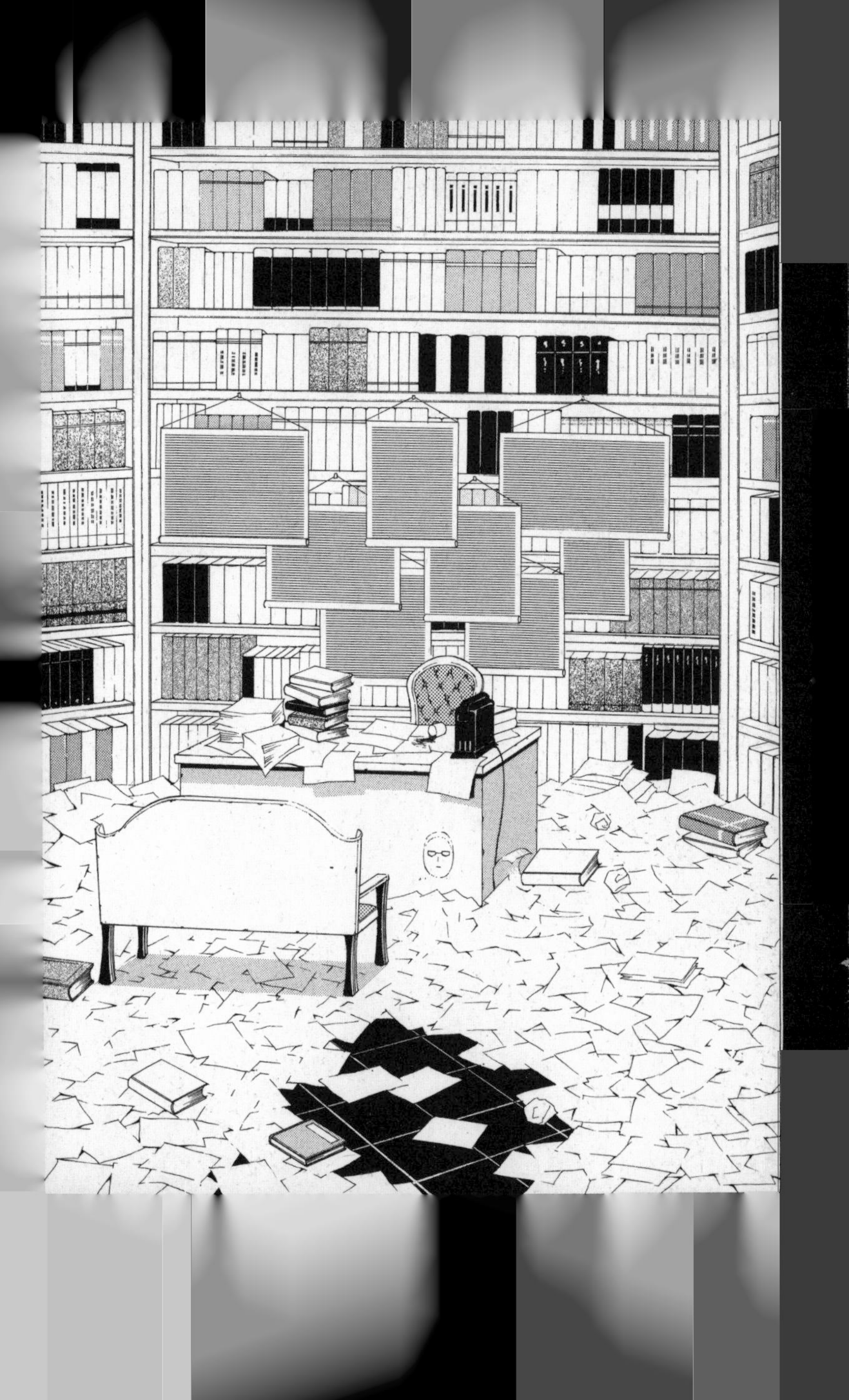

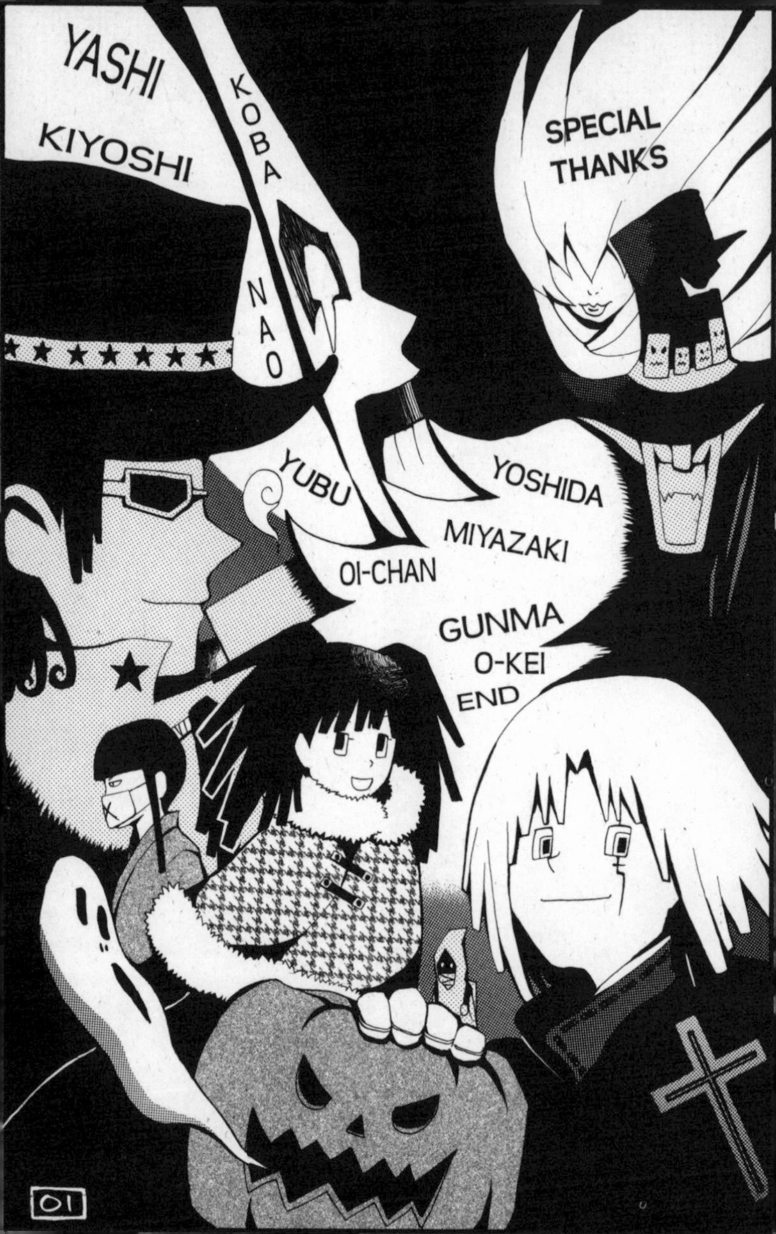
YASHI
KIYOSHI
KOBA
NAO
SPECIAL THANKS
YUBU
YOSHIDA
MIYAZAKI
OI-CHAN
GUNMA
O-KEI
END
01

IN THE NEXT VOLUME...

Prepare for another bizarre adventure as teenage exorcist Allen Walker and Lenalee of The Black Order are dispatched to a city where time has stood still, a place where the townsfolk forget that every day is the same day repeating itself. Oddly enough, a woman named Miranda is the only one who is unaffected by the time warp. What's her secret?

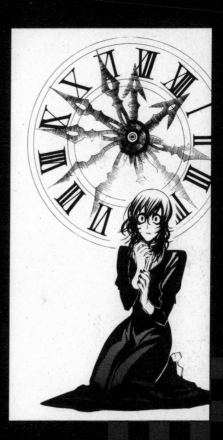

Available Now!

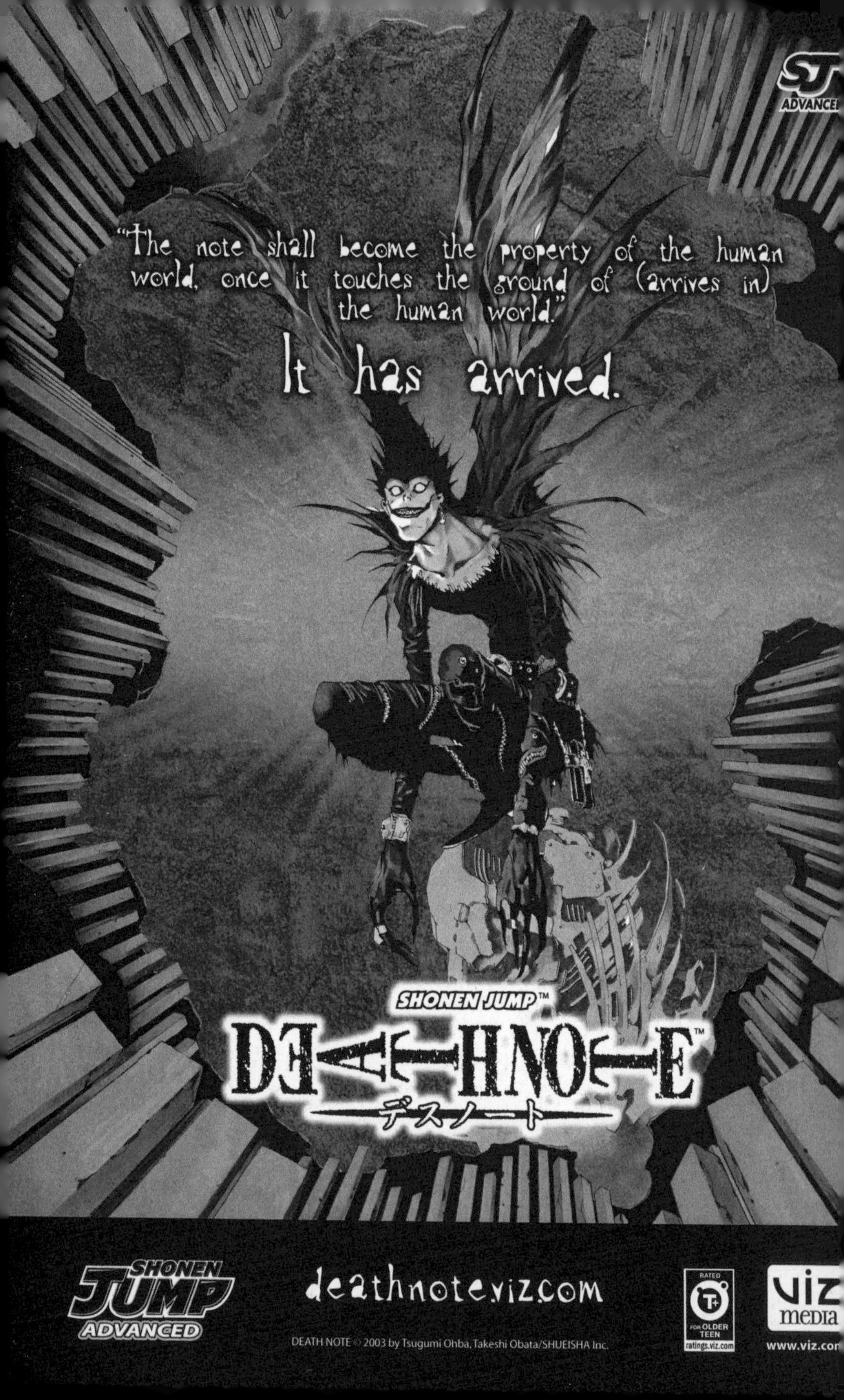

SJ ADVANCED
"The note shall become the property of the human world, once it touches the ground of (arrives in) the human world."
It has arrived.
SHONEN JUMP™
DEATH NOTE™
デスノート
SHONEN JUMP ADVANCED
deathnote.viz.com
RATED T+ FOR OLDER TEEN ratings.viz.com
VIZ media
www.viz.com
DEATH NOTE © 2003 by Tsugumi Ohba, Takeshi Obata/SHUEISHA Inc.

SHONEN JUMP
DEATH NOTE
デスノート

"The human whose name is written in this note shall die."

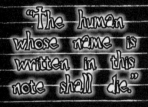

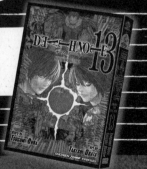

READ WHERE IT ALL BEGAN IN THE MANGA—ALL 12 VOLUMES AVAILABLE NOW

AN ORIGINAL NOVEL BASED ON THE CHARACTERS AND CONCEPTS FROM THE POPULAR MANGA SERIES

A GUIDE TO THE MANGA SERIES, COMPLETE WITH CHARACTER BIOS, STORYLINE SUMMARIES, INTERVIEWS WITH CREATORS TSUGUMI OHBA AND TAKESHI OBATA, PRODUCTION NOTES AND COMMENTARIES, AND BONUS MANGA PAGES

SHONEN JUMP ADVANCED

ON SALE AT
deathnoteviz.com
ALSO AVAILABLE AT YOUR LOCAL BOOKSTORE AND COMIC STORE

VIZ media
www.viz.com

DEATH NOTE © 2003 by Tsugumi Ohba, Takeshi Obata/SHUEISHA Inc.
DEATH NOTE: ANOTHER NOTE LOS ANGELES BB RENZOKU SATSUJIN JIKEN © 2006 by NISIO ISIN, Tsugumi Ohba, Takeshi Obata/SHUEISHA Inc.
DEATH NOTE HOW TO READ 13 © 2006 by Tsugumi Ohba, Takeshi Obata/SHUEISHA Inc.

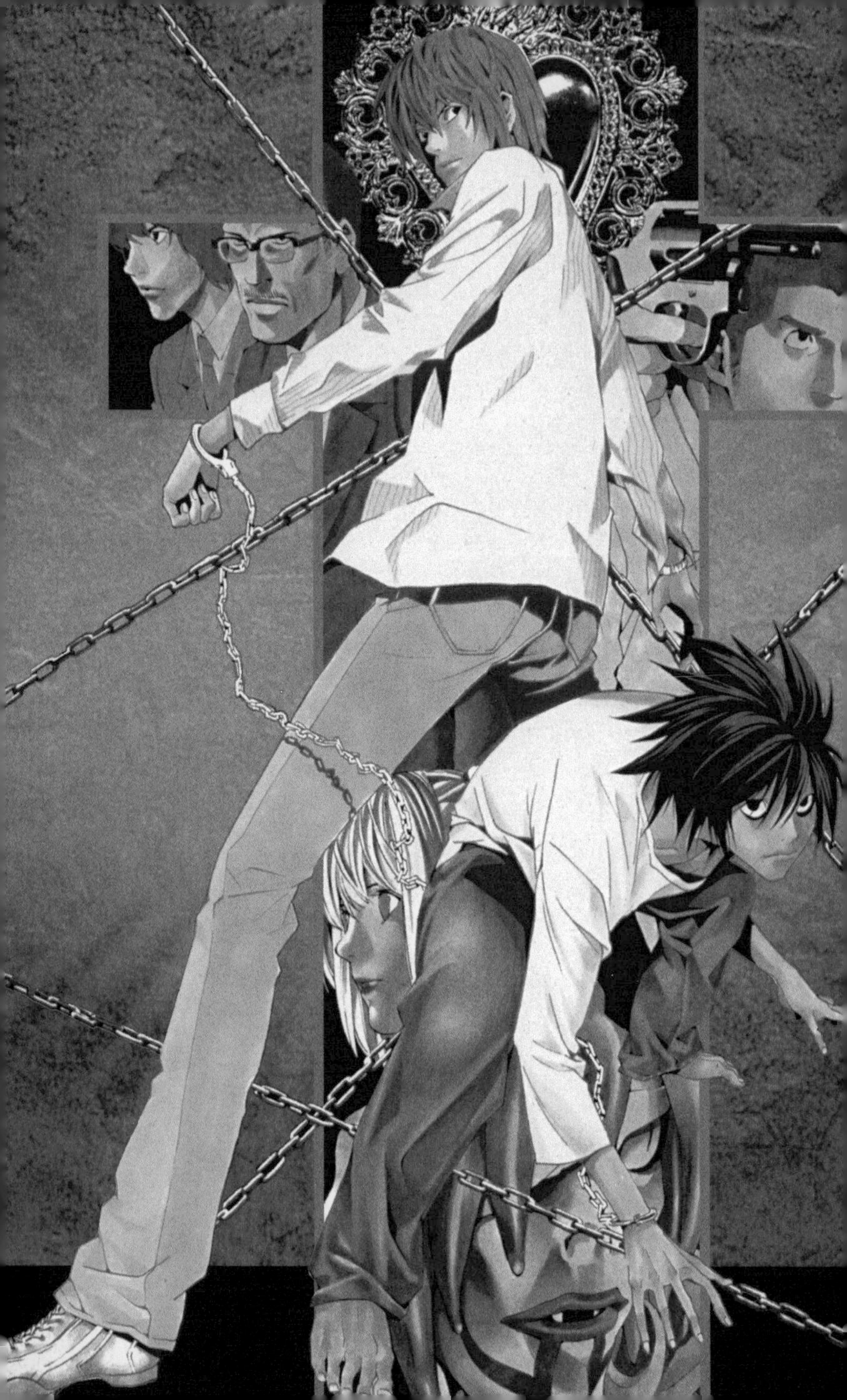

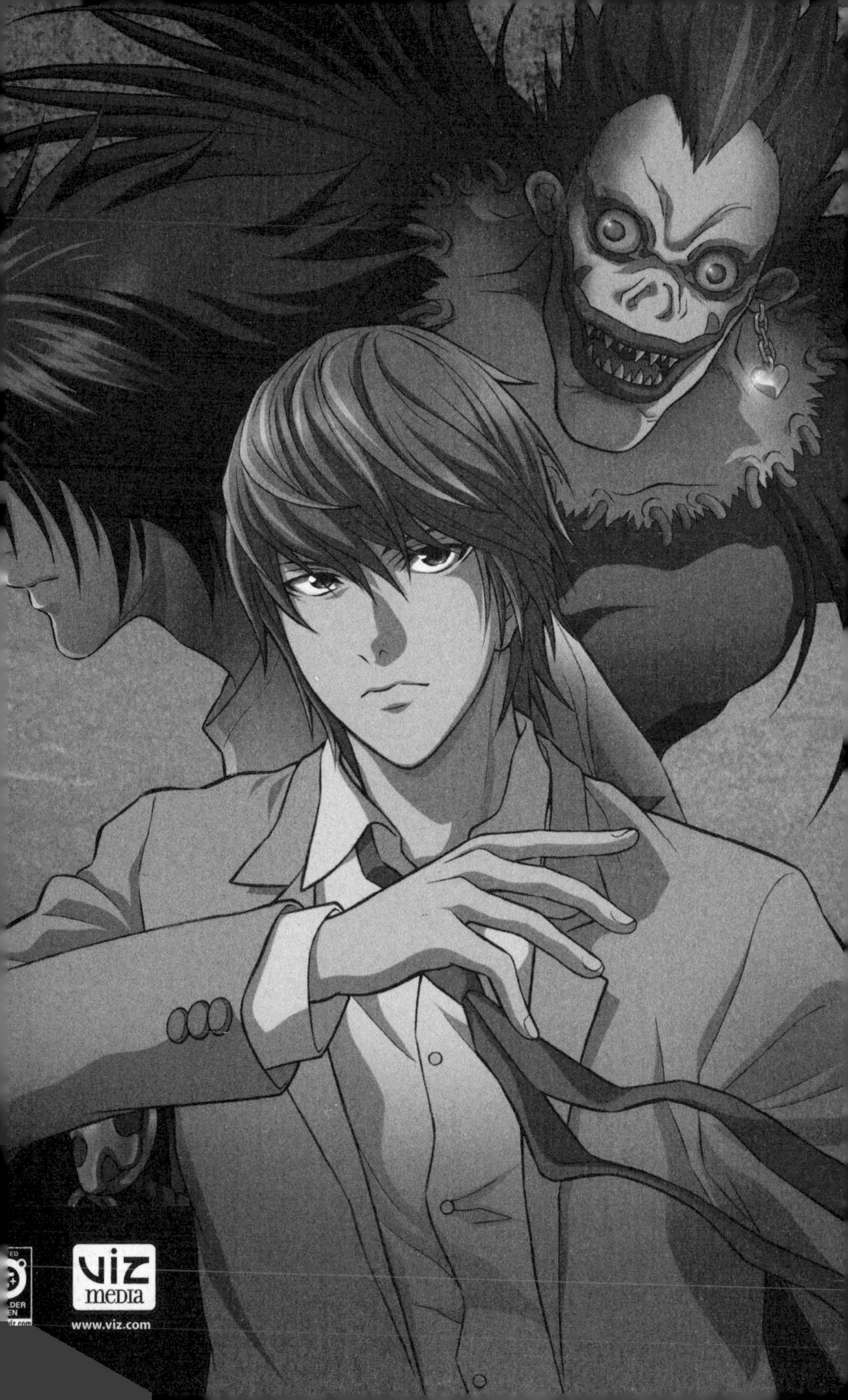
viz media
www.viz.com

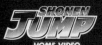

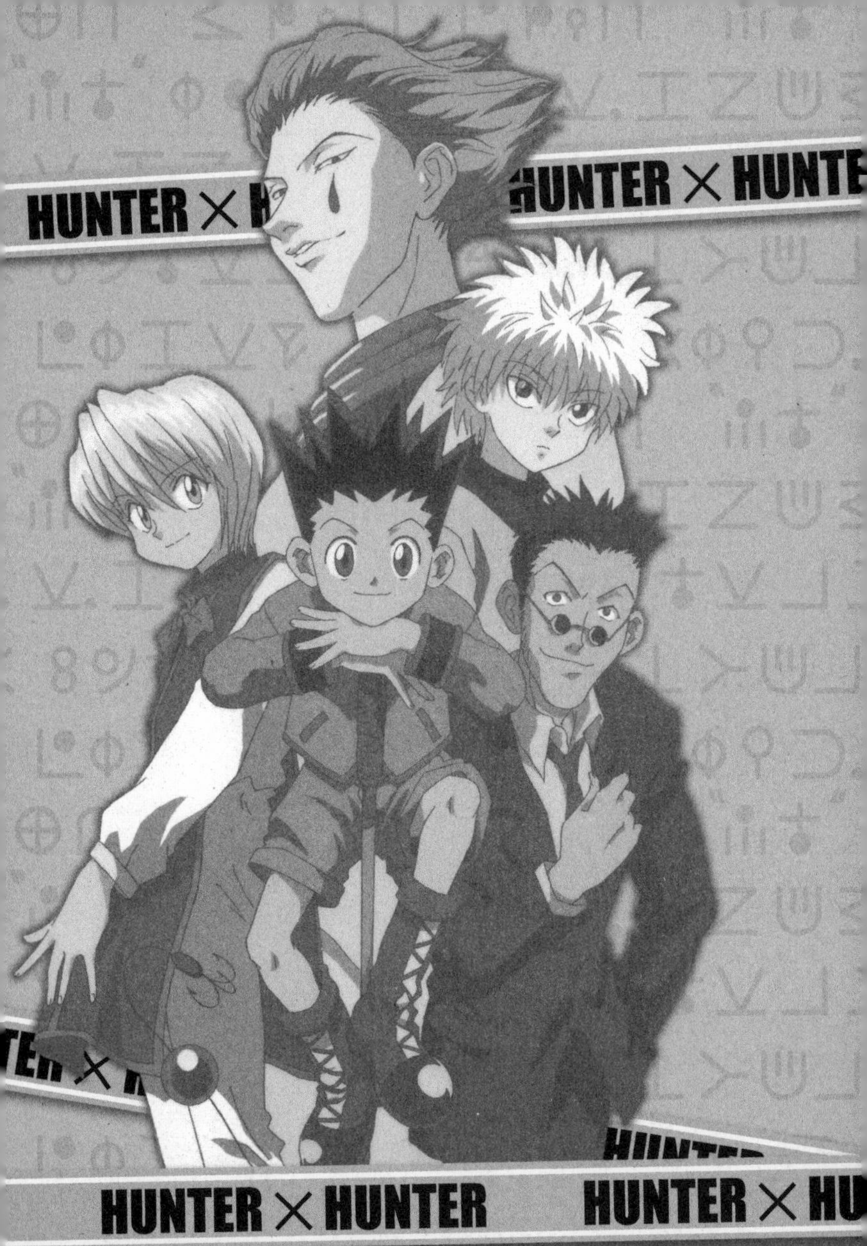
HUNTER × HUNTER

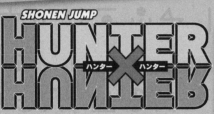
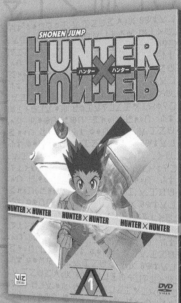
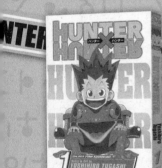
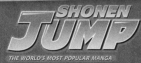

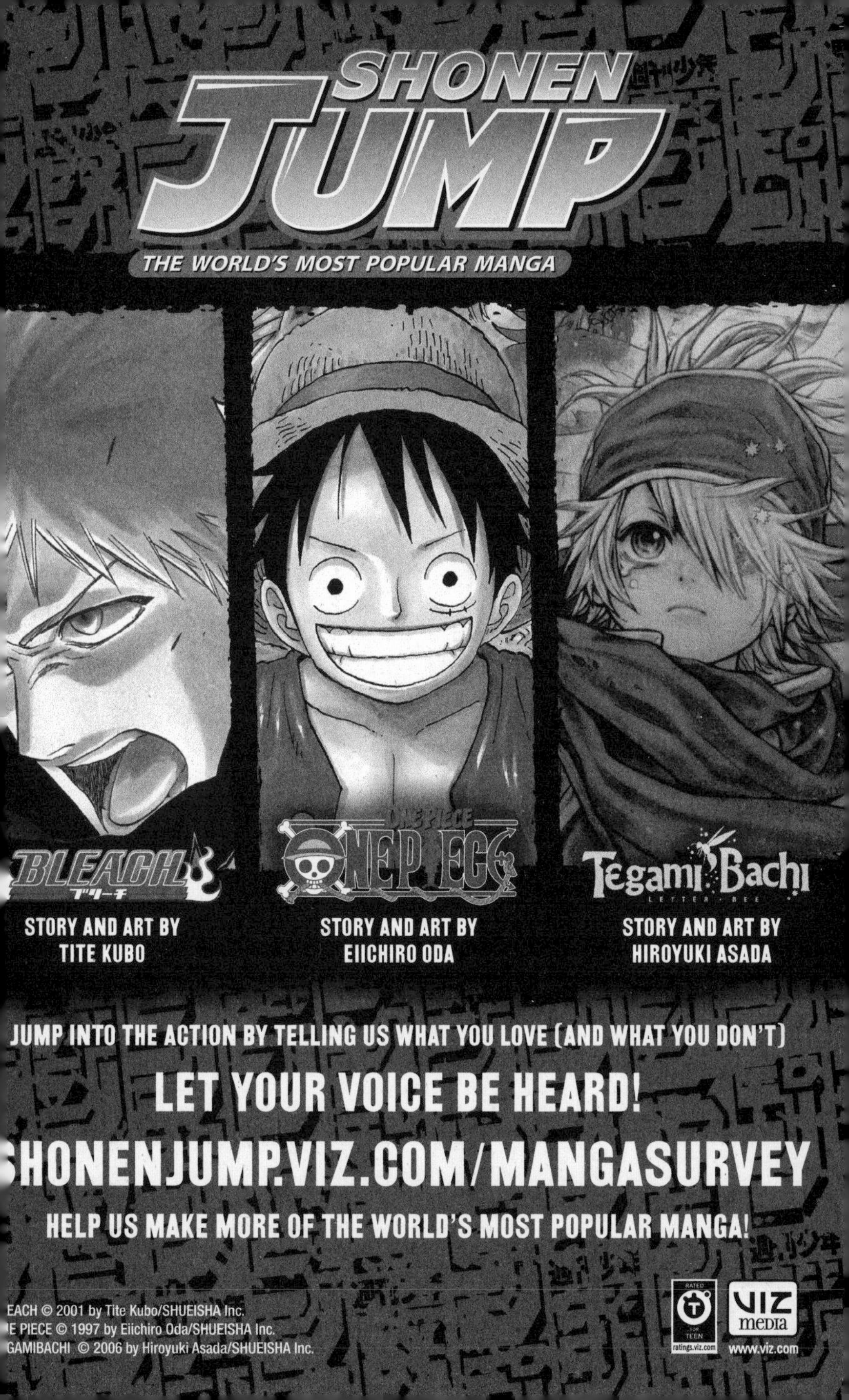
SHONEN JUMP
THE WORLD'S MOST POPULAR MANGA
BLEACH
ブリーチ
STORY AND ART BY
TITE KUBO
ONE PIECE
STORY AND ART BY
EIICHIRO ODA
Tegami Bachi
LETTER BEE
STORY AND ART BY
HIROYUKI ASADA
JUMP INTO THE ACTION BY TELLING US WHAT YOU LOVE (AND WHAT YOU DON'T)
LET YOUR VOICE BE HEARD!
HONENJUMP.VIZ.COM/MANGASURVEY
HELP US MAKE MORE OF THE WORLD'S MOST POPULAR MANGA!
EACH © 2001 by Tite Kubo/SHUEISHA Inc.
E PIECE © 1997 by Eiichiro Oda/SHUEISHA Inc.
GAMIBACHI © 2006 by Hiroyuki Asada/SHUEISHA Inc.
RATED
T
FOR
TEEN
ratings.viz.com
VIZ
media
www.viz.com

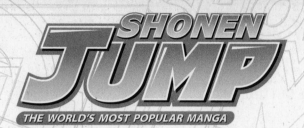
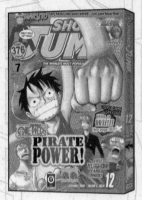
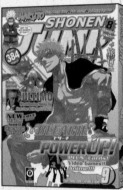
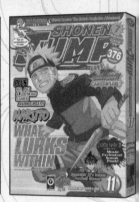

SAVE 50% OFF
THE COVER PRICE!

IT'S LIKE GETTING 6 ISSUES
FREE!

OVER 350+ PAGES PER ISSUE

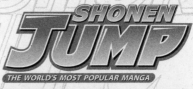

THE WORLD'S MOST POPULAR MANGA

This monthly magazine contains 7 of the coolest manga available in the U.S., PLUS anime news, and info about video & card games, toys AND more!

❏ **I want 12 HUGE issues of SHONEN JUMP for only $29.95*!**

NAME

ADDRESS

CITY/STATE/ZIP

EMAIL ADDRESS   **DATE OF BIRTH**

❏ YES, send me via email information, advertising, offers, and promotions related to VIZ Media, SHONEN JUMP, and/or their business partners.

❏ **CHECK ENCLOSED** (payable to SHONEN JUMP)   ❏ **BILL ME LATER**

CREDIT CARD: ❏ **Visa** ❏ **Mastercard**

ACCOUNT NUMBER

SIGNATURE

CLI
SHONEN JUM

Mount M   GNC1